Government Lawyers

STUDIES IN GOVERNMENT AND PUBLIC POLICY

GOVERNMENT LAWYERS

The Federal Legal Bureaucracy and Presidential Politics

EDITED BY
CORNELL W. CLAYTON

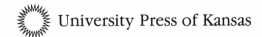 University Press of Kansas

Published by the University Press of Kansas (Lawrence, Kansas 66049),
which was organized by the Kansas Board of Regents and is operated
and funded by Emporia State University, Fort Hays State University,
Kansas State University, Pittsburg State University, the University of Kansas,
and Wichita State University

Library of Congress Cataloging-in-Publication Data

Government lawyers : the federal legal bureaucracy and presidential
    politics / edited by Cornell W. Clayton.
        p.   cm.—(Studies in government and public policy)
    Includes bibliographical references and index.
ISBN 0-7006-0706-4 (cloth : acid-free paper)
    1. Government attorneys—United States.   2. Practice of law—
Political aspects—United States.   I. Clayton, Cornell W., 1960–
II. Series.
KF299.G6G68   1995
353.008′8—dc20   95-6288

British Library Cataloguing in Publication Data is available.

Printed in the United States of America

10 9 8 7 6 5 4 3 2 1

The paper used in this publication meets the minimum requirements of
the American National Standard for Permanence of Paper for
Printed Library Materials Z39.48-1984.

CONTENTS

Government Lawyers

INTRODUCTION: POLITICS AND THE LEGAL BUREAUCRACY

CORNELL W. CLAYTON

A collection of essays examining the legal bureaucracy needs some apology. The term *legal bureaucracy* is not commonly used either in political science or in law schools; but quite simply, it refers to a substratum of government officers who are employed as lawyers.

Why are the activities of government lawyers of interest to students of public policy? A central factor is the fact that control over a growing number of policy areas—consumer protection, environmental and antitrust regulation, civil rights, welfare and entitlement programs, to name only a few—has been shifting out of the legislative arena and into the ambit of courts and the administrative state. A recent body of scholarship has focused on explaining the causes of this shift and its likely effects on the relationship between administrators and judges.[1] Still, relatively little is known about the role of the government lawyers who operate at the nexus of this important policy-making relationship.

The federal government employs nearly forty thousand attorneys. Approximately one-fifth of these work in the Department of Justice, and the rest are scattered among the various other offices, agencies, and departments of the government. A small number are employed by Congress or by the courts, but the vast majority of government lawyers work in the executive branch (including regulatory agencies formally styled "independent").[2] Their principal roles are to prosecute or bring enforcement actions under federal statutes, to advise administrators on the law, and to represent government agencies in court when civil suits are filed against them.

Although attorneys are scattered throughout government, this volume focuses on the offices that are important in representing the federal government and its agencies in judicial proceedings or in framing broad policy issues when providing legal counsel to administrative officials. Even at that, this volume focuses selectively on lawyers who operate at the highest levels of the executive branch's policy-making apparatus. Thus the term *bureaucracy* is used here in a rather limited way: to describe a set of offices related in a functional but not necessarily in an organizational sense. The individual chapters in this volume seek to explore the political (not the bureaucratic) aspects of legal policy-making, but the reader will discover that these two concerns can never be entirely separated.

Previous scholarship on government legal-administrative institutions has tended to focus on individual offices or on the policies of particular administrations. Many of these studies were penned by former occupants of the offices involved.[3] This volume is different in that it sets out to provide a broader and a more integrated overview of the government's legal administrative bureaucracy and of the politics surrounding its operation. Each chapter concentrates on a different office or set of offices where law and politics directly intersect and where the lines between law and discretionary policy-making blur. The aim is to provide the reader with a sense of the history, the present-day functions, and the web of political relationships that exist in and between these offices.

THE GOVERNMENT'S LEGAL OFFICES AND THE CONTRIBUTIONS TO THIS VOLUME

Within offices such as the attorney general's, the solicitor general's, the White House counsel's, or the general counsels' in various departments and agencies of the federal government, lawyers confront a unique set of tensions—tensions that Nancy Baker aptly described in her chapter on the attorney general as "conflicting loyalties."[4] Each lawyer in one of these positions serves as advocate for an agency or a department that has its own organizational objectives, as well as for a partisan administration that expects the individual to fit the law to its political agenda. At the same time, however, each lawyer belongs to a profession that has trained and exhorted its members to maintain a detached and neutral adherence to the law. This tradition is not just a matter of professional culture but a requisite for any system of government that aspires to uphold the rule of law. If law cannot be interpreted objectively and neutrally, then law—like other forms of politics—simply becomes synonymous with the exercise of power. The tensions between political allegiances and professional independence affect all aspects of government lawyering.

As head of the Department of Justice, the attorney general is the federal government's chief legal policymaker and law enforcement official. Attorneys general have always had to be "learned in the law," but today they must also be skillful politicians and administrators, capable of managing a powerful federal bureaucracy of over 90,000 employees.[5] The office, according to Professor Baker, occupies a unique position in American government. Unlike other cabinet secretaries, the attorney general has special obligations to respond to both legal and political demands. An early attorney general, Caleb Cushing, described his role not only as "a counsel giving legal advice to the Government as his client," but also as a "public officer, acting judicially, under all the solemn responsibilities of conscience and of legal obligation."[6] More than in any other office, lawyers in the attorney general's office must make a schizophrenic choice between the office's role as a neutral expositor of the law and its role as a political advocate for the administration. That choice is not the attorney general's to make alone, however; much also depends on the expectations of the president. For example, Professor Baker explains that following the Watergate scandal, Attorneys General Edward Levi and Griffin Bell fit comfortably into the role of neutral expositors, in part because Presidents Ford and Carter both had promised to "depoliticize" the Department of Justice. President Reagan, on the other hand, saw changing the law and the government's legal policies as being integral to the administration's political agenda. Thus it is not surprising that Attorneys General William French Smith and Edwin Meese tended to view their role as being one of partisan advocacy.

The attorney general's dual obligations to the law and to the president's political agenda once led legal scholar Daniel Meador to describe the office as a "unique bridge between the executive and judicial branches."[7] While this description is certainly true with regard to the history and statutory powers of the attorney general's office, it might more accurately be applied to the day-to-day workings of the solicitor general. Within the Justice Department, primary responsibility for the federal government's appellate litigation has been delegated to the solicitor general and to the small staff of attorneys who work in that office. Created by the Justice Department Act of 1870, the office originally served as a general assistant to the attorney general. Over time, however, it evolved into an elite barrister's position, responsible for approving government appeals from lower courts and for arguing the government's cases in the Supreme Court. The solicitor general's close working relationship with the judiciary has led some commentators to attribute to it a quasi-judicial status. For instance, in a controversial book that criticized the Reagan administration's utilization of the office to further its political agenda, Lincoln Caplan argued that the office has traditionally played the part of an apolitical helpmate to the Court—the equivalent of the Court's "Tenth Justice."[8]

Rebecca Salokar's chapter on the solicitor general's office takes issue with such characterizations of the solicitor general's office. After describing the origin and development of the office's close relationship to the Court, Professor Salokar discusses how that relationship has been used historically as an instrument of presidential policy-making. Solicitors general, while expected to adhere to the highest standards of professional accuracy and honesty, have traditionally served as mouthpieces for the legal views of the president and his administration. In Professor Salokar's view, individual officeholders have been more or less adamant in presenting their own interpretation of the law and in advocating the strategies they believe will persuade the Court when advising their political superiors; but when it comes time to present an argument to the Court, Professor Salokar concludes, the solicitor general has always been the advocate for the president's views.

Both Professors Baker and Salokar argue that much of the confusion surrounding the function of lawyers at the Justice Department flows from an anachronistic conception of the law—one that tends to view the law as an apolitical institution. Professor Salokar argues that the essence of law in the American system "is inherently political; it is a battle for power, resources, and legitimacy in an arena dominated by lawyers and judges." The "rules of the game are more structured in the judicial arena, and the resources a lawyer uses [are different]. But to argue that the role of the solicitor general is or ought to be apolitical is to ignore reality." Likewise, Professor Baker concludes that a root source of conflict surrounding the role of the attorney general is the "lack of a clear delineation between what is legal and what is political" in American government. The tensions that government lawyers experience thus emerge out of the structure of American constitutionalism, which assumes that law can simultaneously restrict political power and be shaped by the political forces it confines.

Contributors to this volume agree that tensions between political and professional loyalties have always been present in government legal administration, but they also recognize that those tensions have grown more sharp and more public in recent decades. Offices that used to operate in relative obscurity have suddenly become subjects of campaign rhetoric, interest group scrutiny, and popular media attention.[9] For better or worse, Bernard Nussbaum, Lani Guinier, Edwin Meese, William Bradford Reynolds, Charles Fried, Griffin Bell, and John Mitchell are names no longer known by only a handful of academic lawyers; they are widely recognized by the general public.

Much of the recent controversy surrounding government lawyering has focused on the exercise of prosecutorial power and the enforcement of ethics laws by these officials. The attorney general's close relationship to the president has always made the Justice Department vulnerable to charges of corruption and cronyism when it is asked to investigate or prosecute members of the president's administration. Watergate was by no means the first scandal to scar the Justice Department's reputation in this regard, but Katy Harriger argues in her chapter on the independent counsel's office that it was the "focusing event" for reform.

In the wake of the Watergate scandal, a new regime of ethics laws found its way onto the books. At the heart of those reforms was the Ethics in Government Act of 1978, which created the independent counsel's office. Under this statute, independent counsels can be appointed by a federal appellate court and are thus buffered from the conflict of interest that other federal prosecutors confront when investigating the president or members of his administration. Independent counsels were utilized on thirteen separate occasions between 1978 and 1992, against both Republican and Democratic administrations, but the office remained highly controversial. Although the question of the office's constitutionality was settled by the Supreme Court's 1988 decision in *Morrison v. Olson*,[10] the independent counsel provisions of the Ethics in Government Act were allowed to expire at the end of the Bush administration amid bitter partisan wrangling.

Professor Harriger's chapter details the circumstances surrounding the origin of the independent counsel's office, subsequent episodes involving its use, and the arguments made for and against Congress's eventual decision to reauthorize the independent counsel law in 1994. She concludes that, while critics couched their opposition on questions of accountability and separation of powers, their fears have not been realized in how the office has actually performed. Professor Harriger argues that, rather than launching roving inquisitions, the office has thus far been constrained by the same "complex set of accountability relationships that exist for any actor in the political or legal process."

Professor Harriger's study of the independent counsel's office suggests that the real controversy surrounding the office lies elsewhere than in legalistic concerns over constitutional structure. Many observers fear that hypersensitivity to ethical misconduct, together with the politics of scandal that it has spawned in post-Watergate Washington, reflects a deeper malaise in American government. Scandal and investigation have seemingly become ordinary weapons in the conduct of partisan politics, used by political opponents to damage the president and his administration.[11] Following an independent counsel investigation of the Iran-Contra scandal for instance, Republican opposition to the counsel statue in Congress hardened and prevented its reauthorization in 1992. Two years later, however, with Republican leaders eager to institute "independent" investigations of the Whitewater scandal plaguing the Clinton administration, the act was reauthorized; and subsequently, in a controversial move, a panel of judges appointed Kenneth Starr, a former solicitor general during the Bush administration, to take over the investigation into the matter.[12] Although few independent counsel investigations have resulted in criminal prosecutions, critics maintain that the mere appointment of a prosecutor and the media coverage it generates can seriously damage any administration.[13]

Jeremy Rabkin's contribution to this volume argues that the post-Watergate ethics regime and the scandal style of politics associated with it have also transformed the character of the White House counsel's office. This office was originally created by Franklin Roosevelt in 1941. But until the 1970s, Professor Rabkin explains, the title of "counsel" served a largely "honorific" function: individuals who occupied the office during this period advised presidents on a range of policy matters but had no regular legal functions. As late as 1970, when Richard Nixon appointed John Dean to the post, it was a solo office that took on the character of the person occupying it. Since 1970, however, the office has become "an institutionalized presence—indeed, a separate bureaucracy of its own—within the White House." With a staff of more than thirteen associate and assistant counsels, the office today performs a variety of institutionalized roles: advising presidents on the legal implications of legislation and presidential action, managing the administration's judicial selection process, and counseling on ethics.

This last function, Professor Rabkin argues, occupies the bulk of the White House counsel's time and energy. As ethics laws have become more demanding and complex, it has become easier for officials subject to them to make inadvertent mistakes. In an atmosphere where such mistakes are fanned into scandals that damage their administrations, presidents have increasingly turned to the counsel's office to act as their ethics watchdog. Today's counsel is expected to maintain an "ethical tone" in the White House, provide legal clarification of ethics standards to administration officials, and carefully screen and "scrub" prospective nominees to high-level positions in the administration. But the office's dual role of enforcing ethics standards and protecting the administration from scandal is fraught with pitfalls. It is precisely this delicate role-balancing, Professor Rabkin points out, that sealed the fate of John Dean during Watergate and more recently forced the resignation of President Clinton's counsel, Bernard Nussbaum. With some irony Professor Rabkin notes that, in the recent case of Nussbaum, the ethics watchdog himself became the target of—what else?—an independent counsel investigation!

The term *independent counsel* and the need to find alternatives to Justice Department prosecutors exposes another source of conflict within the legal bureaucracy in the United States. While friction between political and professional loyalties is experienced by government legal officers in other countries,[14] representing the "government" in the United States is further complicated by tensions inherent in the separation of powers and the impact that this has on the legal system. Unlike in parliamentary systems, where the "government" *is* the cabinet (an institution that fuses legislative power and executive power), in the United States no such clarity exists.[15] Under the separation of powers, government attorneys must represent and balance competing institutional clients. Congress, the White House, and the courts sometimes clash over the meaning of the law, disagreeing about the interpretation of particular statutes or of provisions of the Constitution. The conflict may even lead to litigation pitting parts of the sovereign against each other. The mere styling of cases such as *United States v. House of Representatives* (1983) and *United States v. United States District Court* (1972) illustrates this problem.[16]

Such clashes present a dilemma to those charged with representing the (singular) legal interest of the United States when in fact those interests are plural. If interbranch conflicts over law and law enforcement cannot be resolved through political compromise, the government's legal bureaucracy may be thrown into crisis. During the Watergate scandal, for example, Attorney General Elliot Richardson promised Congress during his confirmation hearings that the Justice Department would guarantee a thorough and independent investigation of the Watergate break-in. When President Nixon ordered his attorney general to fire the special prosecutor who had been appointed to perform such an investigation, a crisis ensued that could only be resolved by Richardson's own resignation.[17]

A more common consequence of this type of conflict, however, is fragmentation of government legal services. As each branch seeks its own attorneys to advise and advocate its views, the pressures to multiply the number of legal offices in government and to duplicate advising and litigating functions become irresistible. The rise in separation-of-powers confrontations during the 1970s and 1980s had precisely this effect. Faced with a growing incidence of Justice Department refusals to defend against, and in many cases the solicitor general's participation in, court challenges to congressional statutes or prerogatives; Congress in 1978 moved to create an institutionalized alternative to Justice Department legal representation. The Senate legal counsel's office and the counsel to the clerk of the House of Representatives now regularly intervene in judicial proceedings representing Congress or its interests when the Justice Department refuses to do so.[18] Perhaps even more surprisingly, the Supreme Court in 1972 also created an in-house legal counsel's office. Although the Supreme Court legal office's primary function is to advise the Court and its members, the office has on occasion hired private counsel to represent the Court in litigation.[19]

But the real fragmentation of the legal bureaucracy has occurred within and not outside the executive branch. Of course, the struggle to centralize control over a relatively decentralized administrative state is an old theme in American political history, and it is no different as applied to the administration of government legal work. Indeed, Congress's creation of the Department of Justice in 1870 came in response to repeated pleas from presidents and attorneys general for the efficiency and the uniformity in legal position that centralization promised. Prior to this time, each department and agency had its own solicitors or counsel, who worked entirely independently of one another (and often at cross-purposes), espousing potentially conflicting legal positions in the courts. Because it was intended to centralize the government's legal resources, the Justice Department was expected to cure this confusion and to reduce the cost of the federal government's sprawling legal bureaucracy.[20]

Even after the Justice Department was established, however, the practical extent of centralized authority over the conduct of government legal work remained subject to the ebb and flow of larger efforts to centralize control over the administrative state. As with other areas of the administrative state, centralizing control over agency legal work meant strengthening presidential influence over it. Decentralization, on the other hand, usually worked to enhance the power of Congress.[21] Thus, despite creation of the Justice Department, Congress continued to allow other agencies to retain legal counsel; and these agencies jealously guarded their independent authority—especially the authority to represent themselves in court. Not until Franklin Roosevelt (within the broader context of governmental reorganization surrounding the New Deal) issued an executive order requiring Justice Department management of all government litigation did any semblance of truly centralized control emerge. And even then, the order (which was later codified into law) dealt only with agency litigation; legal advising continued to be the function of attorneys inside the agencies.[22]

Legal scholar Donald Horowitz described this post–New Deal division between the Justice Department and agency legal counsel as "a division of labor and a divorce of function."[23] With few exceptions, litigation became the domain of the Justice Department, while advising administrators on the legal ramifications of regulatory programs became the responsibility of the agency counsel. This division reflected an implicit agreement among Congress, the White House, and agency administrators about the nature of the litigating and legal advising functions. Litigation was more closely associated with the president's constitutional duty to execute the law, and centralizing control over it was thus seen as an appropriate way to enhance presidential supervision over the presidency's constitutional functions. Providing legal counsel to agencies regarding the development of their regulatory program, on the other hand, seemed more closely associated with the quasi-legislative powers that Congress intended to delegate directly to agency heads. Centralizing control over this function was therefore viewed as being neither desirable (as a matter of administrative policy) nor required (as a matter of constitutional principle).

During the past three decades, however, the division of functions between the Justice Department and agency counsel and the agreement that undergirds it have come under pressure from several sides. During the 1970s and 1980s, presidents, faced with increasingly hostile Congresses (usually controlled by the opposing party), began to rely heavily on administrative rather than legislative strategies of policy-making.[24] An important element in such strategies consisted of strengthening White House control over both agency litigation and agency legal advising during the regulatory process. To this end, presidents (with the possible exceptions of the Ford and Carter administrations) sought simultaneously to strengthen Justice Department authority over agency legal policy-making and to strengthen White House oversight of the Justice Department. Congress and agency bureaucrats, on the other hand, became increasingly distrustful of White House oversight of agency decision-making, especially with regard to the threat that Justice Department supervision of government litigation posed to agency enforcement autonomy. Consequently, Congress set about making statutory exceptions to Justice's litigating monopoly for agencies and areas of law that were most vulnerable to White House incursions.[25] Thus, as the White House sought to gain greater control over the legal advising function, Congress and agency bureaucrats sought to decentralize the litigating function. Justice Department officials were caught in the middle: trying to convince Congress that they could be relied on to remain professionally independent and neutral on the one hand, but attempting to reassure the president and White House policy-makers that they were politically loyal on the other.[26]

The final four chapters of this volume capture this rich political interplay among agencies, the White House, Congress, and the Justice Department during the past couple of decades. Michael Herz and Neal Devins examine the role of the agency general counsel's office. After describing the history and functions of the counsel's office, Professor Herz examines the conflicting pressures on the office's legal advising role. Using a case study involving a legal interpretation of the Clean Air Act by attorneys in the Environmental Protection Agency, Professor Herz illustrates how various offices inside the White House (the White House counsel, the Office of Management and Budget, and—during the Bush administration—the vice-president's Council on Competitiveness) influence the legal advice given to agency regulators. Often, Herz points out, the White House uses opinions from the White House legal counsel and from the

Justice Department (which in theory are binding on executive branch agencies) to counter the legal opinions of agency lawyers. Professor Herz concludes his chapter with an analysis of the advantages and disadvantages of a decentralized system of legal advising in the executive branch. While endorsing the current agency-centered approach, Professor Herz suggests a way to lessen the political tensions that plague the agency counsel's role.

Professor Devins directs his attention away from the advising function and toward the distribution of litigating authority between the Justice Department and independent regulatory agencies. After describing how competition for control of agency litigation is part of the broader power struggle between Congress and the president, Professor Devins seeks to explain why some agencies possess independent authority and others do not. He concludes that, rather than reflecting any systematic approach to governance, the current distribution of litigating authority is the result of individual will and political circumstance. Congress has "crafted an extraordinarily incoherent system of varying, unpredictable degrees of litigating authority. Some agencies are virtually independent; others are entirely dependent; and most fall somewhere in the middle. Specific political circumstances, not cohesive thinking about the attributes of independent agency autonomy, explain this patchwork structure." Moreover, while grants of independent authority may have limited presidential control over certain regulatory agencies, they did not necessarily make those agencies more responsive to Congress, as some lawmakers had hoped. Instead, Professor Devins argues, independent authority generally has the effect of strengthening the influence of courts, not Congress, over agency decision-making.

Finally, Nelson Lund and Michael Strine examine the legal advising function in their two chapters which address the relationship between the White House counsel's office and the Justice Department's Office of Legal Counsel (OLC). These two offices have in recent years become organizational competitors in advising the president about his constitutional powers and the legal ramifications of presidential actions. The nature of that competition, however, is a source of dispute in these chapters. Taking a historical approach, Professor Strine argues that, while each office seeks to advise the president, the character of the advice they provide depends on the institutional cultures within which they operate. As presidents have sought greater control over legal policy, they have tended to rely on the White House counsel for supportive legal advising. Strine contends that this has occurred because, unlike the attorneys in the Justice Department, lawyers in the White House have no institutional interests outside those of the individual president they serve. Legal advising in the White House counsel's office is thus marked by political expediency and personal loyalty rather than by principled jurisprudence. The OLC, on the other hand, has developed a distinct organizational mission that centers on championing the interest of the presidency as an institution. Usually the two sets of interests coincide, and the White House counsel and the OLC operate in harmony. At other times the interests diverge, however, and competition for control of legal advising ensues. In recent decades, Professor Strine concludes, that competition has been between an office dedicated to providing the president with personally supportive (some might say sycophantic) advice and an office that sought to define an independent role for itself as the guardian of a principled view of executive authority.

Professor Lund provides an alternative explanation of the motives underlying the behavior of those advising the president. Using the Bush administration as a case study, Professor Lund argues that the perceived self-interest of individual advisers, not principled jurisprudence or institutional culture, is the most significant determinant of the legal advice given to the president. Lund argues that the Bush administration makes an excellent case study because, more than any of its recent predecessors (including the Reagan administration), it was committed to "shoring up the legal defense of the presidency" and advancing a principled view of the separation of powers. Moreover, this mission was uniformly embraced at the outset by the president and all of his major advisers, including the attorney general, the head of the OLC, and President Bush's White House counsel, C. Boyden Gray.

Despite this uniform commitment to principle, Professor Lund argues that the Bush administration failed to carry it through. In several important separation-of-powers conflicts, the administration abandoned principle for remarkably trivial political gains. These instances involved decisions to acquiesce in Congress's use of the legislative veto and in the statutory appointment of an executive-branch regulator, the Justice Department's defense of a statute transferring executive authority from the Department of Transportation to a unique regulatory body composed of members of Congress, and a bungled effort to prevent the Postal Service from exercising independent litigating authority. In each instance, Professor Lund concludes, the president and his legal advisers compromised legal principle in order to obtain short-term political or personal objectives.

SOME COMMON THEMES

Many government legal offices are not directly involved in policy-making at a general level, and these are not represented in this volume. Examining the work of lawyers in the United States attorneys offices or in the field offices of other agencies would undoubtedly enhance our understanding of federal prosecution or of how bureaucratic relations and culture influence the routine practice of law by government lawyers. But this volume focuses on the political (not the bureaucratic or other) aspects of government legal work. This focus drives both the scope of coverage and the substance of analysis in the individual chapters. As the preceding discussion indicates, a few common themes emerge from this focus and tie together the discussions in each chapter.

Politics: The Separation of Powers and the Rule of Law

Like other government officials, lawyers must interpret and enforce the law, be it constitutional, statutory, or common in origin. Unlike other officers, however, their professional training and institutional roles lend their pronouncements about the law a certain degree of authority. This includes laws that are the subject of administration and laws that govern administration. The latter category comprises not just the narrow band of law that has come to be called *administrative law* but the entire gamut of legal rules, both formal and informal, that constrain the behavior of government officials. The relationship between the modern administrative state and law in this broader sense is extraordinarily complex. Good administration requires discretion. More than two centuries ago—long before the federal government evolved into a massive welfare and regulatory state—Hamilton wrote that "the steady administration of the laws" requires a certain amount of "energy in the executive."[27] Not even Hamilton could have foreseen a future in which the federal government distributes monthly cash benefits to individuals and federal laws regulate such things as air quality and the placement of seatbelts in automobiles. Inevitably, the more responsibility government assumes and the more complex those areas of responsibility become, the more discretion must be delegated to administrative officials.[28]

Although the enormous expansion of the administrative state since the New Deal has altered constitutional relations in the United States, the problem of controlling administration is an old one in the science of government. Unbounded discretion is the very definition of tyranny—the evil that constitutions are designed to prevent. Indeed, the limitless quality of royal discretion in late medieval England gave rise to modern constitutionalism and the idea of limiting power by the rule of law. The historical milieu of this origin is reflected in the words of William Pitt that stand carved in stone on the Justice Department building in Washington: "Where law ends tyranny begins."

Pitt's pronouncement is nevertheless too stark. Law does not simply end anywhere. No bright lines mark where the legal authority for government action begins or ends. This is particularly the case in the modern administrative state, where Congress has delegated vast amounts of discretion under sweeping, sometimes vaguely written statutes.[29] Today, most government action takes place in a twilight zone that exists between what the clear commands of law authorize and what they prohibit. Within this zone, custom, convention, professional norms, and institutional cultures merge to authorize and constrain discretionary conduct. The rule of law thereby obtains content even when no formal legal enactment or judicial degree binds governmental behavior. It is the work of government attorneys, whether located in the Department of Justice, the White House, or in one of the various administrative and regulatory agencies of the government, to construct and define these informal understandings and to assist their political superiors in navigating through them.

But granting that government lawyers at least initially provide the substance to the rule of law, the matter of how they should go about this task is less clear. The lines produced by convention and professional norms are not hard and fast, and during periods of interbranch conflict these lines fluctuate all the more. This is not to suggest that the law is wholly indeterminate, however. The rule of law requires faith in the notion that law can be objectively interpreted; and at some point, the exercise of discretion ceases to enjoy the color of law. For example, when members of Ronald Reagan's National Security Council secretly channeled "profits" generated from covert arms sales to Iran to the Nicaraguan Contras and then lied to Congress to cover up their involvement, they violated the law. No theory of administrative discretion or presidential power can change this conclusion.[30] The law, in this case the Boland Amendment, an amendment to an appropriations bill that Ronald Reagan himself had signed, might not have been good policy (as defenders of the Reagan administration are quick to assert); but disagreement with the wisdom of a law does not justify willful violation of its express provisions, even by a president or his immediate staff. Such conduct violates the very idea of the rule of law, which is implicit in the Faithful Execution Clause of Article II, among other places in the Constitution.[31]

Still, the Iran-Contra enterprise was an extreme example. Debates about the legality of administrative action are usually fought on murkier ground, where the dictates of law are less clear or where different branches and agencies of government disagree about the law's meaning. Consider, for example, the case of the EPA interpretation of law related in Michael Herz's chapter. Under provisions of the Clean Air Act Amendments of 1990, the EPA is required to hold public hearings prior to granting air pollution permits. But while the act clearly requires public scrutiny of new applications for permits or significant changes to existing permits, does the EPA violate the law if it grants minor changes in existing permits without public notice or hearings? Professor Herz describes how lawyers in the EPA came under pressure from members of the Bush White House to interpret the law in one way and from members of Congress and EPA administrators to interpret it in another. According to Herz, EPA lawyers initially sided with Congress and the agency in the dispute, but eventually they were forced to change their interpretation of the statute to conform with White House policy, which sought to decrease regulatory burdens on industry.

Did the regulation that emerged from the EPA's interpretation of the Clean Air Act violate the law? Some members of Congress thought so. The EPA's lead counsel, who was forced to publicly reverse his own independent interpretation of the law, also seems to have thought so. Evidently, however, lawyers in the White House were convinced otherwise; and so, it seems, were lawyers in the Department of Justice, which in the event issued a legal opinion siding with the White House.

One way to answer this particular question would be to report what the courts decided. This, however, misses the point that the vast majority of such decisions never get reviewed by any court; and even when they do, courts tend to display great deference to the legal positions advanced by lawyers for the executive. The solicitor general's office is extremely influential not only in setting the agenda for federal courts but also in persuading them to accept its view of the law. Professor Salokar points out that, during the past thirty years, the Supreme Court has granted nearly 70 percent of the government's petitions for review and, in rendering a decision on the merits, has accepted the legal position advanced by the office nearly 68 percent of the time.

The political import that attaches to legal decision-making in the executive, especially during periods of interbranch conflict, is amply illustrated in another controversial episode during the Reagan and Bush years. On advice from counsel in 1988, the Department of Health and Human Services reinterpreted the meaning of a twenty-year-old law so as to bring it into accord with the Reagan administration's political goal of restricting access to abortion services. Under Title X of the Public Services Act of 1970, federal agencies are prohibited from granting funds to "programs where abortion is a method of family planning." For more than eighteen years, during four different presidential administrations, the statute had been interpreted by administrators and judges alike as restricting abortions only, not counseling about abortion services. Under the administration's new interpretation, however, HHS issued new regulations prohibiting federally funded clinics from providing counseling on abortion as well.

In *Rust v. Sullivan* (1991) the new regulations were challenged on First and Fifth Amendment grounds and attacked as an unreasonable interpretation of Title X under the act.[32] After dismissing the constitutional objections to the regulation, the Court turned to the question of the executive branch's new interpretation of the statute. Upholding the administration's radical policy change, Chief Justice Rehnquist, writing for the Court, framed the issue as being whether the new regulation could be justified under "any plausible construction" of the statute. Explaining that the Court accords "substantial deference" to executive branch interpretations of the law, Rehnquist said that, when a statute is silent or ambiguous with respect to a specific action, the question for the courts is not whether the agency has adopted the best or most reasonable or most accurate interpretation, but only whether it has adopted a "permissible construction." In dissent, Justices Blackmun, Marshall, O'Connor, and Stevens pointed out that the Court's broad standard of deference to the solicitor general allowed HHS to reverse the most obvious interpretation of its statutory duty in order to adopt one that raised serious constitutional objections and that congress clearly did not intend.[33]

Stunned by the administration's reinterpretation of its statute and the Court's deference to it, Congress shortly thereafter passed legislation specifically overturning the HHS regulation. President Bush vetoed the measure, however, and the House of Representatives fell eleven votes shy of the two-thirds majority required to override.[34] In this case the Court's deference to executive branch interpretation of the law led it to condone not only the reversal of a long-established policy under the statute, but a new interpretation that was constitutionally dubious and specifically rejected by a majority in Congress. The practical effect, an editorial in the *New York Times* pointed out, was to make law backward, with administrators exercising broad discretion to make policy and Congress forced to muster a two-thirds vote to stop them.

Cases such as these raise serious questions about government lawyering in a system of separated powers. Few would argue that an administration is bound to a particular interpretation of a law simply because it was adopted by a previous administration. Nor would many argue that it is inappropriate for the President to override legal interpretations made by subordinates in the executive branch. But what should guide administrative interpretation and enforcement of the law, especially when the three branches disagree? And how should courts treat those interpretations during a period of interbranch conflict?

Cases of this type are far more common than cases of the Iran-Contra variety. Rather than being marked by bright lines, the relationship between administrative action and the rule of law resembles a continuum: at one end are administrative actions that have the intent and effect of

enforcing a shared understanding of what the law is; at the other are administrative actions that either intend or have the effect of violating that
clear understanding; in between are many shades of legality, where the
commands of law are more or less explicit and more or less consistent
with each other, in a political context that produces more or less controversy over their interpretation. The continuum expands outward and
variations in its shades grow more intense as the scope of government responsibility increases and the ability to legislate in detail diminishes. The
following chapters recount many episodes in which government attorneys struggle to establish workable interpretations along this continuum,
sometimes during the routine give-and-take of the policy-making process
and other times under intense pressures of political scandal or crisis.

Partisan Loyalty and Partisan Abuse: Two Types of Politics

The charge that the administration of law has been "politicized" is a frequent refrain in post-Watergate American politics. But what this charge
means is less than clear. The term *politics* often has more than one meaning in such discussions: politics as ideology and philosophy of government, and politics as corruption and abuse of power. While the influence
of one over the administration of law is clearly improper, the extent to
which the other might properly influence it is a matter of debate. Making
the charge of "politicization" without clearly distinguishing what it
means has confused discussions and efforts to reform the administration
of justice in the United States.

The Clinton administration's handling of Whitewater and its use of
the FBI during the White House travel office episode are only the latest
instances in which critics of an administration have charged that it has
abused or corrupted federal law enforcement.[35] The Bush administration
was alleged to have obstructed the criminal investigation of influence
peddling in the Department of Housing and Urban Development and to
have been guilty of misconduct in the investigations of the BCCI (Bank
of Commerce and Credit International) and savings and loan scandals of
the late 1980s.[36] The Reagan administration was the subject of a series of
scandals involving obstruction of justice and other efforts to cover up
wrongdoing by administration officials, including the Iran-Contra scandal and the Justice Department's attempt to conceal criminal activity by
officials in the EPA.[37] The latter scandal led to the appointment of an independent counsel who later became the subject of the Supreme Court's
1988 decision in *Morrison v. Olson* upholding the constitutionality of
the independent counsel's office.

But charges of political abuse in the administration of justice are not
unique to this period. In fact the Justice Department has been near the

center of almost every major political scandal of the twentieth century. During Woodrow Wilson's administration, for instance, Attorney General A. Mitchell Palmer provoked public outrage as a result of the so-called "Red Raids." In what historian Luther Huston called the "most bizarre performance by any Attorney General," Palmer ordered the investigation of more than 60,000 Americans who were alleged to be anarchists or extremists.[38] More than 5,000 individuals were eventually arrested or deported. The arrests were carried out in a draconian fashion; and although Palmer survived in office, the episode severely damaged the Wilson administration and led to widespread condemnation of its management of the Justice Department.[39]

Two years later, in 1921, Attorney General Harry M. Daugherty embroiled the Justice Department in the Teapot Dome scandal, nearly destroying the Harding administration. The Justice Department was accused of failing to prosecute individuals involved in bribing Interior Secretary Albert Fall in connection with an oil-reserve leasing program, and Daugherty was personally accused of trafficking in pardons and liquor permits. In the face of investigations by an independent prosecutor and a Senate Select Committee, Daugherty was forced to resign and was indicted on fraud and conspiracy charges. Although the charges against Daugherty were dropped after two separate trials resulted in hung juries, the scandal prompted congressional calls to remove the Justice Department from presidential control.[40]

In 1952, Attorney General James Howard McGrath and an assistant attorney general, Lamar Caudle, were forced to resign as the result of a tax conspiracy scandal and the Justice Department's mishandling of the matter. President Truman appointed a special prosecutor to investigate the affair, and Caudle was eventually convicted. Again there were calls in Congress to restructure the Justice Department in order to insulate it from political influence. In an effort to restore confidence in the department, McGrath's successor, James McGranery, recommended that Congress remove the U.S. attorneys and other front-line prosecutors in the department from partisan politics and make them part of the civil service.[41]

By far the most injurious scandal of corruption and abuse to involve the Justice Department was Watergate. No institution outside the presidency itself was so badly damaged by the affair. During a three-year period between 1972 and 1975, the scandal consumed five separate attorneys general, six deputy attorneys general, and two special prosecutors. The scandal, involving a cover-up of illegal campaign activity by members of the Nixon administration, reached its nadir in 1973, when President Nixon ordered Attorney General Elliot Richardson to dismiss the Watergate special prosecutor. The subsequent firings of the attorney general and the special prosecutor led Congress to consider initiating impeachment proceedings; and to forestall these, Nixon was forced to appoint another prosecutor and eventually to resign the presidency.[42] Although the president's legal authority to fire the attorney general was never seriously challenged, the controversy surrounding "political" control of federal prosecution lingered long after Nixon left the White House.

The Watergate scandal led to enactment in 1978 of the independent counsel law, which has been used to investigate allegations of misconduct during each of the five presidential administrations since.[43] Prior to settling on the independent counsel law, however, Congress considered more radical proposals for restructuring the Justice Department. In hearings titled "Removing Politics from the Administration of Justice," Senator Sam Ervin's Subcommittee on the Separation of Powers considered a proposal to create an "independent" Department of Justice by buffering the attorney general from the president's removal authority.[44] The Ervin proposal was rejected by most constitutional scholars at the time as violating the separation of powers: it would have removed from the president's control certain functions that are at the heart of the executive's constitutional duty to "faithfully execute the laws."[45]

In addition to these constitutional objections critics also questioned whether it would be desirable to shield federal law enforcement from direct political accountability. This question loomed large in light of a growing fear of "subsystem governments" and "agency capture" by special interests. The policy stagnation during the 1970s led to a major change in normative theories of public administration;[46] and as older theories favoring "neutral competence" gave way to newer ones emphasizing "responsiveness" and "accountability," the idea of creating another large independent bureaucracy became less appealing.

Finally, the assumption that the administration of law could be "depoliticized" simply by removing it from presidential control was criticized for relaying on an unsophisticated view of politics. The very title of the Ervin hearings illustrates the confusion that emerges from the dual meaning of *politics*. It is one thing to say that the president should not obstruct a criminal investigation of his own administration; it is quite another to deny the president any influence over government legal policy. Nixon's intervention into the Watergate investigation is a clear example of impropriety, but some White House interventions into decision-making by the legal bureaucracy are entirely appropriate, and few are unambiguously improper. The problem is that it is virtually impossible to erect legal obstacles that prevent partisan corruption and cronyism without also interfering with political policy influence of a proper kind.

Two examples illustrate the difficulty that efforts to distinguish between the different types of politics encounter. The first occurred in early 1971, when the Justice Department was preparing to file a major antitrust suit against ITT Corporation. The Johnson administration initiated the action, and it was ongoing when the Nixon administration came to power. The day the suit was to be filed, Attorney General Richard Kleindienst received a call from President Nixon instructing him to drop the suit. Kleindienst subsequently called the department's antitrust division and arranged for the suit to be settled out of court. Under the circumstances, Nixon's intervention in the affair may merely have reflected his interest in changing the direction of antitrust enforcement policy. This had been a major issue during the 1968 campaign, and Nixon had promised to ease federal antitrust restrictions. Kleindienst learned later, however, that ITT had promised to contribute $400,000 to Nixon's re-election campaign in exchange for an out-of-court settlement.[47]

Contrast this intervention by the White House with one that occurred seven years later, during the Carter administration. In *Regents of the University of California v. Bakke* (1978), the Supreme Court was asked to decide whether race-conscious admissions programs used by public universities violated the Civil Rights Act of 1964 and the Equal Protection clause of the Fourteenth Amendment.[48] Intervening in the suit as amicus curiae, the federal government's position was bound to have great influence on the Court. Solicitor General Wade McCree originally drafted a brief taking the position that any race-conscious treatment within the context of a voluntary state program was unconstitutional. Upon learning of the solicitor general's position, however, HEW Secretary Joseph Califano and Vice-President Walter Mondale appealed to the president to modify the Justice Department's position. Carter, who was himself committed to affirmative action programs, instructed Attorney General Griffin Bell to order McCree to rewrite the government's brief. After some protest, McCree did. The government's eventual position was softer on affirmative action, arguing only that numerical quotas (not racial preferences in general) were legally objectionable. The Justice Department's brief no doubt influenced the Court's plurality decision, which not surprisingly adopted the same position.[49]

Long before Watergate, the Nixon administration was criticized for "politicizing" the policy decisions made at the Justice Department. Nixon had made appointing a new attorney general with a new legal direction a pledge during his 1968 campaign; and under John Mitchell, the Justice Department radically altered the government's legal policies from those of the two previous Democratic administrations. From school busing to First and Fourth Amendment cases, the Justice Department switched sides in legal disputes and changed the federal government's positions. The widespread protestations of "political foul-play" that such changes prompted were answered by then–Assistant Attorney General

William Rehnquist: "the basic charge by the 'outs,' as I understand it, is that the 'ins'—the Republicans under Attorney General Mitchell—have 'politicized the Department of Justice.'" There was truth to this charge, he conceded, but "that there should not have been considerable changes in the department's policies, would be unthinkable under any meaningful system of two-party government."[50]

The Nixon administration was not the first to be criticized for "politicizing" the administration of justice in this way either. The Johnson Justice Department was criticized by congressional conservatives for being too soft on crime. The Kennedy and Eisenhower administrations were criticized for pandering to civil rights constituencies. And during the New Deal, Attorney General Homer Cummings and Solicitor General Robert Jackson were criticized for serving as Roosevelt's foot soldiers in a war on the Supreme Court's *Lochner*-era jurisprudence—an appraisal that Supreme Court Justice Jackson later admitted when he characterized his previous role as being that of a "partisan advocate."[51] Nor did the end of the Nixon administration and the reforms it inspired signal the demise of controversial White House influence in Justice Department policy-making. In the wake of Watergate, Presidents Ford and Carter tried to cultivate a more detached relationship to the Justice Department. The appointments of Edward Levi and Griffin Bell to head the department heralded efforts to "depoliticize" and buffer its operations from direct White House influence. But when the policy stakes escalated—as they did during the *Bakke* case, for instance—even Ford and Carter found it impossible to ignore Justice Department decision-making.[52] The Reagan and Bush administrations dropped any pretense of interest in an independent or detached Justice Department, calling earlier efforts to erect barriers between White House policy and Justice Department decision-making "misguided overreactions" or "deliberate efforts to strip from the executive" its powers. Administration officials during the 1980s forthrightly asserted that the Justice Department should play "an active role in effecting the principles upon which Ronald Reagan campaigned."[53]

The tendency to conflate pejorative and affirmative meanings of *politics* is deeply rooted in the antistatist nature of American political culture.[54] But the confusion that results from that conflation, especially in the period since Watergate, has hindered most efforts to reform the administration of justice and federal law enforcement. Quite apart from considerations of how to prevent corruption and abuse, questions about how responsive law enforcement should be to the president's policy agenda go to the heart of any theory of the rule of law. In both the ITT case and the *Bakke* case, the White House intervened to change the federal government's legal posture. Just because President Nixon's encroachment in the ITT case may have

been motivated inappropriately does not mean that the president is not entitled to have some say about executive-branch enforcement of antitrust
law. Similarly, just because President Carter's mediation in an affirmative
action case was arguably proper does not mean that the president should
have *carte blanche* to change the government's legal policies and positions.
What should be the extent of presidential influence over the government's
law enforcement policies? The contributors to this volume provide different answers to that question, as well as to the question of how best to guard
against corruption and abuse.

ACADEMIC CULTURES AND UNDERSTANDING LEGAL POLICY-MAKING

A final question raised by this volume involves how best to understand
and analyze developments in federal legal policy and the behavior of
government lawyers. Until recently, scholars paid scant attention to government legal work and the offices that are responsible for it. In part this
stems form the hybrid nature of the subject, which straddles disciplines
in the policy sciences and the law. Writers on the subject must be familiar
with two different academic cultures that have distinct methods of inquiry and analysis. Although government legal policy-making is sometimes mentioned in the policy science literature, just as the work of government lawyers is often alluded to in the law journal literature, such
references usually occasions discomfort in their readers, who may feel
that they have strayed too deeply into the terrain of a foreign discipline.

The problem is compounded by the curricula both in law schools
and political science, which all but ignore this important area of policy-
making. Despite contemporary modes of critical jurisprudence, law
schools continue to treat law as an autonomous science within which
change and development can be explained by focusing narrowly on the
process of judicial interpretation. The curriculum in the policy sciences,
on the other hand, tends to treat law as just another arena of political
struggle: interpretations of the law outside the courts are generally
treated as mere epiphenomena of other policy processes, not a unique
form of decision-making. The result is that lawyers and political scientists have tended either to ignore or to underappreciate each others'
work. This volume makes an effort to bring scholarship from law and political science into a common dialogue, but it is not immune to the tensions that remain between the two disciplines.[55]

There is also disagreement (rooted within larger debates in the social
sciences and the legal academy) over what factors are most important in
explaining the way legal policy is made. The contributors to this volume

use different analytical models to explain the behavior of government lawyers. Nancy Baker and Rebecca Salokar, for example, tend to focus on the behavior of individual officeholders and particular choices they make when balancing competing political and legal obligations. This agent-behavior model assumes that individuals are relatively free to define their roles. Offices are seen as institutional shells in which individual behavior and choice occur rather than as separate cultural environments that fundamentally shape the occupant's view of law and politics. Thus, changes in legal policy are usually traced to changes in personnel. If the professional self-image of the individual attorney general or solicitor general emphasizes the role of partisan advocate, the individual is likely to view the law as being a continuation of politics and is likely to be more willing to challenge precedent and push the courts to advance the president's agenda. If, on the other hand, the person's professional self-image emphasizes the role of a more neutral adviser, the official will be more likely to strive to offer principled interpretations of the law and to avoid actions that challenge the existing status of the law. For Baker and Salokar, this agent-behavior analysis explains why the Justice Department has been controversial during some periods (such as during the Reagan administration when William French Smith, Edwin Meese, and Charles Fried identified strongly with the partisan advocate role) and relatively noncontroversial during others.

The picture of agency attorneys presented by Neal Devins and Michael Herz builds on this agent-behavioral model. Although they acknowledge that individual attorneys choose between competing roles and obligations, Devins and Herz emphasize the complex multidimensional nature of those choices. The decision is not simply between being an advocate for the administration and being a more professionally independent adviser. Rather, government lawyers must choose among multiple competing political constituencies: the White House, Congress, the agency or department for which they work, and the courts. Legal policy is the result of choices made by all of the individual players in the policymaking process. Professor Herz uses this model to explain why attorneys in the EPA moved from advocating one view of the Clean Air Act to endorsing an altogether different one in the space of a few months. Likewise, Professor Devins uses the model to explain how the current haphazard pattern of distributing litigating authority to some agencies but not to others results from the exercise of political will by individual members of Congress and agency heads in resisting subordination to the executive. Here the analysis continues to focus on individual officeholders but with emphasis placed on understanding the number of players involved and the complexity of the choices that they make.

Nelson Lund extends this approach further still, into a rational-choice model. Professor Lund argues that legal policy is dictated neither by adherence to a principled jurisprudence nor by choices between competing but relatively well-defined political interests. Rather they are usually the result of highly idiosyncratic influences linked to the personal interests and powers of individuals occupying key offices at any given time. This analysis retains its focus on the choices made by individual office-holders, but it assumes that those choices are driven by the agents' own self-interests, not those of the agency or administration they represent. This model enables Professor Lund to explain why, despite a commitment to a general legal strategy aimed at bolstering the authority of the presidency as an institution, legal policy-makers in the Bush administration nevertheless failed to carry it through when making decisions affecting their personal interests.

Elsewhere I have argued that changes in government legal policy and the role of the legal bureaucracy must be understood against a backdrop of larger structural changes in the American political system and society.[56] In recent decades, three developments in particular have shaped the political context of legal policy-making and the role that government lawyers play: the growth of discretionary power in the regulatory state; the more central and autonomous role that courts have assumed in public policy-making; and the emergence of electoral dealignment and the prolonged experience with divided government during the past quarter-century. These structural-institutional developments have all served to heighten the political value of government legal policy and have generated controversy around the offices responsible for it. Thus, for example, I have argued that, to understand the separation-of-powers arguments advanced by the Justice Department during the Reagan and Bush administrations, these arguments must be removed from the narrow realm of individual choice and placed in the broader political contexts that generated them—such as the president's policy agenda and the lack of political support it enjoyed in Congress.[57]

From this perspective, the individuals who serve in office in any given time have only relative autonomy to shape the roles those offices play in the political system. The choices they make are largely determined by the broader contextual frameworks within which they operate and by the views and values that these frameworks generate. Michael Strine and Katy Harriger have employed similar contextual-institutional models of analyses to explain the behavior of attorneys recently serving in the independent counsel's office, in the White House, and in the OLC. Focusing on the complex institutional relationships and expectations that surround the independent counsel's office, Professor Harriger explains how, despite the office's formal independence, the behavior of individual counsels has nevertheless been restrained. These institutional constraints, she contends, lend accountability and should calm the fears of critics of the office.

Professor Strine advances the analysis further by examining not only the institutional constraints external to such offices but also those that are embedded within the offices themselves. Professor Strine argues that, rather than representing choices made by individual attorneys, the roles of the White House counsel and of the OLC reflect the institutional cultures that have developed inside those offices. The proximity of the White House counsel to the Oval Office has led to an institutionalized view of the law that supports the individual president; meanwhile the need to develop a role distinct from that of the White House counsel, together with the values of professionalism within the Justice Department, has led lawyers in the OLC to adopt a view that centers on defending the presidency as an institution. Accordingly, individual officeholders may marginally or temporarily alter the role of their office, but changes in one office necessarily implicate and influence the roles of others.

CONCLUSION

While it is true that government lawyers,—especially those in policy-making positions—share certain characteristics across agencies and departments, it is equally true that important differences separate them as well. Each office tells a different story, and in this volume experts familiar with the history and operation of the individual offices have tried to tell those stories. Nevertheless, by treating the offices and institutions involved in government legal policy-making as a system rather than as discrete entities, one can identify three themes that recur in the discussions in this volume: the conflict between political loyalties and the commitment to the rule of law; the importance of the separation of powers in establishing the political context of government legal work; and the general academic and pedagogical debate about how best to describe and understand the forces that drive legal policy.

This volume does not and has not sought to provide common answers to the questions posed by these themes. Instead it represents the diversity of opinion and the array of scholarship that exists. To this extent it should serve at once as a valuable introduction to this increasingly important area of public policy-making and as a catalyst for future research.

NOTES

1. Recent examples include Shep R. Melnick, *Between the Lines: Interpreting Welfare Rights* (Washington, D.C.: Brookings, 1994); Shep R. Melnick, *Regu-*

lation and the Courts: The Case of the Clean Air Act (Washington, D.C.: Brookings, 1983); Jeremy Rabkin, *Judicial Compulsions: How Public Law Distorts Public Policy* (New York: Basic Books, 1989); and Martin Shapiro, *Who Guards the Guardians? Judicial Control of Administration* (Athens, Ga.: University of Georgia Press, 1988).

2. The question of what constitutes an executive agency has been controversial at least since the Supreme Court's decision in *Humphrey's Executor v. United States* (1936). My reference to the executive branch here merely encompasses agencies that are primarily charged with carrying out the law and is not meant as an analysis of presidential authority to control these agencies' functions.

3. Most book-length studies were either histories of the Justice Department or biographical accounts of individual officeholders. See, for example, Albert Langeluttig, *The Department of Justice of the United States* (Baltimore: John Hopkins University Press, 1927); Homer Cummings and Carl McFarland, *Federal Justice: Chapters in the History of Justice and the Federal Executive* (New York: Macmillan, 1937); Francis Biddle, *In Brief Authority* (Garden City, N.Y.: Doubleday, 1962); Luther Huston, *The Department of Justice* (New York: Preager, 1967); Richard Harris, *Justice* (London: Bodley Head, 1970); Elliot Richardson, *The Creative Balance* (New York: Holt, Rinehart & Winston, 1976); Victor Navasky, *Kennedy Justice* (New York: Atheneum, 1971); Griffin Bell and Ronald Ostrow, *Taking Care of the Law* (New York: William Morrow, 1982); Richard Kleindienst, *Justice* (New York: Frederick Praeger, 1985); William French Smith, *Law and Justice in the Reagan Administration: Memoirs of an Attorney General* (Stanford, Calif.: Hoover Press, 1991); and Charles Fried, *Order and Law: Arguing the Reagan Revolution—A Firsthand Account* (New York: Simon & Schuster, 1991).

More recent scholarship has tended to focused on the political functions of particular offices. See, for instance, Luther Huston, Arthur Miller, Samuel Krislov, and Robert Dixon, *Roles of the Attorney General of the United States* (Washington, D.C.: American Enterprise Institute, 1968); Lincoln Caplan, *The Tenth Justice: The Solicitor General and the Rule of Law* (New York: Alfred A. Knopf, 1987); Cornell Clayton, *The Politics of Justice: The Attorney General and the Making of Legal Policy* (Armonk, N.Y.: M. E. Sharpe, 1992); Nancy Baker, *Conflicting Loyalties: Law and Politics in the Attorney General's Office, 1789–1990* (Lawrence, Kans.: University Press of Kansas, 1993); Katy Harriger, *Independent Justice: The Federal Special Prosecutor in American Politics* (Lawrence, Kans: University Press of Kansas, 1992); Rebecca Mae Salokar, *The Solicitor General: The Politics of Law* (Philadelphia: Temple University Press, 1992).

4. See also Baker, *Conflicting Loyalties.*

5. The phrase "learned in the law" was the requirement established in the Judiciary Act of 1789, under which the Attorney General's office was first established.

6. *Opinions of the Attorney General* 6 (1854): 326, 333–34.

7. Daniel J. Meador, *The President, the Attorney General, and the Department of Justice* (Charlottesville, Va.: White Burkett Miller Center of Public Affairs, University of Virginia, 1980), p. 26.

8. See Caplan, *The Tenth Justice.*

9. One indication of the changing political nature of these offices can be found in the confirmation process. For instance, before the 1950s, public hearings on the confirmation of attorneys general were not even held. The first time a special-interest group appeared at a confirmation hearing for attorney general was when John Kennedy appointed his brother Robert in 1961. However, the involvement of interest groups steadily increased during the next thirty years. By the time Congress confirmed Griffin Bell in 1977, representatives of some 33 separate groups testified at the hearings; and when Edwin Meese was confirmed in 1986, representatives of more than 50 groups provided testimony. For an extended discussion of growing public interest and scrutiny of the Justice Department during this period, see Clayton, *The Politics of Justice*, pp. 120–58.

10. 108 S. Ct. 2597 (1988).

11. See Suzanne Garment, *Scandal: The Culture of Mistrust in American Politics* (New York: Random House, 1991).

12. "Counsel Bill Clears Congress, and Clinton May Gain by It," *New York Times*, 23 June 1994, p. A-1; Andrew Taylor, "Schedule for Hearings Is Unclear as Starr Takes Over Probe," *Congressional Quarterly Weekly Report*, 13 August 1994.

13. For this criticism of the counsel statute, see Terry Eastland, "The Independent Counsel Regime," *Public Interest* 100 (1990): 68.

14. For a discussion of these tensions in British government, see John Ll. J. Edwards, *The Attorney General, Politics, and the Public Interest* (London: Sweet & Maxwell, 1984).

15. For a discussion of how parliamentary and presidential systems differ with respect to the political implications of the law, see Patrick Atiyah, "Judicial–Legislative Relations in England," in Robert Katzman, *Judges and Legislators* (Washington, D.C.: Brookings, 1988).

16. 556 F. Supp. 150 (D.D.C. 1983); 407 U.S. 297 (1972).

17. For his own account of this crisis, see Elliot Richardson, *The Creative Balance*.

18. Prior to this time, Justice Department refusals to defend Congress and its statutes were rare. When they occurred, Congress hired outside counsel on an ad hoc basis. But statutory creation of these independent offices now provides an institutionalized competitor to Justice Department litigation. For a discussion of the circumstances surrounding the creation and the role of these offices, see Arthur Miller and Jeffrey Bowman, "Presidential Attacks on the Constitutionality of Federal Statutes: A New Separation of Powers Problem," *Ohio State Law Review* 40 (1979): 51; and Note, "Executive Discretion and the Congressional Defense of Statutes," *Yale Law Journal* 92 (1983): 970.

19. One of the few studies of the Legal Office of the Supreme Court is John W. Winkle III and Martha B. Swann, "When Justices Need Lawyers: The U.S. Supreme Court's Legal Office," *Judicature* 76 (1993): 244.

20. For a discussion of early efforts to centralize control over the government's legal work, see Sewall Key, "The Legal Work of the Federal Government," *Virginia Law Review* 25 (1938): 165; and James Easby-Smith, *The Department of Justice: Its History and Functions* (Washington, D.C.: Lowdermilk, 1904).

21. For a general discussion of the effect of centralizing government legal authority, see Clayton, *The Politics of Justice*, pp. 77–80; and Donald Horowitz, *The Jurocracy* (Lexington, Mass.: Lexington Books, 1977), pp. 103–16. Michael Herz in the present volume argues that, while centralization usually works to strengthen White House influence, under some circumstances decentralization of the legal counseling function actually permits the president to "divide and conquer" the administrative state. With multiple sources of legal advice available, the president can pick and choose the ones he prefers.

22. The best treatment of the division of government legal services in the post–New Deal period is Donald Horowitz's *The Jurocracy*. For a general discussion of the relationship between control over government legal services and the rise of the administrative state, see Clayton, *The Politics of Justice*, pp. 73–80.

23. Horowitz, *The Jurocracy*, p. 5.

24. The literature on recent efforts to presidentialize the administrative state is vast. For two of the best recent studies, see Richard Nathan, *The Administrative Presidency* (New York: John Wiley, 1983); and Richard Waterman, *Presidential Influence and the Administrative State* (Knoxville, Tenn.: Tennessee University Press, 1985).

25. For a general discussion of this period, see Griffin Bell, "The Attorney General: The Federal Government's Chief Lawyer and Chief Litigator, or One Among Many," *Fordham Law Review* 46 (1978): 1049.

26. For a discussion of presidential efforts to assert control over agency legal policy-making and the response by Congress and the courts, see Clayton, *The Politics of Justice*, pp. 172–209.

27. *The Federalist* No. 70 (A. Hamilton), p. 423.

28. The case for expanding executive discretion in the face of the growing responsibilities of the federal government has most recently been made in Terry Eastland, *Energy in the Executive: The Case for the Strong Presidency* (New York: Free Press, 1992).

29. The best theoretical discussion of the interaction between law and administrative discretion is still found in Kenneth Culp Davis's *Discretionary Justice* (Urbana, Ill.: University of Illinois Press, 1971).

30. For a discussion of this case by one who served in the Reagan Justice Department during the Iran-Contra investigations, see Eastland, *Energy in the Executive*, pp. 96–105.

31. For elaboration on this point, see Clayton, *The Politics of Justice*, pp. 187–90.

32. *Rust v. Sullivan*, 111 S. Ct. 1759 (1991).

33. Blackmun and Marshall in dissent, 111 S. Ct. 1759 (1991), pp. 1781–86.

34. See Anthony Lewis, "How Freedom died," *New York Times*, 22 November 1991, p. A-15.

35. See chapter 5 in this volume by Jeremy Rabkin for a detailed account of these controversies and the charges that surround them.

36. See Joan Biskupic, "Thornburgh's Bumpy Start," *Congressional Quarterly* (26 August 1989), p. 2215–18; and David Johnston, "Conceding Delay at Justice," *New York Times* (13 November 1992), p. A-10.

37. For a detailed discussion of scandals involving the Reagan administration, see Clayton, *The Politics of Justice*, pp. 200–209.

38. Luther Huston, "The History of the Office of the Attorney General," in Huston, Miller, Krislov, and Dixon, *Roles of the Attorney General of the United States*, p. 13.

39. R. G. Brown and Z. Chafee, *Report upon the Illegal Practices of the United States Department of Justice* (Washington, D.C.: National Popular Government League, 1920).

40. U.S. Congress, Senate, *Hearings Before the Select Committee on Investigation of the Attorney General*, 68th Cong., 1st sess. (1924). See in particular the testimony of Assistant Attorney General John Crim.

41. U.S. Congress, House of Representatives, Committee on the Judiciary, *Hearings on Investigation of the Department of Justice*, 82nd Cong., 2d sess. (1952–1953).

42. Probably the best blow-by-blow account of the prosecution and legal proceedings surrounding Watergate is Leon Jaworski's *The Right and the Power: The Prosecution of Watergate* (Houston: Gulf Publishing, 1976).

43. See chapter 4 in this volume by Katy Harriger for a discussion of the office's operations. Although the law was allowed to lapse in 1992, the Clinton administration nevertheless felt compelled to have the Attorney General appoint an "independent counsel" to investigate the Whitewater affair. That counsel, Robert B. Fiske, Jr., was later replaced by Kenneth Starr, after the act was reauthorized by Congress in 1994.

44. U.S. Congress, Senate Committee on the Judiciary, Subcommittee on the Separation of Powers, *Removing Politics from the Administration of Justice*, 93rd Cong., 1st sess., 1974.

45. Of the seventeen witnesses who testified about the constitutionality of the plan, fourteen concluded that it would violate the separation of powers. See Clayton, *The Politics of Justice*, pp. 104–7.

46. On the changing attitudes in public administration during this period, see Roger H. Davidson, "Breaking Up Those 'Cozy Triangles': An Impossible Dream?" in Susan Welch and John Peters (eds.), *Legislative Reform and Public Policy* (New York: Frederick Preager, 1977); E. Lewis, *American Politics in a Bureaucratic Age* (Framingham, Mass.: Winthrop Publishers, 1977); Paul Quirk, *Industrial Influence in Federal Regulatory Agencies* (Princeton, N.J.: Princeton University Press, 1981); and Robert Rabin, "Federal Regulation in Historical Perspective," *Stanford Law Review* 38 (1986): 1278.

47. This ITT affair is recounted in Kleindienst, *Justice*, pp. 90–109.

48. 438 U.S. 265 (1978).

49. The episode is discussed in Bell and Ostrow, *Taking Care of the Law*, pp. 28–32.

50. William Rehnquist, "The Old Order Changeth," *Arizona Law Review* 12 (1970): 251, 259.

51. For a discussion of controversies during this period, including Jackson's quotation, see Clayton, *The Politics of Justice*, pp. 123–41.

52. Ibid., pp. 141–45.

53. Ibid., p. 147. (The quotations are from Edwin Meese, Stephen Markman, and William French Smith.)

54. The antistatist nature of American political culture and its impact on general views of politics are exposed in classics such as Richard Hofstadter's *The American Political Tradition* (New York: Random House, 1973) and Charles and Mary Beard's, *The American Spirit* (New York: Scribner's, 1943).

55. Note Nelson Lund's discussion of the limitations that the subject matter places on analysis by nonlawyers, in chapter 8 of this volume. Compare Rebecca Salokar's view of the law in chapter 3.

56. For a more general discussion of these developments, see Clayton, *The Politics of Justice*.

57. Ibid.

2

THE ATTORNEY GENERAL
AS A LEGAL POLICY-MAKER:
CONFLICTING LOYALTIES

NANCY V. BAKER

A U.S. attorney general has served the president since 1790, when Edmund Randolph joined the administration of George Washington. As of 1994, seventy-six men and one woman have filled the post. Initially the attorney general had only two statutory responsibilities: to argue federal cases before the Supreme Court and to "give his advice and opinion upon questions of law when required by the President of the United States, or when requested by the heads of any of the departments, touching any matters that may concern their departments."[1] The attorney general also began to participate in policy formation, once Randolph joined the cabinet in 1792.[2]

The courtroom function is the oldest attorney general duty, dating from fourteenth-century England, when king's attorneys represented the Crown in court. Albert Langeluttig in 1927 called this one of the most important powers, because the attorney general may decide "which infractions of law shall be prosecuted and which shall not."[3] The significance of this role has increased in the current legal climate, where litigation is perceived as an effective political strategy, which in turn has led to an explosion in interest-group litigation. Cornell Clayton notes that these factors "have led to the judicialization of larger and larger areas of public policy" and to a more politically strategic role for the attorney general.[4]

Advising the chief executive on legal matters is also a long-standing function of the office, with antecedents in seventeenth-century England and in the American colonies. In this capacity, the attorney general assists the president in fulfilling the Constitution's requirement to "take care that the laws be faithfully executed."[5] The traditional method of providing this advice is in the form of a written opinion. Until challenged, official opinions provide authoritative answers to legal questions and so may affect the development of the law.[6] They "are likely to become powerful controlling elements in the determination of governmental policies, not only through the adoption of such opinions by the heads of the departments, but as a result of the course followed by the courts of the country."[7]

A third function—administering a government bureaucracy—formally dates from the establishment of the Department of Justice in 1870, although administrative duties began to devolve onto the office even earlier. Since the 1930s, this role's scope and importance have grown. Among the factors contributing to their growth are the expansion of the federal government as a whole during this time and increased regulatory responsibilities for the attorney general.[8]

Currently the department has six divisions that handle distinct substantive legal areas: civil, criminal, environment and natural resources, tax, civil rights, and antitrust. There also are offices of the inspector general, intelligence policy and review, legal counsel, justice programs, and policy and communication. Other administrative functions of the attorney general include supervision of U.S. attorneys and marshals, the Federal Bureau of Investigation, the Drug Enforcement Agency, the Immigration and Naturalization Service, federal prisons, parole, pardons, and the Board of Immigration Appeals.[9] The department budget illustrates the dramatic growth in the nation's legal business. In 1963, the actual budget outlay was $319 million,[10] rising to $1.25 billion in 1971[11] and to $9 billion in 1991.[12] Even controlling for inflation, budgetary growth has been dramatic.[13] The budget increased 207 percent between 1967 and 1971; Clayton found that it grew 300 percent in the seven years following 1970. Recently, the department has experienced another surge of growth.[14]

Because of these heavy and diverse demands, the attorney general necessarily operates less as a lawyer than as the head of a large bureaucracy. Most of the office's functions have been delegated to subordinate officials. Responsibility for the six divisions is delegated to assistant attorneys general. Since its creation in 1933, the Office of Legal Counsel (OLC), also headed by an assistant attorney general, has promulgated most of the department's legal opinions. Administrative tasks are divided between a deputy attorney general (since 1953) and an associate attorney general (since 1977). Supreme Court responsibility has rested primarily with a solicitor general since 1870; that office works with the attorney general to determine what cases will be appealed and what amicus curiae or "friend of court" briefs will be filed.

In addition to his or her roles as litigator, legal adviser, and administrator, the attorney general serves as a political or policy adviser to the president. First, as the head of the Justice Department, he or she is required by the Constitution to provide advice and information on matters relating to that department. In that role, the attorney general testifies before Congress on legislation related to justice and the federal court system, and assists in selecting potential judicial nominees. Second, the attorney general may participate as a member of the cabinet in policy discussions of issues outside the department—for instance, issues affecting education policy or national security—and may be expected to lobby Congress on general administration policy proposals. Third, as a trusted friend or political ally, the attorney general may assist the president on a broad range of issues, from campaign strategies to personal advice.

SERVING TWO MASTERS: THE LAW AND POLITICS DEBATE

The attorney general's position is unique within the American polity because, unlike other cabinet secretaries, the attorney general has special obligations to respond to both legal and political demands. The attorney general is the chief law officer of the nation, an important legal adviser, and an officer of the court. Yet he or she also is an appointed member of a partisan administration, accountable to a democratically elected chief executive. The tension between these responsibilities faces any law officer "who tries to adjust the demands of law-in-the-abstract with the realities of politics and power," writes Victor Navasky in his 1971 portrait of the Kennedy Justice Department.[15]

This makes the position, in the words of one scholar, a "unique bridge between the executive and the judicial branches."[16] Another observer characterizes the office as "schizophrenic" because of this duality.[17]

There are two sources of this tension. One is structural, inherent in the different roles that the attorney general must play. Former attorney general Griffin Bell notes that "the attorney general wears so many hats that his independence is difficult to establish or sustain," because each role requires different degrees of contact with and independence from the executive branch.[18] The other source—which pervades the American system of government—is the lack of a clear delineation between what is legal and what is political. As Tocqueville found 150 years ago, "There is hardly a political question . . . which does not sooner or later turn into a judicial one."[19]

Attorneys general who identify strongly with one or the other role may not feel torn by a sense of competing loyalties. Edwin Meese III, for example, considered himself President Reagan's attorney first and foremost.[20] As such, he championed the president's conservative legal agenda, including a pro-life policy where his own views reportedly were more moderate.[21] He described his role in investigating the Iranian arms sale as being not the involvement of the attorney general, but that of a "friend" or adviser to the president, according to his own account, and those of Oliver North and John Poindexter.[22]

But other attorneys general do feel torn between their competing roles in direct and dramatic ways when "these two functions collide with each other head on," as Whitney North Seymour, Jr., notes they often do.[23] One such collision jarred Attorney General Francis Biddle, when Franklin Roosevelt decided to intern Japanese-Americans during World War II. Biddle felt great admiration for the president[24]; yet he also had been a long-time advocate of civil liberties.[25] In the end he acquiesced, despite his belief that the internment plans were unnecessary, cruel, and probably unconstitutional. Twenty years later, he still struggled with the memory of his compliance, wondering if he should have protested more loudly or perhaps directly to Secretary of War Henry Stimson, who might have been able to influence Roosevelt.[26]

The inherent duality of the office may be ignored for long periods, even by the president and the attorney general. Traditionally, the president enjoys the political leeway to name a close associate to the attorney general's post, and little controversy is raised thereby in the press or the Senate confirmation hearings. Most modern presidents have named a campaign manager, a campaign aide, or a national party figure as attorney general sometime during their administrations.[27] But in the aftermath of scandal, critics in Congress, the media, and academia—sensitized to the political dimensions of the office—demand an attorney general who is neutral and nonpartisan. This has happened on at least three occasions in the past 200 years.[28] The first instance occurred in 1881, when a post office scandal involving bid-fixing and route manipulation exploded just as James Garfield died and Chester Arthur became president.[29] The second episode, in 1923–1924, implicated Attorney General Harry Daugherty in such scams as selling influence, stealing confiscated liquor, and securing immunity from prosecution for clients; allegations about Daugherty broke at about the same time as the Teapot Dome scandal, intensifying the public outcry.[30] The third occasion was the Watergate break-in and cover-up in 1972, in which Attorney General John Mitchell was implicated. Mitchell was indicted on six felony counts involving obstruction of justice and perjury, and he was found guilty of five. The first attorney general to be convicted, he served nineteen months in prison.[31]

The debate diminished somewhat after the tenures of Edward Levi in the Ford administration and Griffin Bell in the Carter administration. It resurfaced in the early 1990s, although not as intensely as it had in the mid-1970s. Media and congressional critics again have called for neutrality in the office, a refrain that President Clinton was not able to ignore.[32] In part these are simply continuing echoes of Watergate that reverberate through the Washington political atmosphere. But the reinvigorated debate also stems from the specific actions of the four Reagan/Bush appointees—William French Smith, Edwin Meese, Richard Thornburgh, and William Barr. Their actions contributed to the public perception that the department has been more sharply politicized. Some scholars and writers share this view. Lincoln Caplan argues that the Reagan Justice Department "read cases, construed statutes, and represented both trial records and legislative history in radically unorthodox ways" in order to advance the president's agenda.[33] Clayton writes that department appointees "possessed a thoroughly politicized view of the law and a sense of mission about how it might be utilized for political reform."[34] Under Meese in particular, the department selectively enforced the law, "refusing to prosecute under statutes which it opposed."[35] Rebecca Salokar concedes that other administrations have taken cases to court to advance their policy views, but the Reagan Justice Department publicized this strategy and applied it to perspectives that were "significantly different from what had been publicly perceived to be the norms of American politics."[36]

Contributing to the heightened scrutiny of the office is the fact that Meese was investigated by three independent counsels after his nomination. In the first probe (which interrupted Meese's confirmation hearings), Jacob Stein investigated Meese's financial dealings while White House counsel. The second special prosecutor, James McKay, examined his associations with the Wedtech Corporation and an Iraqi oil pipeline project, as well as his handling of telecommunications cases while he held AT&T stock. Meese's activities also were scrutinized by Lawrence Walsh during the Iran-Contra investigation, although he was not the focus of this inquiry. Meese was not indicted after any of these investigations; even so, the repeated questions about his judgment that they raised undermined the credibility of the attorney generalship.

The outcome of such episodes is a hypersensitivity that constrains the choices of post-scandal presidents in naming their law officers. The Senate assumes a more aggressive posture during confirmation hearings. Thus, for example, questions about independence from White House control came up repeatedly during the hearings on Edward Levi, Ford's nominee, yet he was asked relatively few questions about traditional areas of concern to the department—law enforcement, antitrust, the death penalty, gun control, and the Voting Rights Act.[37] The issue of independence also dominated the hearings on Levi's successor, Griffin Bell.[38] One result of this heightened scrutiny is that the confirmation hearings tend to last longer. Compare, for example, the thirty-minute confirmation hearings for Nicholas Katzenbach in 1965 to the twenty-four days for Richard Kleindienst in 1972. On occasion, Congress holds special hearings to examine the attorney general's actions in office. A Senate select committee investigated Daugherty after he left office; the two months of hearings produced almost 3,000 pages of testimony.[39] In the wake of Watergate, the Senate Judiciary Committee held hearings to consider removing the Department of Justice from White House political control. The subcommittee concluded that insulating the attorney general posed other dangers, such as the loss of accountability, and was probably unconstitutional.[40] Senate ethics hearings in 1988 investigated the relationship between Meese and Wedtech Corporation officials, many of whom had been indicted on felony charges of bribery and racketeering in military procurement fraud.[41] Congressmen also may propose new legislation to weaken the attorney general's political ties to the White House. for example, in response to a recommendation by the Watergate special prosecutor,[42] Senator Lloyd Bentsen amended the Ethics in Government Act in 1977 to exclude anyone "who had served as a high-level campaign advisor to the President" from being appointed attorney general or deputy attorney general. Although it passed the Senate, the amendment was deleted in the conference committee.[43] The press also mobilizes after a scandal. Toward the end of Meese's troubled three years, the press was especially active; news reports abounded that people in the Republican party, the White House, and the Justice Department wanted his resignation.[44]

Under this pressure, presidents generally eschew personal and political associates in favor of eminent professional attorneys who have not been active in politics or partisanship.[45] Because the Watergate scandal implicated both an attorney general and a president, Gerald Ford in 1975 was especially sensitive to the need for a respected outsider to head the Justice Department. He chose a man he did not know—Levi, a former University of Chicago president. Nor was Levi partisan; he testified at his Senate hearings that he had not registered with either political party for many years, to avoid any hint that the University endorsed one party over the other.[46] Ford said at Levi's swearing-in that he consciously looked for an attorney general who could restore confidence in the "integrity and trust of our legal system."[47] Jimmy Carter a few years later responded to the same political climate when he named a federal judge, Griffin Bell, to be his attorney general. Although he was a fellow Georgian and a close friend of Carter's cousin, Bell saw himself as independent of the White House. He had Carter pledge during the campaign to place the Justice Department in a "neutral zone" outside politics, and he promised to operate "on a nonpolitical basis."[48]

Presidents ignore these external pressures at their own peril. For example, only a year after Daugherty left office, Calvin Coolidge unsuccessfully named a highly partisan nominee, Charles Beecher Warren, to be attorney general. Warren had been convention floor leader for Coolidge in 1924; furthermore, he was implicated in the Sugar Trust monopoly then under indictment. When the Senate rejected the nomination, Coolidge stubbornly renominated Warren. The Senate rejected him again. Coolidge finally selected someone less controversial.[49]

Since Watergate, a recurring normative argument has been made that the attorney general should be above politics. Critics charge that officers with partisan backgrounds or close friendships with the president will distort the law to achieve political ends. Such attorneys general may be more inclined to sanction illegal or unethical behavior in the interest of political exigency.

Justice insiders often take a different view, however. As former Nixon-era attorney general Elliot Richardson was written, "The perversion of the legal process by political pressure" cannot be permitted, but that is distinctly different from the legitimate and inescapable role that politics plays in the formation of legal policy.[50] "Laws, after all, are instruments of policy," he explained.[51] Ramsey Clark, a former attorney general in the Johnson administration and assistant attorney general under Robert Kennedy, said that "basic policy decisions are for the agencies involved" with the legal questions left to the Justice Department, "but invariably legal and policy questions become intertwined."[52] Charles Cooper, head of the OLC during the Reagan years, expressed surprise at finding that attorneys general have existed who were not sympathetic to their presidents' policy positions. Cooper said that he tried to be objective and thorough, but he was not unfriendly to the president's programs or his underlying legal philosophy. "Policy preferences plug into legal analysis at different levels," he added. "This is true of anyone who considers legal questions. All one can ask is that conscious objectivity be the operating rule."[53]

The president is constitutionally free to ignore all advice. The attorney general simply serves the president, who has the electoral legitimacy to provide general policy direction in legal areas. Arguing to the contrary ignores both the connection between law and politics and the principle of majority rule as it is embodied in the president's election. "The controversy," writes Salokar, "is rooted in the belief that the law should somehow be above politics."[54] As Homer Cummings speculated almost sixty years ago, "Law and government are probably thought of too much as if they were opposites or as if the body social had two organs, one political and one legal."[55] He and other legal realists were able to dismantle the notion that law is simply a neutral mechanism applying formal rules. While that earlier theory of legal positivism carries less weight today in studies of American courts, the conception of law as an apolitical process continues to be applied to the attorney general.

A HISTORICAL OVERVIEW OF THE OFFICE

The role, relationships, and influence of the attorney general within the American political system can be understood better in the context of historical developments. Not only is the tension between law and politics evident at an early stage, but so is another tension: fragmentation versus centralization of the nation's legal business.

The attorney generalship as an institution began 500 years ago in England, when law officers served as litigators and later as legal advisers to the Crown. The office was transplanted to the New World to ensure that colonial governments respected the Crown's interests. Between 1643 and 1683, attorneys general were appointed to the pioneer governments of Virginia, Rhode Island, Pennsylvania, and Maryland.[56] Most of the thirteen colonies had attorneys general by the beginning of the eighteenth century.[57] These law officers were not formally independent, since their authority was delegated by the English attorney general,[58] yet they were able to operate virtually autonomously because of the great distances involved. In fact, some of the colonial officials assumed broader responsibilities within their governments than their English superior possessed.[59]

The tension between loyalty to the law and loyalty to the chief executive surfaced during the colonial period. In 1752, Peyton Randolph of Virginia clashed with the colonial governor over Randolph's refusal to implement one of the governor's orders. Without the approval of the colonial legislature, the governor had imposed a fee on the signing of land grants, which Randolph considered an unlawful act. The governor removed him from office, but the new attorney general, George Wythe, also thought the governor had acted illegally, and he promptly relinquished his position to Randolph.[60] In another colonial confrontation, a New York attorney general named Graham told his governor, the Earl of Bellomont, that the latter did not have the unilateral authority he claimed to create a court system. Instead, Graham argued, Bellomont had to receive authorization from the New York General Assembly. Bellomont ignored the advice and established the courts as he had planned, claiming that his authority came from the king.[61]

By the time of the American Revolution, the system of attorneys general was well established, and it evolved with little change from a colonial to a state office. However, no attorney general existed on the national level throughout the years of the Confederation, which meant that the

Continental Congress had to hire costly outside attorneys to argue in court on behalf of the new government.[62] Early in 1781, the Continental Congress discussed the idea of establishing an office of national attorney general, but nothing came of the proposal.[63] The legislators were influenced by their strong opposition to any centralization of power. As one historian has written, "having just paid the price of war to snap the bond of a government which they considered tyrannical, the States were fiercely protective of their independence and sovereignty."[64] They did not want a national law office adding to the power of a new national government. With ratification of the Constitution, however, a U.S. attorney general represented a logical addition in the context of the new national legal order.

The first Congress created the office of attorney general in the Judiciary Act of 1789, which also established the federal court system; early drafts had proposed that the officer be appointed by the Supreme Court. The final version, leaving the appointment authority vague, implied a presidential selection.[65] The legislative history suggests that the attorney general's status was perceived to be at least quasi-judicial.

Anti-federalists opposed the measure because they saw it as an attempt to aggrandize the central government's power. The act passed, but the position of attorney general was made weaker than other cabinet posts. The officer's salary was half that of the others, which meant that the attorney general was compelled to continue in private practice. Nor was the attorney general given clear authority over the district attorneys who argued the government's side in federal cases at the trial court level. In addition, Congress for many years refused the office any funding for a clerk, or even a law book.[66] The first incumbent, Edmund Randolph, complained of the conditions under which he worked: "I am a sort of mongrel between the State and the U.S.; called an officer of some rank under the latter, and yet thrust out to get a livelihood in the former,—perhaps in a petty mayor's or county court . . . could I have foreseen it, [it] would have kept me at home to encounter pecuniary difficulties there, rather than add to them here."[67] Randolph and subsequent attorneys general advocated reform, but Congress was slow to respond.

The first major improvement to the office occurred in 1819, when William Wirt, James Monroe's attorney general, persuaded Congress to provide him with a clerk and contingent expenses, and to raise his salary from $3,000 to $3,500—still far below that of other cabinet members.[68] Wirt, who served as attorney general for twelve years, also contributed to the office by keeping records of his legal opinions. He was aghast when he discovered, upon taking office, that none of his predecessors had done so. But following Wirt's tenure, increases in congressional support were rare. The next salary boost did not come until 1831, when the office also received a small appropriation for furniture and law books.[69]

Institutionalization came slowly. Before real progress could be made, the attorney general's post had to be made full time. As it was, attorneys general often were away from the capital, preoccupied with their private practice. They could be neither active participants in administration policy-making nor effective presidential advisers.[70] All of this changed in 1853, when the able and energetic Caleb Cushing became the first attorney general to receive a salary comparable to those of his cabinet peers. Cushing interpreted this to mean that his post was now full-time. Because of his intelligence, ambition, and political skill, Cushing dominated the Pierce cabinet, eagerly assuming more responsibility than any of his predecessors had.[71] While the office remained small, with only two clerks and a messenger, Cushing already began to describe himself as the head of a law department,[72] although actual formation of the Justice Department was almost twenty years away.

Congressional debates over creating a department of justice began as early as 1829, when President Andrew Jackson proposed expanding the attorney general's responsibilities. Anti-Jackson resistance led to passage of an alternative bill that created a solicitor's post but placed it in the Treasury Department.[73] Congress continued to be skeptical of centralized legal authority, instead dispersing the nation's legal affairs to various other departments over the next eighty years. By 1915, separate legal offices operated in the departments of treasury, state, interior, commerce, labor, agriculture, navy, post office and internal revenue. These separate legal staffs were nominally brought under the attorney general's control by the Judiciary Act of 1870, but in reality they retained much of their independence.[74] Today, executive departments continue to rely on their own law staffs, but generally those offices are limited to rendering legal advice on issues relating only to their department. Most of the government's litigation now proceeds under Justice Department control. When executive departments take contradictory stands in a case, the attorney general and the solicitor general must determine which position will be argued as the government's.[75]

Another concern of the attorney general from the very beginning was the lack of clear authority over the U.S. attorneys. Early in Washington's administration, Randolph tried unsuccessfully to amend the Judiciary Act, which had made them answerable only to the president.[76] They were nominally brought under the attorney general's supervision in 1861.[77] In reality, however, Justice Department control continues to be limited. Even though the attorney general establishes broad policies with which the U.S. attorneys cooperate, the latter still enjoy considerable latitude in interpreting and applying those policies.[78]

THE ATTORNEY GENERAL'S RELATIONSHIPS

Getting Along with the President

The attorney general interacts with numerous political actors both inside and outside government, but the most important of these relationships is the one with the president. The attorney general does not operate in a narrow hierarchical channel, receiving orders only from the president and in turn dispensing orders to subordinates. In fact, despite formal organizational charts and democratic theory, a clear hierarchical arrangement does not always operate, as norms of independence influence several of the participants in legal policy-making, including the attorney general.[79]

Usually attorneys general have acted in concert with their chief executives. Compliance is neither sinister nor unusual, given that many presidents have selected attorneys general who are political allies. They may agree with the president. They may act out of a strong sense of personal loyalty. They may view compliance as legitimate and consistent with the demands of majority rule. They may even share a president's sense of mission about a policy goal.

One example of a sense of shared mission was that felt by Attorney General Ramsey Clark for Lyndon Johnson's civil rights stand.[80] Despite LBJ's occasional use of racist rhetoric in his House and Senate career, he had been raised in the nonplantation South, and his father and grandfather had supported black political participation; Johnson himself believed that poverty and racism were twin evils. For his "basic fairness" on race issues, he always received solid support from black voters.[81] As vice-president and chairman of the President's Committee on Equal Employment Opportunity, Johnson began to advocate civil rights more openly. On becoming president, he moved quickly and aggressively for passage of the Civil Rights Act of 1964.[82] After this major legislative success, Martin Luther King, Jr., characterized Johnson's commitment to civil rights as genuine.[83] Ramsey Clark, a fellow Texan, had become active in civil rights activities while an assistant attorney general in 1962, when he participated in the federal effort to desegregate the University of Mississippi. The next year, he oversaw other desegregation efforts of Southern schools and colleges, and helped initiate early discussions of civil rights legislation.[84] In early 1965, he worked with others on a draft of a voting rights bill, under continual prodding by Johnson.[85] When he became LBJ's attorney general in 1967, Clark easily assumed an advocacy role in this policy area. His Justice Department initiated the first desegregation case in a Northern school district, and he lobbied on behalf of the Open Housing Act of 1968.[86]

President Reagan and his attorneys general agreed on such social issues as the restoration of prayer in public schools; curtailment of the legal rights of the accused; and an end to busing, affirmation action, and abortion. Reagan spoke often on these subjects, but he relied on Justice Department lawsuits to achieve substantive change, since his legislative efforts were focused primarily on economic issues.[87] His three attorneys general—William French Smith, Edwin Meese III, and Richard Thornburgh—reflected these policy positions in their speeches, litigation priorities, and recommendations for judicial appointments.[88] Litigation proved a viable avenue for shifting the legal/policy direction of earlier administrations. Since the federal government was seldom a party in these cases, the solicitor general's office would file amicus curiae briefs to advance the administration's position.[89] In the area of abortion law, for example, the solicitor general's office supported efforts to overturn or limit *Roe v. Wade* (1973) in cases decided in 1983,[90] 1986,[91] and 1989.[92] Although *Roe* stands, a 1992 ruling[93] vindicated the Reagan policy on two counts: the court majority rejected the trimester framework of *Roe,* and it upheld a number of state restrictions on abortion. Judicial appointments also were utilized to advance policy goals in the Reagan years. Meese explained that societal problems with drugs, pornography, racial quotas, and "social issues" resulted from the liberal rulings of federal judges in the 1960s and 1970s. He and Reagan concluded, "Something had to be done about the judges."[94] The Justice Department employed rigorous screening of potential nominees through the Office of Legal Policy (OLP), established by Smith, Reagan's first attorney general. The OLP scrutinized the speeches, articles, and opinions of judicial candidates, and interviewed them to ascertain both their judicial philosophy and their likely positions on various hypothetical cases, including ones involving the constitutionality of abortion.[95]

Leading the Way for the White House

Attorneys general usually act as agents of their presidents, but on a few occasions the attorney general has successfully advocated a policy that differed form the chief executive's. Respecting the legal expertise of their attorneys general, some presidents defer to them, particularly when a question of constitutionality exists on which the attorney general feels strongly.

As early as 1953, Attorney General Herbert Brownell wanted to move the executive branch more quickly in civil rights reform and enforcement than President Dwight Eisenhower did. Eisenhower was not opposed to civil rights; one of his first presidential acts had been to end racial segregation in all public accommodations and parks in the District of

Columbia.[96] But being sensitive to claims of states' rights, the president preferred a gradual evolution toward desegregation rather than federally mandated change.[97] Brownell, however, was able to advance a more aggressive civil rights agenda in two areas. First, he was instrumental in framing the administration's response to the first major desegregation case, *Brown v. Board of Education* (1954), which the president preferred to ignore. He persuaded Eisenhower that the Justice Department had to file an amicus brief pertaining to the Fourteenth Amendment in the case. Later, in Court, Brownell was able to link his brief to the earlier Truman administration brief, which explicitly opposed segregation, thus implying to the justices that the Eisenhower administration also was opposed.[98] In fact, the president privately was disappointed in the decision, and he refused to permit wording in the 1956 party platform that his administration supported it.[99] Second, Brownell played a significant role in framing and pushing through Congress the Civil Rights Bill of 1957, the first since Reconstruction. Accounts differ as to Eisenhower's sympathy with this goal. Brownell himself writes that he merely followed Eisenhower's orders[100]—a view shared by Eisenhower's biographer Stephen Ambrose, who notes that Ike told his attorney general to draft a civil rights bill.[101] But political historian John Anderson writes that Brownell was the architect and promoter of a much stronger bill than Eisenhower contemplated. Brownell reportedly used Eisenhower's absence after a heart attack to maneuver the bill past the cabinet and then employed political tactics in Congress to make the bill difficult for the president to repudiate in an election year.[102] While not publicly opposed to the measure, Eisenhower was "not badly disappointed" when the bill initially died in the Senate Judiciary Committee.[103] It eventually passed Congress in a measurably weakened condition.

A second example of an attorney general leading a reluctant president occurred in 1968. That spring, the Poor People's Campaign began to march on Washington, D.C., with plans to camp near the Lincoln Memorial. Lyndon Johnson, who feared that the march would lead to a violent and televised confrontation with poor blacks, pressured Attorney General Clark to deny them a permit and so prohibit the march.[104] Possibly he worried that the march would create a situation that would make him look either weak or repressive in the eyes of the nation.[105] LBJ had difficulty accepting public criticism; he did not see his actions designed to discourage dissent as an exercise in stifling debate, but as a question of utility.[106] But Clark refused; he believed that the marchers were acting within their constitutional rights of assembly and free speech.[107] In persuading Johnson, he also stressed a more pragmatic argument—that the marchers were more likely to become disorderly if denied a legal means of protest. A legal march would draw more responsible participants.[108] In the end, the march was held, with Clark and others from Justice meeting repeatedly with organizers to work out logistics and to ensure nonviolence. After Martin Luther King, Jr., was assassinated and rioting swept through Washington, Clark faced renewed pressure to call off the demonstration and use federal troops to restore order.[109] He withstood the pressure, explaining in his 1970 book his aversion to using force to silence public protest, "To be constitutional, commitment of troops against citizens presupposes insurrection beyond the control of state and local law enforcement,"[110] which was not the case in 1968.

An incident in the Carter administration also illustrates that attorneys general may assert positions at variance from their presidents'. In 1973, a twelve-year-old Hispanic boy was killed by a Dallas policeman in the back of a squad car; the officer was convicted in state court but sentenced to only five years in prison. In 1978, when Carter heard of the mild sentence, he was outraged and asked the attorney general to review the case personally. Bell and the Civil Rights Division did so, but they decided against federal prosecution of the police officer; the case had been prosecuted vigorously in the state court, they concluded, even though the jury had imposed a light sentence.[111] Bell believed a second prosecution would be unconstitutional, placing the officer in double jeopardy and thus violating the Fifth Amendment. After he refused to undertake a federal prosecution, Carter was furious, calling the decision a disgrace. Bell remembers telling the president, "You can't tell me who to prosecute. You delegated the prosecutorial discretion to me. I have to exercise it. But you can get rid of me." Bell now notes, "He almost fired me for that decision."[112]

The Attorney General and Competing Power Centers

Other relationships are important to the attorney general as well, and some of these may create greater tension than the relationship with the president. Griffin Bell discovered as attorney general that his greatest conflicts were with White House aides, and not with Jimmy Carter. He identifies five power centers in the White House that compete with the attorney general in making legal policy: the domestic policy staff, the Office of Management and Budget (OMB), the National Security Council (NSC), the White House counsel, and the vice-president.[113]

The attorney general's primary competitor is the White House counsel. Created by Franklin Roosevelt and situated in the White House, the office of White House counsel provides a wide range of legal and nonlegal advice to the president. The counsel's status as a staff aide is not coequal with the attorney general's cabinet rank; nor do his or her opinions influence the courts. Even so, proximity to the Oval Office enhances the counsel's authority in some administrations. This is particularly so when a close friend of the president occupies the position, as in the Ford administration when Philip Buchen was White House counsel or in the Bush administration when C. Boyden Gray was counsel. Such appointments tend to draw legal policy-making into the White House and out of the Justice Department. In the Ford administration, for example, the president consulted Buchen, a former fraternity brother and law partner, when the Cambodian government seized the *Mayaguez* in 1975; Attorney General Levi was not included in the discussions.[114] Buchen also advised Ford on the legal issues raised by pardoning Richard Nixon, particularly the question of constitutional powers; in fact, Buchen was one of only four insiders informed in advance that Ford was considering a pardon.[115] Buchen himself denied that his close advisory relationship with Ford created tension with Levi.[116]

A similar situation arose in the Bush administration. As Bush's "trustiest aide,"[117] Gray had singular access to the Oval Office.[118] Gray, not the attorney general, provided advice on the legal ramifications of various international crises of 1989, 1990, and 1991, including those associated with freezing Iraqi assets and sending troops into the Persian Gulf.[119] One incident suggests that he had an impact on domestic as well as international legal policy. In 1990, the Justice Department issued new sentencing guidelines for companies convicted of crime; the guidelines, supported by Deputy Attorney General Donald Ayer, were especially strict. Several business leaders protested to Gray, who then contacted the Justice Department. Ayer immediately withdrew his support of the guidelines and, two weeks later, resigned. His successor was a close associate of Boyden Gray's.[120]

Bill Clinton also named a long-time family friend, Bernard Nussbaum, to the White House counsel's post. Attorney General Janet Reno had to compete with Nussbaum after her belated arrival in Washington. Because the attorney general for the first few months of the administration was a Bush holdover, Nussbaum was given responsibility to begin staffing the Justice Department and to set the administration's legal policy on such issues as the handling of Haitian refugees. Even after Reno was confirmed, the White House counsel continued to have substantial input into the appointment of individuals to top Justice Department posts, including the politically bungled nomination of Lani Guinier to head the Civil Rights Division. Reno reportedly had a veto power over such appointments, but did not use it.[121] Her lack of input in legal policy vis-a-vis the White House was especially notable in the crime bill submitted to Congress in 1993 and passed the following year. The administration's bill, usually drafted by the attorney general, came out of the White House instead. A number of its features—such as the expansion of the number of federal crimes punishable by the death penalty, continued mandatory minimum sentences for first-time nonviolent drug offenders, and funding for an increase in police forces—did not have Reno's support.[122] Department insiders were reportedly frustrated that she was not able "to restore the department's primacy at the juncture of law and politics."[123]

The office of White House counsel has had its critics; Justice Felix Frankfurter, for example, blamed the counsel for President Harry Truman's flawed decision to seize and operate the nation's steel mills before a threatened strike in 1952—an action later struck down by the Supreme Court.[124] Another vocal critic has been Griffin Bell, who recounts in his memoir several incidents where he clashed with the counsel, particularly on control of judicial nominations.[125] This was the case even when the office was occupied by Robert Lipshutz, Carter's first counsel, a low-key lawyer.[126] Conflict increased when the savvy Washington lawyer Lloyd Cutler replaced Lipshutz.

Among the other competing power centers is the office of the vice-president, invigorated with new political clout during Carter's term in office and sustained at that level in the Reagan, Bush, and Clinton administrations. Bell reports that Walter Mondale and his staff sought to define the administration's legal position on the question of whether (and to what extent) church schools could receive federal CETA (Comprehensive Employment and Training Act) funding. Justice Department attorneys in the OLC had counseled Carter that CETA funds could be used only for health aides and kitchen personnel, but not for teachers, counselors, or clerical staff. The Catholic community responded angrily, and Mondale and Stuart Eizenstat of the domestic policy staff persuaded Carter to ignore that opinion. CETA funding of sectarian schools was later overturned in the federal courts.[127] Mondale also reportedly tried to control the government's amicus position in the Allan Bakke affirmative action lawsuit, and the drafting of a charter for the FBI.[128]

Clinton's vice-president and attorney general have also had occasion to clash over the direction of legal policy. As part of his proposal to streamline government, Al Gore recommended in 1993 that the Drug Enforcement Administration be consolidated with the FBI. Reno, whose department houses both agencies, seemed initially in favor of the merger.[129] In the following weeks, however, she repudiated the proposal. Her public disapproval contributed to the administration's decision to drop the plan—a major early setback for Gore's proposals to eliminate government redundancy.[130]

Others in the White House also may exercise influence in legal policy-making, in competition with the attorney general. In the first Reagan term, for example, the Justice Department received direction from the White House, particularly from Edwin Meese. Meese writes that Reagan was concerned with "matters of law enforcement, drugs, family policy, civil rights [and] the courts" from the outset and that, as counselor to the president, he played an active role in setting policy in these areas and in screening judicial appointments.[131] He also influenced a number of government litigation positions; in at least two cases, he was able to convince the department to change its position in the middle of litigation. Both of those cases reversed long-standing government positions. One was brought by Bob Jones University, which had been denied tax exempt status because it had a racially discriminatory admissions policy.[132] The other dealt with Grove City College's violation of Title IX rules in connection with its refusal to file certain mandatory federal forms.[133]

Others have disagreed with the notion that the White House and the Justice Department compete in the arena of legal policy-making. Two members of the Reagan Justice Department noted in 1986 that the attorney general and the department were the principle legal advisers in the executive branch, responsible for formulating the more important and controversial opinions.[134] This may have been true at the time, when Fred Fielding was White House counsel and Meese, a longtime Reagan aide, was attorney general. Fielding, an old friend of Chief Justice Warren Burger, does not appear to have been a Reagan intimate.[135] Even under Fielding, however, the White House counsel exercised significant authority in screening judicial nominations by chairing the President's Committee on Judicial Selection.[136] Furthermore, the assertion about Justice Department primacy ignores the evidence that the Justice Department during Reagan's first term received ideological direction from Meese and the White House.

The tension between the attorney general and the White House counsel or the vice-president has emerged out of institutional changes in the modern presidency. But another source of competition for the attorney general is much older: the conflict with a department secretary on legal questions relating to policies in the other department's jurisdiction. Historic examples may be found as early as the tenure of Edmund Randolph, the first attorney general. Randolph clashed with Secretary of State Thomas Jefferson over U.S. policy toward the French revolutionaries; Washington, believing that Jefferson was too partisan on the matter, relied on Randolph's advice. Jefferson was sufficiently annoyed to characterize Randolph as, "the poorest chameleon I ever saw, having no color of his own and reflecting that nearest him."[137] This long-standing tension continues in contemporary administrations. For example, Attorney General Meese and William Bradford Reynolds, head of the Civil Rights Division at the Justice Department, clashed with Labor Secretary William Brock III over Executive Order 11246. The order, first signed by Lyndon Johnson, prohibits federal contractors from discriminating in employment and requires them to institute affirmative action plans. In 1985, Meese and Reynolds tried to persuade Reagan to rewrite and weaken the executive order. The Labor Department became involved because it is responsible for implementing the order. Secretary Brock consistently opposed the proposal to weaken the order and eventually succeeded in convincing the president to retain the policy.[138]

Although this is somewhat more unusual, competition can even come from within the department. The second-ranking person in the Clinton Justice Department, Associate Attorney General Webster Hubble, has a close relationship with the Clintons that affords him more access to the president than Reno enjoys. As partner to Bill Clinton on the golf course and as Hillary Clinton's former partner in a Little Rock law firm, Hubble had a direct line to the White House. His authority grew in the months between the inauguration and Reno's confirmation, because he served as administration liaison with acting Attorney General Stuart Gerson of the Bush Justice Department.[139]

Congress is another potentially difficult arena for the attorney general. Griffin Bell argues that an attorney general must carefully maintain independence from Congress: "If you bow to the Congress, you can do just as much damage as if you're not independent of the White House."[140] Janet Reno is the latest attorney general to be accused of caving in to congressional pressure. In July 1993, she permitted Congressman John Dingell's staff to interview attorneys in the Justice Department's environmental crimes section.[141] Dingell wanted to investigate why several cases involving alleged violations of federal environmental law never were prosecuted by the department.[142]

In the Carter years, Bell sought to neutralize the political pressure brought into the department through these varied relationships. He established guidelines to clarify the areas where the Justice Department should make independent decisions, and he set up rules to prohibit contact between career attorneys and either Capitol Hill or the White House on specific investigations. Through an OLC memorandum, he reiterated the importance of independence for the solicitor general.[143] In these ways, he tried to insulate the professional staff from political demands. These buffers, however, were dismantled in the Reagan Justice Department.

CONCLUDING THOUGHTS

Attorneys general have played a pivotal role in policy-making and implementation since the beginning, but their importance as players has expanded with the emergence of the administrative state and the explosion of litigation. They operate at the nexus of law and politics—as the nation's chief law office on one hand, and as presidential appointee on the other. Among the diverse and sometimes competing roles required of every incumbent are those of federal litigator, legal counsel, presidential adviser, and administrative department head. Different attorneys general have emphasized different roles, interpreting their responsibilities in light of their own understanding of the office. Many have not recognized the tension inherent in the position.

Attorneys general who share a close association with the president have been among the most influential political actors, particularly in administrations that utilize the law as a policy tool. As Robert Kennedy and Edwin Meese illustrate, such advisers are trusted to provide guidance on a wide range of issues. But not all attorneys general operate with this high level of presidential trust. Even if their professional eminence and integrity are widely recognized, such attorneys general may find that their authority is diminished by competitors who are closer to the president. This "outsider" law officer is more likely to be appointed in the aftermath of scandal, when presidential choice is circumscribed by a more rigorous press, a more aggressive Senate, and a more attentive public.

Legal scholars as well as public officials have wrestled with the nature of the attorney generalship. Among the individuals who have recommended distancing the office from politics have been Arthur Goldberg,[144] Archibald Cox,[145] and Mitchell Rogovin.[146] Law scholar Daniel Meador argues that "inappropriate political entanglements" are one of the twin problems facing the office. The other problem, lack of time, is related to the first, since the multiple nonlawyering functions "distract the Attorney General."[147] The trend was noted as early as 1927, when Albert Langeluttig wrote, "His duties as administrative head of the Department of Justice require his entire attention, and since the creation of the office of Solicitor General, the Attorney General has not always been appointed primarily for his legal ability."[148]

Constitutional and institutional factors—including such notions as "shared" powers, rule of law, and majority rule—create the broad contours in which the attorney general acts as a legal policy-maker. Within this general landscape, however, the attributes, values, abilities, and relationships of individual law officers provide the environmental details that may help explain certain policy outcomes. This chapter has used case studies and historical examples to examine how the attorney general as a political actor both affects and is affected by the institutions in which he or she operates.[149]

NOTES

1. Judiciary Act of 1789, 1 Stat. 73, sec. 35.

2. Homer Cummings and Carl McFarland, *Federal Justice: Chapters in the History of Justice and the Federal Executive* (New York: DaCapo Press, 1970, reprint ed), pp. 25, 495.

3. Albert Langeluttig, *The Department of Justice of the United States* (Baltimore: Johns Hopkins University Press, 1927), p. 21.

4. Cornell Clayton, *The Politics of Justice: The Attorney General and the Making of Legal Policy* (Armonk, N.Y.: M. E. Sharpe, 1992), pp. 6–7. He adds that the importance of judicial selection has been enhanced for these same reasons.

5. U.S. Constitution, art. II, sec. 3.

6. Dee Ashley Akers, "The Advisory Opinion Function of the Attorney General," *Kentucky Law Journal* 38 (1950): 561; Robert Toepfer, "Some Legal Aspects of the Duty of the Attorney General to Advise," *University of Cincinnati Law Review* 19 (1950): 201–2.

7. Arthur J. Dodge, *Origin and Development of the Office of Attorney General*, H.R. Doc. 510, 70th cong., 2d sess. (Washington, D.C.: U.S. Government Printing Office, 1929), p. 17.

8. Clayton, *The Politics of Justice*, p. 40.

9. Nancy Baker, "Justice, Department of," in Louis Fisher and Leonard Levy (eds.), *Encyclopedia of the American Presidency* (New York: Simon & Schuster, 1993).

10. "New Obligational Authority by Agency," *Budget of the United States Government, Fiscal Year 1965* (Washington, D.C.: Government Printing Office, 1964), p. 44.

11. "Budget Authority and Outlays by Agency," *Budget of the United States Government, Fiscal Year 1973* (Washington, D.C.: Government Printing Office, 1972), p. 497.

12. "Current Services Budget Authority by Agency," *Budget of the United States Government, Fiscal Year 1993* (Washington, D.C.: Government Printing Office, 1992), pp. 2–21.

13. See Figure 2.2, "Justice Department Budget 1920–1990 in Constant Dollars," in Clayton, *The Politics of Justice*, p. 28.

14. "Budget Authority and Outlays by Agency," *Budget of the United States Government, Fiscal Years 1969, 1973, 1985, 1989, 1993* (Washington, D.C.: Government Printing Office, 1968, 1972, 1984, 1988, 1992); Clayton, *The Politics of Justice*, p. 27.

15. Victor S. Navasky, *Kennedy Justice* (New York: Atheneum, 1971), p. xx.

16. Daniel J. Meador, *The President, the Attorney General, and the Department of Justice* (Charlottesville, Va.: White Burkett Miller Center of Public Affairs, University of Virginia, 1980), p. 26.

17. Robert Palmer, "The Confrontation of the Legislative and Executive Branches: An Examination of the Constitutional Balance of Powers and the Role of the Attorney General," *Pepperdine Law Review* 11 (January 1984): 349.

18. Griffin B. Bell and Ronald J. Ostrow, *Taking Care of the Law* (New York: William Morrow, 1982), pp. 183–84.

19. Alexis de Tocqueville, *Democracy in America*, ed. J. P. Mayer (Garden City, N.Y.: Anchor Books, 1969), pp. 269–70.

20. Interviews with Terry Eastland and Charles Cooper, Washington, D.C., 19 October 1987. Eastland was the director of the Office of Public Affairs in the Meese Justice Department, and Cooper was the assistant attorney general for the Office of Legal Counsel.

21. Lou Cannon, *President Reagan: The Role of a Lifetime* (New York: Simon & Schuster, 1991), p. 812. Cannon writes, "[Terry] Eastland remembers that Meese while at Justice expressed personal and policy views on abortion that would be regarded as 'middle of the road.' That is also my own recollection from California."

22. "November 1986: The Attorney General's Inquiry," *Report of the Congressional Committees Investigating the Iran-Contra Affair, with Supplemental, Minority, and Additional Views*, November 1987, 100th Cong., 1st sess., H. Rept. No. 100-433; S. Rept. No. 100-216. (Washington, D.C.: Government Printing Office, 1987), p. 305, 305n.

23. Whitney North Seymour, Jr., *United States Attorney: An Inside View of "Justice" in America Under the Nixon Administration* (New York: William Morrow, 1975), pp. 228–29.

24. Francis Biddle, *In Brief Authority* (Garden City, N.Y.: Doubleday, 1962), pp. 4–5.

25. In fact, he had some success in ensuring free speech and press critical of the president and of American involvement in World War II, despite Roosevelt's pressure on him to do something to stop the "anti-war talk." Biddle, *In Brief Authority*, pp. 234–38.

26. Peter Irons, *Justice at War* (Oxford: Oxford University Press, 1983), pp. 17, 32; Biddle, *In Brief Authority*, pp. 205–26. In fairness to Biddle, there was little he could do, since FDR used an executive order to implement the program, evidently without first sending it to the attorney general for a legal opinion.

27. Notable recent examples include Robert Kennedy in the Kennedy administration, John Mitchell in the Nixon administration, and Edwin Meese in the Reagan administration. The exceptions are Lyndon Johnson, Gerald Ford, and Jimmy Carter.

28. Nancy Baker, *Conflicting Loyalties: Law and Politics in the Attorney General's Office, 1789–1990* (Lawrence, Kans.: University Press of Kansas, 1993), ch. 1, 4, and 5.

29. For a description of the "Star Route" scandal, see Eugene C. Savidge, *Life of Benjamin Harris Brewster* (Philadelphia: J. B. Lippincott, 1891), pp. 119–49.

30. James N. Giglio, *H. M. Daugherty and the Politics of Expediency* (Kent, Ohio: Kent State University Press, 1978).

31. *Watergate Special Prosecution Force Report* (Washington, D.C.: Government Printing Office, 1975), pp. 52, 156. The cases were *Mitchell et al. v. Sirica,*

D.C. Cir. No. 74-1492, 502 F.2d 373 (1974), and *U.S. v. Mitchell*, D.C. Cir. No. 75-1384.

32. See, for example, Anthony Lewis, "Challenge of Justice," *New York Times*, 25 December 1992, p. A-31; David Kaplan, "No More Hacks or Cronies: Clinton, for a Change, Should Pick an Attorney General Who Is Above Politics," *Newsweek*, 23 November 1992, p. 64. Part of the appeal of Janet Reno was that she had weathered significant public scrutiny already as Dade county prosecutor, and she was known for her integrity. Richard L. Berke, "Clinton Picks Miami Woman, Veteran State Prosecutor, to Be His Attorney General: President Appears Eager to Move Past Turmoil of Baird and Wood," *New York Times*, 12 February 1993, pp. A-1, A-22.

33. Lincoln Caplan, *The Tenth Justice: The Solicitor General and the Rule of Law* (New York: Alfred A. Knopf, 1987), p. 271.

34. Clayton, *The Politics of Justice*, p. 146.

35. Ibid., p. 6.

36. Rebecca Mae Salokar, *The Solicitor General: The Politics of Law* (Philadelphia: Temple University Press, 1992), pp. 99–100.

37. U.S. Congress, Senate, Judiciary Committee, *Hearings on the Nomination of Edward H. Levi to Be Attorney General*, 94th Cong., 1st sess. (Washington, D.C.: Government Printing Office, 1975).

38. U.S. Congress, Senate, Judiciary Committee, *Hearings on the Nomination of Griffin Bell to Be Attorney General*, 95th Cong., 1st sess. (Washington, D.C.: Government Printing Office, 1977), pp. 10, 33, 44–46, 137, 142–44.

39. U.S. Congress, Senate, *Hearings before the Select Committee on Investigation of the Attorney General*, 68th Cong., 1st sess. (Washington, D.C.: Government Printing Office, 1924). Among the charges were obstruction of justice in war fraud and land fraud cases; failure to prosecute illegal monopolies; and sale of jobs, including judgeships.

40. U.S. Congress, Senate, Judiciary Committee, *Hearings on S. 2803 and S. 2978 Before the Subcommittee on the Separation of Powers on Removing Politics from the Administration of Justice*, 93d Cong., 2d sess. (Washington, D.C.: Government Printing Office, 1974).

41. U.S. Congress, Senate, Subcommittee on Oversight of Government Management of the Committee on Governmental Affairs, *Office of Government Ethics' Review of the Attorney General's Financial Disclosure*, 100th Cong., 1st sess. (Washington, D.C.: Government Printing Office, 1988).

42. *Watergate Special Prosecution Force Report* (Washington, D.C.: Government Printing Office, 1975), p. 136.

43. *Congressional Quarterly Almanac 1977* (Washington, D.C.: Congressional Quarterly, 1978), pp. 581, 584.

44. A sampling of press reports in spring 1988: "Should Ed Meese Resign? An Enemy of the People," *ABA Journal* 74 (1 February 1988): 39, Editorial, "For an Earlier Meese Exit," *Christian Science Monitor*, 5 February 1988. Editorial, "The D-p--tme-t of J-st-ce." *New York Times*, 31 March 1988. Philip Shenon, "High Justice Aides Quit Amid Concern Over Meese's Role," *New York Times*, 30 March 1988. Philip Shenon, "More Justice Aides Expected to Resign," *New York*

Times, 31 March 1988. Fox Butterfield, "Ex-Justice Aide Deeply Troubled by Meese Role," *New York Times*, 31 March 1988. "Dumping Meese: Close Reagan Advisers Mount Drive to Force Attorney General Out," *Wall Street Journal*, 27 April 1988. "Meese Told He Is Hurting GOP and Bush Presidential Campaign," *New York Times*, 26 May 1988.

45. Baker, *Conflicting Loyalties*, ch. 5.

46. Gerald R. Ford, "Attorney General Edward H. Levi," *University of Chicago Law Review* 52 (Spring 1985): 284–285; U.S. Congress, Senate, *Hearings on the Nomination of Edward H. Levi*, pp. 2–3, 7.

47. Memo on the president's talking points at the swearing in ceremony of Edward Levi, 7 February 1975, folder "FG 17/A 8/9/74 - 2/10/75," Box 88, FG 17/A—Department of Justice, Gerald R. Ford Library, Ann Arbor, Michigan.

48. U.S. Congress, Senate, *Hearings on the Nomination of Griffin Bell*, pp. 20, 33; Griffin Bell, "Office of Attorney General's Client Relationship," *Business Lawyer* 36 (March 1981): 791.

49. Donald McCoy, *Calvin Coolidge: The Quiet President* (Lawrence, Kans.: University Press of Kansas, 1988), pp. 278–81.

50. Elliot Richardson, *The Creative Balance* (New York: Holt, Rinehart & Winston, 1976), p. 26.

51. Interview with Elliot Richardson, 20 October 1987, Washington, D.C.

52. Ramsey Clark, Transcript of Oral History Interviews, 30 October 1968, Lyndon Baines Johnson Library, Austin, Texas, p. 6.

53. Interview with Charles Cooper, Washington, D.C., 19 October 1987.

54. Salokar, *The Solicitor General*, p. 71.

55. Homer Cummings, *Liberty under Law and Administration* (New York: Scribner's, 1934), p. 114.

56. For good early histories, see James Norton-Kyshe, *The Law and Privileges Relating to Colonial Attorneys General and to the Office Corresponding to the Attorney General of England in the United States* (London: Stevens & Haynes, 1900); Hugh S. Bellot, "The Origin of the Attorney General," *Law Quarterly Review* 25 (1909): 403; Sewall Key, "The Legal Work of the Federal Government," *Virginia Law Review* 25 (1938): 165; George W. Keeton, "The Office of Attorney General," *Juridical Review* 58 (1946): 108; Rita Cooley, "Predecessors of the Federal Attorney General," *American Journal of Legal History* 2 (1958): 306.

57. Lewis W. Morse, "Historical Outline and Bibliography of Attorneys General Reports and Opinions," *Law Library Journal* 30 (April 1937): 102, 195, 200, 226–27; Oliver W. Hammonds, "The Attorney General in the American Colonies," in *Anglo-American Legal History*, series 5, vol. 1, no. 3 (New York: New York University School of Law, 1939), pp. 3, 13, 15, 20, 22. Georgia was not established until 1733; it named its first attorney general in 1752.

58. James Hightower, "From 'Attornatus' to the Department of Justice," The Library of Congress, Legislative Reference Service, 17 August 1966, cited in U.S. Congress, Senate, *Hearings on S. 2803 and S. 2978 on Removing Politics*, p. 407.

59. John Ll. J. Edwards, *The Law Officers of the Crown* (London, Sweet & Maxwell, 1964), p. 9.

60. Edmund Randolph, *History of Virginia* (Charlottesville, Va.: University Press of Virginia, 1970), pp. 161–62, 183. See also Hammonds, "The Attorney General in the American Colonies," pp. 9–10, 35.

61. Cummings and McFarland, *Federal Justice*, p. 12.

62. U.S. Congress, *Journals of the Continental Congress*, vol. 19 (23 January 1781), ed. by Gaillard Hunt (Washington, D.C.: Government Printing Office, 1912), pp. 75, 354.

63. U.S. Congress, *Journals of the Continental Congress*, vol. 19 (16 February 1781), pp. 155–56, 190.

64. Hightower, "From 'Attornatus' to the Department of Justice," pp. 408–9.

65. Charles Warren, "New Light on the History of the Federal Judiciary Act of 1789," *Harvard Law Review* 37 (1923): 108–9.

66. Ibid., pp. 58, 130–31. Hightower, "From 'Attornatus' to the Department of Justice," p. 412. Key, "The Legal Work of the Federal Government," p. 176.

67. Letter, 1790, reproduced in Moncure Daniel Conway, *Omitted Chapters of History in the Life and Papers of Edmund Randolph* (New York: G. P. Putnam's Sons, Knickerbocker Press, 1888), p. 135.

68. John P. Kennedy, *Memoirs of the Life of William Wirt*, vol. 2 (Philadelphia: Lea & Blanchard, 1850), p. 65.

69. Langeluttig, *The Department of Justice of the United States*, pp. 4, 6.

70. Henry B. Learned, *The President's Cabinet* (New Haven, Conn.: Yale University Press, 1912), pp. 176–77.

71. Claude M. Fuess, *The Life of Caleb Cushing* (New York: Harcourt, Brace, 1923), vol. 2, pp. 136–137; Cummings and McFarland, *Federal Justice*, pp. 149–50, 156. In part this was due to his high energy and inclination, but in part it was also due to his ability to devote himself full time to the office.

72. Caleb Cushing, "Office and Duties of the Attorney General," *American Law Register* 5 (December 1856): 86–87.

73. Senate, *Register of Debates*, 26 March 1830, 13 April 1830, and 30 April 1830, pp. 276, 322–24, 404; Key, "The Legal Work of the Department of Justice," pp. 177–79.

74. Cummings and McFarland, *Federal Justice*, p. 487.

75. One example is the Tellico Dam controversy during the Carter administration. The Tennessee Valley Authority wanted to continue construction of the dam despite an Interior Department ruling that construction had to cease because the snail darter fish in the area was endangered. The Justice Department in the Ford administration had sided with the TVA, and Carter's attorney general believed that he should maintain that position. The Interior Department was permitted to file an appendix to the Justice Department brief explaining its interpretation of prior court rulings. See Baker, *Conflicting Loyalties*, pp. 159–60.

76. Langeluttig, *The Department of Justice of the United States*, p. 12.

77. Ibid., p. 8.

78. James Eisenstein, *Counsel for the United States* (Baltimore: Johns Hopkins University Press, 1978).

79. See discussions about claims of independence in Salokar, *The Solicitor General*, p. 174, and Baker, *Conflicting Loyalties*, pp. 32–33.

80. Lloyd Cutler, Transcript of Oral History Interviews, 12 April 1969, LBJ Library, p. 4. Cutler was executive director of the Commission on Violence during the Kennedy administration. He had heard the president, Robert Kennedy, and Johnson speak on civil rights and found Johnson's speech the most moving. Cutler said, "I have no question but that [Johnson] had a deep personal conviction about the matter."

81. Mark Stern, *Calculating Visions: Kennedy, Johnson and Civil Rights* (New Brunswick, N.J.: Rutgers University Press, 1992), pp. 115–17, 119, 121. See also Robert Dallek, *Lone Star Rising: Lyndon Johnson and His Times, 1908–1960* (New York: Oxford University Press, 1991), pp. 276–77, 287–89, 369.

82. Stern, *Calculating Visions*, pp. 153–55, 160–64, 170.

83. Ibid., p. 185.

84. Clark, Transcript of Oral History Interviews, 11 February 1969, LBJ Library, pp. 3–4, 8–16.

85. Stern, *Calculating Visions*, p. 223.

86. Richard Harris, *Justice: The Crisis of Law, Order, and Freedom in America* (New York: E. P. Dutton, 1970).

87. Barbara H. Craig and David M. O'Brien, *Abortion and American Politics* (Chatham, N.J.: Chatham House Publishers, 1993), pp. 164–65, 169–72; Ronald Reagan, "Address to National Association of Evangelicals," Orlando, Florida, 8 March 1983; Ronald Reagan, "Second Inaugural Address," 21 January 1985.

88. See, for example, Elder Witt, *A Different Justice: Reagan and the Supreme Court* (Washington, D.C.: Congressional Quarterly, 1986), pp. 139–47; Richard Wiley and Laurence Bodine, "Q & A with the Attorney General," *American Bar Association Journal* 71 (July 1985): 46; John A. Jenkins, "Mr. Power: Attorney General Meese is Reagan's Man to Lead Conservative Charge," *New York Times Magazine*, 12 October 1986, pp. 19, 92.

89. Salokar, *The Solicitor General*, p. 76.

90. *City of Akron v. Akron Center for Reproductive Health*, 462 U.S. 416, 103 S. Ct. 2481 (1983).

91. *Thornburgh v. American College of Obstetricians*, 476 U.S. 747, 106 S. Ct. 2169 (1986). Thornburgh, then governor of Pennsylvania, later served as attorney general under both Reagan and Bush.

92. *Webster v. Reproductive Health Services*, 492 U.S. 490, 109 S. Ct. 3040 (1989). The Justice Department persuaded Missouri's attorney general to appeal the lower court decision invalidating the state's abortion restrictions.

93. *Planned Parenthood of Southeastern Pennsylvania v. Casey*, 112 S. Ct. 2791 (1992).

94. Edwin Meese III, *With Reagan: The Inside Story* (Washington, D.C.: Regnery Gateway, 1992), pp. 315–16.

95. Craig and O'Brien, *Abortion and American Politics*, p. 173; Cannon, *President Reagan*, pp. 802–3; Clayton, *The Politics of Justice*, pp. 64–65.

96. Herbert Brownell and John Burke, *Advising Ike: The Memoirs of Attorney General Herbert Brownell* (Lawrence, Ks.: University Press of Kansas, 1993), pp. 186–87. Eisenhower felt on solid ground here; this was clearly a federal issue. Furthermore, the congressional committees that governed the District of Columbia—dominated by Southern Congressmen—had ignored for decades a Reconstruction-era ordinance making such segregation illegal in the nation's capital.

97. John W. Anderson, *Eisenhower, Brownell and the Congress: The Tangled Origins of the Civil Rights Bill of 1956–57* (Tuscaloosa, Ala.: University of Alabama Press, 1964), p. 29.

98. Brownell and Burke, *Advising Ike*, pp. 189–94; Stephen E. Ambrose, *Eisenhower* (New York: Simon & Schuster, 1984), pp. 124–26, 142. In fact, Ambrose reports that, at a White House stag dinner, Eisenhower appeared to try to influence Chief Justice Earl Warren to uphold the Topeka, Kansas, school board. Warren and a unanimous Court did not. Ambrose, *Eisenhower*, pp. 189–90.

99. Ambrose, *Eisenhower*, pp. 190–91, 328.

100. Brownell and Burke, *Advising Ike*, pp. 216, 217, 220.

101. Ambrose, *Eisenhower*, p. 30.

102. Anderson, *Eisenhower, Brownell and the Congress*, pp. 4–5, 18–20, 27–28, 39, 42–43, 60–61, 135.

103. Ambrose, *Eisenhower*, p. 327.

104. Harris, *Justice*, pp. 61–62. In a similar incident the previous October, Clark convinced LBJ that the protest march on the Pentagon was constitutional; p. 64.

105. Philip Geyelin, *Lyndon B. Johnson and the World* (New York: Frederick Praeger, 1966), p. 154.

106. Ibid., p. 140.

107. Harris, *Justice*, pp. 18, 61.

108. Memo from Clark to Larry Levenson of the White House, 3 June 1968, on the permit for the June 19 demonstration, in Box 74 of the Personal Papers of Ramsey Clark, LBJ Library. Clark wrote, "I plan to authorize the issuance of a permit, with appropriate conditions and restrictions, because I believe it will give us by far the best chance to have the June 19 demonstration on an orderly and peaceful basis. It will tend to maximize the number of responsible people who will participate, and provide the best opportunity to control the troublemakers."

109. Harris, *Justice*, pp. 61–62.

110. Ramsey Clark, *Crime in America* (New York: Simon & Schuster, 1970), p. 278.

111. Bell and Ostrow, *Taking Care of the Law*, pp. 32–34.

112. Interview with Bell, Washington, D.C., 21 October 1987.

113. Bell and Ostrow, *Taking Care of the Law*, pp. 35, 39.

114. Richard Head, Frisco Short, and Robert McFarland, *Crisis Resolution: Presidential Decision-making in the* Mayaguez *and Korean Confrontation* (Boulder, Colo.: Westview Press, 1978), pp. 51, 56, 71, 108–9, 113, 115, 122,

141, 240; Baker, *Conflicting Loyalties*, pp. 146–48; see also relevant files at the Gerald R. Ford Library.

115. Comments of Philip Buchen and Robert Hartmann, Seventh Presidential Conference: Gerald R. Ford, 8 April 1989, Hofstra University, published in *Gerald R. Ford and the Politics of Post-Watergate America*, Bernard Firestone and Alexej Ugrinsky (eds.) (Westport, Conn.: Greenwood Press, 1993), pp. 57–58, 60–61. The other three insiders, including Hartmann, were all White House advisers.

116. Buchen letter to journalist Nina Totenberg, specifically refuting the allegation that their relationship was "anything but highly satisfactory," 31 March 1976, folder "FG 17 1/1/76 - 3/31/76," Box 87, FG 17—Department of Justice, Ford Library.

117. W. John Moore, "The True Believers," *National Journal* 17 August 1991, p. 2018. Columnist William Safire described the relationship between Bush and Gray as being comparable to that between father and son. Safire, "A Tale of Three Counsels," *New York Times*, 28 December 1992, p. A-15.

118. Michael Wines, "A Counsel with Sway over Policy," *New York Times*, 25 November 1991, p. A-16.

119. Bob Woodward, *The Commanders* (New York: Simon & Schuster, 1991).

120. Andrew Rosenthal, "Bush Nominates Deputy as Head of Justice Dept." *New York Times*, 17 October 1991, p. A-1. The successor was William Barr, soon to succeed to the attorney generalship itself.

121. Ruth Marcus, "The Man Behind the President: White House Counsel Bernie Nussbaum Rises to the Defense," *Washington Post*, 1 July 1993, p. B-1; David Margolick, "At the Bar," *New York Times*, 11 June 1993, p. A-26, also published in "At the Bar," *Washington Journal*, 21 June 1993, p. 38.

122. Anthony Lewis, "Where Was AG Reno Through Crime Bill?" *New York Times*, 22 November 1993; Bob Cohn and Eleanor Clift, "The Contrary Voice of Janet Reno," *Newsweek*, 11 October 1993, p. 30; Bill Turque, "The Politics of Crime," *Newsweek*, 6 December 1993, pp. 20–22; author's interview with Peter Boyer, staff writer, *New Yorker*, 2 November 1993.

123. David Johnson and Stephen Labaton, "Doubts on Reno's Competence Rise in Justice Dept.," *New York Times*, 26 October 1993, pp. A-1, A-18.

124. Bruce Allen Murphy, *The Brandeis/Frankfurter Connection* (Garden City, N.Y.: Anchor Press/Doubleday, 1983), pp. 325–26. The case was *Youngstown Sheet and Tube Company v. Sawyer*.

125. Bell and Ostrow, *Taking Care of the Law*, pp. 24–38, 40–42.

126. Ibid., pp. 35, 39.

127. Ibid., pp. 25–27. When his successor, Benjamin Civiletti, later tried to defend CETA funding of Wisconsin church schools, a U.S. district court judge issued a nationwide injunction, and the U.S. Court of Appeals for the Seventh Circuit affirmed this injunction. The Justice Department decided not to appeal to the Supreme Court.

128. Bell and Ostrow, *Taking Care of the Law*, pp. 29–38, 40–42.

129. Neil A. Lewis, "White House Seeks to Combine FBI with Drug Agency; Gore and Reno Back Plan," *New York Times*, 19 August 1993, pp. A-1, A-21.

130. Stephen Labaton, "Administration Drops Plan to Merge Justice Agencies," *New York Times*, 22 October 1993, p. A-12.

131. Meese, *With Reagan*, pp. 304–5, 317.

132. *Bob Jones University v. United States*, 461 U.S. 574 (1983); Caplan, *The Tenth Justice*, pp. 51–60.

133. *Grove City College v. T. Bell*, 104 S. Ct. 1211 (1984); Terrel H. Bell, *The Thirteenth Man: A Reagan Cabinet Memoir* (New York: Free Press/Macmillan, 1988), p. 101.

134. Interviews with Charles Cooper and Terry Eastland, Washington, D.C., 19 October 1987.

135. Fielding resigned as White House counsel prior to the breaking of the Iran-Contra scandal. Donald T. Regan, *For the Record: From Wall Street to Washington* (New York: Harcourt, Brace, Jovanovich, 1988), pp. 64, 330.

136. Clayton, *The Politics of Justice*, p. 65.

137. Conway, *Omitted Chapters of History*, pp. 148–51, 190–91; Cummings and McFarland, *Federal Justice*, pp. 36–39.

138. "Law/Judiciary: Affirmative Action Disputes," *Congressional Quarterly Almanac*, 1985, p. 221.

139. David Von Drehle, "Out of the Shadows: A Clinton Pal has been Justice's Mystery Man," *Washington Post National Weekly*, 12 April 1993, p. 34; Holly Idelson, "Hubbell, Nominee for No. 3 Job, Quizzed About All-White Club," *Congressional Quarterly*, 22 May 1993, pp. 1298–99.

140. Bell and Ostrow, *Taking Care of the Law*, p. 65; Bell, interview with author, Washington, D.C., 21 October 1987.

141. "General Dingell," editorial, *Wall Street Journal*, 8 July 1993, p. A-12.

142. Bryan Abas, "Dingell's Justice Probe Is Justified," *Wall Street Journal*, 22 July 1993, p. A-15.

143. Bell and Ostrow, *Taking Care of the Law*, pp. 58, 65, 78; Caplan, *The Tenth Justice*, pp. 48–50.

144. Goldberg testimony, "Hearings on Removing Politics," pp. 61–63.

145. Cox testimony, "Hearings on Removing Politics," pp. 198–99.

146. Mitchell Rogovin, "Reorganizing Politics out of the Department of Justice," *American Bar Association Journal* 64 (June 1978): 855.

147. Meador, *The President, the Attorney General, and the Department of Justice*, pp. 57–58.

148. Langeluttig, *The Department of Justice of the United States*, p. 2.

149. This approach, while focusing on individual decision-making, is not necessarily inconsistent with the "New Institutionalism" of such public law scholars as Rogers M. Smith, "Political Jurisprudence, the 'New Institutionalism,' and the Future of Public Law," *American Political Science Review* 82 (March 1988): 89–108.

3

POLITICS, LAW, AND THE OFFICE OF THE SOLICITOR GENERAL

REBECCA MAE SALOKAR

On May 28, 1993, Drew S. Days III was quietly confirmed by the U.S. Senate and later that afternoon sworn in as the fortieth solicitor general of the United States. Surprisingly, the occasion received little press coverage despite its representing the culmination of a twelve-year experience that revealed the potential power of this office as a policy-making tool of the White House. As the senior practicing attorney in the Department of Justice, the solicitor general represents the administration and, thus, the "United States" before the U.S. Supreme Court. The most frequent litigant before the Supreme Court, the solicitor general is responsible for defending both the constitutional and the statutory powers of the executive branch, as well as the policies promoted and supported by the administration that the office serves. At the same time, however, the individual officeholder must work to maintain the office's traditional reputation for integrity before the Supreme Court by presenting the government's arguments in a highly professional manner. In essence, this political appointee operates in an environment dominated by both politics. and law.

In recent years, scholars have debated the nature of the solicitor general's office, on grounds rooted in the theoretical distinction between law and politics. Lincoln Caplan, in *The Tenth Justice: The Solicitor General and the Rule of Law,* argues that the history of this office is marked by independence from the political whims of the White House and a long-standing dedication to the "rule of law," commonly interpreted as meaning the development of legal principles in a "neutral" fashion. Thus, the title of Caplan's book explicitly suggests that the solicitor general is intimately tied to the functions of the Supreme Court and ought to be immune to the politics of the executive branch.

Caplan's view can be substantiated by the numerous comments of former solicitors general in describing their work. Consider, for example, Francis Biddle's comment, "The Solicitor General has no master to serve except his country,"[1] or more pointedly, the words of Simon Sobeloff: "My client's chief business is not to achieve victory, but to establish justice."[2] Even Robert Bork's assessment of his role as solicitor general for the Nixon administration suggests that law and the judicial processes took precedence over his work as advocate for the executive branch: "The Court and its functions under our Constitution are far more important than a Government victory in any given case."[3]

Interpreting the "rule of law" as an apolitical aspect of our government's framework, however, overlooks the very nature of the American constitutional tradition. To assert that law is a static institution that ought to be impervious to political change is to ignore the important roles that the adversarial process and the Supreme Court have played in that tradition. Unlike several European judicial systems, which employ a neutral legal adviser or consultant for their constitutional courts (for example, the advocate-general in the European Community or the French *commissaire du gouvernement*), the American tradition of separated powers does not provide for such a disinterested participant. Rather, the justices rely on the arguments presented by opposing parties through an adversarial process, and each of those parties works to invoke the "law" to their own end. The solicitor general is simply one of the many advocates who appears before the Court—albeit more frequently than others, and on issues that touch the very heart of our governmental processes.

That the solicitor general professionally presents the government's case and adeptly employs the norms of precedent and legal reasoning, should not be taken to minimize the office's role as an advocate who wants to prevail on the merits for a client (namely, the executive branch and its interests). The essence of law and the adversarial process is inherently political; it is a battle for power, resources, and legitimacy in an arena dominated by lawyers and judges where the strategies differ significantly from the politics of electoral campaigns or of the legislative process. Clearly, the rules of the game are more structured in the judicial arena, and the resources a lawyer uses to prevail in a court of law do not necessarily depend on constituency support, compromise, or negotiation. But to argue that the role of the solicitor general is or ought to be apolitical is to ignore reality. The solicitor general is, first and foremost, an advocate for the institutional power of the executive branch, its coordinate departments, and its agencies. One should expect that the decisions and arguments of this political appointee will advance the policy goals of the administration he or she serves.

Prior to the 1980s, very little research existed on the solicitor general and on the office's various functions. Largely invisible, most scholarly writings on the topic were penned by former solicitors general seeking to explain their role to the legal community.[4] One exception was the work of Robert Scigliano, a political scientist who sought to flesh out the various aspects of the relationship between the Supreme Court and the executive branch. His chapter on the solicitor general, published in 1971, stood as the only scholarly treatment of the topic for more than twenty years.[5]

The election of Ronald Reagan to the presidency ended the shadowy work of the office. What was different about the early 1980s (and to a lesser extent, about the Nixon administration) was the greater degree of systemic political conflict over what the law should be on a range of important policy issues. With divided party control both within Congress (during the early years of the Reagan administration) and between the legislative and executive branches, political tensions were heightened on a national scale. In the face of resistance by Congress to the president's legislative strategy, the administration turned to the courts as a potential ally for political change. This focus on a legal strategy meant that the work of the solicitor general was even more important and more visible as salient issues like abortion, the separation of church and state, and civil rights reappeared on the Supreme Court's docket.

Unquestionably, the work of the solicitor general was visibly political during the Reagan administration. But this experience should not be interpreted to mean that the solicitor general's work had historically been apolitical. Rather, the experiences of the Reagan era suggests that the work of the solicitor general reflects the degree of conflict evident in national politics. When consensus exists among the three branches on the major issues of the day, the solicitor general's decision may predictably be less controversial and less visible; but they are nonetheless based on political considerations. Thus, an appraisal of the role of the solicitor general during any administration should not be cast as a matter of law or politics. Rather, the issue for scholarly examination should be one of degree—the extent to which the work of the office reflects the political debates of the day. Ultimately, what the Reagan administration taught us is that the solicitor general can be a valuable operative for an administration seeking policy change through the courts.

The importance of the solicitor general is clearly evident from the frequency with which the United States government appears before the Supreme Court. Between 1959 and 1989, the federal government participated either as a party or as an amicus (friend of the court) in 48.5 percent of all cases decided on the merits by the Supreme Court. The solicitor general's office also appeared in 59 percent of the cases that were scheduled for oral argument.[6] But more important is the apparent success of the government's attorney on the merits. During this thirty-year period, the arguments advanced by the solicitor general prevailed in 67.6 percent of the cases in which the government participated.[7]

In this chapter, I discuss the history of the solicitor general's office, its internal organization, and its role in the political qua judicial process. The decision-making strategies of the solicitor general and the degree to which politics and the policy concerns of the administration play a role in these decisions are examined in some detail. Also explored are the relationships between the solicitor general and other governmental actors. Finally, throughout this chapter, I have integrated references to recent scholarly research on the solicitor's office in the belief that the scope of inquiry is still in its early stages of development.

As a scholar trained in political science rather than in the law, my perspective on this office will trouble those who view the law as having a fixed meaning or as constituting a body of rules for which we can always find reasoned arguments and rational developments. The thesis that runs throughout this chapter is that the solicitor general has historically been a political actor in the arena of legal policy-making. Thus, while certain presidents have been more aggressive or systematic in their use of government litigation in pursuit of their political agenda, all have viewed the office and its work as a tool for attaining their administration's goals and policy objectives. To expect the Clinton administration, or the administration of any modern president, to ignore one of the most important offices for controlling government legal policy is to misunderstand not just the realities of contemporary American politics, but the nature of American law and the American legal system. While the legal tools have been modified over time, the motivations for solicitors general to defend the executive branch and to serve as advocates for administration policy have remained the essential attributes of this office.

HISTORY AND ORGANIZATION OF THE OFFICE

The solicitor general's office was established under the Justice Department Act of 1870. Two factors contributed to the creation of the office. First, Congress had traditionally established a separate position of solicitor for each of the large executive departments. Thus, by 1870, the Treasury Department, Internal Revenue Service, State Department, and the Naval Judge Advocate each had its own legal representatives. The practice led to duplicity and conflicts between agencies. More important, however, was the resulting lack of cohesive national legal policy. The second factor that contributed to the development of the position of solicitor general was a fiscal concern: departments that did not enjoy the resources of an in-house solicitor or that were faced with cases docketed at appellate courts in other areas of the country had to hire private counsel at great expense.

It is clear from the legislative history of the Justice Department Act, that Congress envisioned the solicitor general as an attorney who could be a generalist. Representative Jenckes from Rhode Island, the congressional sponsor of the bill, argued that: "If a sugar case is to be tried today, the Attorney General can send his solicitor to attend the trial. The champagne cases and the whiskey cases and other revenue cases in New York could be postponed until the solicitor general can go there and try them. In the course of a year one competent lawyer could try all these important cases . . . ."[8] Although the vision of a traveling solicitor general was abandoned in practice, the broad, generalized nature of the office's work remains a visible element of its operation today. Indeed, this aspect particularly appealed to former solicitor general and Supreme Court Justice Thurgood Marshall. Upon his retirement from the Court, a reporter asked him which of his three careers—as attorney for the NAACP, solicitor general, or justice of the Supreme Court—he had most enjoyed. Marshall's response suggested that it was the variety of his work as solicitor general that gave him the most pleasure: "As solicitor general," he noted, "you are in the dead middle of everything that's legal and you have your two cents to put in."[9]

The only qualification for office under the 1870 statute was that the solicitor general must be "learned in the law."[10] The office was to serve as second in command at the Department of Justice, and the solicitor general was to assist the attorney general "and with the attorney general, conduct and argue" cases before the Supreme Court. The first solicitor general, Benjamin Bristow, was appointed to office by President Ulysses Grant with an annual salary of $7,500. A list of Bristow's successors includes some of America's most renowned attorneys: John W. Davis, William Mitchell, Stanley Reed, Robert H. Jackson, Francis Biddle, Charles Fahy, Archibald Cox, Thurgood Marshall, Erwin Griswold, and Robert Bork, to name only a few.

The work of the solicitor general has changed very little over time. The establishment of the office of deputy attorney general in 1953 removed many of the administrative functions that the solicitor general had performed in the Justice Department and allowed the solicitor general to focus more on litigation. Still, when Erwin Griswold became solicitor general in 1967, he found that"the work was exactly the same as it had been nearly forty years before," during his tenure as a young assistant in 1929.[11] Although the volume of cases has grown significantly over the years, necessitating an increase in the number of attorneys assigned to the office, the nature of the work and the general processes of handling cases have remained virtually unchanged. The office is steeped in tradition and history. Even the solicitor general's traditional apparel for argument before the Supreme Court—a morning coat with striped trousers—continues to be worn in contemporary practice.

The office is staffed by a small cadre of twenty-five or so career attorneys who remain in office from one administration to the next. These career attorneys are divided into deputy solicitors general and assistant solicitors general. They provide continuity to the work of the office and serve as the key repository of institutional knowledge about the organization. Most of the career attorneys come to the office from outside the Department of Justice and bring with them law degrees from elite law schools, superb academic records and clerkship experiences with federal appellate courts. Given the massive volume of cases that flows through the office each year (between July 1984 and July 1985, 4,083 substantive matters), these attorneys spend a great deal of time screening cases and preparing briefs. Unlike the heads of most executive agencies, however, solicitors general have traditionally exhibited a reluctance to expand the size of the office.[12]

One significant organizational change within the office that occurred during the Reagan administration involved the addition of a position formally entitled, "Deputy Solicitor General and Counselor to the Solicitor General." The position emerged as a result of an extraordinary set of circumstances surrounding the 1983 case of *Bob Jones University v. United States*.[13] The case involved denial by the Internal Revenue Service (IRS) of tax-exempt status to a private, religiously based university whose admissions policy was racially discriminatory. Solicitor General Rex Lee's former position as counsel to the Mormon church led him to recuse himself from the case, so Lawrence Wallace, the senior deputy in the office, was assigned to develop the administration's legal arguments as acting solicitor general. White House officials, led by presidential counselor Edwin Meese, wanted the solicitor general to side with the university, but Wallace, viewing the dispute as well-settled by case law, supported the IRS. Nonetheless, Wallace devised a compromise in accordance with which he submitted a brief advancing the White House's views but added a footnote indicating that he personally disagreed with the brief's legal position.[14] To avoid having this embarrassing scenario recur, the administration shortly thereafter established the position of political deputy.

Critics of the Reagan administration have pointed to the political deputy's post as evidence that the administration "politicized" the work of the solicitor general in a manner antithetical to its role as an independent, legal office dedicated to the "rule of law."[15] In fact, however, the development of such a position was long overdue. As in many of the divisions inside the Justice Department and within other executive agencies, having a deputy secretary avoids placing career staff members in the personally distasteful or ethically difficult situation of reversing policy positions that they previously were involved in developing or implementing. It is hardly surprising that neither the Bush administration nor Clinton administration has eliminated the political deputy's position.

The selection and appointment process for solicitors general is another indicator of the office's political nature. Subject to Senate confirmation, the White House, in consultation with the attorney general, seeks to nominate a person who is not only "learned in the law" but shares the basic ideological concerns of the administration. Drew S. Days III, for example, seems to have been chosen by President Clinton on the basis of his previous experience as Assistant Attorney General for the Civil Rights Division during the Carter administration, his advocacy work for the NAACP's Legal Defense and Educational Fund, and his academic record as a professor of law at Yale University. Robert Bork was nominated and confirmed to be solicitor general during the second term of the Nixon administration and brought to the office his own conservative economic and social ideology. To suggest that the president or attorney general would nominate someone who did not share the partisan leanings of the administration ignores both the history and the strategic political role of the office. Whatever insulation or independence the solicitor general enjoys from White House policy direction—a characteristic of the office examined later in this chapter—is made possible by the selection process's guarantee that the incumbent will share the political philosophy of the administration.

Although deputy and assistant solicitors general have the opportunity to make a career out of their assignments, few do. During both the Nixon and Reagan administrations, sources reported staff discontent and a more rapid turnover of attorneys than at other times in the past. Four deputy solicitors general who had served less than three years each resigned during the Nixon administration. In 1986, press reports announced similar staff dissatisfaction with the Reagan administration and noted the departure of four of the five civil service attorneys, who were allegedly discontent with political positions being taken by Charles Fried, Reagan's second solicitor general.[16] But whatever frustrations existed with the particular administration, several other factors might have led to these departures, including the relatively low salary for attorneys in the office (especially when compared to what they could command in private firms) and the personal management style of the political appointee. Notably, the one deputy who had the most compelling reason to leave during the Reagan administration, Lawrence Wallace, did not abandon his career. On the record, none of the attorneys have pointed to the politicization of the office as the impetus for their departure—and probably for good reason. Like all civil service staff, they are well aware that changes in administration and leadership are to be expected; it is the nature of their position within the executive bureaucracy.

Despite differences in management style that political appointees bring to the office, the actual processing of cases has remained relatively constant over the years. The initial screening of cases is performed by the assistants, who prepare their own evaluation of the merits of each case, including a written recommendation about whether the solicitor general should consider pursuing an appeal to the Supreme Court (or permitting an appeal to the circuit courts of appeal in noncriminal cases lost in district court). The assistants' assessments are then reviewed by one of the five deputy solicitors general.[17] Although the deputy solicitors general traditionally divide case responsibilities by policy area and thus may appear to specialize in certain types of cases, changes in their assignments ensure that they remain generalists.

Once the deputy solicitor general involved has added his or her evaluation of the case, the solicitor general reviews the recommendations and makes a decision. When attorneys in the office disagree on the disposition of the case, the solicitor general may request further information from the agency or division of the Justice Department that referred the case or may arrange conferences with the appropriate players. Once the decision is made to seek the Supreme Court's review, an assistant or deputy is generally assigned to prepare the petitions for certiorari (jurisdictional statements in appeals) and to craft the government's position on the merits. The deputies work closely with the assistants, and all documents filed with the Supreme Court receive some level of review by the solicitor general, but much of the work in the office is performed independently by the assistant solicitors general.

Perhaps the most coveted assignment is to argue the government's case before the justices. Each attorney in the office typically argues one to two cases a year; and for assistants, these cases are generally the ones that they have prepared. The solicitor general traditionally reserves for himself or herself what are viewed as the most important cases—namely, the cases likely to receive a great deal of press attention, the ones the government simply cannot afford to lose, and the ones in which the solicitor general's presence is likely to "send a message" to the Court. Solicitor General Archibald Cox, for example, personally argued the landmark reapportionment case, *Baker v. Carr*, in hopes of persuading the middle-of-the-road justices.[18]

The institutionalization of the case-management process within the office and the expertise of a skilled corps of attorneys who can draw on the full range of information and resources available to the executive branch produce the ideal model of what Marc Galanter has called "the

Repeat Player."[19] As the most frequent litigant before the Supreme Court, the solicitor general enjoys the advantages of advance intelligence, access to specialists and to a wide range of resources, expertise, opportunities to build informal relationships with members of the Court, and a reservoir of credibility with the justices. Unlike the "One-Shotter," whose single case is of critical importance, the solicitor general's office has the opportunity to choose its cases so as best to protect its client's interests. According to Galanter, the "Repeat Player" enjoys greater success in the courtroom than the litigant who is a one-time player. As discussed in the next section, this success is evident in the solicitor general's record before the highest court in the nation.

ROLES OF THE SOLICITOR GENERAL

The responsibilities of the solicitor general include both organizational tasks within the Department of Justice and (more importantly) management of cases in which the government is a party. This latter category includes not only Supreme Court litigation, but also decisions on whether to pursue an appeal in noncriminal government cases lost in the lower courts. Although decisions to allow agency attorneys or U.S. district attorneys to pursue appeals have policy implications and consume a great deal of office resources,[20] this area of the office's work has rarely been the subject of scholarly research. Rather, the more visible and arguably more important decisions involving Supreme Court litigation have received the bulk of scholarly attention.

The roles of the solicitor general with respect to Supreme Court litigation are many. Perhaps the most important cases are those in which the government is named as a party. First, the solicitor general is responsible for deciding which cases lost by the government at the appeals court level merit a petition for certiorari to the Supreme Court.[21] In making these decisions, the solicitor general is in a position to act as a gatekeeper for the Court, culling out only the "best" cases for its attention. In the 1984 Supreme Court term, for example, Solicitor General Lee reviewed over 700 cases lost by the government in the courts of appeals but filed only 43 requests for review by the Supreme Court.[22]

Deciding which cases to send to the Court involves anticipating the outcome of the rather blurry criteria that the justices use in granting certiorari review. Generally, the stipulations of Rule 17 of the Rules of the Supreme Court serve as the initial guideline. Solicitors general and their staff look for conflicts in case law between circuits, conflicts between federal appellate courts and state courts of last resort, radical departures by federal courts from well-established legal principles, or cases that involve important federal questions that need to be settled.[23] But beyond this rather structured assessment, other factors must also be considered. For example, the fact situation in a particular case may not provide an ideal basis for making legal policy, and a similar but better-framed case might be in the "pipeline." External events, such as the civil unrest surrounding school desegregation, are sometimes taken into consideration. In certain other cases, the government simply cannot afford not to appeal an adverse ruling, because the lower court's decision seriously undermines the authority of the executive branch and/or one of its agencies or departments. Although many cases lost by the government in the lower courts may meet each of these criteria, solicitors general must ultimately establish priorities among the eligible cases, given the limited nature of the Supreme Court's docket.

Once the cases for review are identified, the solicitor general's office works closely with lawyers in the appropriate division of the Justice Department or with counsel for the department or agency involved in the litigation. Access to a broad range of legal expertise within the various departments and agencies of the federal government is one of the office's most important assets. Essentially it has available what amounts to the country's largest law firm, with all of the legal and policy expertise, nearly unlimited resources, and access to information needed to present a compelling rationale to the Supreme Court for granting certiorari.

Several studies of the office have confirmed the success of the solicitor general in gaining the Court's review. Robert Scigliano found that 70 percent of the government's petitions for certiorari and 78 percent of the government's appeals were granted in the 1958 to 1967 Supreme Court terms.[24] Doris Marie Provine established that, "Now, as in earlier years, no other litigant receives nearly as much attention as the United States."[25] Finally, in my own study of the 1959 to 1989 Court terms, I found that the solicitor general was successful in gaining review in more than 69 percent of the 1,294 cases that the government filed, while slightly less than 5 percent of private litigants' petitions were granted during that same time period.[26]

Certiorari work also includes arguing against petitions for certiorari that name the United States as a respondent. Private litigants and governmental bodies (states and local governments) that have lost to the United States in the courts of appeals frequently try to obtain Supreme Court review of those decisions. Between 1959 and 1989, over 38,000 such certiorari petitions were filed, but 96 percent of those against which the U.S. government argued were subsequently denied review. When one considers that the justices routinely dismiss 91 percent of all certiorari petitions, however, the government's "success" is somewhat less impressive.[27]

When a litigant files a petition for certiorari naming the United States as a respondent, the solicitor general has four options: respond to the petition and argue against granting certiorari; waive response; acquiesce; or confess error. Since the 1970s, the practice by the solicitor general's office of "waiving response" has significantly reduced the burden of responding to every case filed against the United States. Today, the solicitor general simply sends a short memorandum to the Court implying that the cases are "so frivolous and so unworthy of Supreme Court attention" that they do not even merit a full response by the solicitor general's office.[28] In other cases, however, a full treatment of the petition is submitted, with specific arguments for denying certiorari.

On occasion, in a practice that appears to be unique to the solicitor general, the United States may "acquiesce" in a case. In such instances, the solicitor general tells the Court that, even though the government prevailed at the appellate court, the issue needs the Supreme Court's attention. On this basis, the office urges the Court's review. It would be easy to interpret this action as signaling the independence of the solicitor general and the office's dedication to "justice"; but there may be other motivations behind acquiescing that suggest otherwise. These cases generally involve principles of law that are unsettled and evoke serious conflicts among the various circuit courts of appeals. The government may have numerous cases pending on the issue in multiple jurisdictions throughout the federal courts, and it may be winning some cases while losing others on the same basic facts; consequently, both the solicitor general's office and the judicial system may benefit from having the Supreme Court issue a clear statement about how certain laws or principles should be applied. Furthermore, since the United States prevailed at the lower appellate court, the solicitor general may deem it likely that the fact situation of an acquiesced case is a relatively favorable one for the government to use in pursuing a clarification of the law.

Another practice unique to the solicitor general's role as attorney for the United States is the strategy of confessing error. In one or two cases each year, the solicitor general concedes that an error was made by a lower court in a case in which the government's position was upheld. Two types of error have historically been asserted by the solicitor general. The first type of error is procedural, where an overzealous prosecutor may have pursued a criminal charge or sentence that was, by acceptable practices, extreme or technically incorrect under the circumstances.[29] The Supreme Court, reserving its power to review the case, generally accepts this type of confession as dispositive and vacates the judgment of the lower court.

The other type of confessed error involves cases where a prosecutor has obtained a conviction that on its face is legitimate, but that violates the internal policies of the Justice Department. The classic example is a 1960 case, *Petite v. U.S.*,[30] in which a district attorney violated a department directive not to pursue federal criminal charges after a state prosecutor had successfully won a conviction under state law for the same criminal behavior. Although the Court recognized that the solicitor general's confession was being made for policy reasons, it granted a reversal for the petitioner. Confession of error by the solicitor general is often exasperating to the government attorneys who prevailed in the initial litigation and to the lower court judge who is thereby reversed on appeal. Chief Justice William Rehnquist has also been a vocal critic of the practice. As an associate justice dissenting in *Rinaldi v. United States* (1977)—a case very similar to *Petite*—Rehnquist noted the irony of allowing the solicitor general to confess error when, in fact, no error of law was involved: "Here . . . the Court again fails to enunciate why federal courts must reverse a valid conviction because of the Government's admission of administrative error not going to the guilt or innocence of the defendant."[31] In a later discussion with Solicitor General Bork over yet another case involving the practice, Justice Rehnquist bluntly suggested that, "Justice is our business, not yours."[32]

Once the Supreme Court has agreed to review a case on the merits, regardless of whether the government is the petitioner or the respondent, the solicitor general's office takes on the task of crafting the legal position of the United States. Again, the office can draw on the many resources within the government to put together the most compelling arguments to use before the Court. If and when the Court grants time for oral argument, the solicitor general, a member of the staff, or someone designated by the solicitor general presents the government's case to the justices.

During the Court terms from 1959 to 1986, the government won nearly 70 percent of the cases decided by a written opinion to which it was a party. But this success varied significantly depending on whether the government was the petitioner or respondent. In cases decided on the merits in which the United States was the petitioner, the office of the solicitor general was successful 80 percent of the time. As respondent, however, the government's position was upheld only 54 percent of the time.[33] This is not particularly surprising in view of the conventional wisdom regarding the Supreme Court's selection of cases; it generally does not grant certiorari simply to affirm a lower-court decision. Rather, the Court's decision to grant review seems most often to be based on an early assessment that the lower court's decision was flawed. In this light, the government's 54 percent success rate is more impressive.

Cases that involve the United States as a party most frequently deal with the executive branch's constitutional role (as enunciated in Article

II) "to take care that the Laws are faithfully executed" or with matters that involve the institutional powers of the president. In these cases, partisan differences between administrations are less likely. All administrations, regardless of the incumbent's party or ideology, are committed to protecting the institutional powers of the executive. This is especially true, for example, on issues that involve criminal procedure. Regardless of the party in office, the executive branch is always the "prosecutor" and, as such, traditionally argues the pro-state position in criminal matters.

Distinctions between administrations are more likely to be evident in the selection by the solicitor general of cases to be appealed to the Supreme Court. This is an area of decision-making that simply has not been explored. It is likely, for example, that differences exist between the substantive issues raised in cases selected by the Carter administration for Supreme Court review and those advanced in cases championed by the Reagan or Bush administrations (issues such as the enforcement of civil rights, environmental standards, or economic regulations). The discretion the solicitor general enjoys in selecting cases, much like prosecutorial discretion or the arrest discretion of a police officer, can be imbued with policy considerations. Unfortunately—and this no doubt accounts for the lack of scholarly research in this area—it is difficult to identify accurately the rationale for the solicitor general's denial of review in a given case. A study that closely examined the substantive issues of cases eligible for appeal and the policy agenda of the administration, while operationalizing the factors that make for a worthy certiorari petition (federal interest, conflict between circuits), would contribute significantly to our understanding of work of the solicitor general.

Consider, for example, the recent cases involving homosexuality and military service. In *Steffan v. Aspin*, the District of Columbia Circuit Court of Appeals declared in November 1993 that the policy as applied to the discharge of a gay man from the U.S. Naval Academy was unconstitutional.[34] Earlier in the year, in *Meinhold v. Department of Defense*, a federal district court judge in California also ruled that the military policy was unconstitutional and further ordered the Defense Department to suspend its discharge of homosexuals.[35] To the surprise of many gay activists, Solicitor General Days approved the Department of Defense's request to seek an en banc hearing by the full membership of the Court of Appeals in the *Steffan* case. In *Meinhold*, Clinton's solicitor general went even further, successfully obtaining a Supreme Court ruling that permits the military to continue discharging homosexuals pending the full litigation of the *Meinhold* case.[36] If the policy position of the Clinton administration had consisted of a firm commitment to end the blanket ban on gay men and lesbians in the military, the solicitor general could simply have chosen not to seek further review in each of these cases; the lower-court decisions would then have remained intact, fulfilling the campaign promises of candidate Clinton.

Other considerations arise when the scenario is reversed. Suppose that a lesbian army officer who lost her case in a federal court of appeals then successfully obtained the Supreme Court's review. Now "forced" to defend a policy with which it did not agree, how would the Clinton administration, through the office of the solicitor general, craft its legal position? The most common practice in such a case would be for the solicitor general to defend the ban vigorously, thus holding the executive branch to its constitutional obligation to enforce the law. Although there might be some political costs to defending the statute outright, solicitors general would be inclined to take this approach in order to maintain their reputation before the Supreme Court.

Such a policy contradiction arose during the Carter administration in a case that pitted the Tennessee Valley Authority (TVA) against several environmental groups. Litigated initially by the Ford administration in response to a suit brought by environmentalists, the United States argued in support of TVA's authority to build a dam at a site near the habitat of a small endangered species of fish (the snail darter). The case had reached the Supreme Court's docket and was accepted for review when the transition from one administration to the other took place. The Carter administration, having committed itself to support stronger environmental protection policies, was placed in the delicate position of inheriting responsibility for a legal argument that was viewed as anti-environmental. Although he felt some pressure from the White House to abandon the position taken by the Ford administration, Solicitor General Wade McCree ultimately defended the TVA, and the government prevailed on the merits.[37]

A second tactic that might be used by the solicitor general in such cases is to allow the executive branch to speak with a "forked tongue." Consider, once again, the matter of gays in the military. While the solicitor general, acting on behalf of the administration, may file a separate brief arguing against the statute or policy, the government's attorney can permit the appropriate branch of military service to actively defend the ban. This arrangement allows the administration to preserve its public commitment, while simultaneously providing the government agency most affected by the issue an opportunity to argue its case. In the past, this strategy has been employed particularly often in cases that involve independent agencies or conflicts between various departments within the executive branch, where the arguments on both sides have merit. Although the strategy is used infrequently, it is a workable tactic to preserve the policy commitments of the administration while simultaneously ensuring that the law is adequately defended.

The appearance of the solicitor general before the Supreme Court is not limited to cases in which the government is a party. The increased use of the amicus curiae (friend of the court) brief and Rule 36 of the Rules of the Supreme Court have permitted and even encouraged the government to express an opinion in cases in which the United States is not named as a party.[38] By filing an amicus curiae brief, the solicitor general can provide the justices with the executive branch's "viewpoint" on legal/policy issues at both the petition stage and the merits stage of a case. Amicus briefs were submitted by the solicitor general in 518 cases decided by a written opinion of the Supreme Court between 1959 and 1986.[39]

Although many of these amicus submissions are filed at the discretion of the solicitor general, on numerous occasions the Supreme Court "invites" the solicitor general's office to participate. These invitations are not viewed by the office as discretionary, but rather as orders from the Supreme Court.[40] In addition, requests for amicus filings are made by many other political actors. Members of Congress, interest groups, and legal counsels in other departments may urge the solicitor general to file an amicus in a particular case pending before the Court.[41] The ultimate decision to do so, however, rests with the solicitor general.

The office of the solicitor general transfers the success it enjoys as a litigant before the Supreme Court to the private parties whom it supports as amicus. In my study of the 1959 to 1986 Court terms, the government's position was upheld in nearly 72 percent of the cases in which it filed an amicus brief. Again, a distinction arose between cases in which the United States supported the petitioner and cases in which it favored the respondent party. When the solicitor general weighed in on the side of the petitioner, the Supreme Court ruled for the petitioner in just over 78 percent of the cases. Respondents with governmental support, however, prevailed only 58.67 percent of the time.[42]

The amicus activity of the solicitor general's office has been the subject of several scholarly studies employing different methodological approaches to assess the importance of the government's amicus participation. One of the earliest works on the amicus brief was Steven Puro's research on its use in the Supreme Court generally. Puro not only documented the increased use of the amicus brief between the 1920 and 1966 Court terms, he also noted the frequency with which the United States participated and succeeded before the Court.[43]

Karen O'Connor examined the filings of three separate solicitor generals: Erwin Griswold, who was solicitor general under Lyndon Johnson and during Richard Nixon's first term; Robert Bork, who served during the second term of the Nixon administration; and Wade McCree, solicitor general for the Carter administration. By classifying the position taken by the government in amicus briefs filed on civil rights/liberties issues, O'Connor was able to identify differences among the solicitors general that suggested that the government's amicus advocacy was strongly influenced by the ideological and policy preferences of the administration in office.[44]

In a subsequent study, S. Sidney Ulmer and David Willison sought to develop a predictive model of the government's success in utilizing the amicus brief as a function of five variables, including the individual solicitor general in office at the time and whether the United States had been invited to participate by the Court.[45] Jeffrey Segal extended this line of research by including whether the government had participated in oral argument, the substantive content of the amicus briefs, and the side of the case that the United States supported.[46]

Finally, in an earlier work, I examined the use of the amicus brief by administration and by the party controlling the White House, by solicitor general, by whether the United States has been invited to participate, and by the side that the government supported (either petitioner or respondent) at both the aggregate level (all cases between 1959 and 1986) and for cases that raised issues involving individual rights and liberties. I found differences not only in the types of arguments presented by the government, depending on the administration in office, but also differences in their subsequent success before the Supreme Court.[47]

The use of the amicus brief is probably the most political of the decisions made by solicitors general, for several reasons. Except with regard to cases in which the government is invited by the Court to file an amicus, the solicitor general exercises a great deal of discretion in determining whether or not to participate in a case. A decision not to file an amicus in an uninvited case may be based on an assessment by the office that the parties involved in the litigation have fully expounded the legal issues, so that the solicitor general's office has little to add. Alternatively, the solicitor general may feel that the United States simply has no interest in the case that would merit its participation; the issues do not affect governmental power and are not of substantial concern to the administration.[48]

But when the solicitor general does decide to file an amicus brief, very few institutional constraints are imposed on that participation. Rule 36 of the Supreme Court Rules exempts the solicitor general from the general requirement that private litigants must obtain permission to file from the parties to the case. The government's brief may address a range of issues including questions of institutional power stemming from constitutional arguments, established principles of law or judicial precedents as interpreted by the solicitor general, or even the policy concerns and commitments of the administration. Likewise, when the office is invited by the Court to participate, the solicitor general is free to weigh in on either side of the legal controversy and to craft the government's legal arguments as he or she deems appropriate.

Over the past few decades, we have witnessed two distinct trends in the government's use of amicus advocacy. First, the frequency of the government's amicus participation has increased significantly. Between 1959 and 1964, for example, the solicitor general filed an average of eleven amicus briefs per term as compared to an average of thirty briefs per year between 1985 and 1989.[49] Second, and perhaps more important, some observers have suggested that recent solicitors general were more willing to file briefs in cases that traditionally would not have called for the federal government's participation. For instance, Archibald Cox, solicitor general during the Kennedy administration, noted that the Reagan administration used amicus advocacy in cases that he would not even have considered entering in the early 1960s.[50] More specifically, Cox pointed to litigation that primarily involved controversies between states and individuals claiming constitutional protection for their conduct (abortion and obscenity cases, for example), and he cited the lack of what he considered a legitimate federal interest that would have justified the solicitor general's appearance.

The increased use of the amicus brief by the government in recent years is at least partly the result of the willingness of the Supreme Court to accept the amicus filings from a broad range of interest groups, private parties, and other governmental actors such as states and municipalities.[51] In some respects, one might argue that the government would be remiss in not taking the opportunity to have its voice heard on issues of national importance. As Charles Fried noted, "You more or less view your office as sort of a constitutional ombudsman, to make sure that all areas of public interest, particularly with regard to constitutional issues, are explored, debated and discussed as issues are decided."[52] Solicitors general have filed amicus briefs in some of the most important and controversial constitutional cases of the last half-century, including *Brown v. Board of Education of Topeka*[53] (school desegregation), *Baker v. Carr*[54] (reapportionment), and *Regents of the University of California v. Bakke*[55] (reverse discrimination). Not to have participated in these landmark cases might have constituted an error of omission.

THE SOLICITOR GENERAL'S CLIENT

Francis Biddle, solicitor general for Franklin Roosevelt, once argued that "He [the solicitor general] determines what cases to appeal, and the cli-

ent has no say in the matter, he does what his lawyer tells him, the lawyer stands in the client's shoes, for the client is but an abstraction."[56] Biddle's statement implies that the lawyer-client relationship is virtually
nonexistent for the attorneys working in the solicitor general's office. But
this is misleading; the solicitor general does not operate in a vacuum.
Rather, various constituencies both within and outside of government
apply pressures to which the solicitors general must respond.

The solicitor general's most important client is necessarily the president of the United States. The solicitor general is appointed by and serves
at the pleasure of the president and can be dismissed at the president's
direction. Although functionally little direct communication occurs between the White House and the solicitor general, the president generally
can make his wishes heard through the attorney general or, more recently through the OLC. Rarely does the president get directly involved
in government litigation. The snail darter case has already been discussed. It is also known that President Eisenhower personally reviewed
(and edited) the government's brief in *Brown v. Board of Education*
prior to its filing.[57] Some observers suggested that President Kennedy and
Attorney General Robert Kennedy desired a more aggressive litigation
strategy on civil rights than Solicitor General Cox was willing to pursue,
although Cox has explicitly denied that his office was subjected to any
interference from the White House.[58]

On several occasions during Griswold's tenure as solicitor general for
the Nixon administration, however, the White House and the attorney
general became directly involved in matters traditionally left to the solicitor general.[59] Rather than put his name to a brief that he did not support
regarding public funding of religious schools, Griswold recused himself
and had his deputy sign the brief as acting solicitor general, a practice
that Simon Sobeloff had employed during the Eisenhower administration. In a school desegregation case, the attorney general filed an application for a stay in light of Griswold's determination that the government's
position was in error. In other cases, Griswold was asked to seek an extension of a filing deadline in order to forward the government's brief to
the attorney general for review prior to filing it with the Supreme Court.

The various executive departments, other divisions within the Justice
Department, and independent regulatory agencies are also the solicitor
general's clients. Except in the case of a few independent agencies, the
solicitor general is the only attorney federal agencies can engage to defend their interests before the Supreme Court. Even agencies with independent litigating authority would rather have the solicitor general's expertise and support on their side than "go it alone" or, even worse, find
the solicitor general filing a brief in opposition.

As explained earlier, executive-branch agencies, departments, and divisions are often the initial sources of information for attorneys within the solicitor general's office. Staff attorneys at the various bureaucratic departments prepare what amount to draft briefs as part of their agencies' request that the solicitor general seek a reversal of a lower court's adverse decision before the Supreme Court. Attorneys in these agencies are also consulted by the solicitor general's office when the Court accepts for review a case that significantly affects the interests of the agency. Within the context of interdepartmental relations, cases assume a life of their own. Departmental or agency advocates often think that their case should be a priority for the solicitor general's efforts; and many are disappointed when (as frequently happens) the solicitor general's office disagrees.

On occasion, the solicitor general must act as mediator. As might be expected, given the size and multiplicity of interests within the executive bureaucracy, conflicts between agencies and departments often arise. When such disputes cannot be resolved, the solicitor general may be put in the extremely awkward position of having to argue both sides of a case. In *St. Regis Paper Co. v. U.S.*,[60] Solicitor General Cox was forced to manage a conflict between the Census Bureau, the Department of Commerce, and the Bureau of the Budget, on one side of the issue, and the Federal Trade Commission (FTC) and the antitrust division of the Justice Department on the other. Although he argued both sides of the case, Cox further urged the justices to avoid making a decision altogether on grounds that the issue was moot. The Supreme Court ultimately decided in favor of the FTC and the antitrust division.

The solicitor general may also find interest groups expressing concerns over litigation pending before the Court. As Karen O'Connor and others have noted,[61] interest groups recognize the reputation and success of the solicitor general and seek the government's support in their own cases. Although it is difficult to determine how much contact takes place between attorneys in the solicitor general's office and representatives of interest groups and whether the "lobbying" is successful, those familiar with the office confide that phone calls and written correspondence urging the solicitor general to file an amicus curiae on particular matters are not uncommon.

Finally, the solicitor general has an important relationship with Congress. Historically, unless the solicitor general approved of its participation, the legislative branch did not have access to the docket of the Supreme Court. This complicated the office's role in cases that juxtaposed the powers of the executive branch against those of Congress and in cases in which the solicitor general decided not to defend the constitutionality of a statute endorsed by Congress. When such cases arose in the past, solicitors general usually negotiated ad hoc arrangements permitting Congress to hire its own private counsel to represent its interests. In the late 1970s, however, the Senate established an office of Senate legal counsel and the House of Representatives strengthened the powers of its general counsel to the clerk. As part of the statute governing the Senate legal counsel, the solicitor general is now required to notify Congress in the event that the government chooses not to defend the constitutionality of a statute. In cases such as *Immigration and Naturalization Service v. Chadha* (legislative veto)[62] and *Bowsher v. Synar* (Gramm-Rudman Act),[63] Congress was able to depend on the arguments of its own counsel.

Although I have argued that the solicitor general is an important political actor and an integral part of the president's administration, the office's advocacy role is tempered by various factors. First, in order to succeed as an advocate for the executive branch, the solicitor general must recognize the constraints imposed by the legal system and must act accordingly. Legal arguments supporting significant departures from established precedent, for example, tend not to be given respectful treatment by the justices and may only serve to undermine the solicitor general's position in the case and the office's long-term reputation before the Supreme Court. Second, more than most attorneys, the solicitor general has an interest in seeing the Court develop "good law" that the executive branch can both understand and use in the future. Finally, the solicitor general must be an expert adviser to the administration. Like private attorneys who ought to tell a prospective litigant when a case lacks merit, solicitors general must carefully and fairly assess the executive branch's case and soberly estimate its prospects of winning before the Supreme Court.

CONCLUSION

The picture painted by the foregoing discussion suggests that the solicitor general operates in a complex environment of competing institutional and political interests. The real work of the solicitor general is multifaceted; solicitors general are advisers to the Supreme Court, advocates for the institutional power of the executive branch, and advocates for the policy goals of the specific administration they serve. If each case that came under the solicitor general's review had fit neatly into but one of these roles and had had no impact on the others, the work of the solicitor general might have continued to occur in the shadows of government. But the reality of the office is such that solicitors general must occasionally choose between the various hats they have been assigned to wear by statute and by tradition. Returning to a theme suggested earlier in this chapter: the nature of the solicitor general's work is such that the office can easily become embroiled in controversies that arise when legal developments, institutional power, and public policy goals diverge.

The solicitor general is expected to be both a gatekeeper for the Supreme Court, allowing only the most important government cases to reach the Court's docket, and an adviser to the justices on the proper development of law, presenting high-quality arguments couched in precedent and rigorous legal reasoning. Solicitors general believe that they have a special reputation to uphold before the Supreme Court; and therefore, they behave in a manner that maintains that reputation. During the Reagan and Bush administrations, however, Solicitors General Fried and Starr each submitted briefs that explicitly asked the Supreme Court to reverse or move away from a number of well-established precedents regarding abortion, the separation of church and state, and civil rights. Some observers have argued that these officers' roles as advocates for the policy goals of the White House took precedence over their concerns for the reputation of the office as a reliable adviser to the Court.[64] By focusing on the politically oriented task, these solicitors general risked devaluing the reputation of the office by violating gatekeeper norms, offering less-than-rigorous arguments to the justices, and showing a general lack of respect for legal precedent. Nonetheless the arguments of these solicitors general were not dismissed by the Supreme Court out-of-hand; the government's positions may not have mustered the support of a majority of the nine justices, but they did manage to secure some votes on each of these issues. I suggest that the arguments advanced by these solicitors general merely reflected the controversies that were being debated both within the Court and in the broader political environment—specifically the lack of agreement that these issues were "settled" areas of law.

The solicitor general is also expected to be an advocate for the institutional power of the executive branch, as well as an advocate for the policy goals of the administration. That these two roles could come into conflict was clearly evidenced in two cases previously discussed. In the Bob Jones University controversy, the Reagan administration subordinated its institutional interests and powers to its political desires by ordering the acting solicitor general to argue against the Internal Revenue Service and to support the policy agenda of the administration on behalf of tax exemptions for private schools. Had the administration's argument been sustained, the result might have been a critical limitation on the power of executive agencies to interpret and enforce statutory law—a matter of institutional executive power. A similar conflict, but in reverse, occurred in the TVA case, when the solicitor general offered a brief that clearly supported the rule-making and implementation authority of an executive agency to the detriment of the Carter administration's policy goals on protection of the environment.

For the most part, such conflicts between various roles of the solicitor general arise infrequently. When they do, however, the White House and the attorney general are likely to provide some direction to their lawyer. But as the government's chief litigator, the solicitor general usually operates with little direct interference from the White House or the attorney general. This functional independence is the norm and is allowed to flourish because the nature of the selection process assures that the solicitor general not only will know how best to use the law to protect the institution's power, but also will share the ideology of the administration. As a result, the executive branch enjoys the benefits of having both an advocate and a highly successful attorney in the government's litigation before the Supreme Court.

NOTES

1. Francis Biddle, *In Brief Authority* (New York: Doubleday, 1962), p. 98.

2. Simon E. Sobeloff, "Attorney for the Government: The Work of the Solicitor General's Office," *American Bar Association Journal* 41 (March 1955): 229.

3. Robert H. Bork, "The Problems and Pleasures of Being Solicitor General," *Antitrust Law Journal* 42(3) (1973): 701.

4. See, for example, Bork, "The Problems and Pleasures of Being Solicitor General," pp. 701–5; Archibald Cox, "The Government in the Supreme Court," *Chicago Bar Record* 44 (1963): 221–29; Charles Fahy, "The Office of the Solicitor General," *American Bar Association Journal* 28 (1942): 20–22; Erwin N. Griswold, "The Office of the Solicitor General—Representing the Interests of the United States Before the Supreme Court," *Missouri Law Review* 34 (1969): 527–36; Rex E. Lee, "Lawyering for the Government: Politics, Polemics and Principle," *Ohio State Law Journal* 47 (1986): 595–601; Wade H. McCree, "The Solicitor General and His Client," *Washington University Law Quarterly* 59 (1981): 337–47; Philip B. Perlman, "The Work of the Office of the Solicitor General of the United States," *Maryland State Bar Association* 54 (1949): 265–90; and Sobeloff, "Attorney for the Government," pp. 229–32, 279.

5. Robert Scigliano, *The Supreme Court and the Presidency* (New York: Free Press, 1971).

6. Rebecca Mae Salokar, *The Solicitor General: The Politics of Law* (Philadelphia: Temple University Press, 1992), p. 21.

7. Ibid., p. 29.

8. Remarks of Representative Jenckes, United States House of Representatives, April 27, 1870, in *Congressional Globe* 90: 3035 (Washington, D.C.: Government Printing Office, 1870).

9. Linda P. Campbell, "Health May Be Fading, but Marshall's Wit Still Sharp," *Chicago Tribune*, June 29, 1991, p. C1.

10. "An Act to Establish the Department of Justice," ch. 150, sec. 2, 5, 10; 16 Stat. sec. 162–163 (1870) [commonly known as the "Judiciary Act of 1870"].

11. Interview with Erwin N. Griswold, May 22, 1990, Washington, D.C.

12. See the comments of Charles Fried in U.S. Congress, House of Representatives, Committee on the Judiciary, Hearing Before the Subcommittee on Monopolies and Commercial Law of the Committee of Judiciary on Solicitor General's Office, 100th Cong., 1st sess., March 19, 1987 (Washington, D.C.: U.S. Government Printing Office, 1988), pp. 4, 14.

13. *Bob Jones University v. United States*, 461 U.S. 574 (1983).

14. This practice is known as "tying a tin can." See Lincoln Caplan, *The Tenth Justice: The Solicitor General and the Rule of Law* (New York: Alfred A. Knopf, 1987) for an extended discussion of the *Bob Jones University* case.

15. See especially Caplan, *The Tenth Justice*.

16. Nancy Blodgett, "Solicitor General: Has Office Been Politicized?" *American Bar Association Journal* 72 (May 1, 1986): 20.

17. The "political deputy" performs the same functions as the other deputy solicitors general and only takes on the role of acting solicitor general in the solicitor general's absence or recusal from a case.

18. *Baker v. Carr*, 369 U.S. 186 (1962). See Cornell W. Clayton, *The Politics of Justice: The Attorney General and the Making of Legal Policy* (Armonk, N.Y.: M. E. Sharpe, 1992), p. 134, for a discussion of the role Solicitor General Cox played in tempering the aggressive civil rights litigation agenda of the Kennedy administration.

19. Marc Galanter, "Why the 'Haves' Come Out Ahead: Speculations on the Limits of Legal Change," *Law and Society Review* 9(1) (Fall 1974): 98; see also Doris Marie Provine, *Case Selection in the United States Supreme Court* (Chicago: University of Chicago Press, 1980).

20. An example of the policy implications of these decisions can be seen in *Meinhold v. U.S. Department of Defense* (808 F. Supp. 1445 [1993]), where a federal district court ruled against the military's ban on homosexuals in the service. That the solicitor general has permitted an appeal in this case seems to go against the well-known policy goals of the Clinton White House.

21. Certiorari is the process by which litigants request that the Supreme Court review the decision of the lower court. As such, the certiorari process invokes the discretionary jurisdiction of the Supreme Court. Although a technical distinction exists between cases in which appeal is mandatory and those considered under a petition of certiorari, in practice the Court treats the cases similarly. For this reason, I make no distinction between the two types of cases in this chapter.

22. Salokar, *The Solicitor General*, p. 114.

23. For an extended discussion of the criteria for case selection, see Salokar, *The Solicitor General*, pp. 107–16.

24. Scigliano, *The Supreme Court and the Presidency*, pp. 174–75.

25. Provine, *Case Selection in the United States Supreme Court*, p. 89.

26. Salokar, *The Solicitor General*, p. 25.

27. Ibid., p. 25.

28. Ibid., p. 25 (based on an interview with A. Raymond Randolph, former deputy solicitor general).

29. See, for example, *Saldana v. United States*, 365 U.S. 646 (1961).

30. *Petite v. United States*, 361 U.S. 529 (1960).

31. *Rinaldi v. United States*, 434 U.S. 22 at 26 and 34 (1977).

32. Interview with Robert Bork, June 14, 1990, Washington, D.C. The full story is recounted in Salokar, *The Solicitor General*, p. 122.

33. Salokar, *The Solicitor General*, p. 126.

34. 8 F.3d. 57 (1993).

35. D. Ct. C. Calif., No. CV 92-6044 (January 29, 1993).

36. *U.S. Department of Defense v. Volker Keith Meinhold*, 114 S. Ct. 374 (1993).

37. Griffin Bell and Ronald J. Ostrow, *Taking Care of the Law* (New York: William Morrow, 1982).

38. Rule 36 specifically exempts the office of the solicitor general from obtaining the consent of the formal parties to a case prior to filing an amicus curiae brief. *United States Courts, Rules of the Supreme Court*, Appendix, 28 U.S.C. 1982 ed. (Washington, D.C.: U.S. Government Printing Office, 1983).

39. Salokar, *The Solicitor General*, p. 145.

40. Between the 1959 and 1986 Supreme Court terms, the government was invited to participate as an amicus in 440 cases (Salokar, *The Solicitor General*, p. 144).

41. See, for example, Karen O'Connor, *Women's Organizations' Use of the Courts* (Lexington, Mass.: Lexington, 1980); Clement E. Vose, *Caucasians Only* (Berkeley, Calif.: University of California Press, 1959); Lee Epstein, *Conservatives in Court* (Knoxville, Tenn.: University of Tennessee Press, 1985); and Susan Lawrence, *The Poor in Court: The Legal Services Program and Supreme Court Decision Making* (Princeton, N.J.: Princeton University Press, 1990).

42. Salokar, *The Solicitor General*, p. 146.

43. Steven Puro, "The Role of the Amicus Curiae in the United States Supreme Court: 1920–1966." Ph.D. dissertation, State University of New York at Buffalo, 1971.

44. Karen O'Connor, "The Amicus Curiae Role of the U.S. Solicitor General in Supreme Court Litigation," *Judicature* 66(6) (December–January 1983): 256–64.

45. S. Sidney Ulmer and David Willison, "The Solicitor General of the United States as Amicus Curiae in the U.S. Supreme Court, 1969–1983 Terms." Paper presented at the American Political Science Association Annual Meeting, New Orleans, 1985.

46. Jeffrey A. Segal, "Amicus Curiae Briefs by the Solicitor General During the Warren and Burger Courts: A Research Note," *Western Political Quarterly* 41(1) (March 1988): 135. See also Jeffrey A. Segal, "Supreme Court Support for the Solicitor General: A Longitudinal Analysis." Paper presented at the annual meeting of the Midwest Political Science Association, Chicago, 1986; and Jeffrey A. Segal and Cheryl D. Reedy, "The Supreme Court and Sex Discrimination: The

Role of the Solicitor General," *Western Political Quarterly* 41(3) (September 1988): 553.

47. Salokar, *The Solicitor General*, pp. 165–70.

48. Ibid., p. 137–42; Puro, "The Role of the Amicus Curiae," p. 138.

49. Salokar, *The Solicitor General*, p. 19.

50. Interview with Archibald Cox, May 21, 1990, Cambridge, Massachusetts.

51. For documentation of this trend, see Puro, "The Role of the Amicus Curiae," pp. 54–62.

52. U.S. Congress, House of Representatives, *Hearing Before the Subcommittee on Monopolies*, p. 19.

53. *Brown v. Board of Education of Topeka*, 347 U.S. 483 (1954), 349 U.S. 294 (1955).

54. *Baker v. Carr*, 369 U.S. 186 (1962).

55. *Regents of the University of California v. Bakke*, 438 U.S. 265 (1978).

56. Biddle, *In Brief Authority*, p. 98.

57. Salokar, *The Solicitor General*, p. 72; Caplan, *The Tenth Justice*, pp. 30–32.

58. Victor S. Navasky, *Kennedy Justice* (New York: Atheneum, 1971), pp. 280–315; Caplan, *The Tenth Justice*, p. 188; but see Archibald Cox, *The Court and the Constitution* (Boston: Houghton Mifflin, 1987), pp. 290, 395–97.

59. For a fuller discussion of these cases, see Salokar, *The Solicitor General*, pp. 73–74, and Caplan, *The Tenth Justice*, pp. 35–36.

60. *St. Regis Paper Company v. United States*, 368 U.S. 208 (1961).

61. O'Connor, *Women's Organizations' Use of the Courts*. See also Epstein, *Conservatives in Court*, and Lawrence, *The Poor in Court*.

62. *Immigration and Naturalization Service v. Chadha*, 462 U.S. 919 (1983).

63. *Bowsher v. Synar*, 478 U.S. 714 (1986).

64. See especially Caplan, *The Tenth Justice*.

4

INDEPENDENT JUSTICE: THE OFFICE OF THE INDEPENDENT COUNSEL

KATY J. HARRIGER

The temporary office of independent counsel was created in 1978 as part of post-Watergate ethics reform.[1] The office was born in the aftermath of constitutional crisis, and its constitutional and political legitimacy has remained a source of controversy throughout its existence. It was designed to address the conflict between professional independence and political loyalty of attorneys within the Department of Justice, by providing for independent investigation of alleged criminal wrongdoing by high-level executive branch appointees. Thus it offers an ideal case study in how a legal institution designed to eliminate the problem of political loyalty operates within the federal legal system. An examination of the experience with the independent counsel since 1978 demonstrates that this office is less independent than its supporters hoped but more accountable than its critics claimed. Further, it offers insights into the nature of prosecutorial power and the considerable influence of the president and attorney general in federal criminal law enforcement, even in instances where, technically, control of that enforcement has been removed from the executive. The potential for abuse of power by the independent counsel lies not in the independence of the office but rather in the nature of prosecutorial discretion possessed by all prosecutors, independent or not.

HISTORICAL BACKGROUND

While using special prosecutors to investigate and prosecute allegations of executive misconduct antedates to Watergate,[2] that scandal was, until Iran-Contra, the one most clearly identified with the institution. During the five years in which the scandal unfolded, four special prosecutors were appointed by the president, after some consultation with Congress. The first, Harvard law professor Archibald Cox, was fired in the infamous "Saturday Night Massacre" of October 1973. That firing was the "focusing event"[3] that caused Congress to begin considering a statutory arrangement that would provide independence for the special prosecutor.[4] Although the appointment of Leon Jaworski with executive guarantees of independence reduced the immediate demand, interest in a statutory arrangement for future cases persisted.

Between 1973 and 1978, Congress considered a number of possible solutions, ranging from creating a completely independent Department of Justice[5] to establishing a permanent independent office of public attorney.[6] Ultimately, it settled on the special prosecutor provisions of the Ethics in Government Act of 1978. (The name of the officer was changed to independent counsel as part of the act's reauthorization in 1982.[7]) The provisions were again reauthorized in 1987, and their constitutionality was upheld by the Supreme Court in 1988.[8] They were permitted to expire in December of 1992. The Clinton administration supported their reauthorization, and an effort to revive the provisions began in Congress in 1993. Republican critics of the bill, still angry about the independent counsel investigation of the Iran-Contra matter, resisted these reauthorization efforts until that winter, when the Whitewater scandal implicating the Clintons gained prominence. Suddenly the advantages of independent investigation became more apparent to erstwhile opponents of the office. The Senate passed a new bill in November of 1993, and the House passed a similar one in February of 1994. By this time, bowing to public pressure, the attorney general had been forced to appoint a "special counsel" for the Whitewater affair without benefit of the statute. The provisions were reauthorized in June of 1994; and shortly thereafter, in a controversial move by the special court panel, "special counsel" Robert Fiske was replaced with a statutory independent counsel, Kenneth Starr.[9]

During the five years that Congress debated the adoption of a statutory independent counsel arrangement, the debate centered on constitutional issues. Would the separation of powers doctrine be violated if some control over law enforcement was removed from the direct control of the executive branch? Did Congress have the power to vest appointment of an independent prosecutor with the judiciary instead of with the executive? This debate pitted different parts of Article II against each other. Opponents of a judicially appointed prosecutor argued that the responsibility for faithful execution of the laws resided with the executive. Advocates of the independent arrangement noted that the appointments clause permitted Congress to vest the appointment of inferior officers with "the courts of law." As is the case with most legislation, the final product sought to reach a compromise position in this debate.

The special prosecutor provisions of the Ethics in Government Act of 1978 attempted to strike a balance between executive responsibility for enforcement of the laws and Congress's desire to ensure the appearance of independence for a special prosecutor assigned to investigate the executive branch. This balance was accomplished by dividing the responsibility for implementing the act between the attorney general and a special panel of judges created under the act. It required the attorney general, upon receiving specific allegations of federal criminal law violations by certain high-ranking executive branch officials, to conduct a preliminary investigation into the charges. The attorney general was allowed ninety days within which to conduct the investigation but was not permitted to utilize the compulsory process to obtain information during that time. At the end of this limited investigation, the attorney general had to determine whether the charges warranted further investigation (and/or prosecution). If so, a report of the attorney general's findings was to be filed with a special division of the Court of Appeals for the District of Columbia, requesting appointment of a special prosecutor. If preliminary investigation of the charges led to the conclusion that they did not warrant further action, the attorney general was required to file a report with the panel, explaining the decision not to proceed with the case. Under the statute, the attorney general's decision about whether to appoint a special prosecutor was not reviewable.[10]

The special division of the court consisted of three senior or retired circuit judges, appointed by the chief justice of the Supreme Court. The panel was responsible for selecting a special prosecutor, defining his or her jurisdiction, receiving the reports of the attorney general and the special prosecutor, and determining whether the reports should be made public.[11] Although the panel appointed the prosecutor, the attorney general was empowered to remove the appointee in instances of "extraordinary impropriety." Should the attorney general remove the special prosecutor, the court could review that decision at the special prosecutor's request. The standard for removal was lowered to "good cause" during the 1982 reauthorization.[12]

Between 1978 and 1992, thirteen independent counsel investigations were conducted under these provisions, eleven of which were publicly announced by the court panel. During the Carter administration, two White House staff members, Hamilton Jordan and Timothy Kraft, were separately investigated for alleged cocaine use. In each case the special prosecutor found no grounds for prosecution.[13] The remaining cases arose during the two terms of Ronald Reagan. These included two investigations (by the same independent counsel) of allegations of bribery and organized crime activity by Secretary of Labor Raymond Donovan, which ended in decisions that insufficient evidence existed to support indictment.[14] Two different investigations prompted by allegations of misconduct in the filing of financial disclosure forms and tax returns and of misuse of office by White House counsel (and later attorney general) Edwin Meese were closed with decisions not to seek indictment.[15] Illegal lobbying allegations against former White House staff members Lyn Nofziger and Michael Deaver resulted in criminal indictments and convictions of both officials, although Deaver's conviction was for perjury.[16] Nofziger's conviction was overturned by the D.C. Circuit Court of Appeals.[17] Theodore Olson of the OLC in the Justice Department was accused of lying to Congress during its investigation of improprieties at the Environmental Protection Agency during the early 1980s. After his case became the vehicle for a constitutional challenge to the independent counsel's office, the independent counsel found insufficient evidence to indict Olson on these charges.[18] A variety of charges relating to the Iran-Contra affair involving a number of administration officials led to the most controversial of the independent counsel investigations. The Iran-Contra investigations produced a number of guilty pleas and convictions, although the chief convictions of Oliver North and John Poindexter were overturned on appeal because the independent counsel was unable to prove that the testimony of prosecution witnesses was unaffected by the defendants' immunized congressional testimony.[19] The pardons by George Bush in late 1992 of others involved in the scandal effectively brought that investigation to a close.[20] The investigation of former officials of the Department of Housing and Urban Development continued in 1994.

The independent counsel arrangement was controversial throughout its first incarnation, although the nature of the debate shifted over time. Initially, the dispute over the constitutionality of the arrangement served as the focus of controversy. The differences in opinion regarding the constitutional issue depended on different interpretations of the separation-of-powers doctrine. Those who subscribed to a "formalist" approach to the doctrine emphasized the separateness of the branches and viewed the functions of each branch as being clearly defined and delineated. They viewed the independent counsel statute as a prime example of an "imperial" Congress impermissibly intruding on executive power. The law enforcement powers exercised by the independent counsel were powers intended by the Constitution to be controlled exclusively by the executive. Appointment by the judiciary and limited removal power by the executive branch constituted unacceptable arrangements under this view of the separation of powers.[21] This view was adopted by Justice Scalia in his lone dissent in *Morrison v. Olson*, the decision upholding the constitutionality of the provisions. Scalia contended that law enforcement power belonged wholly to the executive and could not be delegated to an independent officer. He also claimed that, by removing the independent counsel from the direct control of the executive, Congress had created an officer answerable to no one.[22]

Supporters of the independent counsel arrangement and the majority of the Supreme Court in *Morrison* based their arguments on a "functionalist" approach to the separation of powers and focused on the appointments clause of Article II for their textual justification for the provisions. Article II, section 2 grants Congress the power to "vest the Appointment of such inferior Officers, as they think proper, in the President alone, in the Courts of Law, or in the Heads of Departments." Given the limited and temporary nature of the office, supporters viewed the independent counsel as an "inferior officer" covered by this clause.[23] The majority opinion argued that the limited scope of the counsel's jurisdiction and of the court panel's oversight, the temporary status of the office, and the attorney general's continued role in triggering appointment and in removal made the arrangement constitutionally acceptable. The Court concluded that the provisions did not interfere with the president's ability to perform his constitutional duties to faithfully execute the laws and that they were carefully crafted to meet a legitimate congressional interest in impartial law enforcement.[24]

After the Court's decision in *Morrison*, the debate shifted away from constitutional arguments toward issues of political accountability and cost. While some critics continued to disagree with the Court's constitutional analysis,[25] the Iran-Contra investigation offered the opportunity for opponents to attack the arrangement on other grounds. Critics accused Independent Counsel Lawrence Walsh of incompetence, excessive spending, and partisanship and claimed that his statutory independence made him uncontrollable and unaccountable.[26] The question of accountability remains the central issue of debate about the independent counsel arrangement, and it is the issue to which this chapter speaks.

INDEPENDENCE AND ACCOUNTABILITY

Few critics explicitly invoke a formalist theory of the separation of powers to justify their attack on the independent counsel's accountability, but that perspective continues to underlie their argument. The argument for lack of accountability assumes that unless an office is subject to direct control by one of the three major branches of government, it is subject to no control. And since independent counsels exercise law enforcement power but are not subject to direct control by the chief law enforcement officer in the government, they are ipso facto unaccountable. A corollary assumption should also be exposed. The argument against the independent counsel assumes that prosecutors who are subject to executive control are less likely to abuse their power than those who are not. Thus regular prosecutors exercise prosecutorial discretion responsibly, whereas independent prosecutors have numerous incentives, given their freedom, to abuse their power. One critic argues that "These counsels have oppressively enforced criminal justice because they enjoyed unlimited budgets, were ambitious for fame and its cash value, and attracted biased and overzealous staffs"; another asserted that the law has "produced savage injustices to individuals."[27]

In contrast, supporters of the independent counsel arrangement have focused their attention on the informal relationships within the executive branch that underlie the formal relationship and that seem to justify resort to independent investigation. Noting how often attorneys general are close friends and political allies of the president, they argue that the opportunities for real and perceived conflicts of interest to develop are too great to allow the executive to investigate itself. The "accountability" that the formalists view as an argument in support of executive appointment of special prosecutors is identified as the source of the conflict-of-interest problem that justifies independence by supporters of a separate arrangement.

An examination of the use of independent counsels since 1978 challenges the formalist reading of the situation on several grounds. The accumulated evidence demonstrates a major flaw in the formalist theory that has also been revealed in other critiques of the approach. While neat conceptually, formalism fails to account for how the separation-of-powers system functions in practice, the "bundle" of accountability relationships that exist within the system, and the transformation of the American system that has attended the rise of the administrative state.[28] Further, formalist assumptions about the differences between regular prosecutors and independent ones are not supported by the evidence to date. These assumptions ignore the complexity of the separation of powers generally and the nature of prosecution specifically.

Except with regard to the source of the prosecutor's appointment, independent counsel operate within substantially the same constraints as regular prosecutors. They exercise substantially the same discretion and possess the same potential for abuse in exercising their power. Prosecutorial discretion has long been recognized as creating the possibility for abusive prosecutions. Critics have noted that this danger is greatly enhanced when such discretion is backed by the awesome power of the federal executive, and they have observed that the courts have permitted prosecutorial discretion to grow virtually unchecked.[29] Recent developments at the federal level suggest that the political popularity of anti-crime positions taken during the Reagan era (and afterward) has encouraged the abuse of prosecutorial discretion by federal prosecutors. In recent years, federal judges, not the executive, have begun to act to rein in these prosecutors.[30] Meanwhile the absence of an institutional power base comparable to the Justice Department and the presence of stringent reporting requirements under the enabling statute mean that the independent counsel's discretion must be publicly justified in a manner rarely demanded of regular prosecutors.[31]

THE EXECUTIVE BRANCH AND THE INDEPENDENT COUNSEL

In creating an independent counsel arrangement, Congress sought to limit the traditional supervisory authority of the attorney general over the attorneys who handled cases of executive branch misconduct. Thus, appointment of the special counsel was vested in a judicial panel instead of the attorney general; the independent counsel was granted the "full power of independent authority" to exercise all investigative and prosecutorial functions and powers of the Department of Justice; the independent counsel was given the power to select a staff and determine its duties and salaries; and ongoing Justice Department investigations relating to matters within the independent counsel's jurisdiction were to be suspended unless the counsel permitted their continuation.[32] On the other hand, the provisions contained a number of opportunities for the attorney general and the Department of Justice to exercise power. The attorney general was given authority to make the initial determination of whether independent investigation was warranted and to outline the jurisdiction of the independent counsel in making his or her request to the judicial panel for counsel appointment under the statute. The independent counsel was encouraged to consult with the U.S. attorney for the district within which the alleged crime occurred and to comply with established criminal enforcement policies of the Justice Department. Finally, the attorney general could remove the independent counsel for "good cause."[33]

In practice, attorneys general have exercised significant influence in implementing the provisions. Identification of the precise number of times attorneys general have exercised their discretionary judgment under the act is difficult, since much of the earliest stage of the process is intentionally obscured from public view. A formal estimate obtained in connection with the 1987 reauthorization hearings found that thirty-six cases implicating covered officials had been handled by the Department of Justice between 1982 and 1987. Eleven triggered preliminary investigations, and eight led to the appointment of independent counsel. Two of these appointments never received public attention and were not officially announced by the court panel.[34] In 1992 Attorney General William Barr publicly refused to seek appointment of independent counsel on three different occasions, despite considerable congressional pressure on him to do so. Twice, his refusal was in response to requests from congressional Democrats for an independent investigation into the Iraq/BNL scandal and once it involved rejection of a request from congressional Republicans seeking an independent investigation of the Iran-Contra independent counsel, Lawrence Walsh.[35]

Clearly, the attorney general has more than once exercised discretionary judgment in the early stages of the process. This filtering role is desirable to the extent that it eliminates frivolous and unfounded charges against always vulnerable public officials; but it also indicates that the critics' suggestion that the attorney general has no choice but to seek appointment of independent counsel whenever allegations against covered officials arise is incorrect. A review of specific cases that have arisen under the provisions of the independent counsel law demonstrates the significant degree of control retained by the attorney general in deciding whether a preliminary investigation is needed, in declining to seek appointment of an independent counsel, in defining the jurisdiction of the independent counsel when one is sought, and in influencing the outcome of cases taken to trial.

Attorney General Edwin Meese III was subjected to more scrutiny and oversight in his handling of Ethics Act cases than were any of his predecessors. In part this was attributable to the ethics cloud that hung over him when he entered office, and in part it reflected the adversarial relationship he had with congressional Democrats. Consequently, Meese experienced greater political pressure than did other attorneys general to use the independent counsel arrangement. Even so, several important examples illustrate how Meese exercised his discretion to interpret the provisions in a way that maximized his control of the process.

Faith Whittesley, the Reagan administration's ambassador to Switzerland and a personal friend of Meese's, was the subject of several allegations of official misconduct in 1986. She was accused of improperly using money that had been donated to the embassy, of giving a job to the son of one of the donors of the money shortly after the gift was received, and of obstructing justice by threatening to dismiss the deputy chief of mission for cooperating in an investigation of the first two allegations.[36] Meese's conclusion that no independent counsel was warranted in this case was based on assessments of the evidence that did not conform to the standards established to guide the attorney general's discretion under the statute. His report asserted that, while the funds had been improperly used, no evidence suggested that the ambassador knew that use of the funds was restricted under law. Regarding the job to the donor's son,

Meese found no compelling evidence that a quid pro quo arrangement existed, despite the timely conjunction of the gift and the job. Finally, Meese concluded that the conflicting versions of the events at issue in connection with the obstruction of justice charge indicated that, under similar circumstances, a private citizen would not be prosecuted, and if prosecuted, would not be convicted.[37]

The Whittesley case demonstrates the extensiveness of the discretion exercised by the attorney general during the earliest stages of the process. Without press attention, which in turn prompts inquiries from congressional overseers, there is no way to know what allegations were made and what interpretations of facts and law were devised in disposing of the case.[38] If no report is made to the court panel, there is no legal basis for holding the attorney general accountable at this stage of the process. The 1987 congressional oversight investigation found that, since 1982, the Justice Department had closed more than two-thirds of the cases involving covered officials (twenty-five of the thirty-six) prior to conducting a preliminary investigation—the event that would trigger the statutory requirement of a report by the attorney general to the court panel. In most of these cases, the department conducted "threshold inquiries," taking an average two and one-half months, that resulted in determinations that evidence was insufficient to justify undertaking a preliminary investigation. In some of these cases, including the original investigation into the Whittesley allegations, that determination was based not on the specificity or credibility of the evidence (the statutory standard), but rather on a preemptive judgment that the subject lacked criminal intent.[39]

In the Whittesley case, the Justice Department took six weeks to investigate the allegation, sending two investigators to Switzerland, to France, and around the United Sates. Nearly fifty interviews were conducted. "Elaborate factual and legal analyses" were developed. This in-depth investigation led the attorney general to conclude that no statutory preliminary investigation (requiring a report to the court panel) was warranted. Later, congressional investigators suggested that the department had been "conducting preliminary investigations in all but name to avoid statutory reporting requirements."[40]

In a later investigation into the obstruction-of-justice allegations against Whittesley, Meese did submit a report to the court panel explaining his conclusion that no appointment of independent counsel was warranted. Meese argued that "a reasonable prosecutor would not seek an indictment" in this case and that appointment of an independent counsel would be "unjust" because no harm had resulted from Whittesley's behavior and because she was under a great deal of stress at the time of the incident.[41] In reaching these conclusions, Meese interpreted his decision-making power under the independent counsel statute in a manner that conflicted with the intent of Congress. One critic noted that Meese's judgment appeared to be based, in part, "on sympathy that he believed the Ambassador should be accorded. Reliance on grounds of compassion is precisely the sort of consideration inappropriate for one involved in a conflict of interest."[42] A congressional staff member noted that the Whittesley case demonstrated "the one big flaw in the process. We still have to trust the attorney general to trigger the statute and we don't know if he doesn't"[43]

The attorney general's influence is illustrated further in the Theodore Olson case, which arose out the EPA controversy of 1981–1982. In this case, Meese did seek the appointment of independent counsel. But in exercising his power to establish the jurisdiction of the investigation, he significantly shaped the work of the counsel. The allegations in this case emerged from a bitter confrontation between Congress and the president over supposed political manipulation of the EPA by the Reagan administration. Two House subcommittees became embroiled in a legal dispute with the EPA, the Justice Department, and the White House over a claim to executive privilege covering certain documents that congressional investigators deemed necessary to conduct oversight of the agency. Eventually the parties reached a political settlement, but resentment lingered in Congress over the role the Department of Justice played in the controversy about executive privilege. A House Judiciary Committee investigation into the department's role resulted in a 3,000-page report suggesting that Theodore Olson, assistant attorney general for the OLC, had lied to the subcommittee during its investigation. It also accused Deputy Attorney General Edward Schmults and Assistant Attorney General (for the land and natural resources division) Carol Dinkins of obstructing the congressional investigation by withholding needed documents.[44]

After a lengthy preliminary investigation the public integrity section of the Department of Justice recommended that the allegations against Schmults, Dinkins, and Olson be investigated by an independent counsel. It concluded that the case appeared to involve a "seamless web of events" and that any effort to separate the allegations and individuals would be "artificial" and "may impede the independent counsel's ability to fully explore the allegations."[45] The head of the criminal division concluded that only Olson should be subjected to investigation. A special assistant to Meese, appointed to give advice in this case because of the large number of recusals, recommended that Schmults and Olson, but not Dinkins, be investigated by an independent counsel. Meese decided to refer only the allegations against Olson (for lying to Congress) to the special divisions of the court for independent investigation.[46]

Meese's decision to refer only the Olson allegations to special counsel placed significant limitations on the independent counsel's ability to investigate the case. One of her deputies in the investigation described it as "requiring us to go into the investigation with clipped wings."[47] Independent Counsel Alexia Morrison noted that "the jurisdiction problem demonstrated the difference between a normal prosecution where you get a file on a case or a person and you follow it wherever it may lead you. In this case the focus on a particular person and the Attorney General's ability to place limits on the jurisdiction, clearly limited the ability to investigate the case along whatever lines it led us."[48] Early in the investigation Morrison and her staff concluded that, taken alone, Olson's behavior was probably not criminal. But they had serious concerns about the role Olson might have played in a broader conspiracy with Schmults and Dinkins to obstruct the congressional investigation: "The House Judiciary report did not think it was just a problem of whether Olson told the truth. The report suggested a conspiracy at the highest levels of the Department of Justice to obstruct the inquiry into the EPA dispute. We were concerned that the committee may have had a point about what was going on at Justice. Our jurisdiction had been carved up in a very peculiar way and on the basis of what we could see, without being able to include Dinkins and Schmults in our review, there was a lot more reason to ask questions about them than about Olson."[49]

As a result of these concerns, Morrison requested an expansion of her jurisdiction in a letter to the attorney general. That request was denied. She turned to the special court panel responsible for her appointment and requested that it expand her jurisdiction to include Dinkins and Schmults. The court panel concluded that it lacked the legal authority to overrule the attorney general's decision.[50] This decision was consistent with three earlier court decisions during former attorney general William French Smith's tenure that found that discretionary judgments by the attorney general in deciding whether to investigate allegations and whether to seek appointment of independent counsel were not reviewable.[51]

The Iran-Contra case provides further evidence of the attorney general's power to affect the conduct and outcome of independent counsel investigations. Given the very complex problems with classified documents raised by these cases, it is remarkable that Oliver North and John Poindexter ever went to trial.[52] Decisions by the executive branch—and particularly by Attorney General Richard Thornburgh—regarding the use of classified documents by the defense seriously hampered the prosecution, delaying the proceedings and ultimately forcing the independent counsel to drop central conspiracy and theft charges against the defendants (North, Poindexter, Richard Secord, and Albert Hakim).

Throughout 1988 and 1989, the trial of Oliver North was delayed by complicated legal wrangling among the attorney general, the independent counsel, the defense, and the district court over the best way to handle the myriad classified documents that the defense claimed were relevant to its case.[53] The procedures for deciding on the admissibility and availability of classified information in federal criminal trials are prescribed in the Classified Information Procedures Act of 1980 (CIPA).[54] The statute was designed to avoid "graymail" by criminal defendants whose job or alleged crime might make classified information relevant to their defense. CIPA attempts to balance the defendant's right to a fair trial and the government's need to protect classified information, by establishing pretrial discovery and trial procedures governing the use of such information. The act requires defendants to give advance notice of their intent to use classified information in their defense, and the trial court is required to conduct an in camera hearing as to the use, relevance, and admissibility of the information thus identified. If the court decides that the classified information is necessary to the defense, the government (that is, the Department of Justice) ultimately decides whether the classified information may be used at the trial. The attorney general may submit an affidavit certifying that the disclosure would lead to "identifiable damage" to the national security; the validity of the certification as a matter of fact is not contestable by any of the litigants in the case. Once the affidavit is filed, the court must decide whether the case can go forward without the classified information. If not, the court will dismiss the indictment.[55]

The CIPA procedures were designed to ease the "friction" between the Justice Department and intelligence agencies that occurs when prosecutions involving classified information arise.[56] No one anticipated that a CIPA case might pit an independent counsel against the attorney general and the intelligence agencies combined.[57] In the Iran-Contra prosecutions, however, this is precisely what happened. The attorney general and the agencies worked in tandem, usually as the independent counsel's adversaries, in the proceedings before the district court. Final authority over what information could be disclosed remained with the attorney general and the agencies. "That authority," argued one observer, "enabled them to impose broad de facto limits on [Independent Counsel] Walsh's freedom to prosecute, even though the independent counsel law barred them from controlling his prosecution directly."[58]

Only significant compromises by the independent counsel allowed the North case to go forward at all. In November 1988, Judge Gesell announced that he would begin North's trial in January of 1989 and that he intended to give North "wide latitude" to use documents to challenge the credibility of prosecution witnesses. Gesell indicated that he did not intend to dismiss the case unilaterally and that if the trial was to be stopped, it would have to occur through the exercise of the presidential pardon or the filing of CIPA affidavits by the attorney general.[59] President Reagan announced that he would not pardon North prior to trial but that he would have to move to prevent the disclosure of some of the secrets North claimed were essential to his defense.[60] After intense negotiations between Walsh and Thornburgh, during which the attorney general made it clear that the government would not permit the disclosure of some of the information Judge Gesell had found to be essential to North's defense, Walsh was forced to seek dismissal of the main conspiracy and theft charges against North. Thornburgh submitted an affidavit certifying that the documents had to be kept secret, and Gesell granted the dismissal. "There is no way known to the court," said the judge, "or found in any of the cases, to force the attorney general to prosecute a case the attorney general doesn't want to prosecute."[61] During the next year, Walsh also dropped the same conspiracy counts against North's co-defendants. The impact of the executive branch's control of the CIPA process on the independent counsel's case was profound. It permitted Walsh to focus only on the narrower charges involving North's personal behavior and not on the central issue in the scandal: the organized effort to conduct foreign policy in contravention of specific laws of the United States. "The guts of the original indictment lay in its first two counts . . . the rest . . . focused upon epiphenomena, not the heart of the affair."[62]

Finally, the December 1992 pardons of six Iran-Contra defendants show how the constitutional prerogatives of the president continue to influence the work of the independent counsel. All six of those pardoned had been accused of withholding information or lying to Congress. Independent Counsel Walsh had obtained guilty pleas in three of the cases, a conviction in another, and was preparing to go to trial in the other two.[63] In his fourth interim report to Congress in early 1993, Walsh reported that the pardons prevented him from presenting new evidence of the Reagan administration's efforts to cover up the arms-for-hostages deal that precipitated the scandal in the first place.[64] The pardons effectively brought the independent counsel's investigation to a close.[65] Critics have treated the Iran-Contra investigation as prime evidence of an out-of-control special prosecutor operating without any legal restraint, but the outcome of the conflict over classified documents and the significance of the presidential pardon power suggest otherwise.

THE COURTS AND THE INDEPENDENT COUNSEL

The independent counsel statute's provisions mandate a judicial role in the appointment of prosecutors that does not exist in relation to regular prosecutors. This permits a degree of judicial influence, since the panel sets out to appoint persons with well-established reputations within the legal community, who do not have a conflict of interest in taking the case, and whom they trust not to be publicity seekers.[66] The cases of Lyn Nofziger, Michael Deaver, and the Iran-Contra principals reveal an important role for the judiciary beyond appointment of the independent counsel because these cases involved criminal indictments, trials, and appeals to higher courts. The cases demonstrate that, as it does with regard to regular prosecutors, the judiciary provides an extremely important check on the use of power by independent counsel.

Trial judges supervise grand juries, preside over trials, and rule on the various motions involving the conduct of the trial. Appellate judges reexamine the case with an eye to procedural fairness and the application of the law. There is no reason to believe that the impartial federal judiciary acts any differently toward independent counsel than it does toward other federal prosecutors. One might argue that, in the independent counsel cases, the trial judges proceed even more carefully because of the greater likelihood of heightened media attention and of appellate review.

The trial judge in the North trial clearly played a key role in deciding the complex questions of what evidence the defendant should be permitted to claim as essential to his defense in the trial. As demonstrated previously, his rulings on the CIPA procedures, in conjunction with the attorney general's refusal to permit declassification of the documents involved, forced the independent counsel to drop some of the charges he originally planned to pursue and to alter his approach on others.[67] Further, the Court of Appeals for the D.C. Circuit, in setting aside the verdicts in the Nofziger, North, and Poindexter cases, acted as an additional check on both the trial court and the independent counsel.[68] In the Deaver case, the trial judge's refusal to permit the independent counsel to subpoena the Canadian ambassador ensured that the ambassador would not offer evidence on one of the charges against Deaver; ultimately, Deaver was acquitted by the jury on that charge.[69] In the EPA-related investigation, the special court panel's refusal to overrule Meese's denial of Morrison's request for expansion of her jurisdiction limited the scope of her inquiry to Olson alone.[70] Clearly, judges provide as meaningful a check on special prosecutors as they do on regular prosecutors. In bringing a case against a covered official, independent counsel are subject to the same impartial review of their actions, the same rules of evidence, and the same procedural limitations on their powers that regular prosecutors are.

A related check lies in the use of grand juries and trial juries. Prosecutors, both independent and regular, must have sufficient evidence to convince a jury that the defendant has committed a crime. This is easier with grand juries, because of the lower standard of proof required for indictment, but that is true regardless of independence. "One clear constraint on independent counsel," argued a deputy independent counsel, "is one that is on all prosecutors. They must ask themselves whether their case will pass 'the smell test' in front of a jury. Will they find criminal action beyond a reasonable doubt?"[71] To argue then that there are no checks on the independent counsel ignores the most obvious check of all: independent counsel cannot operate outside the established legal system in their pursuit of a successful prosecution. They cannot escape the requirement that their case against an individual be reviewed by an impartial judge and jury.

CONGRESS AND THE INDEPENDENT COUNSEL

Congress's limited statutory role in the process of seeking an appointment of independent counsel is structured along partisan lines. The act permits a majority of either party's members of the Judiciary Committee of either house to "request in writing that the Attorney General apply for the appointment of an independent counsel." The attorney general is not required to comply but must explain any failure to do so. Members of both parties have exercised this right in past cases, and attorneys general have resisted such pressure on several occasions. This congressional role has little effect on the actual conduct of an investigation.

Other congressional powers of oversight and investigation act as more significant constraints on the independent counsel. Congress's investigatory powers are perhaps the most important to examine in this regard. When Congress investigates a case involving a covered official, the conflicting institutional goals of Congress and the independent counsel can pose a substantial impediment to the criminal investigation. Congressional investigations have frequently played an important role in exposing misconduct in the executive branch. This sort of oversight is an important way for Congress to resist abuse of power by the executive. Individual members of Congress may also be motivated by personal ambition or partisan desires to harm the opposition, but congressional investigations certainly can be important and appropriate means by which Congress checks the executive. Further, investigations can serve a valuable educational function for the public, exposing misconduct and teaching citizens about the workings of government.

When congressional exposure of misconduct leads to criminal investigation and prosecution, however, the needs of a representative institution like Congress are frequently at odds with the needs of an office of the criminal justice system. Congressional inquiries raise major barriers to criminal prosecution, including the publicity that inheres in investigations of this type and the willingness of Congress under some circumstances to grant immunity from prosecution in exchange for congressional testimony. For Congress to accomplish exposure and educational goals, publicity is necessary. Prosecutors desire minimal publicity because of the adverse impact extensive exposure has on both the investigative and prosecutorial stages of their cases. Publicity may alert targets of investigation, witnesses, and informants to the purposes of the investigation and the nature of each other's testimony. In both Watergate and Iran-Contra, the prosecution stage of the case was complicated, and in some cases severely damaged, by the granting of immunity to witnesses appearing before the congressional investigative committees.[72] When congressional immunity is granted, prosecutors are forced to prove that their case is not tainted by protected testimony. They may be forced to forgo the use of some evidence available to them because of the difficulty of proving that it is untainted, and they may have to litigate these issues before proceeding with their case in chief. They must also prove that none of their cross-examination of defense witnesses is tainted. These problems are only aggravated by the attendant publicity. In both Watergate and Iran-Contra, members of Congress perceived their interests in exposure and public education to be sufficiently compelling to justify the risk to the effective prosecution of criminal activity in the scandal.[73] The problems of the Iran-Contra investigation created by the congressional grants of immunity were extensive, requiring elaborate procedures within the prosecutor's office to avoid tainting the investigation and significant delays in bringing the case to trial.[74] The congressional grants of immunity to North and Poindexter for their televised testimony ultimately negated much of the work of the independent counsel in these cases.[75]

Congressional committee investigations have coincided with many of the independent counsel cases. For example, the Senate Labor and Human Resources Committee carried out its own investigation of Raymond Donovan, during which the first allegations of ties to organized crime surfaced. The first allegations against Edwin Meese surfaced during the Senate Judiciary Committee's hearings on his nomination for attorney general. The Olson investigation followed on the heels of a House Judiciary Committee investigation. Independent Counsel Morrison noted the problem of parallel or preceding investigations in the Olson case: "Everyone knew what everyone else had said. The Public Integrity Section had investigated and written a 160-page report. Congress had issued a four-volume report. Consequently, it was a very difficult case for us to get into. It had been well chewed over and we were handed a very cold trail. It had been chewed over in a way no other case I had ever been involved in had been."[76]

CONCLUSIONS

Critics of the independent counsel arrangement have focused on the wrong evidence in arguing that the independent counsel is unaccountable and that the executive has no real influence in the process. Their theoretical assumptions about the separation of powers have forced them into assumptions about how the arrangement works in practice that are not supported by the facts. Critics have focused on the lack of restraints in the statutory language creating the independent office and on the formal insulation of the counsel from the immediate control of the executive. That focus has blinded them to the much more complex set of accountability relationships that exist for any actor in the political or legal process. The attorney general and the president continue to exercise constitutional prerogatives of prosecutorial discretion and national security protection that have had a substantial and limiting impact on independent counsel investigations. The federal judiciary continues to play the role it must always play in the criminal law. The institutional interests of Congress have, at times, conflicted with and done great harm to the interests of the independent counsel. Independent counsel would perhaps be better named "interdependent counsel." They do not and cannot operate in a vacuum. An approach to the separation of powers that eschews neat compartmentalization in favor of flexibility and adaptiveness provides a substantially better framework for understanding the politics of independent counsel and the constraints within which the entire federal legal bureaucracy operates.

NOTES

1. Ethics in Government Act of 1978, 28 U.S.C. 591–598 (Public Law 95-521).

2. Special prosecutors were appointed to investigate the Teapot Dome scandal of the 1920s and the tax scandal of the Truman administration. See Burt Noggle, *Teapot Dome: Oil and Politics in the 1920's* (Baton Rouge, La.: Louisiana State University Press, 1962); and Robert H. Ferrell, *Harry S. Truman and the Modern American Presidency* (Boston: Little, Brown, 1983).

3. John W. Kingdon, *Congressmen's Voting Decisions*, 2d ed. (New York: Harper & Row, 1981), p. 285. Kingdon says, "Once a matter is in the congressman's attention field, events may take place which have a powerful focusing effect."

4. U.S. Congress, House of Representatives, Committee on the Judiciary, *Special Prosecutor and Watergate Grand Jury Legislation: Hearings Before the Subcommittee on Criminal Justice*, 93rd Cong., 1st sess. (Washington, D.C.: Government Printing Office, 1973).

5. U.S. Congress, Senate, Committee on the Judiciary, *Removing Politics from the Administration of Justice: Hearings Before the Subcommittee on the Separation of Powers*, 93rd Cong., 2d sess. (Washington, D.C.: Government Printing Office, 1974).

6. U.S. Congress, Senate, Committee on Government Operations, *Watergate Reorganization and Reform Act of 1975, Part I*, 94th Congress, 1st sess. (Washington, D.C.: Government Printing Office, 1975).

7. U.S. Congress, Senate, Committee on Governmental Affairs, *Ethics in Government Act Amendments of 1982: Hearings Before the Subcommittee on Oversight of Government Management*, 97th Cong., 2d sess. (Washington, D.C.: Government Printing Office, 1982); House of Representatives, Committee on the Judiciary, *Amendment of the Special Prosecutor Provisions of Title 28: Hearings Before the Subcommittee on Administrative Law and Governmental Relations*, 97th Cong., 2d sess. (Washington, D.C.: Government Printing Office, 1982).

8. *Morrison v. Olson*, 487 U.S. 654 (1988).

9. Holly Idelson, "Whitewater Boosts Prospects of Independent Counsel Bill," *Congressional Quarterly Weekly Report*, 15 January 1994, p. 73; Andrew Taylor, "Former U.S. Prosecutor Named as Whitewater Investigator," *Congressional Quarterly Weekly Report*, 22 January 1994, p. 108; Holly Idelson, "Stage Is Set for Swift Renewal of Independent Counsel Law," *Congressional Quarterly Weekly Report*, 12 February 1994, pp. 333–34; Holly Idelson, "House Clears Bill Reauthorizing Independent Counsel Law," *Congressional Quarterly Weekly Report*, 25 June 1994, p. 1718; Andrew Taylor, "Schedule for Hearings Is Unclear as Starr Takes over Probe," *Congressional Quarterly Weekly Report*, 13 August 1994, p. 108.

10. 28 U.S.C. 591–92 (1978).

11. 28 U.S.C. 49 (appointment of judges); 28 U.S.C. 593(b)–(c) and 595 (b)(3) (duties of court panel) (1978).

12. 28 U.S.C. 596(a) (1978). Change of removal standard is at 28 U.S.C. 596(a)(1) (1983).

13. Arthur Christy, *Report of the Special Prosecutor on Alleged Possession of Cocaine by Hamilton Jordan in Violation of 21 U.S.C. 844(a)*, New York, May 28, 1980; Gerald Gallinghouse, *In re Investigation of Allegations Concerning Timothy Kraft: Report of the Special Prosecutor in Compliance with 28 U.S.C. 595(b)*, New Orleans, January 15, 1982.

14. Leon Silverman, *Report of the Special Prosecor*, Washington, D.C., June 25, 1982.

15. Jacob Stein, *Report of Independent Counsel Concerning Edwin Meese III*, Washington, D.C., September 20, 1984; James McKay, *Report of Independent Counsel in re Edwin Meese III*, Washington, D.C., July 5, 1988. Stein found insufficient evidence to warrant prosecution. McKay found that Meese was technically

in violation of the law, but he declined to prosecute because similar violations by a private citizen would not be prosecuted by the Justice Department.

16. Ben A. Franklin, "Former White House Aide Is Acquitted on 2 Counts—Sentencing Is Set for Feb. 25," *New York Times*, 17 December 1987, p. 1; David Johnston, "Nofziger Is Convicted on 3 Counts of Violating Federal Ethics Law," *New York Times*, 12 February 1988, p. 1.

17. *United States v. Nofziger*, 878 F.2d 442 (D.C. Cir. 1989).

18. Alexia Morrison, *In re Theodore B. Olson and Robert M. Perry: Report of the Independent Counsel*, Washington, D.C., December 27, 1988.

19. *United States v.North*, 910 F.2d 843 (D.C. Cir. 1990); *United States v. North*, 920 F.2d 940 (D.C. Cir. 1990); *United States v. Poindexter*, 951 F.2d 369 (D.C. Cir. 1991).

20. Carroll J. Doherty, "Walsh Says Pardons Thwarted New Evidence on Arms Deals," *Congressional Quarterly Weekly Report*, 13 February 1993, p. 325; James J. Brosnahan, "Pardoning Weinberger Belittles Democracy," *National Law Journal*, 18 January 1993, pp. 17–18.

21. See, for example, Terry Eastland, *Ethics, Politics and the Independent Counsel: Executive Power, Executive Vice 1789–1989* (Washington, D.C.: National Legal Center for the Public Interest, 1989); and William French Smith, "Independent Counsel Provisions of the Ethics in Government Act," in L. Gordon Crovitz and Jeremy A. Rabkin (eds.), *The Fettered Presidency: Legal Constrains on the Executive Branch* (Washington, D.C.: American Enterprise Institute, 1989).

22. *Morrison v. Olson*, 487 U.S. 654 (1988), pp. 697–734 (J. Scalia, dissenting).

23. See, for example, Donald J. Simon, "The Constitutionality of the Special Prosecutor Law," 16 *University of Michigan Journal of Law Reform* (1982): 45–73; Carl Levin, "The Independent Counsel Statute: A Matter of Public Confidence and Constitutional Balance," *Hofstra Law Review* 16 (Fall 1987): 11–22.

24. *Morrison v. Olson*, 487 U.S. 654 (1988).

25. See, for example, Eastland, *Ethics, Politics and the Independent Counsel*, pp. 99–120; Stephen Carter, "Comment: The Independent Counsel Mess," *Harvard Law Review* 102 (1988): 105–41.

26. Bruce Fein, "Don't Restore Counsel Law," *USA Today*, 15 December 1992, p. 10A; Robert Bork, "Against the Independent Counsel," *Commentary* 95 (February 1993): 21–26; Michael Ledeen, "Lawrence Walsh, Grand Inquisitor," *American Spectator* (March 1993): 18–24.

27. Fein, "Don't Restore Counsel Law"; Bork, "Against the Independent Counsel," p. 21.

28. William Haltom, "Separating Powers: Dialectical Sense and Positive Nonsense," In Michael W. McCann and Gerald L. Houseman (eds.), *Judging the Constitution* (Glenview, Ill.: Scott, Foresman, 1989), pp. 127–53; Louis Fisher, "Judicial Misjudgments About the Lawmaking Process: The Legislative Veto Case," *Public Administration Review* 45 (November 1985): 705; Peter Strauss, "Formal and Functionalist Approaches to Separation of Powers Questions—A Foolish Inconsistency?" *Cornell Law Review* 72 (1987): 492.

29. Kenneth Culp Davis, *Discretionary Justice: A Preliminary Inquiry* (Bat-

on Rouge, La.: Louisiana State University Press, 1969); James Vorenberg, "Decent Restraint of Prosecutorial Power," *Harvard Law Review* 94 (May 1981): 1521; Robert Palmer, "The Confrontation of the Legislative and Executive Branches: An Examination of the Constitutional Balance of Power and the Role of the Attorney General," *Pepperdine Law Review* 11 (1984): 331–53.

30. Jim McGee, "Do Prosecutors Play Fair?" *Washington Post National Weekly Edition*, February 1–7, 1993, pp. 6–7; and "When the Defendant Doesn't Get a Fair Shake," pp. 8–9.

31. One critic of prosecutorial discretion argues that all prosecutors ought to be required to generate a more formal record of their decisions, especially for the early, less visible decisions relating to charges. Vorenberg, "Decent Restraint of Prosecutorial Power," p. 1565. Virtually every discretionary decision made by the independent counsel is subject to public exposure because of press attention and the office's reporting requirements.

32. 28 U.S.C. 49, 593 (appointment); 28 U.S.C. 594(a) (investigative powers); 28 U.S.C. 594 (c) (staff selection); 28 U.S.C. 597(a) (ongoing investigations).

33. 28. U.S.C. 592 (role in appointment); 28 U.S.C. 594(a)(10) and (f) (consultation/compliance); 28 U.S.C. 596(a)(1) (removal).

34. U.S. Congress, Senate, Committee on Governmental Affairs, *Independent Counsel Reauthorization Act of 1987*, Sen. Report 100-123, 100th Cong., 1st sess. (Washington, D.C.: Government Printing Office, 1987), pp. 6–7.

35. Carroll J. Doherty, "Barr Nixes Independent Counsel, Cites 'No Reasonable Grounds'," *Congressional Quarterly Weekly Report*, 12 December 1992, p. 3809; and "Barr Rejects Call for a Counsel to Probe a Counsel," *Congressional Quarterly Weekly Report*, 12 December 1992, p. 3798.

36. The allegations and the department's handling of them are discussed in American Bar Association, Section on Criminal Justice, *Report to the House of Delegates* (August 1987), p. 13.

37. Ibid., pp. 13–14.

38. Interview with Elise Bean, counsel for the Senate Subcommittee on Oversight of Government Management, Washington, D.C., 14 July 1989; interview with Mary Gerwin, minority counsel, Washington, D.C., 17 July 1989.

39. Sen. Report 100-123, pp. 6–7.

40. Ibid., p. 9.

41. Cited in *Testimony of Archibald Cox, Chairman of Common Cause, on the Independent Counsel Provisions of the Ethics in Government Act, Before the Subcommittee on Administrative Law and Governmental Relations of the House Judiciary Committee*, April 23, 1987, p. 18. (Xerox obtained from Common Cause.)

42. Ibid., p. 19.

43. Interview with Mary Gerwin, Washington, D.C., 17 July 1989.

44: U.S. Congress, House of Representatives, Committee on the Judiciary, *Report on the Investigation of the Role of the Department of Justice in the Withholding of Environmental Protection Agency Documents from Congress in 1982–1983*, 98th Cong., 1st sess. (Washington, D.C.: Government Printing Office, 1985).

45. Public integrity section memo of April 4, 1986, cited in Morrison, *In re Theodore Olson and Robert Perry*, p. 11.

46. Ibid., pp. 10–15.

47. Interview with Earl Dudley, Jr., deputy independent counsel, Arlington, Virginia, 13 July 1989.

48. Interview with Alexia Morrison, independent counsel, Washington, D.C., 21 July 1989.

49. Interview with Earl Dudley, Jr., Arlington, Virginia, 13 July 1989.

50. *In re Olson*, 818 F.2d 34 (D.C. Cir. 1987).

51. *Nathan v. Attorney General*, 737 F.2d 1069 (D.C. Cir. 1984); *Banzhaf v. Smith*, 737 F.2d 1167 (D.C. Cir. 1984); and *Dellums v. Smith*, 797 F.2d 817 (9th Cir. 1986).

52. Ann Pelham, "Can North Be Tried? Who's to Be Trusted?" *Legal Times*, 20 February 1989, p. 1.

53. Glenn Craney, "Classified Data, Immunity Pose Delay in Iran-Contra Case, *Congressional Quarterly Weekly Report*, 16 April 1988, p. 997; Glenn Craney, "Access to Secret Papers Snarls Iran-Contra Case," *Congressional Quarterly Weekly Report*, 30 April 1988, pp. 1157–58; Glenn Craney, "Secrecy Spat Jeopardizes Iran-Contra Trial," *Congressional Quarterly Weekly Report*, 3 December 1988, p. 3455; Ann Pelham, "Walsh Clashes with Justice Department over Secrets," *Legal Times*, 31 July 1989, p. 2.

54. Public Law No.1. 96-456, 94 Stat. 2025.

55. 18 U.S.C. §§ 5(a) and 6.

56. Brian Z. Tamanaha, "A Critical Review of the Classified Information Procedures Act," *American Journal of Criminal Law* (Summer 1986) 13: 280.

57. Pelham, "Can North Be Tried?" p. 11.

58. Harold Hongju Koh, *The National Security Constitution* (New Haven, Conn.: Yale University Press, 1990), p. 31.

59. Glen Craney, "Judge Won't Derail North's Iran-Contra Trial," *Congressional Quarterly Weekly Report*, 26 November 1988, p. 3403.

60. Craney, "Secrecy Spat Jeopardizes Iran-Contra Trial," p. 3455.

61. Glenn Craney, "Two Iran-Contra Charges Against North Dismissed," *Congressional Quarterly Weekly Report*, 14 January 1989, p. 99.

62. Koh, *The National Security Constitution*, p. 26.

63. Holly Idelson, "Bush Leaves Partisan Mark with Surprise Pardons," *Congressional Weekly Report*, 2 January 1993, pp. 31–32.

64. Doherty, "Walsh Says Pardons Thwarted New Evidence on Arms Deals," p. 325.

65. Brosnahan, "Pardoning Weinberger Belittles Democracy." Brosnahan contended that Bush's pardons "nullified the very office that he was supposed to leave alone" (p. 18).

66. Interview with Judge Edward Lumbard, New York City, 29 January 1985; Interview with Judge George MacKinnnon, Washington, D.C., 17 July 1989.

67. Glen Craney, "Split Trials Could Be Blow to Iran-Contra Case," *Congressional Quarterly Weekly Report*, 11 June 1988, pp. 1625–27; Craney, "Access to Secret Papers Snarls Iran-Contra Case"; "Two Iran-Contra Charges Against North

Dismissed"; and Lawrence Walsh, *Independent Counsel's Report to the Subcommittee on Legislation of the Permanent Select Committee on Intelligence of the House of Representatives*, September 19, 1989. (Xerox obtained from Office of Independent Counsel.)

68. *United States v. Nofziger*, 878 F.2d 442 (D.C. Cir 1989); *United States v. North*, 910 F.2d 843 (D.C. Cir. 1990); *United States v. North*, 920 F.2d 940 (D.C. Cir. 1990); *United States v. Poindexter*, 951 F.2d 369 (D.C. Cir. 1991).

69. Telephone interview with Whitney North Seymour, independent counsel, 30 November 1989.

70. *In re Olson*, 818 F.2d 34 (D.C. Cir. 1987).

71. Interview with Earl Dudley, Jr., Arlington, Virginia, 13 July 1989.

72. Lawrence Walsh, "The independent Counsel and the Separation of Powers," *Houston Law Review* (January 1988) 25: 1–11.

73. Interview with John Nields, chief counsel for the House Select Committee to Investigate Covert Arms Transactions with Iran, Washington, D.C., October 16, 1989; interview with Archibald Cox, Harvard Law School, Cambridge, Massachusetts, February 5, 1985; Joel M. Woldman, *Congress and the Iran-Contra Affair*, CRS Report 88-765F, November 1988, p. 15; and Samuel Dash, *Chief Counsel: Inside the Ervin Committee—The Untold Story of Watergate* (New York: Random House, 1976), pp. 124, 142–44.

74. Walsh, "The Independent Counsel and the Separation of Powers." Judge Gerhard Gesell describes the procedures taken in the office in one of his rulings on a pretrial motion to dismiss the case because of the immunity grants. *United States v. Poindexter*, 698 F. Supp. 300, 312–13 (D.D.C. 1988).

75. *United States v. North*, 910 F.2d 843 (D.C. Cir. 1990); *United States v. North*, 920 F.2d 940 (D.C. Cir. 1990); *United States v. Poindexter*, 951 F.2d 369 (D.C. Cir. 1991).

76. Interview with Alexia Morrison, Washington, D.C., 21 July 1989.

5

WHITE HOUSE LAWYERING: LAW, ETHICS, AND POLITICAL JUDGMENTS

JEREMY RABKIN

The U.S. Department of Justice proclaims this motto on the wall of the attorney general's rotunda: "The United States wins its point whenever justice is done its citizens in the courts." Even when it loses a legal battle, in other words, the Justice Department may still console itself that its clients have been served—at least when the opposing party is also an American citizen. Attorney General Griffin Bell articulated the premise of this thought in 1977 when he affirmed that, for the Justice Department, "the people are your client"[1]

The counsel to the president of the United States, often known as the White House counsel, has no such easy consolation. The White House counsel has only one client—the president. If the president loses his legal "point," the counsel has failed his client. Yet the counsel may be accused of failing in his duties even when his legal views prevail.

The sad experience of Bernard Nussbaum, who served as President Clinton's counsel, nicely illustrates the difficulty. After a series of controversial interventions into the activities of various federal agencies—in each case, it seemed, simply to protect the personal reputation or political standing of Mr. Clinton—Nussbaum was forced to resign, having served little more than a year in office. Nussbaum may well have been telling the truth when he claimed in his resignation letter that he had neither broken any laws nor violated any of the accepted ethical obligations of an attorney. Whatever his transgressions, he was joined in them by several other officials, but no one else was forced to resign. So it appeared that Nussbaum had not transgressed any definite ethics boundaries. At most, it appeared, he had exercised bad judgment and provoked controversies that made the president look bad. For most critics, this was sufficient reason to dismiss him.

Nussbaum protested (in his resignation letter) that his critics failed to understand the duties of a lawyer, "even one acting as White House Counsel," to defend his client's interest with zeal.[2] Another White House aide elaborated: "The duty that a lawyer has to represent a client zealously within the bounds of the law applies just as much to a lawyer whose client is the President of the United States as it does to a private lawyer."[3] To this defense, a number of critics responded that the client of the White House counsel is the presidency rather than the particular incumbent of the office, so the counsel should not have let himself be overly swayed by the immediate short-term concerns of Bill Clinton.[4]

This formulation has an edifying ring to it, which is perhaps why it was quickly picked up by Nussbaum's replacement, experienced Washington attorney Lloyd Cutler. Cutler emphasized that questions dealing with Mr. Clinton's personal affairs would be handled by private attorneys and that the White House counsel's office would attend only to questions concerning the official duties of the president.[5] This makes some sense when the president's personal affairs include, as they have for President Clinton, the need to mount legal defenses against charges of financial abuse and sexual misconduct dating to a period before his election to the presidency.[6] President Clinton secured different private attorneys to deal with these personal problems and acknowledged that these attorneys would have to be paid from his own pocket.[7]

Yet there remains something decidedly odd about the notion that the counsel to the president serves only the presidency, not the actual president. No one suggests that the presidential press office should only defend the abstract interests of the presidency, simply because the press office is funded by the taxpayers. No one contends that the president's political advisers should be barred from considering the particular political interests of the incumbent president. Even in the present era of "heightened ethical sensitivity," no one thinks it improper that presidents take top campaign advisers into the White House, where, at taxpayers' expense, they continue to devote most of their effort to advancing the political fortunes of their leader, just as they did during the campaign.

It can be said, of course, that other White House aides are expected to deal with politics, whereas the counsel is responsible for dealing with questions of law. But on genuine questions of law, the president already has extensive professional support: it is called the Department of Justice.

The White House counsel thus seems to be caught in a dilemma. If he bends too much to the immediate personal or political concerns of the president, the counsel is accused of betraying his office. Yet if the counsel's office were simply there to provide legal advice, it would not be necessary.

The dilemma is more apparent than real. There is not, in strict legal terms, any actual office involved when one speaks of the counsel to the president. The counsel (or the counsel's office) is entirely a creation of presidential will and has accordingly played quite different roles in different administrations. Yet the pressures that have driven presidents to inflate the counsel's office in recent decades have had enduring force. Contemporary presidents thus rely on a strangely undirected office that, if not hard to account for, remains very difficult to judge.

CHANCE ORIGINS, VARIED STATUS

In President Washington's day, the attorney general operated without any staff—and at that, performed the duties of chief law officer as a part-time job.[8] The White House counsel's office, which now encompasses an extended staff, also began as the position of a single person, and most of the work was only tangentially (if at all) related to official legal duties. The similarities end there, however.

The position of attorney general was created by congressional enactment; and from the outset, most of the duties performed by the attorney general—or at least, most of the formal responsibilities carried by the attorney general—have been assigned by law. The attorney general is unambiguously an "officer of the United States," whose appointment is subject to Senate confirmation. Like other executive officers, the attorney general is regularly subject to congressional requests for information, explanation, and appearances for direct questioning by congressional committees.

The White House counsel has no formal responsibilities assigned by statute. Indeed, no statute even acknowledges the existence of the office. Neither the counsel nor any of the counsel's assistants is subject to Senate confirmation. And just as it is assigned no duties by Congress, the counsel's office makes no answer or report to Congress: the counsel's office regards most of its activities as shielded from outside inquiry by executive privilege, and counsels are almost never asked to testify before congressional committees.[9]

The attorney general presides over a large department, now embracing over 90,000 employees. Most of these are specialized careerists (with civil service protection), guided by well-developed institutional routines and office traditions.[10] Most of their working priorities are fixed by the annual budget appropriation for the Department of Justice.

The counsel and all the members of his staff serve at the pleasure of the president who appoints them. Each administration entirely restaffs the counsel's office from scratch. Even the precise size of the staff is left undetermined in the general appropriations for the White House staff.[11]

In almost every way, the organization and operation of the counsel's office reflect the fact that it is the creation of the president.

As befits an office created by personal fiat, the origin of the counsel's office reflects a certain degree of presidential caprice. President Franklin Roosevelt was the first president to designate one of his staff as a legal adviser. But he did so only in his third term and then almost surreptitiously. During his second term, Roosevelt sponsored an extensive study of "administrative management."[12] On the basis of this study, he persuaded Congress to fund a formal staff of official presidential assistants at the White House. The resulting Reorganization Act of 1939[13] is often taken by scholars as the origin of the modern White House staff. Yet this statute did not mention a legal adviser, and the initial arrangements for the White House staff made no provision for one.

The position of counsel to the president seems to have been created almost by accident. President Roosevelt had long relied on informal advice from Samuel Rosenman, who had grown close to Roosevelt during his earlier service as governor of New York. In New York (where the state attorney general is a separately elected official, not under the direct control of the governor), Rosenman had held the title "Counsel to the Governor." When Rosenman, after much urging, finally agreed to take up a full-time position in the White House in 1941, Roosevelt rewarded him with the title "Special Counsel to the President." The post was subsequently given the more abbreviated title "Special Counsel" to mollify FDR's attorney general at the time, who insisted that the attorney general was the sole proper channel of legal counsel for the president.[14] In addition to truncating the title, Roosevelt took the precaution of announcing Rosenman's appointment at a moment when the attorney general was out of the country and thus in no position to make a public protest.[15]

As it turned out, Rosenman was no rival to the Justice Department. He worked without any special staff and devoted himself for the most part to drafting public messages for the president. He did not vet speeches for legal problems; he was himself the principal speechwriter.[16] Clark Clifford, who succeeded Rosenman as "Special Counsel" in the Truman White House, summed up the position as consisting of doing "whatever the President wanted."[17] Clifford involved himself in a wide range of matters, but few of them had any distinctly legal component. The man he describes in his memoirs as "my closest associate and collaborator" on the White House staff was not even a lawyer.[18] Clifford was deeply involved in campaign strategy for the 1948 election and also played a role in deliberations on American recognition of the new Jewish state in Palestine—a role resented by the secretary of state, not because it involved intruding legal considerations, but because it consisted of "pressing a political consideration" (as Secretary Marshall saw it).[19]

The protean character of the counsel's office is reflected in the shuffling and reshuffling of titles over the next decade. President Eisenhower, adapting his military experience to the White House, designated one top aide to serve as "Chief of Staff" in the White House, while lengthening the title of "Special Counsel to the President" and applying it to a legal adviser who was clearly a less central figure. Presidents Kennedy and Johnson eliminated the formal title "Chief of Staff" and instead designated their top aides—who served, in effect, as office managers in the White House—as "Special Counsel to the President." Johnson briefly conferred the unqualified title "Counsel to the President" on a particular aide, but when that aide departed soon thereafter, the president designated his replacement as "Special Counsel."[20]

President Nixon revived the Eisenhower practice of naming a formal "Chief of Staff" in the White House. At the outset, he also conferred the title "Counsel to the President" on top aide John Ehrlichman; then he retired the title (after redesignating Ehrlichman as counselor for domestic policy) and gave the title "Special Counsel to the President" to three separate political advisers simultaneously.[21]

Thus, for the first three decades after the term "Counsel" or "Special Counsel" was brought to the White House, the legal resonance of the term seems largely to have been honorific. White House staffers who served under this title might occasionally call on their legal training to scrutinize the language of specific legislative measures (particularly in connection with White House deliberations over whether to sign or to veto a particular measure). They might serve on occasion as trusted interpreters of Justice Department recommendations on complex legal matters (Truman, Eisenhower, Kennedy, and Johnson had no formal legal training). But on the whole, the title of "Counsel" or "Special Counsel" seems never to have been a meaningful description of a full-time position. It was, like "Chancellor of the Duchy of Lancaster" in the pre-war British cabinet, a title to dignify a political adviser, without requiring any significant separate duties.

President Nixon's designation of John Dean to serve as "Counsel to the President" in 1970 strikingly indicates how little weight was accorded to the specifically legal duties suggested by the title. Dean was a young lawyer in the Justice Department when he was recommended for the White House post by Attorney General Mitchell. He had no particular achievements to his name and had never even met the president (nor the president's chief of staff) prior to his appointment. For almost two years after his appointment, he saw the president only a few times a month and then mostly on ceremonial occasions.[22] He was genuinely a legal adviser, which meant that he was at that time considered a very minor figure in the White House.

Dean began the process of building up the counsel's office into a separate bureaucracy. And after the Watergate debacle—in which Dean came to play a central role, first in helping to arrange the cover-up of wrongdoing and then in exposing the cover-up to congressional investigators and to special prosecutors—no president ever treated the counsel as casually as Nixon did. But the counsel's role has continued to vary a good deal.

None of Dean's successors as "Counsel to the President" attained the status of Theodore Sorensen in the Kennedy administration or Harry McPherson in the Johnson administration—men who functioned as virtual chiefs of staff under the title "Special Counsel."[23] But a number of subsequent counsels were key figures in the White House, and all of Dean's successors were much more prominent or at least much more widely known and professionally established figures than the young John Dean had been in 1970.

President Ford accorded the title "Counsel" to Philip Buchen, his old friend and former law partner who had taken the initiative in making plans for Vice-President Ford's elevation to the presidency even before President Nixon's resignation.[24] Buchen was clearly a key figure in a close-knit White House. President Carter also appointed a close personal associate to be his counsel—Robert Lipshutz of Atlanta, who had served as counsel to Carter's successful presidential campaign in 1976. But Lipshutz, described as "relatively unassertive" by Carter's attorney general,[25] did not take a prominent role in policy debates within the White House. Lipshutz was replaced in the summer of 1979 with prominent Washington attorney Lloyd Cutler in an effort to "add prestige to a flagging White House."[26] Cutler proceeded to involve himself in an extraordinary range of high-level undertakings, from lobbying for the Strategic Arms Limitation Treaty with the Soviet Union to arranging safe places of exile for the deposed shah of Iran.[27]

By contrast, the men who served as counsel in the Reagan White House were far less visible figures and generally played only a secondary role in policy debates. None had close personal ties to Reagan before they assumed their positions. But given President Reagan's penchant for delegating details to subordinates, it was more important that each counsel had close ties with the White House chief of staff. Fred Fielding, who served as counsel under Chief of Staff James Baker, had ties to Baker from the Ford administration (even earlier, he had served as assistant to John Dean in the Nixon White House).[28] In Reagan's second term, when James Baker was succeeded as chief of staff by Donald Regan (who had been secretary of the treasury in Reagan's first term), Regan brought Peter Wallison, one of his top aides at the Treasury Department, to serve as counsel in the White House. When Regan was replaced in turn as chief of staff by former senator Howard Baker, Baker replaced Wallison with A. V.

Culvahouse, who was a top aide to Baker prior to Baker's retirement from the Senate and who had followed Baker into private law practice.

President Bush retained C. Boyden Gray as counsel to the president. The two men had a solid working relationship after Gray's long service to Bush as counsel to the vice-president during the Reagan years. Gray was clearly a much more central figure in White House policy debates than counsels during the Reagan years had been, taking a prominent role in (among other things) negotiations with congressional leaders over disputed provisions in major pieces of legislation of the Bush era (including the Clean Air Act Amendments, the Americans with Disabilities Act, and the Civil Rights Act of 1991).[30] But Gray was far from being the dominant staff assistant in the Bush White House. His subordinate position was underscored when he was publicly scolded, on one occasion, by Chief of Staff John Sununu for having made politically unseemly remarks to the press.[31] No one but the president could have publicly rebuked Theodore Sorensen or Harry McPherson.

Bernard Nussbaum had ties to the Clintons going back almost twenty years, to the time when Hillary Clinton served with him on the House Impeachment Committee in 1974. Unlike other counsels, moreover, Nussbaum was backed up by deputy and assistant counsels who also had close ties to the president—closer indeed than Nussbaum's, as they had been law partners with Mrs. Clinton in Arkansas. On the other hand, none of these individuals had any previous experience in high executive office in the federal government, nor recent experience of any sort in Washington. In this respect, the Clinton team in the counsel's office was similar to John Dean—and in marked contrast to almost all the counsels in between. But when Nussbaum was forced to resign, the White House immediately indicated that he would be replaced by an experienced Washington figure "like Lloyd Cutler." The president then proceeded to hire Lloyd Cutler himself, to lend credibility to the Clinton White House, just as he was hired to do for the Carter White House some fifteen years before. When Cutler left the position in August 1994 (having agreed to serve only on a temporary basis), he was replaced by another experienced Washington player, D.C. Circuit Judge (and former Democratic Congressman) Abner Mikva.

Presidents since Nixon may have made a point of relying on more trustworthy figures than John Dean, but they still have not made equal use of the men they hired nor used them in the same ways. Lloyd Cutler was "in and out of the Oval Office several times a day" during his service in the Carter White House and seemed to follow the same pattern with President Clinton. By contrast, Boyden Gray, despite his prominent role in major policy disputes and his long personal connection with George Bush, recalls seeing President Bush no more than once a week, on average, during the Bush presidency.[32] Bernard Nussbaum, like Cutler, reported having direct discussions with President Clinton several times a day.[33]

In at least one respect, though, the counsel's office has followed a consistent pattern: it has grown steadily. When Dean was named counsel, he started all by himself. He was soon able to hire an assistant, however, and then to hire two additional attorneys, all working full-time on legal issues.[34] By 1980, Lloyd Cutler needed a staff of six attorneys to assist him.[35] By 1986, the counsel reported a staff of eight to ten lawyers.[36] A year later, there were fourteen lawyers.[37] The Clinton administration started out with a full staff of "associate counsels" and "assistant counsels," with thirteen lawyers in all[38]—all of them in place many weeks before the administration had announced its nominations for top positions in the Justice Department.

Although the personal influence or prominence of individual counsels still varies, over the past two decades the counsel's office has become an institutionalized presence—indeed, a separate bureaucracy of its own—within the White House. The process began with John Dean, and Dean's fate goes a long way toward explaining the trend.

COUNSELING ETHICS

When Harry McPherson joined the White House staff in 1964 as an "understudy" to Counsel Lee White, the legal chores of the counsel were so limited that he did not feel "fully employed" in his official position.[39] Six years later, Counsel John Dean found that, by devoting close attention to "conflict of interest" questions regarding White House aides and prospective presidential appointees, he could "produce new business' for what he viewed as his "law firm" within the White House.[40] The first full-length treatises on federal conflict-of-interest requirements had appeared only in the early 1960s, and President Johnson opened a still undeveloped field by issuing his 1965 executive order on standards for executive personnel to avoid conflicts of interest.[41]

In its early years, the staff of the Nixon White House was particularly cautious about appearances of impropriety in relation to personal finances and conflicts of interest.[42] Perhaps Nixon's circle remembered financial scandals that had marred the Truman and Eisenhower administrations. Perhaps they were already gripped by that obsessive suspicion of enemies in the press that would later lead to so many abuses. At any rate, Counsel Dean had little trouble in promoting his services. Indeed, he soon found himself besieged with requests for technical legal advice from White House aides. Even after hiring additional lawyers, Dean found his staff "hopelessly overworked."[43]

But the ethics concerns of the Nixon administration were as nothing compared to those imposed on subsequent administrations in reaction to the ethical lapses of the Nixon administration. In the aftermath of the Watergate scandals, allegations of wrongdoing took on fearful momentum, with a press poised to unmask new sources of corruption. Politicians were especially fearful of charges that might lead to the appointment of independent prosecutors. President Ford was forced to appoint a special prosecutor to investigate charges that he had improperly received gifts from labor leaders when serving as House minority leader, years before.[44] The Carter administration, which had promised to restore trust and integrity in government, quickly discovered that Democratic administrations could be equally subject to crippling suspicions under the standards of post-Watergate morality. The Reagan administration would learn in due course that these new standards—and the climate of suspicion that sustained them—did not notably dissipate with the passage of time.

At the outset of the Carter administration, publicized allegations of financial manipulation (before assuming office) forced the resignation of the Director of the Office of Management and Budget; the adviser on drug policy was forced to resign amidst allegations that he had improperly provided staffers with drug prescriptions; even Carter's chief of staff was nearly forced to resign over allegations of recreational drug use. In the first year of the Reagan administration, the National Security Director and then the Secretary of Labor were forced to resign amidst charges of bribe-taking[45]; extended charges of financial impropriety forced the resignation of Attorney General Edwin Meese in Reagan's second term.[46] In none of these cases (including those from the Ford and Carter administrations) did allegations result in criminal convictions; in all but one case (that of Reagan's Labor Secretary Ray Donovan, who was eventually acquitted of all charges after a full trial), investigations by special prosecutors came to the conclusion that evidence of serious wrongdoing was insufficient to justify prosecution. But bad publicity from these episodes was still bitterly resented in the White House.

The post-Watergate climate of suspicion prompted passage of the Ethics in Government Act of 1978,[47] which established a mechanism by which a panel of federal judges could appoint a special prosecutor to investigate allegations of wrongdoing by executive officials. In practice, the special prosecutor then operated without any hierarchical supervision or constraining accountability. There proved to be no effective limits to the size of the staff that the special prosecutor might recruit or to the length or breadth of the investigation. Though investigations by special prosecutors rarely resulted in actual prosecutions, the mere appointment of a special prosecutor often generated a great deal of damaging publicity, and the White House had no effective means of countering such publicity.[48]

The provisions regarding the special prosecutor were allowed to lapse at the end of the Bush administration, but the pattern was so well established that President Clinton ultimately felt constrained to let his attorney general appoint a "special prosecutor," Robert Fiske (with promises of complete independence), to investigate evidence of misconduct by Clinton during his tenure as governor of Arkansas (along with allegations that his White House staff had subsequently conspired to prevent proper investigation of these abuses). Congress then reenacted the relevant statutory provisions in the spring of 1994. In a surprising move, the panel of federal judges replaced Fiske with a more openly partisan special counsel, Kenneth Starr, a former federal judge and solicitor general during the Bush administration.[49]

Quite apart from its special prosecutor provisions, the Ethics in Government Act laid down elaborate and very demanding public disclosure requirements for the financial assets and income sources of government officials (and prospective appointees), and these provisions have never been allowed to lapse. The heightened disclosure requirements were designed to make it much easier for journalists and other investigators to detect possible conflicts of interest. As the disclosure requirements began to approach the complexity of the tax code, affected officials more frequently made inadvertent mistakes in their disclosure forms—a serious danger in an atmosphere in which the withholding of information could readily be fanned into a scandal or perhaps indeed into a criminal offense.[50]

The complexity and seriousness of disclosure and reporting requirements put pressure on the counsel's office to provide close scrutiny of potential nominees for high positions, before congressional committees and the press conducted their own examinations. Reagan counsel Fred Fielding warned prospective appointees "facing difficult financial and other decisions" (regarding compliance with new standards) that they might find it "worthwhile" as well as "comforting" to hire their own attorneys to assist them in preparing for a confirmation battle.[51] But the counsel's office did not rely on such help. In five years, Fielding later estimated, the counsel's office in the Reagan administration scrutinized the records of almost five thousand prospective appointees for "conflict of interest and other problems."[52]

Meanwhile, the tightening of disclosure and conflict-of-interest requirements for those already in office created new demands for legal clarification, putting further burdens on the counsel's office. Subsequent changes increased this burden. In 1989, Congress enacted new ethics legislation that not only extended financial reporting requirements for executive personnel but also imposed waiting periods on former officials before they could begin private-sector work as lobbyists or consultants.[53] These requirements had to be digested and interpreted by White House lawyers, in turn. Thus, during the Bush years, lawyers in the counsel's office found that the great bulk of their time and energy was taken up with technical questions involving ethics standards or with careful screening of prospective nominees in a process known to lawyers in the office as an "ethics scrub."[54]

Apart from questions arising under ethics laws in the precise sense, numerous legal issues were generated by related post-Watergate restrictions, such as the 1976 Federal Records Management Act,[55] controlling the disposal of office memos and other records. In an atmosphere of "heightened sensitivity to the appearance of impropriety," even long-standing prohibitions—such as the prohibition against using government property for personal or campaign purposes—had to be treated with more seriousness, which meant that they had to be considered with more care by White House lawyers. During the Bush administration, Chief of Staff John Sununu provoked a minor scandal when he was found to be using government limousines for private outings to New York; the Clinton White House faced a similar outcry when a White House official was found to have used the president's helicopter for a golf outing in Maryland. White House counsels in both cases were called on to establish tighter guidelines on the use of government transportation, where (as was claimed in these cases) mixed public and private errands were involved.[56]

The demand for legal guidance on such matters helps explain the proliferation of official legal advisers throughout the executive branch and even within the Executive Office of the President (EOP). Throughout the 1940s and 1950s, the president had a designated legal counsel within the White House, but none of the advisory or managerial units within the extended EOP had its own counsel—not even the Bureau of the Budget. By 1976, six of these units, including the Council on Environmental Quality and the National Security Council had their own separate legal staffs headed by an officially designated counsel or general counsel. By the 1980s, it had become routine for each unit, including even the Office of White House Administration to have its own separate counsel.[57] Thus, for example, when the EOP acquired an Office of National Drug Control Policy Coordination in 1989, that office immediately obtained a separate general counsel as well, although it did not engage in any direct law enforcement activity of its own and was merely an intra-administration coordinating body.

Considering how many legal advisers were in the executive branch, one might have expected the demands on the White House counsel to diminish. Part of the reason they did not was that no other counsel could speak with the same authority as the counsel to the president. Other legal advisers, aware of the media focus on the president's own counsel, were eager to borrow the distinctive prestige of his office. Thus, when President Bush's "Drug Czar" Bob Martinez was accused of mishandling campaign funds (from an unsuccessful race for reelection as governor of Florida), the general counsel for the Office of National Drug Control Policy Coordination immediately invoked the say-so of the White House counsel's office to back up his own explanations to journalists of the relevant standards.[58]

But the prestige of the president's counsel does not fully explain the demands on the office. By law, the attorney general is officially responsible for interpreting legal requirements for executive agencies.[59] There is also an independent Office of Governmental Ethics, which can provide specialized guidance on the requirements of existing ethics laws. General counsels for agencies and departments routinely seek legal guidance from the Ethics Office or the Office of Legal Counsel (OLC), which acts for the attorney general in interpreting the law and has, in some ways, much more prestige (at least for legal expertise) than does the White House counsel. In fact, the White House itself (along with the various units within the EOP) often refers questions to the OLC.

That the White House counsel's office has nonetheless retained so much business in connection with interpreting and applying ethics standards reflects the reluctance of recent presidents to rely on the Justice Department in connection with especially sensitive questions. And since Watergate, ethics questions affecting presidential nominees to high office or affecting officials within the EOP are almost by definition sensitive questions, since they can so readily be fanned by the press into a scandal (or in the worst case, pursued by a special prosecutor in a criminal investigation).

The main attraction of the counsel's office is not its prestige, but rather its proximity to the White House. Presidents have come to trust the counsel's office and feel more comfortable relying on it for sensitive chores. Guidance on ethics questions may occupy the most man-hours in the counsel's office, but this is by no means the most important of the responsibilities of the counsel. The same factors that have made contemporary presidents reluctant to rely on the Justice Department for advice on ethics questions have made them reluctant to rely on that department in other areas, as well.

ALTERNATE JUSTICE

Relations between the president and the attorney general have varied a good deal from one era to the next in American history. But it was certainly accepted practice, for most of this century, for the president to install a close political associate at the head of the Justice Department. Presidents Theodore Roosevelt, Wilson, Harding, Franklin Roosevelt, Truman, and Eisenhower appointed party chairmen or top campaign aides to be attorney general.[60] President Kennedy appointed his campaign manager, who was also his brother. A retrospective (and generally admiring) study of the Kennedy Justice Department cheerfully described it as "a 32,000 man addition to the White House staff for random presidential business."[61] President Nixon was thus following a long-standing tradition by appointing his campaign chairman, John Mitchell, to serve as attorney general. But John Mitchell ultimately went to prison for assisting the White House in the cover-up of the Watergate scandals. Since then, presidents have been a good deal more careful to preserve at least the appearance of professional propriety in dealing with the Justice Department.

President Ford was so anxious to restore credibility to the Justice Department that he appointed Edward Levi, a nonpolitical university president to be attorney general, though he had never even met the man until he interviewed him for the position.[62] President Carter's attorney general, Griffin Bell, was an old friend from Georgia; but Bell had served fifteen years as a federal judge, had taken no part in the campaign, and assured the Senate during his confirmation hearing that he would organize the Justice Department as a "political neutral zone."[63] President Reagan was less careful about appearances. His appointment during his second term of longtime political counselor Edwin Meese to the post of attorney general aroused much protest about "politicizing the Justice Department."[64] But even Reagan reverted to the standard post-Watergate pattern by naming as his last attorney general Richard Thornburgh, a relative outsider to the Reagan circle after two terms as governor of Pennsylvania. President Bush kept Thornburgh in that post for almost two years and then replaced him with a relatively colorless Justice Department subordinate, William Barr, who had developed close ties to C. Boyden Gray. Although President Clinton departed from the hands-off pattern of his recent predecessors in some respects, he followed the new pattern in his most visible appointment: as his attorney general he appointed Janet Reno, a local prosecutor from Florida with whom he had had no previous dealings.

Recent presidents, in short, have generally sought to adopt the appearance of respectful detachment from the legal deliberations of the Justice Department. And this is not simply a matter of appearances. The Justice Department has long cultivated a reputation for detached professionalism. Partly, this reflects the need for credibility in litigation: judges and juries are not likely to give much weight to the pleadings of Justice Department attorneys who are seen merely as representing the striking arm of a partisan president. Similarly, in appellate briefs, the government is likely to do better in the long run if it advances consistent positions, building on precedents that it has itself helped to establish and cultivate in prior cases. Ad hoc political interventions can prove dangerously disruptive to long-term legal strategies. More generally, the concern for detached legal professionalism in the Justice Department seems to reflect the inevitable bureaucratic culture that develops around the main mission of an agency: the Justice Department promotes a certain degree of piety about professional determinations of the law, just as the State Department invokes the mystique of diplomatic finesse and the Defense Department cultivates the ideals of professional soldiering.

Even partisan presidents have bowed to the ideals of detached professionalism at the Justice Department. For example, in his successful campaign for the presidency in 1968, Richard Nixon attacked the Supreme Court for permissiveness on crime and excessive zeal in desegregation; and his campaign rhetoric also directly criticized the legal positions and leadership of the Justice Department under President Johnson's attorney general, Ramsey Clark.[65] Nonetheless, after the election, President Nixon retained as solicitor general the Harvard law professor appointed by President Johnson to supervise government briefs for the Supreme Court.[66] Similarly, at the OLC, the Nixon administration honored the tradition whereby the political appointee who heads the OLC relies on a career attorney at the Justice Department to serve as one of his principal deputies.[67]

But the president would be violating his own constitutional duty if he allowed the attorney general to run the Justice Department as if it were an entirely independent agency. The president is the chief executive, charged by the Constitution to "take care that the laws be faithfully executed." The attorney general, like all of the top officials of the Justice Department, serves at the pleasure of the president and is indisputably subject to the President's duty to "take care." If the attorney general adopts an interpretation of the law that the president disapproves, the president is entitled to overrule—or replace—the attorney general.

More to the point, modern presidents are expected to advance a political agenda that includes many matters of legal dispute, even on constitutional questions. When, for example, the Justice Department prepared to file a brief in the celebrated *Bakke* case on the constitutional limits of affirmative action, top officials in the White House (led by Vice-President Mondale) legitimately insisted that the matter be reconsidered at the White House. The Justice Department was eventually induced to change the brief it had initially intended to submit to the Supreme Court. Attorney General Bell could not reasonably object, notwithstanding his avowed intention to preserve the Justice Department as a "political neutral zone."[68]

Affirmative action was only one of a number of new constitutional issues on which presidents were pressed to take a stand by the 1970s. Disputes about abortion, church-state relations, pornography, and other new issues frequently engaged aroused political constituencies who in turn engaged the political attention of the White House. *Bakke* was not the first case in which the White House intervened to influence Justice Department filings before the Supreme Court,[69] and it was certainly not the last. The Reagan White House secured different stands from the Justice Department in the *Bob Jones University* case, involving tax exemptions for a private college accused of race discrimination, as well as in cases involving abortion, affirmative action, and free speech. Such interventions were denounced by critics for improperly "politicizing" the Department of Justice.[70] On the other hand, when President Bush pressed the Justice Department to alter its briefs in a case involving traditionally black colleges in the South, it encountered almost no criticism for this intervention.[71]

High-level interventions not only risk criticism and controversy, however; they also are usually ineffective—as was President Bush's intervention and most of those pressed by the Reagan White House.[72] The Supreme Court is not easily moved by last-minute shifts in legal argument. Efforts to influence Court rulings are more likely to succeed in the context of a larger, more sustained legal strategy, encompassing the initial selection of cases and the pleadings in lower courts. On any particular issue, many different White House aides may be concerned about ensuring that the Justice Department—or its official clients in other executive agencies and departments—develops an appropriate legal stance. But most administrations have sought to channel promptings from the White House to the Justice Department through the counsel's office.[73]

Part of the reason for this is that the counsel's office is presumed to have special expertise on legal matters. Since the mid-1970s, moreover, the growth in the size of the Counsel's office has allowed particular lawyers within the office to develop an even more specialized familiarity with the issues and governmental personalities involved in particular areas of dispute. White House lawyers are in regular contact with political appointees in the departments (including the Justice Department) on a variety of matters, large and small. Such continuous, informal contact may allow the White House to head off an awkward last-minute choice between overruling the attorney general (or another high departmental official)—which is likely to bruise egos and to arouse outside critics—and simply swallowing an unexpected departmental decision.

But a dozen lawyers in the White House counsel's office cannot try to manage the legal strategy of the Justice Department, let alone the legal strategy of the entire executive branch. And at some point, excessive intervention by the White House will arouse resentment among responsible officials outside and stir complaints about manipulation among critics in Congress or in the press. One reason for channeling White House interventions through the counsel's office is that the counsel and his staff are presumed to have some sense of what sorts of interventions are seemly and proper.[74] The problem for the counsel's office is that this sense of limits is not always a matter of law, nor does it always accord with the needs and expectations of more powerful figures in the White House.

ON THE BOUNDARIES OF SCANDAL

The role of the White House counsel is thrown into sharp relief when major scandals reach the White House. But counsels have played very different roles in the major scandals of the past quarter century. These differences reflect not only the protean character of the office, but the conflicting pressures on the counsel's performance.

Nixon's White House counsel, John Dean, emerged as a central figure in the Watergate scandals that finally brought down the Nixon presidency. In one sense, this was ironic, even paradoxical, given Dean's generally minor and peripheral status within the Nixon White House. In another sense, Dean's prominent role in the scandal was a perfect reflection of the schizophrenic character of the Nixon White House. Some prominent public figures in the Nixon White House, such as national security adviser Henry Kissinger and urban policy adviser Daniel Patrick Moynihan, emerged unscathed from the Watergate scandal, because their claims to have known nothing about the scandal were generally accepted. The same thing happened with regard to certain very close intimates of the president, including speechwriters William Safire and Patrick Buchanan. Only a handful of senior figures knew anything about the succession of illegal buggings and break-ins and campaign dirty tricks that eventually came to light in the course of extended congressional hearings and investigations by a team of special prosecutors. And even they seem to have been unsure about what was being done by the strange collection of misfits hired for squalid spying missions and petty skullduggery by midlevel White House officials and by the 1972 Nixon reelection campaign.[75]

Whether Dean personally ordered the break-in at the Democratic Party offices in the Watergate complex in Washington—a question that continues to be disputed in recent literature on the scandal—he clearly had ongoing connections with the operatives who perpetrated the bungled break-in (and were apprehended by Washington policemen before they could get away). Dean was also directly involved in efforts to buy the silence of these "burglars" with cash contributions from Nixon campaign funds.[76]

Dean came to be centrally involved in the cover-up of the scandal because he was one of the few figures in the White House who had some ongoing involvement in murky schemes that needed to be covered up. Thus he was in regular contact with the director of the FBI during the period when the White House was assuring the public that the FBI was undertaking a thorough investigation of the Watergate break-in. Dean personally provided the FBI director with inculpating evidence from the White House safe regarding one of the burglars—evidence that the compliant director then destroyed to keep it away from his own agents.[77] In March of 1973, when President Nixon asked Dean to prepare a report describing what had really happened in Watergate, it is clear (from the tape Nixon made of this conversation and others) that Nixon was not really seeking an honest, fully revealing account. But it is also clear that he turned to Dean for this sensitive task because Dean had as much to hide as anyone else in the White House.[78]

In sum, it was not Dean's status as counsel but his readiness to embark on scandalous enterprises that led him into a central role in Watergate. The wonder is that President Nixon ended up resting his presidency on a young lawyer whose competence and loyalty the president had no particularly strong reason to trust. But perhaps this was no more remarkable than the readiness of senior figures (including the president) to countenance reckless and illegal acts that could hardly promise any commensurate benefit.

The so-called Iran-Contra scandals that engulfed the Reagan administration in its second term differed from Watergate in many respects, and they certainly featured the counsel in a very different role. After the Reagan administration had repeatedly denounced the idea of supplying military aid to terrorist states (including Iran), top administration officials arranged for secret sales of arms to Iran in the spring of 1985; then, in violation of the Arms Export Control Act, they did not report this to Congress. The prices charged for the weaponry and parts sold to Iran were greatly inflated, yielding a secret surplus slush fund controlled by a small group of administration officials and private individuals. Some of the money in this secret fund was surreptitiously used to buy military and other supplies for the Contra rebels (who were seeking to overthrow the Marxist government of Nicaragua), even though the so-called Boland Amendments to annual foreign aid legislation prohibited direct aid to the Contras. When rumors of these transactions began to emerge, President Reagan asked Attorney General Meese to determine whether any legal infractions or improprieties had occurred. But Meese's investigation was so inadequate that it was derided in subsequent congressional hearings as being tantamount to a cover-up.[79] These hearings—along with subsequent investigations by an independent counsel—had an extremely demoralizing and debilitating effect on Reagan's second term.

In contrast to the shady skullduggery of Watergate, however, the main policies involved in this scandal—both with regard to the secret arms sales and with regard to the resupply of the Nicaraguan Contras—were repeatedly considered by top figures in the Reagan Cabinet. There is uncertainty (amidst conflicting accounts and heated denials) about whether the president, the secretary of defense, and the secretary of state knew the precise details of these operations, when they knew of them, and what position they took toward them. But they certainly were involved in deliberations on the general policies to which these operations pertained. It is also clear that the national security adviser and the director of Central Intelligence were closely informed and directly involved. But it is equally clear that the White House counsel at the time was generally uninformed and uninvolved.[80] The independent counsel's report on the affair subsequently expressed some amazement that Chief of Staff Donald Regan, who had brought Counsel Peter Wallison into the White House and who relied on his legal advice, did not tell Wallison many things that Regan himself knew about these policies.[81]

Wallison's exclusion is all the more remarkable in view of the numerous complex legal issues involved. The Arms Control Export Act, for example, allowed exceptions to its congressional reporting requirements in special cases, when these are properly certified as such by the president. But Wallison was not even consulted in the hasty efforts that were made (after the fact) to document this certification, much less being consulted in advance to determine whether the arms sales to Iran qualified under the law for this treatment.[82] Similarly, two of the principal figures in this operation subsequently claimed that they thought their activities could be interpreted as being consistent with the law, but they did not consult the White House counsel (nor with the OLC) to find out whether such an interpretation was sustainable.[83]

When the Reagan administration was scrambling to provide a public accounting of its actions, the president assigned responsibility for these efforts to the attorney general, who in turn delegated his investigative and reporting responsibilities to the assistant attorney general for legal counsel. Wallison tried on a number of occasions to confirm that proposed testimony to Congress by top administration officials was consistent with the emerging facts he had been able to gather. But he was several times rebuked for doing so by other officials, who invoked the authority of the attorney general in dismissing Wallison's qualms. When Wallison tried to enter a White House conference between the attorney general and the national security adviser to discuss his concerns, he was rebuffed with the claim that the top officials were no longer discussing Iran-Contra.[84]

There is no obvious institutional reason why the attorney general should have been given principal responsibility here while the White House counsel was relegated to the sidelines. Most probably, the arrangement reflected the fact that the attorney general at the time, Edwin Meese, was a longtime friend and political adviser to Reagan, whereas Wallison was a relatively young Washington lawyer, trusted by the chief of staff, but not well known to the president nor to other top figures in the administration. At earlier stages, those most closely involved in the Iran arms sales and in Contra resupply projects sought to maintain as much secrecy as possible about their operations and presumably were not interested in obtaining professional advice about the legality or illegality of their efforts. But to the end, the counsel was not regarded as being an essential element in the administration's response to the crisis that ensued when these controversial activities were revealed. Top advisers may have feared that Wallison would not be sufficiently accommodating or sufficiently loyal. In any event, they certainly did not regard him as an indispensable participant, merely because he held the position of White House counsel. A. B. Culvahouse, brought in as counsel in the aftermath of the fiasco, cannot be accused of overstating the case when he remarked that the whole policy was "not well lawyered."[85]

The scandals (or embarrassments) that forced the resignation of President Clinton's original counsel, Bernard Nussbaum, reflect a different political environment. Whereas President Reagan put more trust in his friend Attorney General Meese than in his White House counsel, President Clinton hired close friends for the White House counsel's office and appointed an obscure Florida prosecutor whom he scarcely knew to head the Justice Department. The White House counsel's office was extremely active and aggressive in many areas, not least in trying to manage or contain potential scandals.

Nussbaum got into trouble in the early months of the Clinton administration, when top aides decided to dismiss the staff of the White House travel office—nonpolitical employees who made travel arrangements for journalists accompanying the president—and to replace them with people loyal to close personal friends (and to a distant relative) of President Clinton's. To forestall journalistic suspicions, White House aides (including two deputies from the counsel's office) then pressured midlevel FBI officials into issuing a statement that the fired travel office employees were under investigation for financial abuses. The FBI was thus enlisted into the service of a White House public relations effort, without the knowledge of the attorney general or even the full knowledge of the FBI director.[86]

Then, just as controversy over this matter was coming to a boil, Deputy White House Counsel Vincent Foster was found dead in a park in northern Virginia—an apparent suicide. The location of the body allowed investigation of the death to fall under the jurisdiction of the National Park Police. Counsel Nussbaum, as journalists later discovered, may have attempted to limit the reach of park police discoveries. He insisted on remaining present in the room whenever investigators questioned other White House aides about Foster's activities before his death.[87] Even more questionably, Nussbaum refused to give the park police access to Foster's office until Nussbaum himself (with other top White House aides from outside the counsel's office) had sorted through Foster's papers and decided which were appropriate for policy inspection.[88]

At the time of the Foster investigation, Nussbaum indicted that the files that had been removed prior to police inspection pertained only to Foster's personal affairs. But months later, the White House acknowledged that the files actually dealt with a private, fifteen-year-old land investment by Mr. and Mrs. Clinton (called "Whitewater"), on which Foster had retained working files. By the time of this disclosure, the Whitewater land deal had become the focus of intense journalistic interest, because the Clintons' partner in the deal had simultaneously been involved in running a savings and loan institution that subsequently went bankrupt, leaving federal insurance to make good on depositors' claims running to some $50 million. Journalistic inquiries had unearthed evidence that the Clintons may have received favorable treatment in this land investment and that their partner may have received favorable treatment from Arkansas regulatory officials. Suspicions had mounted to the point where the attorney general, with White House approval, appointed a special counsel to investigate the scandal.

In this context came the accidental discovery that Nussbaum had held secret meetings with Roger Altman, the acting director of the Resolution Trust Corporation (RTC)—an ostensibly independent federal regulatory agency charged with overseeing the assets of failed savings and loan institutions. The RTC was going to recommend a criminal investigation of the Clintons' business partner in Arkansas and intended to name the Clintons as possible beneficiaries of his fraudulent banking practices. Altman, a friend of Clinton's since their college days, held several meetings with Nussbaum to advise the White House on the status of the RTC's investigation. After Altman admitted this fact in a congressional hearing in March 1994, criticism of Nussbaum's actions grew so intense that Nussbaum was forced to resign—although President Clinton expressed "regret" at the resignation and affirmed Nussbaum's claims that he had done nothing wrong. In the summer of 1994, Altman also admitted that he sought to recuse himself from any involvement in the RTC's investigation of the Clintons' business affairs in Arkansas, given potential conflicts of interest arising from his own personal ties to Clinton. But when he advised Nussbaum of this intention, the counsel argued strongly against his doing so. Months after leaving the counsel's office, Nussbaum was subjected to a new round of criticism for this effort (which was unsuccessful in any case: Altman did recuse himself and was eventually forced to resign from government service altogether, after senators of both parties accused him of offering misleading testimony about the frequency and scope of his meetings with White House officials).

There has not yet been a full accounting of the questionable activities involved in "Whitewater," but the initial appearances were certainly unfortunate for the Clinton administration—and for Nussbaum in particular. At the outset of the Clinton administration, Nussbaum had reissued the policy guidance offered by previous counsels, warning White House aides not to discuss specific decisions with officials of independent regulatory agencies. Nussbaum then appeared to flout his own policy guidance. Another policy memorandum issued by previous counsels and reissued by Nussbaum had warned against White House involvement in individual criminal investigations; and the spirit of this directive was certainly broken in the earlier episode involving the FBI investigation into the travel office allegations. The *New York Times* seems to have had the facts on its side when it protested that the Clinton White House was "easily the most reckless in interfering with the integrity of Federal investigative agencies since that of Richard Nixon."[89]

Yet the rules that Nussbaum most clearly violated were, in effect, his own rules. They were not formal executive orders of the president. They did not have the status of law. The counsel had no power to enforce them except by calling on the president (or in practice, the chief of staff) to take direct action against offenders. Previous administrations had also seen violations of such memos, with little more consequence than the issuance of a new memo couched in a more chiding tone.

In retrospect, Nussbaum probably ill-served President Clinton by acting too aggressively on his behalf. But a press secretary who shades the truth too eagerly in order to protect the president's image also ill-serves the president, by undermining the credibility of White House pronouncements. The Clinton administration, like other administrations, has also been criticized for the misleading briefings supplied by its press officers.[90] And the cases are not, in the end, very different. Both involve managing appearances rather than performing some otherwise well-defined duty.

The ultimate point is that the counsel's ability to influence conduct in the White House depends on his being a trusted presidential loyalist. No counsel since the Johnson administration has served as effective chief of staff. An overly fastidious counsel, therefore, risks having White House aides bypass the counsel's office entirely when they fear that the counsel will raise legal or ethical objections—as happened to Peter Wallison in the Reagan White House. In the case of Bernard Nussbaum, it seems clear that President and Mrs. Clinton expected him, at least in general terms, to pursue their interests very aggressively. They defended his conduct for as long as they could, and presumably they would have been much less loyal to him if Nussbaum had not served them in ways they approved.[91]

A counsel who engages in criminal conduct, as did John Dean, obviously risks trouble for himself no less than for his president. But in the wide range of ambiguous actions within the border of the law but at the outer boundaries of acceptable routine conduct, the counsel's office will find it difficult to enforce its own view of propriety against contending claims. That is why the counsel remains under continual pressure to tell higher officials (up to and including the president) what they want to hear. One can see this most clearly in relation to the counsel's most important duties—advising the president on his legal powers.

ADVISING THE CHIEF

The White House counsel's office generates a continuing flow of advisory rulings for White House aides, regarding legal limitations on their personal actions. But the most important advice the counsel provides goes directly to the president, with regard to decisions that the president must make in his own name. The actions of aides can be repudiated and in extreme cases the aides can be dismissed (as President Reagan repudiated and fired aides involved in the Iran-Contra scandal and President Clinton replaced aides involved in early aspects of the Whitewater scandal). The president cannot so easily repudiate his own actions nor correct his own mistakes.

But for all its evident importance, the counsel's role in providing direct advice to the president is the most difficult aspect of his performance to document or even to generalize about. Many advisers have the president's ear. The legal issues on which the counsel might be expected to have the greatest expertise are rarely the most salient aspects of a presidential decision. Inevitably, the counsel is drawn into addressing the larger policy issues in which legal questions are entangled. But even in recent times, presidents have varied a good deal in how much they expected of the counsel and in how far they were prepared to rely on the counsel's broader advice.

On some questions, the counsel is routinely consulted. On presidential appointments, for example, the counsel is always involved because White House lawyers must check for compliance with financial disclosure and conflict-of-interest rules. Expectations seem to vary, however, on how far this responsibility should extend into the area of advising the president on broader aspects of a candidate's suitability for office.

Counsel C. Boyden Gray, for instance, was criticized for not anticipating that President Bush would encounter difficulty in his nomination of John Tower to serve as Secretary of Defense, given background rumors of Tower's problems with alcohol abuse and "womanizing." Gray protested that his "ethics scrub" (involving, among other things, a careful review of FBI background reports on the prospective nominee) was not supposed to yield an ultimate political assessment of the nominee's viability before the Senate.[92] But many questions about ethics are, in effect, questions about political appearances—and the harm that they may do—more than about liability to legal penalties. Tower's ultimate rejection by the Senate was certainly a humiliating setback for the new Bush administration, so it is hardly surprising that other White House aides blamed Gray for not warning the president more strongly against nominating Tower in the first place.

The Clinton administration suffered similar humiliation when its first two nominees to be attorney general turned out to have failed to pay social security taxes for household help. Then, within weeks, the nomination of Lani Guinier to serve as assistant attorney general for civil rights was also withdrawn, in response to controversy over published articles by Guinier involving her views on voting rights and race. Nussbaum, who had screened and defended these nominations, protested that the nominees had been maligned. And in truth, other nominees who failed to pay social security taxes on household help were subsequently confirmed by the Senate, as were other nominees who had taken controversial stands on sensitive social issues. But Nussbaum did not deny that political projections of a candidate's viability were part of his responsibility in the Clinton White House (and he accordingly took credit for supporting the well-received nominations of Ruth Ginsburg to the Supreme Court and Louis Freh to be director of the FBI).[93]

The counsel's office is also routinely called on to advise the president about whether to sign or veto enrolled bills from Congress. But as with appointments, the counsel's office is only one of many voices seeking to influence the final decision of the president. The counsel's office may play a more important role in advising the president on the language of signing statements, which may voice legal or constitutional objections (most often in veto messages, but in the Reagan and Bush administrations' signing statements as well). But even here, many hands are often involved.

If the president has a constitutional objection to a bill, the Justice Department is likely to be involved and to offer its own proposals for the phrasing of objections. On a number of occasions during the Reagan and Bush administrations, Justice Department recommendations for tough veto language were toned down by White House aides; and in a few cases, proposed veto messages were transformed into signing statements. From the point of view of officials at the OLC, the White House counsel was much less ready to champion principled constitutional concerns (usually about presidential prerogatives or separation of powers) than lawyers at the Justice Department thought he should be. But the counsel's office could not so readily focus on the abstract merits of constitutional objections when others in the White House were eager to have a piece of legislation adopted and put into effect.[94]

Of course, the president is not obliged to heed the advice of the counsel or even to consult the counsel. And a counsel who is considered to be overly fastidious risks being circumvented in deliberations. The Iran-Contra activities may have been an extreme case, because they were conducted in so much secrecy. But counsels have been excluded from deliberations even on pending legislative measures. Thus, for example, President Bush's counsel, C. Boyden Gray, developed a reputation for taking a hard line against congressional encroachments on presidential authority. When Secretary of State James Baker sought to win congressional agreement to restore funding for the Contras in Nicaragua by promising to clear the subsequent release of such funds with congressional leaders, Baker used his own legal team from the State Department to negotiate the agreement. Informed of the details at the last minute, Gray characterized this arrangement as creating a mechanism disturbingly similar to a legislative veto (an arrangement the Supreme Court had declared unconstitutional). But by that stage, it was too late to scuttle the agreement—which was clearly why White House Chief of Staff Sununu had allowed Baker to negotiate the agreement without consulting Gray at the outset.[95]

The White House can and does turn to the OLC for well-researched advice on a range of substantive legal questions. But here, too, the White House is not obliged to follow the recommendations offered. Executive agencies and departments are required, by law, to accept the legal determinations of the attorney general (normally, acting through the OLC). But the president is not personally bound by such rulings, so they remain, with respect to the president, purely advisory; and other advisers, including the White House counsel, are free to offer competing advice.

But because the OLC has the advantage of a sizable research staff and extensive records on the handling of past inquiries, its advice tends to be better informed and more carefully considered. C. Boyden Gray claims that, during the Bush years, the counsel's office never made a substantive recommendation to the president that was at odds with advice from the Justice Department's OLC.[96]

But the president is not obliged to seek unwanted advice, either. President Ford did not meet with any top officials of the Justice Department when deciding how to respond to the seizure of the U.S. Navy ship *Mayaguez* by the communist government of Cambodia in 1975. Nor did Ford consult extensively with his counsel, Philip Buchen, before committing American forces to rescue the ship (without seeking authorization from Congress).[97] During the Bush administration, by contrast, the legal grounds for military actions in Panama and in the Persian Gulf were carefully considered by top officials from the Justice Department in meetings with legal advisers from the Department of State and the Department of Defense—but the meetings were chaired by the White House counsel, to emphasize that the Justice Department would not necessarily have the last word.[98]

President Clinton's first counsel, Bernard Nussbaum, may have been less cautious in this respect. When Clinton appointed his wife to head up a task force on health-care reform, he relied on Nussbaum's assurances that Mrs. Clinton was not bound by the Federal Advisory Committee Act (FACA),[99] which requires federal advisory bodies to open their meetings to the public when nongovernment figures participate in the proceedings. Nussbaum issued an opinion holding that Mrs. Clinton was an officer of the government for FACA purposes, although she received no salary. Yet Nussbaum had also advised the president that Mrs. Clinton would not be liable to conflict-of-interest rules and reporting requirements, because she was technically not a government "employee." On both matters, Nussbaum acted without consulting the OLC.[100]

When the closed task force meetings with Mrs. Clinton were challenged by a medical advocacy group, the Justice Department defended Nussbaum's position. Eventually, a divided Court of Appeals upheld the claim that the health-care task force could continue to have closed meetings, because Mrs. Clinton could be considered the functional equivalent of a government official. But the court pointedly noted that Mrs. Clinton might under these circumstances have to comply with ethics norms for federal employees.[101]

With technical matters of this sort—as with controversial appointments or constitutional questions about presidential war powers—the president must decide what is safe and what is proper. If he makes decisions that expose him to criticism or to political controversy, he may want to seek better advice. But he is no more obliged to seek better advice on legal matters than on foreign policy or economic matters, where bad advice and bad decisions can prove far more disastrous.

CONCLUSION: COUNSEL TO THE PRESIDENT, NOT THE PRESIDENCY

The scandals that plagued the Clinton administration led a number of observers to argue that the White House counsel—so entangled in some of these scandals—was led astray by excessive loyalty to the particular president who hired him. Lloyd Cutler, for example, argued that the counsel should serve the institutional interests of the presidency rather than the personal concerns of the incumbent president.

But the conduct of the very counsel who urged this distinction illustrates how hard such a mission is to perform in practice. When President Clinton's private lawyer began to argue that the president could not be sued for sexual harassment, because presidents must be immune to civil suits, the argument was greeted by the press with some skepticism. Cutler made a succession of television appearances, however, to defend the more modest claim that the trial of all such suits must be automatically postponed, on constitutional grounds, until after the president has left office. Cutler acknowledged that this position had not been endorsed by the Justice Department's OLC, but it was soon taken up by the president's private lawyer.[102] Besides providing legal theories for the private lawyers of the president, Mr. Cutler took to the op-ed pages to defend Mrs. Clinton from suspicions that she had acquired some of her investment gains in Arkansas by unlawful means.[103]

Of course, it can be argued that the defense of the presidency requires a defense of presidential immunity from private suits. It can even be argued that the defense of the presidency requires efforts to defend the reputation of the First Lady. But one might as well acknowledge, then, that the defense of the presidency is in many areas nearly impossible to distinguish from the defense of the particular incumbent holding the office.

And the performance of Lloyd Cutler in this regard does not seem notably different from that of his predecessors. James St. Clair, nominally special counsel to the White House in the last months of the Nixon administration, fought to keep special prosecutors from gaining access to incriminating tapes that would have proved (as the world eventually discovered) Nixon's collaboration with the Watergate cover-up. St. Clair acted no differently than a private lawyer for Nixon would have done, and he seems to have been every bit as much directed by his client's personal demands.[104]

But that is the point. Whatever the mystique of the title, the counsel to the president is there to counsel—to advise. It is highly dubious that Congress can, consistent with the Constitution, put any restrictions on the advice that the president receives. If the person occupying the position of counsel were restricted by law, the president could seek counsel from someone not subject to those restrictions, although this would presumably also mean someone not as well informed or as closely in touch with day-to-day White House problems. It is difficult to see how this would benefit the president, the nation, or the public's level of overall trust in the president's conduct.

This reality has been somewhat obscured by the institutional development of the counsel's office over the past quarter century. Although counsels such as Clark Clifford and Harry McPherson were obviously and essentially top political advisers and only in a very secondary way specialized legal counselors, the counsel in recent years has operated with a sizable staff of specialists performing a large volume of specialized legal duties. This development may help the president navigate the far more suspicious climate and the intricate ethical traps established in recent decades. It may also provide the president with important resources to lessen his reliance on the Justice Department for legal advice or to take a more aggressive role in nudging the activities of the Justice Department (and perhaps of other departments with specialized legal duties) in a particular direction. But the counsel remains a creation of, and, in fundamental ways, an extension of the president.

In the end, the responsibility for what is done by White House aides remains the president's. He hires them; he can dismiss them and replace them at will. They are there to assist the president, not to do anything else. If aides behave improperly, the president must discipline them—unless their misbehavior amounts to a violation of criminal law, in which case they should be subject to prosecution like any other felon. Whether they give good advice or bad advice, the president must decide what advice he will accept and where he will seek it. Focusing on the obligations of the counsel distracts attention from the fundamental responsibility of the president.

The Federalist warned of the ill effects likely to result from establishing constraints on executive power within the administrative branch itself—constraints that undermine unity and obscure personal responsibility:[105]

[Executive] unity may be destroyed . . . by vesting [executive power] ostensibly in one man, subject in whole or in part to the control and cooperation of others, in the capacity of counselors to him. . . .

It often becomes impossible, amidst mutual accusations, to determine on whom the blame or the punishment of a pernicious measure, or series of pernicious measures, ought really to fall. It is shifted from one to another with so much dexterity, and under such plausible appearances, that the public opinion is left in suspense about the real author. . . .

[I]f there happened to be a collusion between the parties concerned, how easy it is to clothe the circumstances with so much ambiguity as to render it uncertain what was the precise conduct of any of those parties.

The Constitution provides two mechanisms for holding the president accountable for his actions: impeachment by Congress and denial of reelection by the electorate. It is only sensible for the president to take counsel to improve his odds against these forms of rejection. But if he does not take good counsel, the proper remedy is not to force him to take better counsel but simply to remove him from office.

NOTES

1. Cited in Cornell Clayton, *The Politics of Justice: The Attorney General and the Making of Legal Policy* (Armonk, N.Y.: M. E. Sharpe, 1992), p. 143.

2. Gwen Ifill, "The Whitewater Inquiry: Nussbaum Out as White House Counsel," *New York Times*, March 6, 1994, p. 1.

3. Ruth Marcus and Ann Devroy, "Nussbaum Quits White House Post," *Washington Post*, March 6, 1994, p. A1.

4. For example, Ronald Goldfarb, "Counsel of Confusion," *New York Times*, March 9, 1994, p. A15, arguing that "The White House counsel represents the institution of the presidency" and endorsing the claim that the counsel should serve as "counsel to the office, not the person"; William Safire, "No Client Privilege," *New York Times*, March 7, 1994, p. A17: "The White House Counsel's only real client is the people."

5. "Remarks Announcing the Appointment of Lloyd Cutler as Special Counsel to the President and an Exchange with Reporters," *Weekly Compilation of Presidential Documents* 30 (8 March 1994): 462.

6. But even this conclusion is by no means inevitable. The taxpayers cover the president's room and board, even on days when he is not doing public business. No one suggests that the president is committing an abuse if he makes personal phone calls from the Oval Office. If the president developed any sort of illness, taxpayers would foot the bill for his medical care, even if the illness grew out of a preexisting condition. Federally funded medical care for the president was not provided in earlier times. It is now. The change reflects a new policy but

not a new principle. In the same way that it has decided to finance presidential medical care, Congress presumably could decide to finance presidential legal expenses. In fact, when Congress reauthorized the independent counsel statute in June 1994, it provided for reimbursement of legal expenses incurred by the president or any other office as a result of an independent counsel investigation. The lawyers defending the president against charges of personal misconduct are separated from the government attorneys who might be involved in prosecuting the charges, but this does not necessarily make the personal defense of the president a "private matter": there are now separate counsels for independent commissions, for the House, and for the Senate, all of which are outside the hierarchical control of the Justice Department, but the concerns of these counsels are not for that reason considered "private." What presidential concerns are "private"—and therefore necessarily separated from the concerns of the official presidential staff—is sometimes a matter of law and the law changes, but more often a matter of convention and the conventions change.

7. Michael Isikoff, "Clinton Hires Lawyer as Sexual Harassment Suit Is Threatened; Bennett Opens Aggressive Campaign on Public Relations and Legal Fronts," *Washington Post*, May 4, 1994, p. A1.

8. Leonard D. White, *The Federalist: A Study in Administrative History, 1789–1801* (New York: Macmillan, 1948), pp. 164–72.

9. John Dean was an exception. He testified after being dismissed from office, when the president had no way to stop him and Dean feared being made the scapegoat for the president's continuing campaign to save his own reputation.

10. Most lawyers in the counsel's office are young and have never served before in government. The operation of the Justice Department would be unimaginable if it maintained this sort of personnel practice for staff lawyers.

11. At any given time, many of the lawyers in the counsel's office are "on assignment" from other executive agencies (which continue to cover their salaries).

12. President's Committee on Administrative Management, *Report with Special Studies* (1937), sometimes known as "The Brownlow Report," after the chairman of the committee, Professor Louis Brownlow.

13. 53 Stat. 561 (1939).

14. Clark Clifford and Richard Holbrooke, *Counsel to the President: A Memoir* (New York: Random House, 1991), p. 54.

15. Daniel Meador, *The President, the Attorney General, and the Department of Justice* (Charlottesville, Va.: White Burkett Miller Center of Public Affairs, University of Virginia, 1980), p. 130.

16. Clifford and Holbrooke, *Counsel to the President*, pp. 55–56. William Safire's memoir of the Nixon administration, *Before the Fall* (Garden City, N.Y.: Doubleday, 1975), pp. 15–16, reports on Rosenman's first visit to the White House, some twenty-five years after he left: eager to see what had changed and what had remained the same, Rosenman visited not with President Nixon's counsel but with his speechwriters.

17. Clifford and Holbrooke, *Counsel to the President*, p. 75.

18. Ibid., p. 51.

19. Ibid., p. 12.

20. Harry McPherson assumed the title of "Special Counsel" after serving as "understudy" to Lee White, who was identified as "Counsel." McPherson's memoir, *A Political Education* (Boston: Little, Brown, 1972), p. 235, refers to McPherson's various predecessors as having "held the job" of "Special Counsel" without noticing that their titles had briefly been changed along the way.

21. The changing titles can be followed through successive editions of the *U.S. Government Organization Manual* under entries for "The White House."

22. John Dean, *Blind Ambition* (New York: Simon & Schuster, 1976), pp. 5, 10.

23. When an academic conference was organized to explore the role of White House chiefs of staff, Sorensen and McPherson were invited to describe their experiences in the Kennedy and Johnson White Houses on the assumption (which neither man disputed) that they had served as functional equivalents of chief of staff. See Samuel Kernell and Samuel Popkin (eds.), *Chief of Staff, Twenty-five Years of Managing the Presidency* (Berkeley, Calif.: University of California Press, 1986).

24. Gerald Ford, *A Time to Heal* (New York: Harper & Row, 1979), pp. 23–24.

25. Griffin Bell and Ronald Ostrow, *Taking Care of the Law* (New York: William Morrow, 1982), pp. 37, 40.

26. Colin Campbell, *Managing the Presidency: Carter, Reagan, and the Search for Executive Harmony* (Pittsburgh: University of Pittsburgh Press, 1986), p. 88.

27. Jimmy Carter's memoir, *Keeping Faith* (New York: Bantam, 1982), pp. 5–8, 468–69, 518, 526, describes these various activities. Cutler alludes to the wide range of his activities in Lloyd Cutler, "The Role of the Counsel to the President of the United States," *Record of the Bar Association of New York* 35 (1980): 470.

28. On Fielding's role, see Campbell, *Managing the Presidency*, p. 94.

29. Eric Effron, "Culvahouse Assumes Key White House Legal Post," *Legal Times*, March 9, 1987, p. 1, offers a brief sketch of Wallison's service; Vicki Quade, "The President Is His Only client," *Barrister* 15 (Winter/Spring 1988): 5–6 provides background on Culvahouse.

30. For an early overview of Gray's role, see Philip Combs, "The Distant Drum of C. Boyden Gray," *Washington Post*, March 31, 1989, p. D1.

31. David Hoffman, "Sununu Rebukes Counsel," *Washington Post*, March 28, 1989, p. A1.

32. Interview with C. Boyden Gray, May 12, 1993, reporting on his own experience and that of his Washington law partner, Lloyd Cutler.

33. David Margolick, "An All-Star New York Lawyer Disputes the Idea He's Become a White House Butler," *New York Times*, June 11, 1993, p. A26.

34. Dean, *Blind Ambition*, pp. 28, 30.

35. Cutler, "The Role of the Counsel to the President of the United States," p. 470.

36. David O. Stewart, "The President's Lawyer," *ABA Journal*, April 1, 1986, p. 59.

37. Quade, "The President Is His Only Client," p. 6.

38. *Federal Yellow Book* for Winter 1993 and interview with (then) Associate Counsel Walter Dellinger, February 1993.

39. McPherson, *A Political Education*, p. 250.

40. Dean, *Blind Ambition*, p. 29.

41. New York City Bar Association, *Conflict of Interest and Federal Service* (1960); Bayless Manning, *Federal Conflict of Interest* (Cambridge, Mass.: Harvard University Press, 1964); Executive Order 11222 (1965), 3. C.F.R. 306 (1964–1965), reprinted in 18 U.S.C. 201.

42. Safire, *Before the Fall*, p. 325, recalls feeling obliged to seek guidance from the counsel about whether he could keep the $150 fee he was sent by the *New York Times* for an op-ed piece and being told that, because Safire was then a presidential speechwriter, keeping the fee would amount to a "conflict of interest." As late as 1971, Safire urged the White House chief of staff to "make more of the fact that ours is a scandal-free Administration" (p. 15).

43. Dean, *Blind Ambition*, p. 29.

44. Ford, *A Time to Heal*, p. 418.

45. These scandals are well described in Suzanne Garment, *Scandal: The Crisis of Mistrust in American Politics* (New York: Random House, 1991), pp. 43–47, 51–54, 59–64.

46. For a useful blow-by-blow account, see Kmiec, *Attorney General's Lawyer: Inside the Meese Justice Department* (New York: Frederick Praeger, 1992).

47. 28 U.S.C. §§591–599 (1988).

48. See Terry Eastland, "The Independent Counsel Regime," *Public Interest* 100 (Summer 1990): 68–80. For a different view regarding the accountability of independent counsel, see Katy Harriger, *Independent Justice: The Federal Special Prosecutor in American Politics* (Lawrence, Kans.: University Press of Kansas, 1992).

49. Andrew Taylor, "Schedule for Hearings Is Unclear as Starr Takes Over Probe," *Congressional Quarterly Weekly Report*, August 13, 1994, p. 1.

50. Edwin Meese's main legal difficulties stemmed from his failure to report certain sources of income on his forms. See generally Kmiec, *Attorney General's Lawyer*.

51. Fred Fielding, "Presidential Appointments," *Directors & Boards* (Spring 1983), p. 13.

52. Stewart, "The President's Lawyer," p. 59.

53. Ethics Reform Act of 1989, 103 Stat. 1716; see also Resolution to Technical Changes in the Ethics Reform Act, 104 Stat. 149 (1990).

54. Personal interview with C. Boyden Gray, May 1993, confirming earlier telephone interviews with associate counsels Lee Liberman and Nelson Lund.

55. 90 Stat. 2723 (1976); 44 U.S.C. §§2103, 2108, 2111.

56. AP Wire Service, "Sununu Went to Stamp Action in U.S. Car," *New York Times*, June 17, 1991, p. A16 (reporting consultations with White House counsel over travel practices of chief of staff); Gwen Ifil, "Using Clinton's Helicopter

Costs an Official His Job," *New York Times,* May 27, 1994, p. A20 (reviewing past policy guidance on travel practices from the White House counsel, including a "stern set of guidelines" issued by Nussbaum).

57. The changing pattern can be charted through successive editions of the *U.S. Government Organization Manual,* which has been issued annually since 1940.

58. Michael Isikoff, "Martinez Used His Drug Policy Office to Route Funds for Bush Campaign," *Washington Post,* January 9, 1992, p. A1.

59. 28 U.S.C. §§511, 512 (1988 ed.).

60. See Nancy Baker, *Conflicting Loyalties: Law and Politics in the Attorney General's Office, 1789–1990* (Lawrence, Kans.: University Press of Kansas, 1992), pp. 20–21.

61. Victor Navasky, *Kennedy Justice* (New York: Atheneum, 1971), p. xiv.

62. Baker, *Conflicting Loyalties,* p. 142.

63. Bell and Ostrow, *Taking Care of the Law,* pp. 63–66; Clayton, *The Politics of Justice,* pp. 143–45.

64. Charles Fried, *Order and Law: Arguing the Reagan Revolution* (New York: Simon & Schuster, 1991), pp. 44–54 surveys the attacks directed at Meese.

65. For an account of Nixon's campaign attacks on Clark, see Richard Harris, *Justice: The Crisis of Law, Order, and Freedom in America* (London: Bodley Head, 1970).

66. Rebecca Mae Salokar, *The Solicitor General: The Politics of Law* (Philadelphia: Temple University Press, 1992), p. 55.

67. Frank Wozencraft, "OLC: The Unfamiliar Acronym," *ABA Journal* 57 (1971): 33, 36.

68. Bell and Ostrow, *Taking Care of the Law,* pp. 28–32; for a slightly different account, see Joseph Califano, *Governing America,* (New York: Simon & Schuster, 1981), pp. 237–43.

69. See Philip Elman, "The Solicitor General's Office, Justice Frankfurter and Civil Rights Litigation, 1946–1960: An Oral History," *Harvard Law Review* 100 (1987): 817, for accounts of interventions by President Truman in *Shelley v. Kramer* (dealing with race discrimination in housing sales) and by President Eisenhower in *Brown v. Board:* both cases were initiated by private advocacy groups, and the Justice Department became involved only at a later stage. Similarly, William Safire describes President Nixon's insistence that the Justice Department support state aid to parochial schools in *Lemon v. Kurtzman* (which the Justice Department did, over the Solicitor General's objections, and which the Supreme Court rejected). Safire, *Before the Fall,* p. 559.

70. The most bitter (and detailed) such attack was offered by Lincoln Caplan, "The Tenth Justice," *New Yorker,* 10 August 1987, p. 29 (and continued 17 August 1987, p. 30).

71. Ruth Marcus, "Bush Shifts Stand on Aid to Black Colleges, Administration Now Supports Funding in Mississippi Case," *Washington Post,* 23 October 1991, p. A6. The case was *United States v. Fordice,* 112 S. Ct. 2727 (1992), and the position favored by the Bush White House did not prevail.

72. On the interventions by the Bush White House, see *United States v. For-*

dice, 112 S. Ct. 2727 (1992), and *Mail Order Ass'n of America v. U.S. Postal Service*, 986 F.2d 509 (1993). The political background of these cases is described in Jeremy Rabkin, "At the President's Side: The Role of the White House Counsel in Constitutional Policy," *Law and Contemporary Problems* 56(4) (Autumn 1993): 85–86, 92. On the Reagan administration's interventions, see *Bob Jones University v. United States*, 461 U.S. 574 (1983). For a review of other cases where the solicitor general was pressed by political superiors, see Fried, *Order and Law*, chapter 6.

73. Bradley H. Patterson, Jr., *The Ring of Power: The White House Staff and Its Expanding Role in Government* (New York: Basic Books, 1988), p. 141.

74. The policy of the Ford administration, where Counsel Philip Buchen served as a "buffer between the political world and the Justice Department," is described in Baker, *Conflicting Loyalties*, p. 146. Attorney General Griffin Bell similarly insisted on having all White House contacts with the Justice Department routed through the counsel, and his aides at the Justice Department protested angrily to the counsel when this rule was not enforced. See J. M. Strine, "The Office of Legal Counsel: Legal Professional in a Political System" (Ph.D. dissertation, Department of Political Science, Johns Hopkins University, 1992), pp. 117–18.

75. On March 21, 1993, John Dean informed President Nixon that the break-in of the Democratic party offices at the Watergate complex seemed to be an offshoot of a plan proposed by G. Gordon Liddy to Attorney General Mitchell, which Dean described as the "most incredible thing I have ever laid my eyes on. All in codes, and involving black bag operations, kidnapping, providing prostitutes, uh, to weaken the opposition, bugging, uh, mugging teams. It was just an incredible thing. Mitchell sat there puffing and laughing." The incident is described, with many other examples of astonishment among top Nixon aides at the antics of these special detail men in H. R. Haldeman, *The Ends of Power* (New York: Times Books, 1978), pp. 122–24. To some extent, White House aides were afraid of the very people working for them.

76. For the most recent sifting of the evidence on this score, see Jonathan Aitken, *Nixon: A Life* (Washington, D.C.: Regnery, 1993), pp. 467–72.

77. Haldeman, *The Ends of Power*, pp. 259–60.

78. Ibid., pp. 237–40; Aitken, *Nixon*, pp. 487–90

79. See U.S. House of Representatives Select Committee to Investigate Covert Arms Transactions with Iran and U.S. Senate Select Committee on Secret Military Assistance to Iran and the Nicaraguan Opposition, *Report of the Congressional Committees Investigating the Iran Contra Affair, with Supplemental, Minority and Additional Views*, November 1987, 100th Cong., 1st sess., H. Rept. No. 100-433 and S. Rept. No. 100-216 (same report): Chapter 20 reviews criticism of Meese's performance, while Chapter 11 of the Minority Report attempts to defend Meese's efforts. The attorney general did subsequently initiate the appointment of an independent counsel to undertake a thorough investigation.

80. See Lawrence E. Walsh, Independent Counsel, *Final Report of the Independent Counsel for Iran/Contra Matters*, report to the U.S. Court of Appeals for

the D.C. Circuit, Division for the Purpose of Appointing Independent Counsels, Division No. 86-6 (Washington, D.C., August 1993), Vol. I ("Investigations and Prosecutions"), pp. 509–23, reviewing material from grand jury testimony, congressional testimony, and diary entries kept by Peter Wallison at the time.

81. "Reagan apparently did not share with Wallison the facts as he knew them, even though he was seeking Wallison's legal guidance. Reagan could not explain why he did not inform Wallison of his own knowledge [of a particular Iran arms shipment] but he denied attempting to hide that fact from Wallison." Walsh, *Final Report of the Independent Counsel for Iran/Contra Matters*, p. 511.

82. Attorney General Meese subsequently claimed to have offered an oral opinion justifying nonnotification on grounds that the arms sales could be construed as a "covert operation," but he did not undertake any serious research to establish that opinion. *Report of the Congressional Committees Investigating the Iran-Contra Affair*, p. 278. When the White House needed to justify its position in public, it relied on a retroactive endorsement of this theory by Assistant Attorney General Charles Cooper. Wallison was distressed to discover, in November 1986, that Cooper was offering this endorsement after working on the question for "about a day," when he "had not even begun to research the question in any depth." Walsh, *Final Report of the Independent Counsel for Iran/Contra Matters*, p. 528.

83. In the aftermath, Attorney General Meese gave conflicting testimony regarding whether he had given advance advice on this to CIA Director William Casey or National Security Advisor John Poindexter or to Poindexter's assistant, Oliver North. No evidence was found to indicate that the Department of Justice had ever researched the question, so the claims of legal support seem at most to have rested on casual oral exchanges. Walsh, *Final Report of the Independent Counsel for Iran/Contra Matters*, pp. 547–48.

84. Walsh, *Final Report of the Independent Counsel for Iran/Contra Matters*, p. 510.

85. Effron, "Culvahouse Assumes Key White House Legal Post," p. 1.

86. For a detailed account of the affair, based on close study of official statements subsequently released by the White House and by the General Accounting Office, see David Brock, "The Travelgate Cover-Up," *American Spectator*, June 1994.

87. Michael Isikoff, "Conspiracy Theorists Find Foster Case Hard to Resist," *Washington Post*, March 13, 1994, p. A10, reviews deficiencies in the investigation and the wild rumors that these subsequently encouraged.

88. Ibid.

89. Editorial, "White House Ethics Meltdown," *New York Times*, March 4, 1994, p. A26.

90. For a review of misleading press briefings, which had to be revised and then re-revised as new information contradicted previous briefings, see R. W. Apple, "Just Too Slick, Willie," *New York Times*, March 11, 1974, p. A1.

91. Top White House officials defended Nussbaum's conduct—almost to the day President Clinton finally accepted his resignation. See Ifill, "The Whitewater Inquiry," p. 1, especially the section under the subhead, "White House In-

transigence." When Clinton finally expressed concern about Nussbaum's secret meetings with ostensibly independent regulatory officials at the RTC, the *Los Angeles Times* noted that "Clinton's remarks were in sharp contrast to earlier statements by him and top aides on Whitewater. Until Thursday, they had brushed aside complaints about appearances, insisting that, because no one has been proved to have engaged in wrongdoing, allegations about appearance were politically motivated." David Lauter and James Risen, "Clinton Voices First Concerns over Whitewater," *Los Angeles Times*, March 4, 1994, p. A1.

92. Combs, "The Distant Drum of C. Boyden Gray," p. D1.

93. Both Nussbaum and President Clinton referred to these appointments in the letters they exchanged in relation to Nussbaum's resignation. Ifill, "The Whitewater Inquiry," p. 1.

94. Charles Cooper, who served as assistant attorney general for legal counsel in the second Reagan administration, subsequently complained about the treatment of his constitutional arguments at the White House: "Preserving presidential prerogatives, protecting the office itself, was not viewed as that important. Far more important was getting a good political result and avoiding a bad one." Quoted in Terry Eastland, *Energy in the Executive: The Case for the Strong Presidency* (New York: Free Press, 1992), p. 330, n. 24.

95. David Hoffman and Ann Devroy, "Bush Counsel Contests Contra Aid Plan: Gray Fears Pact with Congress May Infringe on Presidential Power," *Washington Post*, March 26, 1989, p. A5.

96. Interview with C. Boyden Gray, May 1993.

97. Baker, *Conflicting Loyalties*, pp. 147–49.

98. Interview with C. Boyden Gray, May 1993. Gray claims that the meetings could not have been convened or chaired by the Justice Department, because it is "just one of the departments at the meetings"—not necessarily the decisive one.

99. 86 Stat. 770 (1972); codified at 5 U.S.C. §1 (1988).

100. William Safire, "On Foster's Mind," *New York Times*, August 16, 1993, p. A17.

101. *Association of American Physicians and Surgeons v. Clinton*, 997 F.2d 898 (D.C. Cir., 1993). The court commented at footnote 10, p. 911: "We do not need to consider whether Mrs. Clinton's presence on the Task Force violates . . . any conflict of interest statute."

102. Asked by interviewers what position the Department of Justice might take on the issue, Cutler responded, "I wish I knew, but I don't know what that opinion would be. You've heard me on what I think it ought to be." *MacNeil-Lehrer News Hour*, May 24, 1994.

103. Lloyd Cutler, "No One Bribed Anyone in Clinton Trading," *New York Times*, June 3, 1994, p. A26.

104. Leon Jaworski, the Watergate special prosecutor at the time, recalled: "I felt certain Nixon was telling St. Clair to pull out all the stops to keep the tapes from me." Jaworski, *The Right and the Power: The Prosecution of Watergate* (New York: Thomas Y. Crowell, 1976), p. 146. Jaworski was particularly incensed by this because he believed that the White House had promised him full sub-

poena powers; and St. Clair, in contesting Jaworski's right to particular taped conversations, was going back on this public undertaking from the White House, treating Nixon as simply a private defendant with no such larger obligations (pp. 137–47). Aitken, *Nixon*, p. 499, reports that high White House aides urged Nixon to destroy the tapes but Counsel Leonard Garment insisted that this would be wrong. But even in this case, Garment did not invoke ethical or legal scruples in the abstract, but warned the president that the action might be treated as an impeachable offense in itself. And Aitken, after interviewing all of the participants, attributes Nixon's decision to preserve the tapes not to Garment's advice, but to his own belief that the tapes might prove helpful in countering false accusations about what he had said to Dean and others in the Oval Office.

105. *The Federalist* No. 70 (A. Hamilton), pp. 424, 428.

6

THE ATTORNEY PARTICULAR: GOVERNMENTAL ROLE OF THE AGENCY GENERAL COUNSEL

MICHAEL HERZ

Although the Department of Justice monopolizes academic attention, most lawyers in the executive branch work elsewhere.[1] Virtually every federal agency has its own (often very large) legal staff. Unlike the attorney general, whose tasks and substantive areas of law are as broad as the interests of the federal government, an agency general counsel is an "attorney particular," focused on a specific substantive area for a client with a far narrower set of interests. In many ways the relationship between the agency head and the agency general counsel parallels that between the president and the attorney general. For one thing, there is often the same sort of personal and political bond. More importantly, there is always the same tension between the obligation (and the personal desire) to facilitate the president's or the agency head's policy program, on the one hand, and the obligation to ensure that the program proceeds within legal limits, on the other.[2]

The general counsel is not simply a miniature attorney general, however. First the attorney general has two masters: the law and the president. An agency general counsel has many more authorities to contend with: not only the applicable legal requirements and the administrator's or secretary's wishes, but also the Justice Department, the White House, the Office of Management and Budget (OMB), the regulated community, and constant congressional oversight. No other government attorney sits at such a confluence of conflicting pressures. Second, unlike the attorney general, the agency counsel is indeed a *counselor,* not a litigator. Agency lawyers never bring criminal actions and rarely take the lead role in civil litigation. Third, the lawyers in a general counsel's office are likely to be committed to the agency's particular substantive mission. Many career lawyers choose and stay at the job because they have such a commitment. In contrast, to the (often limited) extent that Justice Department lawyers have a programmatic commitment, it is likely to be to the president's program or to the principle of presidential power generally, both of which can lead to conflict with individual agencies.[3] Fourth, agency lawyers develop significant substantive expertise in their area of specialization. Department of Justice lawyers—and the attorney general most of all—are generalists. Finally, the general counsel is subordinate in the federal legal hierarchy to the attorney general, although in complicated ways.

This chapter addresses the history and tasks of the agency counsel's position. The focus will be on agencies whose heads serve at the pleasure of the president, which I will refer to as "executive" as opposed to "independent" agencies (recognizing that the implication that independent agencies are *not* executive agencies is controversial). In an independent agency, the existence of multiple commissioners, the fact that the general counsel's term does not correspond to the commissioners' terms, the varying routes by which the general counsel is selected, and the reduced level of White House control all affect the independence and influence of the general counsel. As a result, the role of the general counsel in an independent agency can be quite different and is certainly more variable than in an executive agency.[4] I will use a particular example of a legal and policy struggle between the Environmental Protection Agency (EPA), the Justice Department, the White House, and Congress to illustrate the conflicting demands made on an agency general counsel and the overlap of law and policy.

A BRIEF HISTORY OF AGENCY LAWYERS

The First Congress established the "Great Departments"—State, War, and Treasury—without any provision for departmental attorneys. In the Judiciary Act of 1789, it addressed the minimal need for legal staffing by creating the post of attorney general. When the United States became involved in litigation, it relied for representation on the attorney general or retained private counsel. If a department head sought a legal opinion, he turned to the attorney general.[5] For the rest, departmental officials were on their own.

So matters stood until 1830, when Congress created the post of solicitor of the treasury. The treasury solicitor had far-reaching authority, including supervision of U.S. attorneys in cases involving the Treasury Department. For several decades the treasury solicitor remained the sole departmental legal officer; but then, ever so slowly, Congress started to add other posts, although there was hardly a proliferation of agency legal officers, especially by modern standards. Still, by the time the Department of Justice was created in 1870, a half-dozen lawyers served in various departments, including (in addition to the treasury solicitor) a solicitor of internal revenue, a solicitor and naval judge advocate general in the Navy Department, a judge advocate general in the Army Department, an "examiner of claims" in the State Department, and an "auditor" with legal duties in the Post Office Department.[6] In addition, the government frequently turned to private counsel to represent it in court, particularly after the Civil War, when the attorney general was overwhelmed by claims against the government.

Creation of the Department of Justice in 1870 had two primary impetuses. First, Congress concluded that litigation on behalf of the United States should be handled by lawyers who worked for and had a commission from the federal government. Such a scheme would be more efficient, would ensure consistent litigating positions and consistently high-quality lawyering, and (seemingly most important) would be less expensive than relying on outside counsel. Second, and no less weighty, Congress sought to centralize the *counseling* function. As the bill's House sponsor, Representative Jenckes, explained on the floor:

> [W]e have gone on creating law officers in the different Departments of this Government who are entirely independent of the head of the law department and of the Attorney General of the United States. . . . [W]e have found that there has been a most unfortunate result from this separation of law powers. We find one interpretation of the laws of the United States in one Department and another interpretation in another Department. . . .
>
> We have found, too, that these law officers, being subject to the control of the heads of the Departments, in some instances give advice which seems to have been instigated by the heads of the Department, or at least advice which seems designed to strengthen the resolution to which the head of the Department may have come in a particular case.[7]

Accordingly, the 1870 act creating the Department of Justice provided that the legal officers of other departments "shall be transferred from the Departments with which they are now associated to the Department of Justice . . . and shall exercise their functions under the supervision and control of the head of the Department of Justice."[8]

The 1870 reform never quite took hold. Both as to litigation and as to counseling, attorneys within the departments retained significant independence, In large measure, this was because Congress failed to fund its restructuring adequately. Congress never created office space for the Justice Department to house these lawyers; indeed, for the first year of the Department of Justice's existence, the attorney general had an office next to that of the treasury solicitor *in the treasury building*. As the Justice Department moved about Washington, D.C., for the following six and a half decades, the departmental solicitors continued to work within their departmental offices.[9] (The department never had centralized or sufficient office space until the present building was completed in 1934. Such a prosaic concern has real consequences for what a department can accomplish. It is not entirely by chance that the modern centralization of litigating authority in the Justice Department—which, unlike the 1870 initiative, has been effective—coincided with completion of the new building.[10]) In addition, Congress reenacted the statutes that had created the solicitors, without redefining their roles or specifying that they were under the attorney general's control.[11] Finally, Congress continued to create new legal positions within the departments, without placing them under the attorney general's control.[12]

Throughout the post-1870 period, the department counsels' litigating and legal-advising functions were not clearly separated. Although many cases were referred to the district attorneys, the departmental solicitors (or members of their staff) also appeared in court themselves to represent their agency. In 1918, President Wilson imposed a momentary centralization of governmental legal authority within the Department of Justice,[13] but this was temporary and the overall situation remained "chaotic."[14] Thus, on the eve of the New Deal, five departmental solicitors (for the Interior, State, Treasury, Commerce, and Labor Departments) existed nominally within the Justice Department and were presidential appointees; five others were located within their respective departments (Agriculture, Post Office, Navy, War, and Internal Revenue) and were appointed by the department head.[15] In addition, miscellaneous law officers were sprinkled here and there throughout the government (in the ICC, in the Federal Reserve Board, in the United States Railroad Administration, and elsewhere).[16] The functions of counsels nominally inside and of those outside the Justice Department were indistinguishable, and in practice none was subject in any meaningful way to the attorney general's direction.

As in so many settings, the modern era arrived with the New Deal. In 1933, President Roosevelt issued Executive Order 6166, requiring that all litigation to which the United States was or became a party be handled by the attorney general except as otherwise provided by statute.[17] Congress codified this requirement soon thereafter.[18] By this means, the agency lawyers lost their litigating function. At the same time, the explosion of regulatory statutes and the attendant rise in administrative activity increased the role of lawyers in the agencies outside the Justice Department.[19] The silence of both the executive order and the statute with regard to the counseling function by implication cemented its decentralization. No pretense of control by the attorney general was even made. On the other hand, Congress never repealed the provision, dating back to the Judiciary act of 1789, *allowing* (but not requiring) agency heads to obtain legal advice from the attorney general.[20]

Since 1933, this basic structure has remained intact. The numbers, of course, have changed. As the modern administrative state took shape during the New Deal and then grew into its modern form with the health, safety, and environmental initiatives of the 1970s, Congress always included an office of the general counsel (OGC) in new administrative entities. The Department of Justice now employs some 8,000 lawyers,[21] and administrative agencies outside the department employ many times that number.

THE MODERN AGENCY GENERAL COUNSEL

The general counsel is a fixture in the modern administrative agency. Not only cabinet departments and independent regulatory commissions, but also such relatively minor and nonlegal entities as the Inter-American Foundation, the Peace Corps, the Saint-Lawrence Seaway Development Corporation, and the National Capital Planning Commission have OGCs. The OGC can be quite large; in any of the major agencies, it is far larger than the Office of Legal Counsel (OLC) within the Justice Department. And the lawyers are often spread around the country: the Department of Agriculture's OGC, for example, is headquartered in Washington, D.C., but it has five regional and seventeen branch offices; EPA has a regional counsel's office in each of its ten regional offices; and the Department of Veterans Affairs has fifty-four district counsel offices.[22]

The mode of selecting agency lawyers varies, but some generalizations can be made. In all of the executive agencies, the general counsel is appointed by the president with the advice and consent of the Senate. More often than not, however, the general counsel is effectively selected by the head of the agency, to whose judgment the president defers. Thus, the counsel's loyalties may run primarily to the agency head and secondarily to the president. (This is probably somewhat less true of the Clinton administration than of previous administrations. Clinton made a concerted effort to have the White House, rather than the agency, select the second-tier agency positions, largely to ensure that loyalty would run to him.) In any event, the agency head still has an important consultative role in selecting the general counsel, and the same constellation of political forces that led to the selection of the agency head often lead to the selection of a sympathetic general counsel.[23] All that said, the process remains highly variable, depending on the agency, the White House's confidence in the agency head, the happenstance of whether the president or an aide happens to have someone in mind for a particular post, and the particular political debts to be paid.

Deputy or assistant general counsels are generally not presidential appointees, except in a few cases where they serve as counsel to major organs of government within a department (for example, the "chief counsel" of the IRS is a presidential appointee). In general, these individuals are either career lawyers in the office or, in the upper echelons, hired by the incoming general counsel. The staff lawyers in the office are career employees who do not come and go with changes in presidential administrations.

The nuances of the general counsel's role are discussed somewhat later. This section simply describes the general counsel's basic responsibilities.

A general counsel's primary functions are to give legal advice to the head of the agency and to instruct program staff about what is permissible and what not. The agency OGC has a central role in reviewing all proposed programmatic initiatives and rules. Most agencies institute their key policy decisions through rule-making, and all rules must be authorized by and consistent with a governing statute. The general counsel's role in deciding whether they are permissible is therefore critical in determining what activities the agency will undertake. Indeed, in most agencies the OGC is (and certainly ought to be) involved at an early stage in *developing* a proposal, rather than merely being handed the finished product for approval.

Agency general counsels also give advice to the public—in particular, to members of the regulated community who are seeking clarification of their legal obligations. Such advice can be utterly informal, as when a nonlawyer answers questions over the telephone, but it can also take the form of written opinions from the general counsel.[24] IRS revenue rulings, for example, are issued by the service's chief counsel. This role is the least politicized and least controversial part of the OGC's work, because it is the least visible and (partly because of the lack of visibility) has the narrowest consequences.

The general counsels themselves, as opposed to the other lawyers in the office, are likely to be important advisers to the agency heads on issues other than strictly legal ones. As a former attorney in the office of the legal adviser in the State Department has observed, holders of that post did not simply advise on legal matters, but "gave advice from a lawyer's point of view on everything that came up."[25] More often than not, the general counsel is a confidant in the inner circle of the agency's top officials.

Lawyers from the general counsel's office also represent the agency in administrative adjudications. Many agency decisions follow a trial-type hearing before an administrative law judge. To name just a few, these include grants of permits or license by, say, the Federal Communications Commission or the Nuclear Regulatory Commission; resolution of unfair labor practice charges by the NLRB; determination of claims for government benefits by the Department of Veterans Affairs or the Social Security Administration; and imposition of noncompliance penalties by the EPA or the Occupational Health and Safety Commission. In these essentially judicial proceedings the agency is a party—calling witnesses, introducing evidence, cross-examining—and is represented by attorneys from the general counsel's office.

Outside the administrative setting, however, agency lawyers usually do not litigate. The Justice Department handles all federal criminal prosecutions and the great bulk of civil litigation. Thus, should a private party seek judicial review of an agency order or challenge the validity of regulations, or should the agency wish to initiate a judicial enforcement action, the matter is almost always handled by the Department of Justice.[26] Agency lawyers have some input into the litigating strategy, they participate in settlement discussions, and their names appear on the government's briefs; but the Justice Department takes the lead. This is not true across the board, because in some cases Congress has granted agencies independent litigating authority. As of 1982, the count was seventy-two individual exceptions to Department of Justice control.[27] Whether this number represents a lot or a few such "encroachments" (to use the term the Justice Department often adopts) on the Justice Department's litigation authority depends on who one asks. To hear Justice Department attorneys tell the tale, the exceptions are swallowing the rule.[28] The vast majority of exceptions to the department's representation involve independent agencies. For all intents and purposes, it is accurate to say that the Department of Justice represents executive agencies in court.

Although they generally do not have the lead role in litigation, agency lawyers still have an important effect on the agency's litigation in two ways. First, they do participate. The extent of such participation varies from lawyer to lawyer, from case to case, and from agency to agency. But OGC attorneys do participate in settlement negotiations, help write briefs, and advise the lead attorney(s) from the Justice Department. Indeed, the latter usually draws on the agency lawyer's substantive expertise and familiarity with the particular case.[29] The second way in which OGC attorneys are involved in litigation is that they lay the groundwork. For better or worse, the agency lawyers shepherd the case up to the point at which it becomes a lawsuit. Many of the government's most critical decisions are made before any papers are filed in court.

One last aspect of the general counsel's work bears mention. All agency general counsels are members of the Federal Legal Council. Created in 1979 under Executive Order 12,146, the Federal Legal Council originally consisted of the attorney general and the general counsels of fifteen prominent agencies. It was expanded during the Reagan administration to include all general counsels. The council is supposed to promote the resolution of "problems in the efficient and effective management of Federal legal resources," such as "coordination and communication among Federal legal offices," and to develop recommendations to "avoid inconsistent or unnecessary litigation by agencies."[30] In practice, the Council has been a complete nonstarter, described by one Justice Department lawyer as merely "an opportunity for the general counsels to get to know each other."[31] It did at one point have a staff director and a phone number, and it even issued a set of recommendations concerning pro bono work by government attorneys; today it is not even listed in the Department of Justice telephone directory. The failure of the council is symptomatic of the entrenched decentralization of the counsels, the absence of any coordination of their work, and the distance between each of them and the Justice Department.

A CASE STUDY[32]

One of the most significant initiatives contained in the 1990 Clean Air Act Amendments is the new Title V, which requires all "major sources" of air pollution to obtain a permit to operate. The permit is to set out all emissions limits and record-keeping and monitoring requirements that apply to the source under the act. Like many programs mandated under the federal pollution statutes, the permit program is to be administered by the states, subject to federal oversight and consistent with minimum requirements established by the EPA.

Section 502(b) of the act sets out the minimum components of an acceptable state permit program. Needless to say, Section 502(b) is not wholly free of ambiguity. The EPA has the difficult task of writing regulations that flesh out Section 502(b)'s requirements. After a prolonged and bitter struggle within the government, the EPA promulgated such regulations in June 1992. Far and away the most controversial aspect of EPA's "permit rule" was a provision that allowed the state administrator to make minor changes in the conditions governing an existing permit without public notice or a hearing. The act itself is sketchy with regard to permit procedures. Initial applications and significant changes are indisputably subject to public scrutiny; it is unclear whether the EPA has the legal authority to exempt the subset of minor modifications.

The rule-making began in December 1990, when the EPA circulated a draft rule to a working group consisting of industry representatives, environmentalists, and other experts. The EPA hoped that the final rule might be forged out of discussion and consensus. Illustrative of the central role of agency lawyers in the rule-making process, the two EPA representatives who participated in a series of "roundtable discussions" on the draft proposal were William Rosenberg (the assistant administrator for air and radiation) and E. Donald Elliott (the general counsel).[33]

Early drafts of the rule did not exempt proposals for minor permit modifications from public scrutiny. Industry representatives were deeply concerned about this position, and they took their case not just to the EPA but also to the OMB, the White House counsel, and the White House chief of staff. This generated significant pressure from all three external sources on the EPA to loosen the procedures for minor permit modifications. Furthermore, lurking ostentatiously in the background was the Council on Competitiveness—the most visible expression of the Bush administration's commitment to a hierarchical, unitary executive branch and to (de)regulatory reform. Chaired by Vice-President Quayle and run out of his office, the council consisted of the secretaries of commerce and the treasury, the attorney general, the White House chief of staff, the director of the OMB, and the chair of the Council of Economic Advisors. It had a director, an assistant director, and a small staff. With a roving commission to review matters bearing on "competitiveness," the council sat atop the regulatory review process, evaluating agency programs and proposals to ensure that they did not impose excessive regulatory burdens. President Clinton eliminated the council on his second day in office.

During February, March, and April of 1991, the EPA and the OMB had at least eleven meetings to discuss the permit rule; all were attended by a Competitiveness Council staff member or by its executive director. In April, the EPA submitted its final proposal to the OMB pursuant to the regulatory review process established by Executive Order 12,291, still requiring public review of minor modifications. The OMB returned the draft significantly rewritten and minus the public comment provisions. Reluctantly, the EPA yielded to the OMB's changes. On April 24, 1991, it issued its proposed rule, which exempted minor modifications from public scrutiny.

The proposal was extraordinarily controversial. Representative Henry Waxman, a California Democrat who was engaged in a legislative campaign against the Council on Competitiveness, wasted no time in scheduling hearings and attacking the legality of the proposal. The day the rule was proposed, he wrote to the EPA's administrator, William Reilly, to lament that "the White House has again forced illegal changes upon EPA," and to summon him to a May 1 hearing before the House Subcommittee on Health and the Environment.[34] At the hearing, Waxman released a broadside entitled "The Vice President's Initiative to Undermine the Clean Air Act," which argued unrestrainedly that the Council on Competitiveness had forced these changes on the EPA, that they were blatantly illegal, and that the result would be that "[t]he entire clean air regulatory process for stationary sources is rendered largely meaningless."[35] The hearing was an occasion for unmitigated administration bashing by the Democrats on the subcommittee.

Administrator Reilly did not attend the hearing, sending Assistant Administrator Rosenberg and General Counsel Elliott in his stead. It fell to Elliott to defend the proposal's legality. Waxman lectured Elliott on his professional responsibility to ensure that the agency adhered to congressional mandates,[36] and Elliott assured Waxman that he took "very, very, very, personally my sworn responsibility to uphold the law and I view myself in some sense as the vicar of Congress."[37] Elliott's defense of the proposal was rather lukewarm, certainly leaving open the possibility of a contrary conclusion. He stressed the ambiguity of the statute, noted that the proposal was only a proposal, and was careful to state that "[w]e have not made a final decision as to how the law on this point should be read."[38] All in all, the agency was on the defensive at the hearing, and Waxman and the other Democrats were in high dudgeon.

In late summer, the EPA got to work on a new draft. Two things had changed since April, when it had issued the proposed rule. First, the agency had been beaten up badly on the Hill, in the popular press, and in the comments submitted to the docket. Second, on August 16, 1991, the day he left the EPA to return to teaching at Yale University Law School, General Counsel Elliott produced a memorandum concluding that the courts would not uphold the proposed rule, because it failed to provide for public notice and comment on minor revisions. Addressed to Assistant Administrator Rosenberg in response to his request for a legal opinion, the memo was lawyerly and detached. It did not refer to Elliott's earlier testimony, to the long-standing struggle between the EPA and the White House, or to the reaction on the Hill to the proposed rule. One thing, however, had not changed: the apparently sincere conviction of the administrator, the head of the air office, and EPA staffers that minor permit revisions required public scrutiny, both as a matter of law and as a matter of policy. The proposed rule's hostile public and congressional reception and Elliott's memorandum gave the program staff two important weapons to use in warding off the White House, the OMB, and the Competitiveness Council.

In drafting the final regulation, now in consultation with a new acting general counsel, Ray Ludwiszewski, the EPA returned to its original stance. In October, it submitted to the OMB a draft final rule that eliminated the minor permit modification provision that the OMB had forced into the proposal in April. There ensued a flurry of meetings between EPA representatives and unhappy OMB officials and Competitiveness Council staff—including nine such meetings in the first three weeks of November alone. Over the next few months, under pressure from the OMB, the White House, and the Competitiveness Council, the EPA slowly backed away from its position, several times redrafting the rule to restrict, without wholly eliminating, public review of minor permit modifications. Relations between the EPA, on the one hand, and the Council on Competitiveness, the OMB, and the White House counsel, on the other, grew increasingly strained.

At one point, the standoff seemed about to be resolved; the EPA and White House Counsel C. Boyden Gray had reached a loose agreement on a compromise proposal. On January 27, 1992, the EPA submitted a draft that it thought reflected this understanding to the OMB. The next day, EPA Deputy Administrator Henry Habicht met with Gray, Council of Economic Advisors Chairman Michael Boskin, and Vice-President Quayle's chief of staff, William Kristol, all of whom deemed the latest draft unacceptable. We cannot know, but it is at least possible that the January 27 draft *did* reflect an understanding between the EPA and White House counsel but that one day later the deal was no longer viable. What changed? On January 28, the president gave his state of the union address; and in it he emphasized his commitment to regulatory relief and announced a ninety-day moratorium on new regulations. The moratorium surely raised the stakes for the White House, which had come to perceive the minor permit revision issue as an important test of its commitment to regulatory relief. In a memo to EPA, Kristol castigated the proposal as representing "pure paperwork/regulatory/litigation burdens on the private sector" and objected that "our deregulatory initiative won't be taken seriously" if the proposal were adopted.[39] This comment made its way into the *Wall Street Journal*,[40] which of course only raised the stakes higher. The issue ceased to be one of policy in contradistinction to law; it became instead one of politics in contradistinction to policy.

The Department of Justice had been at the periphery of this dispute for some time. As early as April 1991, the department had sent the EPA proposed language regarding permit revisions—language that would have required public review.[41] Richard Stewart, who at the time headed the department's environment and natural resources division, had been present at a meeting of representatives from the EPA, the OMB, and the

Council on Competitiveness (among others), in April 1991 at which the legality of a streamlined procedure for minor permit amendments was discussed.[42] The Justice Department may have been prepared to weigh in with a formal opinion as early as August 1991, but no one seems to have been pressing it very hard to do so. On November 12, 1991, Competitiveness Council director Allan Hubbard formally requested an opinion[43]; and by late November, talks with the EPA were reportedly on hold pending the receipt of the Justice Department's views.[44] According to a later Justice Department memo, the department provided an oral opinion to the EPA's Reilly at some time during the fall of 1991, concluding that public comment was not required.[45] By January 1992, some sort of Justice Department document seems to have been produced, but it was not in circulation. The general understanding at the time was that the department considered both the OMB's and the EPA's positions legally defensible. At that time, one EPA official was reported as saying that a Justice Department memo to that effect was in existence.[46] Yet the opinion was not released: "One day they [the Justice Department] say it's coming out; one day they say it's in draft form; then they say it isn't coming out at all."[47] Thus, in early February, James MacRae from the OMB testified, perhaps disingenuously, that the Department of Justice had not yet given any opinion: "I don't know what the [Department's] opinion could be. . . . EPA and we and others are waiting to see what the opinion is."[48]

But while the Department of Justice may have been silent, Henry Waxman was not. On November 14 and December 10, 1991, he held further oversight hearings of his subcommittee, regarding the implementation of the Clean Air Act and the role being played by the Council on Competitiveness.[49] Again the subcommittee staff had prepared documents lambasting the meddling of the council and of the OMB and arguing that the act plainly required public review of all proposed permit modifications. In questioning Administrator Reilly, Assistant Administrator Rosenberg, and Acting General Counsel Ray Ludwiszewski, the subcommittee members tried hard to get them to endorse the Elliott memorandum, to reveal the nature of White House pressure, and determine the status of the Justice Department's consideration of the issue. As usual, the hearings generated more heat than light, but they did pointedly remind the agency—and the White House—of Waxman's concerns.

On March 25, 1992, Barry Hartman, acting head of the Justice Department's environment and natural resources division, wrote White House Counsel C. Boyden Gray a letter concluding that public review of all permit revisions was *not* required by the act. Someone at the department orally informed Competitiveness Council staff members on April 2 that public comment was not required for minor permit revisions, and they reportedly informed the EPA of this conclusion the same day.[50] Still, no written opinion was released. A press report asserted that the council was "citing a DOJ opinion which no one has seen and some doubt even exists," and that the "Council has repeatedly cited a DOJ opinion to support its position, but has refused to disclose the memo."[51] Moreover, the OLC, from which an opinion would normally have been expected, remained silent.

On April 13, Reilly himself wrote to Attorney General William Barr requesting a formal written opinion, almost five months to the day after Allan Hubbard of the Competitiveness Council had sent the department an identical request. By this stage in the struggle, Reilly's bargaining position had solidified; he would not sign the final permit rule without public scrutiny of minor revisions unless and until the Department of Justice issued a written opinion stating that such a rule was consistent with the Clean Air Act. It is possible that EPA administrators thought that the department might yet side with it rather than with the White House, particularly in light of frequent reports that the department had been reluctant to put its opinion in writing.[52] But whatever the agency's expectation, the Elliott memo no longer sufficed to hold off the White House/Competitiveness Council/OMB axis.

After several cancellations and testy exchanges, the showdown meeting between Reilly and the Competitiveness Council took place on April 22. At this meeting, Reilly was directly informed of Hartman's March 25 letter. Hartman was not at the meeting; but Timothy Flanagan, then the acting head of the OLC, was.[53] The council stood by its insistence that the permit rule specify a minor permit modification procedure that did not include public comment and reiterated its belief that such a rule was permitted by the statute. At this point, it formally made the decision to ask the president to resolve the controversy. Apparently, President Bush had already told Vice-President Quayle that he would side with the council if the issue came before him.

The following day, Competitiveness Council staff drafted a memo for the president's signature; the EPA's acting general counsel, Ray Ludwiszewski, reviewed the document. The eight-page memorandum—a two-page discussion of the council's recommendations, a three-page background memo, and a three-page memo from the EPA setting out its position—went to the president on April 24, and he endorsed the council position sometime in mid-May.

Only after that did the Department of Justice finally produce a formal, written opinion. In an opinion dated May 27 and sent to Reilly by Attorney General Barr that same day, acting environment division head Barry Hartman concluded that the act did not require state administrators to invite public comment prior to making minor permit revisions.[54] Additional discussions and exchanges of drafts ensued, but the EPA was not going to disagree with the Department of Justice's legal opinion and defy the president. It promulgated the final rule, including an exception from the public review requirements for minor permit modifications, on June 25, 1992.[55] In the preamble, EPA explained at some length why the rule *was* valid under the Clean Air Act. Not surprisingly, this portion of the preamble draws heavily on the Justice Department memo. Officially, however, it states the legal conclusion of the agency.

INTERGOVERNMENTAL RELATIONS AND THE CONFLICT OF LAW AND POLICY

The permit rule saga is a revealing example of the buffeting an agency general counsel takes from conflicting political interests. Drawing on this example, the following subsections discuss the different governmental and political forces at work on the agency general counsel.

The General Counsel Within the Agency

The permit rule saga illustrates the tie between the agency head and the agency general counsel. Both Don Elliott and his successor (as acting general counsel) Ray Ludwiszewski, fought the good fight for the agency from start to finish. Of particular interest in this regard is Elliott's change of position between the May 1991 congressional hearing and his August memorandum. We can never know what lay behind the change, but one strong possibility is that, in both settings, he was being a good soldier for the agency. Until April, all of the EPA's drafts of the proposed rule had provided for public scrutiny even for minor revisions. This position was adopted with the participation and concurrence of the agency's OGC; it may be that Elliott's position at this time was (as later memorialized) that such scrutiny was required. In April, however, political pressures led the EPA to a different proposal. Elliott went to the Hill to defend, albeit inconclusively, the agency's position, just as any lawyer-advocate defends a client's action. By August, on the other hand, the agency had regirded itself and was willing to do battle with the White House. Under the circumstances, an OGC opinion that interpreted the statute as requiring what the agency wanted to do anyway would clearly strengthen its position.

Other explanations for the shift are, of course, possible. It may reflect nothing more than a sincere reevaluation of a complicated question of statutory interpretation. Elliott's initial review of the statute and thinking about the matter may have suggested that public review of minor modifications could have been—but then again might not be—required; on further reflection, he may have changed his mind. Or perhaps one of Elliott's stances reflected his "neutral" reading of the statute, while the other reflected a legal judgment colored by Elliott's own policy preferences. As always in complicated legal questions, the two possibilities are difficult to separate. Finally, the most cynical public-choice version is that all along Elliott was trying to shore up his own position with those who mattered to him. In May, these individuals were not just the agency administrators but powerful people in the White House and the OMB. By his last day on the job, the people who mattered were not those in the government at all but those back at Yale or elsewhere, who might be impressed by Elliott's integrity and/or adoption of the more "environmentally correct" position. (This last explanation is unconvincing, however, since the personal or professional benefit to be gleaned from this parting shot is unclear.)

For present purposes, the correct explanation in this particular case is unimportant. Each scenario is realistic, and the examples of each—the interpretation most helpful to the agency head, the interpretation reflecting sincere effort to figure out a complicated statute, the legal interpretation colored by policy views, and the interpretation most helpful to the interpreter—can be found every day in Washington, regardless of which one this is an example of.

The permit rule story shows how the agency OGC can be a critical ally of the program staff. Purely as a matter of policy, the program staff did not want to exempt minor permit modifications from public scrutiny. Their strongest argument—the argument any bureaucrat always tries to fall back on—is that they had no choice: their hands were tied. Low-level bureaucrats can say this all the time; agency heads can say it only if Congress or the president gives them an order. Rosenberg's and Reilly's strongest argument was the one Elliott gave them: the statute forbids the exemption the White House sought.

The permit rule story is less useful for illustrating a second important dynamic of the relationship between the OGC and the rest of the agency. In the modern regulatory state, where agency decision-making is dominated by statutes and court rulings, lawyers play an extraordinarily powerful role. The more complex the statutes and the more common the judicial intervention, the more powerful that role becomes. And these days, the statutes can be enormously complex and the judicial interventions can be frequent.[56] Anyone who is *not* a lawyer will be dismayed by lawyer's influence, which always involves peripheral issues. OGC lawyers unavoidably generate anger and disdain from other agency staff members by virtue of their particular areas of expertise—and as a result of ignorance. After all, the most welcome advice the lawyer can offer is that it is all right for the program staff to do what they wish to do anyway. Except in cases when an official *wants* to be told that he must do what he wishes to do anyway (in order to deflect criticism),[57] such a statement does not advance things; it only does not derail them.

And at worst, OGC advice can indeed derail a developing plan. Because he or she stands on statutory requirements, the general counsel has a particular ability to obstruct policy innovation. Nonlawyers within an agency may have doubts as to whether the general counsel's conclusion that the statute forbids them to undertake a particular initiative truly rests on the statute or merely reflects personal preference and intransigence. Strictly speaking, legal advice from the agency OGC is not binding on the agency head. However, rejecting it is likely to have severe consequences, both politically (by giving a tool to opponents inside and outside the government, including members of congressional oversight committees) and legally (by inviting a lawsuit and increasing the likelihood that it will be successful). For bureaucratic and institutional reasons as well, the agency OGC must have final authority on legal questions if the agency is to run smoothly. Consequently, however frustrated or suspicious they may be, others in the agency are not usually in a position to second-guess the OGC's legal conclusions.

The extent to which a general counsel is seen as an obstacle depends largely on the personal and professional characteristics of the individuals involved. One veteran of intra-agency struggles divides agency lawyers into two categories: the "How-you-can" type and the "Why-you-can't" type.[58] General counsels whose tendencies move them too strongly in the first direction are likely to get the agency into trouble and may give short shrift to their professional obligation to ensure that the agency adhere to legal requirements. Those with the opposite tendency may habitually overstate obstacles to achieving desired results; in so doing, they profoundly irritate others in the agency and may find themselves being left out of the loop entirely. Agency policy-makers feel frustration and anger toward a lawyer who proves to be what one wag has labeled "the abominable no-man."

While can-do policy types may be impatient with the agency OGC's caution and preoccupation with legal technicalities, the scientific staff is likely to consider the OGC too political. For example, one EPA senior scientist has complained that early in the agency's history "the science element of EPA became not only subordinate but *subservient* to the legal element."[59] In the eyes of the scientist, lawyers try to help policy-making clients get where they want. "The scientist's duty, on the other hand, is to uncover nature's secrets and publish his or her findings, irrespective of any 'client's' desires."[60]

One survey asked EPA program staff to rank ten rule-making goals in order of the importance that they thought various offices within the EPA attached to them. The OGC agency was perceived to care most about the rule's surviving judicial review (a 9.5 on a 0–10 scale—the highest single score), and second most about the rule's fidelity to the statute (9.1), while being relatively unconcerned about factors such as timeliness, administrative efficiency, and enforceability.[61] In part out of a concern that rules survive judicial review and in part because the relevant statutes are the ultimate source of authority and guidance for anything and everything the agency does, the OGC attorneys are likely to become involved in scientific and technical issues fairly far afield from pure questions of law. This can increase the level of resentment and hostility among the program staff.[62] Furthermore, while the lawyers were thought to be especially concerned with fidelity to statutory mandates and surviving judicial review, these goals were important for everyone at the agency. The more important these goals are, the more important the lawyers are; and the more important the lawyers are, the greater the resentment toward them. Indeed, as James Q. Wilson has written, "management of the EPA often has been dominated by lawyers, much to the disgust of many engineers and scientists, because the key output of that agency, a regulation, is framed in a political environment that makes it more important to withstand legal attack than to withstand scientific scrutiny."[63]

Intra-executive Relations

Writing in 1977, then–Attorney General Griffin Bell offered this description of the federal legal apparatus:

> Shortly after I took office, the President asked me to determine the total number of lawyers in the government and their functions. . . . We discovered 19,479 lawyers [of whom only 3,806 are in the Department of Justice] who are performing "lawyer-like" functions—litigating, preparing legal memoranda, giving legal advice, and drafting statutes, rules, and regulations. These lawyers are distributed through the departments and agencies, and practically no agency is too small to have its own "General Counsel." . . .
>
> Although I am the chief legal officer in the executive branch, I have learned that I have virtually no control or direction over the lawyers outside the Department of Justice, except indirectly in connection with pending litigation.[64]

Notice the somewhat petulant disappointment Bell expresses—the assumption that, by rights, the attorney general ought to dominate federal legal activities, and the almost audible sneer in the quotation marks around "General Counsel."

Justice Department lawyers distrust agency lawyers for two reasons. The first—difficult to quantify, possible to overcome, but still quite real—

involves the difference in prestige between the two posts. The general perception is that Justice Department positions are more desirable and the corps of lawyers is more elite. Needless to say, the counterexamples are numerous. Still, the relation is something like that between federal and state courts. For all the talk of mutual respect, the usual assumption is that parity is a myth.

Second, Justice Department lawyers tend to assume that agency lawyers are excessively committed to the narrow mission of the agency and that they lack either the detachment necessary to see the big picture or the neutrality to adhere scrupulously to true legal requirements. The suspicion is longstanding; it was part of the justification for centralizing the counseling function in 1870. As was noted earlier, Representative Jenckes asserted prior to passage of the 1870 act, that "[w]e have found, too, that these law officers, being subject to the control of the heads of the Departments, in some instances give advice which seems to have been instigated by the heads of the Department, or at least advice which seems designed to strengthen the resolution to which the head of the Department may have come in a particular case."[65]

These tensions are exacerbated by the fact that the Justice Department represents agencies in court. From the point of view of the agency lawyer, the case is taken away at a critical moment, after months or years of work, and handed over to a know-nothing generalist. From the point of view of the Justice Department lawyer, any challenges or setbacks are easily attributed to mistakes made before the department got the case. For example, the department lawyers given the task of defending the permit rule are presumably cursing Don Elliott's eleventh-hour memo, which makes their task much harder. Within the Department of Justice the same dynamic exists when the solicitor general's office takes over a case from one of the divisions when it reaches the Supreme Court. In both cases, the success of this arrangement depends on two things: clearly designated final authority, and the goodwill and cooperative professionalism of the individuals involved.

As we saw in the permit rule story, which led to a legal opinion from the Justice Department contradicting the agency general counsel's opinion, the department also has some authority over the agencies with regard to counseling. The head of any executive department "may require the opinion of the Attorney General on questions of law arising in the administration of his department."[66] In 1927, Albert Langeluttig wrote:

Though the office of the Attorney General has been in existence for 135 years and during all of that time one of his most important functions has been that of advising the President and the heads of departments in respect to the law, there is still lacking complete agreement in respect to the binding force of the opinion of that officer when rendered.[67]

With the "135" changed to "205," the same statement could be written today. For such an apparently basic issue to remain unresolved, one of two things must be true: the uncertainty must benefit several relevant interests, or it must not matter. The latter cannot be the case here, because in practice the OLC's opinions *do* bind the requesting agency. The OLC will not write an opinion except on that understanding.[68] Agencies perceive the opinions as binding. Indeed, Elliott so testified to Waxman's subcommittee: "We [the EPA general counsel] get to give a final legal ruling and if that final legal ruling by me and my office is made, it is going to stand unless and until it is appealed to the Department of Justice and somebody over there says I am wrong."[69] To be sure, there is no mechanism to monitor compliance, and no empirical study of actual compliance has been performed, so it is possible that some slippage occurs. Outright defiance would certainly be noticed, however, and it is fair to assume that the Justice Department's opinions are binding in fact, whether or not they are in theory.

In a relative handful of cases, the Justice Department gives a binding legal opinion to an agency; but this fact hardly means that the department controls legal advice-giving. Most importantly, it cannot insist on giving an opinion on a question of law facing the agency; the agency must come to it. As a result, the agency holds its own counsel on the huge majority of legal issues, without advice from the OLC.[70]

Indeed, one might wonder why an agency would *ever* submit a question to the Department of Justice. The agency may have doubts about the department's support, interest, and expertise, and it may fear that the department will have a competing agenda. The agency general counsel's office is full of lawyers who are confident of their abilities and who specialize in the statutes that fall within their jurisdiction. Moreover, the costs of seeking an opinion are high. Since it is obliged to comply thereafter, the agency runs the risk of getting news it does not want to hear and then being unable to hide from it. It can, of course, first sound out OLC informally. And in a manual prepared for new general counsels, the Office of Personnel Management hints broadly that it is wise to do so: "You may also seek informal advice from OLC prior to making a decision on whether you wish to submit a formal request for advice."[71] Negotiation can help control the risk involved in placing the question before the Department of Justice, but it does not eliminate it entirely. Therefore, an agency is likely to avoid asking the department for an opinion if possible. In the permit rule struggle, the EPA stayed away from the department as long as it could.

In one set of circumstances, an agency has no choice but to turn to the Justice Department. If two agencies cannot agree on a question of law, Executive Order 12,146 requires them to submit the question to the attorney general for resolution. Here, Department of Justice resolution makes sense. In these circumstances the expertise argument drops away, and a centralized resolution is by definition required. I have written elsewhere that in some such cases the courts can provide that resolution, but the department has generally taken the position that interagency litigation is nonjusticiable, and for the most part it has been able to keep such cases out of the courts.[72]

Absent such an interagency conflict, under what circumstances would an agency turn to the OLC? It is conceivable that an agency head might do so out of genuine uncertainty as to his or her obligations and/or distrust of the agency's general counsel. Such an occurrence must be extraordinarily rare and limited to constitutional or other issues outside the interpretive purview of the agency's statutes. Indeed, the tendency of agencies to negotiate with the OLC in advance suggests that something other than a sincere and disinterested request for advice, without regard to its substance, is involved.[73] In most cases an agency head will turn to the OLC when some political or strategic advantage, as opposed to legal insight, may be gained thereby. The permit rule struggle is an example of this. Ultimately, Reilly asked the Justice Department for an interpretation of the Clean Air Act, refusing to cave in without it. For Reilly, the department's opinion would serve one of two purposes. If it sided with the EPA, the opinion could be used to fend off the forces close to the president. Indeed, by early 1992, the EPA could not adopt its preferred substantive position without such protection. On the other hand, if the department's opinion went against the EPA on the law, the very fact of having insisted on the opinion—of having gone to the mat—would boost the EPA's standing with its natural constituency. Moreover, the bad outcome could be laid at the Justice Department's door, rather than at the EPA's, thus shielding the EPA from criticism.

During the permit rule saga, the EPA had little contact with the Department of Justice but a great deal of consultation with the OMB, the White House counsel, and the Competitiveness Council. These latter meetings did not involve legal matters, strictly speaking, although they did involve many lawyers. The real fight between the EPA and the White House was over policy, or (especially after President Bush imposed the moratorium on new regulations) politics. It took place against the background of contested legal requirements but was not directly about those requirements. It shows, however, how *un*insulated the general counsel is from the political battle.

Interbranch Relations

Formally, Congress communicates with agencies by legislating. Congress's statutes dictate the agency's obligations and the scope of its authority. Statutes, however, can amount to duties expressed in a foreign language; the agency OGC is the translator. In this sense, Congress lays special claim to the general counsel's attention and loyalty. The general counsel is, to quote Donald Elliott's description of himself, "the vicar of Congress."[74]

Informally, Congress communicates with agencies through oversight hearings. Precisely because of the general counsel's role as translator, he or she tends to be a particular target of the oversight process. The general counsel testified at each of the congressional oversight hearings that hammered at the EPA over the permit rule. At the May 1991 hearing, Representative Waxman leaned on Elliott heavily; at the November and December hearings, he invoked the Elliott memorandum to lean heavily on those whom Elliott had left behind, including his successor. Congress inevitably takes the position that the statute already enacted, if properly interpreted, requires or forbids certain actions on the part of the agency. Hence, once the statute is enacted, the oversight committee wants to turn *all* questions into legal questions, not policy questions. The general counsel is placed in unique focus by that argument.

Ironically, in the courts, where one might expect all questions to be legal questions, there often is an incentive to turn them into policy questions. This is because, under the Supreme Court's decision in *Chevron U.S.A. Inc. v. NRDC*,[75] if the court cannot find a clear resolution in the statute—in other words, if Congress seems to have punted on a particular question of policy and left it for agency resolution—the court is supposed to accept as valid any nonarbitrary agency interpretation.

Chevron is a much-discussed case with uncertain effects on judicial decision-making. At least potentially, and probably in fact, it is an interesting illustration of how judicial method can affect intra-agency and intra-branch relations. Read broadly, *Chevron* sends a strong message to lower courts to accept the agency's understanding of a statute. It reduces the role of the courts in reviewing agency decisions; and it frankly acknowledges that the statute is often of no help in resolving the specific question before the court, because that question is one that Congress never thought about or simply delegated to the agency. In such circumstances, it is a fiction to pretend to be doing the lawyer's or judge's job of "interpreting" the statute. Instead, the real decision to be made is a policy decision. Recognizing this, the court should accept any nonarbitrary conclusion about how to proceed that is reached by the agency, which has substantive expertise and electoral accountability (albeit indirect) that the courts lack.[76]

If the decision is read broadly, it should reduce the role of agency lawyers for the same reason that it reduces the role of courts: there is nothing for them to do. A *Chevron* "step-two case"—that is, a case where the statute is silent and the court must defer to the agency—calls for decision-making by the scientific or technical or policy staff, not by the lawyers. Again, the permit rule fight illustrates the point. The Justice Department's ultimate legal conclusion was not that the statute *forbade* public scrutiny of minor permit modifications, but only that the statute was sufficiently vague that the agency could plausibly read it either to require them or not to require them. Under *Chevron,* the agency could do what it wished (or more precisely, what the White House wished). The legal conclusion was that there was no legal conclusion, only a matter of policy. One important aspect of *Chevron* is that it gives the Supreme Court's seal of approval to such a conclusion. Traditionally, lawyers say things like "it can be argued that . . ." or "on the other hand, . . . but on the other, . . ." on their way to a conclusion that seems by no means inescapable. *Chevron* removes the obligation (if not the tendency) to conclude that there is in fact a single correct reading of the statute.

The emotional and intellectual attachment to "a government of laws, not of men," the received wisdom, and the very existence of the Department of Justice and of agency general counsels all rest on the proposition that legal questions are not the same as policy questions. The constant challenge for any government lawyer is to keep the two separate. A broad reading of *Chevron* (and how strong a reading it will or should receive is a matter of dispute) moves the dividing line significantly, increasing the scope of policy and reducing that of law.

THE BASIS OF DECENTRALIZED COUNSELING

The arguments for and against centralized litigating authority have been much explored, and I shall not revisit them here. Instead, this section considers why the system centralizes litigating authority but not counseling. Ultimately, this section endorses this arrangement and suggests certain reasons other than merit for its existence.

At the outset, notice that this arrangement roughly duplicates the one that prevails in the private sector. Corporations rely on their own general counsel, who knows the company and the particular regulatory schemes under which it must operate, unless and until a matter ends up in court, at which point the tendency is to turn to the litigators in a law firm. And within law firms, "litigation" is a separate specialty—the only one not defined by subject matter. The private adoption of such an arrangement suggests that there is indeed a particular set of litigation skills. The question remains, however, why the litigation department cannot be maintained within the agency (as for example, in the case of IRS lawyers who litigate in the Tax Court, or the Judge Advocate General Corps lawyers who litigate in the Court of Military Appeals) or alternatively why the specialized counselors cannot be located within the Department of Justice. The reason may lie in some combination of reasoned judgment and political realities.

Practicalities. Donald Horowitz writes that the consolidation of litigating authority during the New Deal was successful because "it did not also attempt to do the impossible—to vest the counseling function in the Department of Justice at a time when the number of federal agencies and programs and the complexities of their tasks were growing enormously."[77] The Justice Department would have to be expanded beyond recognition—and beyond the power of the attorney general meaningfully to oversee it—if the myriad counseling functions now carried out by agency lawyers were shifted to that department.

Expertise. Even given the separation of the Justice Department into divisions, the lawyers in the department are generalists. This is especially true of the advice-givers in the OLC, who consider all manner of issues, not limited even to environment, antitrust, civil, and so on. Outside of the OLC, Department of Justice lawyers are primarily specialists in litigating. To fully develop expertise in a particular substantive area, an attorney needs to be at the agency. Professor Ron Levin has pointed out that "[a]n agency is surely likely to know more about the statute it administers—about the interrelationships among various provisions, the precedents applying them, the legislative history, and so forth—than does the average federal judge."[78] Substitute "Department of Justice lawyer" for "federal judge," and the comment is no less correct. A group of attorneys quartered in the agency, coming into daily contact with the program and technical staff, will be better able to handle the counseling function than a group of attorneys situated elsewhere, even if the latter devoted themselves to mastering the relevant law in a single substantive area.

"Federalism." The familiar arguments for federalism rather than highly centralized national government—flexibility, the opportunity to experiment in Brandeisian laboratories, familiarity with the particulars of local circumstances—have counterparts in the federal government's legal bureaucracy. By resolving most legal questions within the agencies, the executive branch can take advantage of similar sorts of benefits.

Analogously, it is generally seen as a good thing that not all lawsuits start in the Supreme Court. The Court itself benefits from having legal issues percolate through the lower courts. It even benefits from disagreement among these lower courts, since such disagreement helps highlight important issues and fully flesh out the relevant arguments and concerns of various interested parties.[79] Similarly, allowing the various agencies to take on legal issues as they arise leads to full development of all relevant issues and gives legal problems their fullest possible airing. This helps explain the OLC's rule that it will not give an opinion unless the requesting agency first prepares and submits its own analysis of the problem. Besides preventing an agency from treating recourse to OLC opinions as a way of evading responsibility for difficult decisions, requiring the agency to provide an opinion in advance helps focus the issues and gives the OLC the benefit of the insights of another set of lawyers. (The same is true in the case of requiring an agency's views on whether to appeal a government defeat, even though the final decision lies with the solicitor general.) Viewing the entire executive branch as a single system, similar benefits arise from decentralizing opinion-giving and having legal issues percolate through the branch.

The negative flip-side of federalism is inconsistency and inefficiency. These are real costs of decentralization of the federal legal apparatus, although they are much greater with regard to litigation than with regard to counseling. The variation in the statutes under which the agencies function does reduce the efficiencies that could be achieved by centralized counseling, but the advantages of uniformity are easy to exaggerate. All things considered, the costs of federalism do not outweigh the benefits.

Maximizing Congressional Power. For the foregoing reasons, the decentralized counseling system makes sense. But it has not necessarily been adopted because it makes sense. Perhaps the most important explanation for its existence is that it enhances the power of the body that created it—the United States Congress. Decentralizing advice-giving serves congressional power in at least two ways.

First, Congress requires information. It is more likely to get that information out of an agency than out of the Justice Department. An agency general counsel must maintain good relations with Congress for the sake of the agency's budget and its legislative program and to avoid gruesome oversight hearings and micromanaging legislation. Cooperating by providing information is one of the cheapest ways of accomplishing this. Thus, for example, an agency is never as eager as the Justice Department is to assert claims of executive privilege. Consider Congress's investigation of the EPA's (non)enforcement of the Superfund law in the early 1980s, which led to the resignation of EPA Administrator Anne Gorsuch Burford and (by a circuitous path) the Supreme Court's decision in *Morrison v. Olson*[80] upholding the constitutionality of the independent counsel law. Throughout this episode, the Justice Department, not the

EPA, insisted that certain documents be held back. The EPA's general counsel was more deferential to the department's wishes than were others in the agency, but he too was not eager to defy Congress.[81] Similarly, during the permit rule fight, the EPA was very forthcoming toward Waxman's subcommittee, and it dutifully complied with all requests for additional information. Indeed, the only piece of paper that the EPA hesitated to turn over was the letter from Allan Hubbard, executive director of the Competitiveness Council, to the Department of Justice requesting a legal opinion.[82] Apart from the fact that this letter was not an EPA document, the agency's reluctance reflects its awareness that those closer to the White House are far less obliging about providing information to Congress.

The hearings also provided one especially revealing and entertaining glimpse of the general counsel's willingness to provide information. Congressman Charles Dingell, a Michigan Democrat, sat on Congressman Waxman's Health and Environment Subcommittee, but was also chair of the Oversight and Investigations Subcommittee. During one of Waxman's hearings, Dingell felt that the EPA had provided documents to the Health and Environment Subcommittee that it had told Dingell's subcommittee were privileged. The following exchange ensued:

> MR. DINGELL: I'm wondering if you view us at Oversight as some sort of second class committee or something.
>
> That would distress me, and that would distress the staff up there prodigiously. It would probably cause enormous difficulties for us and for you.
>
> MR. LUDWISZEWSKI: I believe that would cause enormous difficulties for the agency, Mr. Chairman.
>
> MR. DINGELL: There are former Administrators and Deputy Administrators down there who served at EPA who found that that's a very unpleasant experience for them.
>
> MR. LUDWISZEWSKI: I'm confident of that, sir.
>
> MR. DINGELL: I'm wondering if we should commence with the process of getting distressed, because you have given Mr. Waxman things that you have not given to us. . . . I'm just wondering. Should we start getting distressed about now or should we wait a bit?
>
> MR. LUDWISZEWSKI: I would request that you wait a little bit. I will go back to the agency and see if I can't look into this somewhat inconsistent position.
>
> MR. DINGELL: The purpose is not to require the production of documents at this minute, but it is to let you know that the situation is moving towards the point where I will be compelled to re-

gard as more serious, that staff will be compelled to regard as more serious, and the escalation and the ratcheting up of the levels of unpleasantness will commence.

MR. LUDWISZEWSKI: I'm painfully aware of that, sir.[83]

The second way in which decentralized counseling enhances congressional power is that an agency general counsel is much further removed from White House and presidential oversight (or interference) than is the Justice Department. The attorney general is a cabinet officer and is frequently someone who was prominent in the president's election campaign and possesses deep personal loyalty to the president. The general counsel, although appointed by the president, is likely to have less intense loyalty in that direction and stronger ties to the agency head, the agency program, and possibly even to Congress. This is all the more true of the agency's career OGC staff. The permit rule saga again provides a stark example of a general counsel who was closer to Congress in outlook and sympathies than to the Justice Department or the White House. To be sure, the White House *prevailed* in this case. But the story is highly atypical in terms of the high-level (ultimately presidential) attention given to this relatively minor issue. The norm involves much more decentralized decision-making.

Of course, to the extent that Congress controls lawyers by writing the statutes that lawyers construe, it theoretically has equal control over the agency and over the Department of Justice. But statutory interpretation is not mechanical; and of course, Congress also exerts control through oversight hearings, to which agency counsel are frequently (and Justice Department lawyers are rarely) subject. In short, placing more power with the agency means less power for the president, and less power for the president means more power for Congress.[84] In addition, placing power in an agency's OGC in particular puts it precisely where Congress has relatively great influence.

The President's Strategy of Divide and Conquer. Finally, Congress is not the only entity that helped create and now benefits from decentralized counseling. The president, too, *could* centralize legal authority in the Department of Justice to a greater extent than it is now. Indeed, in certain very high-stakes settings, the Department of Justice, the other departments, and the White House coordinate more closely.[85] For example, on questions of war powers, there is quite close cooperation between the Departments of Defense, State, and Justice and the White House, with heavy ultimate reliance on the Justice Department's legal judgment, as informed by the relevant agencies.[86] Similarly, there is some effort at consistency and centralization with regard to assertions of claims of executive privilege, where core presidential interests are at stake. And the

Justice Department does have the last word when two agencies disagree. For the most part, however, the president has left a quite decentralized system in place. Although this comes at the cost of benefiting Congress, as discussed in the previous subsection, it nonetheless also serves the president's institutional interests.

First, the agencies are part of the president's administration, and the arguments on the merits for decentralization (expertise, practicality, "federalism") should matter to him—indeed, more to him than to Congress. An administration that runs effectively can only help the president.

Second, notwithstanding the usually close ties between the attorney general and the president, there is no guarantee that the attorney general's ideological interests are precisely congruent with the president's. For example, as a matter of political strategy (if nothing else), it would have been a mistake for Ronald Reagan to put himself solely in the hands of Ed Meese, who was, in a sense, too good a friend. Richard Nixon had one attorney general who was also too good a friend and another who was not a good enough one. As of this writing, Bill Clinton would be reluctant for Janet Reno to be general counsel to all executive agencies.

Finally, the president is always threatened by too great a concentration of power in anyone else. Centralizing the legal counseling function would not shift the balance of power within the branch fundamentally, making the attorney general tower over the president. But it would give the attorney general a significant role in overseeing the agencies. Since the Nixon administration, and culminating in Executive Order 12,291, that oversight role has gone to the OMB, which in general is more to be trusted than the attorney general.

CONCLUSION

It is hard to speak generally about how best to handle the conflicting obligations of an agency general counsel without falling into unhelpful platitudes. One somewhat useful way of reconciling the conflict is to divide up the tasks sequentially. When initially consulted as to legal constraints on a possible course of action, the general counsel owes the agency (and Congress and the public) an objective and complete evaluation of the relevant law. Once a programmatic decision has been made, however, the general counsel's task is to make the best legal case for it possible—subject, as any advocate is, to the constraints of good faith and professional responsibility. In the long struggle over the permit rule, the EPA's OGC seems to have made this shift twice: defending the legality of both the proposed rule and the final rule, even though they contradicted the counsel's prior legal opinion.

This sequential division falls far short of wholly resolving the tensions within the general counsel's role, however, because it identifies two types of *lawyering* without taking account of the manifold *political* influences on the general counsel. The general counsel plays a central role in administrative agency policy-making. As the long battle over the EPA's permit rule illustrates, the general counsel also bears a unique set of conflicting pressures and obligations. It is neither possible nor desirable for the general counsel to play a wholly nonpolitical role, but it is also pointless and contrary to the traditions of the rule of law for the general counsel to play a wholly nonlegal role. Ultimately, these tensions can only be resolved case by case, in light of the personalities and issues involved.

NOTES

1. As of 1977, the federal government had 19,479 lawyers, of whom 3,608, or 18.5%, were in the Department of Justice. Allison T. Stark, "When the Government Goes to Court, Who Should Speak for Uncle Sam?" *National Journal* 12 (1980): 1098 (citing an OMB report on reorganizing government). Fifty years earlier, 115 out of 919 lawyers (12.5%) were in the Department of Justice. *Annual Report of the Attorney General of the United States* 347 (1928).

2. This much discussed tension in the attorney general's role is captured in the titles of two excellent modern studies of that office, both of whose authors are represented in the present volume: Nancy V. Baker, *Conflicting Loyalties: Law and Politics in the Attorney General's Office, 1789–1990* (Lawrence, Kans.: University Press of Kansas, 1992); and Cornell W. Clayton, *The Politics of Justice: The Attorney General and the Making of Legal Policy* (Armonk, N.Y.: M. E. Sharpe, 1992).

3. This is less true, in general, of the lawyers in the civil rights division. See Brian K. Landsberg, "The Role of Civil Service Attorneys and Political Appointees in Making Policy in the Civil Rights Division of the U.S. Department of Justice," *Journal of Law and Politics* 9 (1993): 275, 277.

4. On general counsels within the independent agencies, see chapter 7 of this volume, by Neal Devins.

5. Judiciary Act of 1789, ch. 20, sec. 35, 1 Stat. 73, 93 (1789). On the early role of the attorney general—and the overwhelming burden of opinion writing, in particular—see Susan Low Bloch, "The Early Role of the Attorney General in Our Constitutional Scheme: In the Beginning There Was Pragmatism," *Duke Law Journal* 1989: 561.

6. *Annual Report of the Attorney General of the United States* (1928), p. 344.

7. *Congressional Globe*, 41st Cong., 2d sess., 3036 (April 27, 1870) (remarks of Rep. Jenckes). Representative Lawrence, who had also sponsored legislation to create a justice department, voiced similar concerns:

[At present, t]here is no law department. These various officers have no common head or superior. Each gives his opinion, and they are the guide for officers, bureaus, or Departments.

One great object of this bill is to provide a law officer whose opinion shall be asked upon all questions admitting of doubt and whose opinions shall become the rule of action for the Departments and for the several heads of bureaus.

Ibid., 3038 (remarks of Rep. Lawrence). See also ibid., 4490 (June 16, 1870) (remarks of Sen. Patterson) (noting the "absolute necessity of harmony in the legal business of the Government" and arguing that a benefit of having a department of justice would be that "the opinions given by the law officers of the Government will be a unit, will be in harmony with each other"); ibid., 3065–66 (April 28, 1870) (remarks of Rep. Lawrence).

    8. 16 Stat. 162, sec. 3.

    9. 118 *Congressional Record* 21,882, 21,882 (1972) (memorandum by Department of Justice regarding litigating authority).

    10. For a plaintive "recital of the vicissitudes and wanderings of the Department of Justice" prior to 1934, see Address by Attorney General Homer Cummings at the Dedication of the Department of Justice Building, October 25, 1934, quoted in Homer Cummings and Carl McFarland, *Federal Justice: Chapters in the History of Justice and the Federal Executive* (New York: Macmillan, 1937) (text accompanying plate between pages 488 and 489).

    11. Griffin Bell, "The Attorney General: The Federal Government's Chief Lawyer and Chief Litigator, or One Among Many?" *Fordham Law Review* 46 (1978): 1049, 1054.

    12. Cummings and McFarland, *Federal Justice*, p. 487.

    13. Wilson's Executive Order 2877 (1918) provided that:

All litigation in which the United States or any Department, executive bureau, agency or office thereof, are engaged shall be conducted under the supervision and control of the Department of Justice; and that any opinion or ruling by the Attorney General upon any question of law arising in any Department, executive bureau, agency or office shall be treated as binding upon all Departments, bureaus, agencies or offices therewith concerned.

Oddly, uncertainty reigns as to the present validity of this order. The consolidation of all *litigation* is redundant with and/or supplanted by later executive and statutory requirements. As to the binding effect of the attorney general's *opinions*, Professor Kmiec, who headed the Office of Legal Counsel (OLC) in the Bush administration, cites the order without any hesitation as to its continuing relevance. Douglas W. Kmiec, "OLC's Opinion Writing Function: The Legal Adhesive for a Unitary Executive," *Cardozo Law Review* 15 (1993): 337, 368–69. The more common understanding, however, is that Executive Order 2877 rested on a statute granting the president special wartime powers and expired soon after its issuance. See, for example, Clayton, *Politics of Justice*, p. 75 ("When the war ended, the statute and executive order were repealed, and centrifugal forces immediately reappeared."). As I discuss later, for all practical purposes opinions of the attorney general (including those from her delegee, the Office of Legal Counsel) do bind the agencies that request them. The uncertainty as to whether this is also true in theory can persist because, even under Executive Order 2877, agencies are not *required* to submit legal questions to the attorney general; as long as submission is voluntary, the question of whether the resulting advice is binding need never come to a head.

14. Baker, *Conflicting Loyalties*, p. 63.

15. Albert Langeluttig, *The Department of Justice of the United States* (Baltimore: Johns Hopkins University Press, 1927), p. 58.

16. *Annual Report of the Attorney General*, pp. 347–51.

17. Executive Order 6166 (June 10, 1933); reprinted at 5 U.S.C.A. 901 (1993) (note).

18. 28 U.S.C. 516 (1988) ("Except as otherwise authorized by law, the conduct of litigation in which the United States, an agency, or officer thereof is a party, or is interested, and securing evidence thereof, is reserved to the officers of the Department of Justice, under the direction of the Attorney General.").

19. The role of general counsels in the new agencies—in particular their constant battles with program staff and the Justice Department over the scope of the agency's authority—is described in Peter H. Irons, *The New Deal Lawyers* (Princeton, N.J.: Princeton University Press, 1982).

20. For the current version, see 28 U.S.C. 512 (1988) (department head "may require the opinion of the Attorney General on questions of law arising in the administration of his department").

21. United States Department of Justice, *Legal Activities 1993–94*, 3 (giving the total number of Justice Department attorneys as 7,894). This is almost exactly twice as many as in 1977. See *supra* note 1.

22. An agency may have additional lawyers outside its OGC. The Department of Transportation, for example, employs 620 attorneys, of whom only 60 are in the OGC. Telephone communication, Department of Transportation, March 21, 1994. These attorneys tend to work on more narrow and routine individual matters, not the questions concerning the scope of agency authority that highlight the lawyer's policy-making role.

23. For example, President Clinton's EPA administrator, Carol Browner, and general counsel, Jean Nelson, came to their posts as protégés of Vice-President Gore. Browner was Gore's legislative director from 1989 until 1991; Nelson came to the EPA from the Tennessee attorney general's office and served as chief of staff to Tipper Gore during the 1992 presidential campaign.

24. For a general summary of agency advice-giving to the public, and the argument that it ought to be more formal, see Burnele V. Powell, "Sinners, Supplicants, and Samaritans: Agency Advice Giving in Relation to Section 554(e) of the Administrative Procedure Act," *North Carolina Law Review* 63 (1985): 339.

25. Panel Discussion, "Law in the U.S. Foreign Relations Process: Opening the Channels," *Proceedings of the Eighty-third Annual Meeting of the American Society of International Law* (1990), p. 425 (remarks of Michael Cardozo).

26. 28 U.S.C. 516 (1988).

27. Clayton, *The Politics of Justice*, p. 200.

28. *See*, for example, Bell, "The Attorney General."

29. For a full description of the pros and cons of centralized litigation, see

Donald L. Horowitz, *The Jurocracy: Government Lawyers, Agency Programs, and Judicial Decisions* (Lexington, Mass.: D. C. Heath, 1977), pp. 128–39; Susan M. Olson, "Challenges to the Gatekeeper: The Debate over Federal Litigating Authority," *Judicature* 68 (1984): 70, 78–83. For the Department of Justices' position see *Congressional Record* 118: 21,882–85 (1972); Bell, "The Attorney General"; United States Department of Justice, Office of Legal Counsel, "The Attorney General's Role as Chief Litigator for the United States," *Opinions of the Office of Legal Counsel* 6 (1982): 47.

30. Executive Order 12,146, sec. 1-201 to 1-203.

31. Olson, "Challenges to the Gatekeeper," p. 77.

32. For a fuller account of the incidents described in this section, see Michael Herz, "Imposing Unified Executive Branch Statutory Interpretation," *Cardozo Law Review* 15 (1993): 219, from which the following draws.

33. Alan W. Eckert, "What You Need to Know About the New Clean Air Act; Operating Permits: The New Program Strategy," *EPA Journal* (January 1991): 38.

34. Letter from Rep. Henry Waxman to William Reilly, April 24, 1991, reprinted in U.S. Congress, House, *Clean Air Act Implementation (Part 1): Hearings Before the Subcommittee on Health and the Environment of the House Committee on Energy and Commerce*, 102nd Cong., 1st sess. (Washington, D.C.: Government Printing Office, 1991), pp. 208–9 [hereinafter cited as *House Oversight Hearings (Part 1)*].

35. House Subcommittee on Health and the Environment, "The Vice President's Initiative to Undermine the Clean Air Act" (May 1, 1991), pp. 1–2, reprinted in *House Oversight Hearings (Part 1)*, pp. 204–5.

36. The following gives the flavor:

> We have to ask you to uphold the law and you, particularly, Mr. Elliott, you are the lawyer—you are the lawyer that is there—you are the linchpin of this whole operation and you are the one that has to say: "Wait a minute, guys, as much as you don't like the law, as much as you want to give in to those industries that are pressing Mr. Quayle and have contributed to the Republican National Committee or whatever, as much as you might want to go along with them, you can't do it because the law says otherwise."

> [Y]ou are the General Counsel, and there are a lot of political pressures, obviously, in something as important as the Clean Air Act, but whatever the political pressures may be, the rule of law in this country states that those pressures cannot prevail if the law, passed by the Congress and signed by the President, states otherwise

> It seems to me that what we have are two issues. What is legal and what is not, and that is your job as the lawyer, but it seems to me you are also a partisan participant in supporting the policy of these regulations.

> [I]t is my firm belief, and I don't know if your role is to be policymaker—it may well be, but you also have the role to be a clearcut, honest lawyer, and that sometimes means saying to your client, no.

House Oversight Hearings (Part 1), 253–54, 279–81.

37. Ibid., p. 254.

38. Ibid., p. 255.

39. "De Minimis Exemption Dropped from Permit Rule; Public Comment Period Provided in Agency Draft," *Environment Reporter* 22 (February 14, 1992), p. 2363.

40. Rose Gutfield and Bob Davis, "EPA Resists Step in Drive to Deregulate," *Wall Street Journal* (February 4, 1992), p. A3.

41. EPA Rulemaking Docket A-90-33, Item No. IV-H-4.

42. An EPA official later testified that Stewart had "concerns about public participation and that it be . . . on a 'retail basis.' " U.S. Congress, House, *Clean Air Act Implementation (Part 2): Hearings Before the Subcommittee on Health and the Environment of the House Committee on Energy and Commerce*, 102nd Cong., 1st sess. (Washington, D.C.: Government Printing Office, 1991–1993), p. 466 (testimony of John Beale) [hereinafter cited as *House Oversight Hearings (Part 2)*].

43. "EPA Unable to Proceed with CAA Permit Without DOJ Legal Guidance," *Inside EPA* (May 22, 1992), p. 2; *House Oversight Hearings (Part 2)*, p. 467 (testimony of William Rosenberg, EPA Assistant Administrator).

44. "EPA, White House CAA 'Minor Permit Amendment' Talks Halt as DOJ Reviews Issue," *Inside EPA* (November 22, 1991), p. 7.

45. Memorandum from Barry M. Hartman, Acting Assistant Attorney Gen., to William K. Reilly, EPA Administrator (May 27, 1992), p. 1, n.1, reprinted in *Environment Reporter* 23 (June 5, 1992), p. 624.

46. "White House, EPA Continue to Work to Reach Agreement on Air Permit Rule," *Environment Reporter* 22 (December 27, 1991): p. 2172.

47. Ibid.

48. *House Oversight Hearings (Part 2)*, p. 534.

49. *House Oversight Hearings (Part 2)*.

50. "Reilly, White House Competitiveness Council Seek Meeting on Disputed Emission Permit Rule," *Environment Reporter* 22 (April 10, 1992): 2691; "Quayle Council, EPA to Review Justice Opinion of Air Permit Rule in Dispute," *BNA Environmental Law Update* (April 7, 1992).

51. "White House Rejects Public Review for CAA Permits, Creating Standoffs with EPA," *Inside EPA* (April 10, 1992), pp. 1, 13.

52. The following report is typical:

The council does not have a written opinion from Justice—the department reportedly has been reluctant to step into the controversy by putting its analysis on paper—but the council hopes it can go over the information it has with EPA and move discussions forward, the official added. Knowing that the Justice Department is reluctant to provide a written opinion, council staff members hope they will be able to appease EPA without it, but if, as expected, the agency presses for a legal analysis in writing, the council will attempt to obtain it, according to the White House official.

"Quayle Council, EPA to Review Justice Opinion."

53. Those present were Flanagan, Boyden Gray, Samuel Skinner, OMB Director Richard Darman, Michael Boskin, Commerce Secretary Barbara Franklin, CEQ chair Michael Deland, and Reilly. "President to Resolve EPA, White House Deadlock over CAA Permit Reg This Week," *Inside EPA* (May 1, 1992), pp. 3–4.

54. The opinion is reprinted at *Environment Reporter* 15 (June 5, 1992). At the time he produced the opinion, Hartman had already announced his resignation, which took place on June 5.

The most cynical view of the Justice Department's role in the controversy is that the decision to deny public scrutiny of minor permit changes was a purely political decision, with the department obligingly producing an ex post facto legal opinion to legitimate a decision that had already been made on nonlegal grounds. First, the president made his decision *before* the department produced the formal opinion concluding that the statute allowed it. Second, the May 27 opinion itself has a tone of struggling to find an ambiguity in the statute that would allow it to be read either way. Third, the department itself seemed to change its position over the course of the dispute. Finally, one cannot help wondering whether the environment division was given the opinion because it could be trusted to come out with the correct answer more than could the OLC. After all, the environment division consists of litigators, whose job is to defend client agencies in court. Although it, too, has a client, the OLC is a more removed, "judicial" type of law office It does not know the answer in advance the way a litigator does. In this case, the environment division may have perceived its client as being the White House or the Competitiveness Council rather than the agency. If this was its understanding, it simply performed its usual task of making the argument in favor of a predetermined position, ensuring only that it cleared a minimum threshold of plausible legal defensibility.

I think this characterization of the Department of Justice opinion as pure post-hoc rationalization severely overstates the case. While the formal opinion came after President Bush's decision, it was consistent with what everyone understood the department's position to have been since at least early January 1992. The opinion itself was important for the EPA and for later defense of the rule in court; the president would not have read it even if it were available.

Nonetheless, I suspect that politics had a good deal to do with the assignment of the opinion to the environment division, a litigating arm of the department, rather than to the OLC, which normally has the counseling function and which everyone assumed would produce the opinion. Perhaps the White House or the attorney general did think that the division would more reliably produce the desired answer. But the more important political factor was, I think, something else: concern over who should take the heat for what was bound to be an unpopular opinion. At the time both the OLC and the environment division had acting heads. Hartman, who wrote the memo, was never nominated to the post; he had announced his resignation on May 1 and left the department about a week after issuing the opinion. In contrast, the acting head of OLC was Timothy Flanagan. Flanagan assumed that responsibility in October 1991; it was understood that he would be nominated for the post, and he was nominated on April 9, 1992. The signals from the Hill (and not only from the House) with regard to the permit rule were extraordinarily loud and clear. If the permit rule opinion had gone out over Flanagan's name, his confirmation would surely have been a struggle; it might well have been derailed altogether. In any event, it was certainly going to be easier for a departing Justice Department officer to take the heat than one whose nomination was before the Senate.

One way to have ensured Flanagan's confirmation would have been to arrange for him to produce an opinion foreclosing the policy pursued by the Competitiveness Council. By doing so, Flanagan would have dazzled the (Democrat-dominated) Congress with his legal acumen and his integrity simultaneously. For the White House, however, that was an excessive and unnecessary price to pay; it sufficed to keep Flanagan out of the fray. On this account, the frequently noted "Justice Department reluctance" to issue an opinion was really *OLC* reluctance, ultimately resolved by having the environment division issue the opinion. On the OLC's occasional desire to delay or avoid controversial opinions, even when the confirmation of its head is not on the line, see John O. McGinnis, "Models of the Opinion Function of the Attorney General: A Normative, Descriptive, and Historical Prolegomenon," *Cardozo Law Review* 15 (1993): 375, 427.

55. Fed. Reg. 57 (1992), p. 32,250.

56. On the increasing specificity of regulatory statutes, see Michael Herz, "Judicial Textualism Meets Congressional Micromanagement: A Potential Collision in Clean Air Act Interpretation,'" *Harvard Environmental Law Review* 16 (1992): 175, 175–82. For (in my view, excessively) negative assessments of judicial intervention in agency decision-making, see Jeremy Rabkin, *Judicial Compulsions: How Public Law Distorts Public Policy* (New York: Basic Books, 1989); R. Shep Melnick, *Regulation and the Courts: The Case of the Clean Air Act* (Washington, D.C.: Brookings Institution, 1983).

57. As I discuss subsequently, Elliott's memorandum did just that for Reilly and Rosenberg. Similarly, the White House looked to the Justice Department for such a memo. Indeed, it is possible that the White House wanted the department to say that the act precluded public scrutiny for minor permit modifications and had to settle for an opinion concluding that the act left the matter to the agency's discretion. See "White House, Competitiveness Council to Craft Options for CAA Permit Rule," *Inside EPA* (April 3, 1992), p. 8 (quoting an administration source as saying that the council was having difficulty generating support at the Justice Department for its legal position, because "DOJ found there is no legal justification" for denying public notice and comment on all permit revisions).

58. Michael E. Abramowitz, "Bureaucrats and Lawyers: Myths and Realities," *Bureaucrat* 2 (1973): 256, 257–58. Abramowitz (who is himself a lawyer) accuses lawyers of too often hiding behind nonexistent legal requirements. He subdivides the "Why-you-can'ts" into those who are merely legally cautious and those who package a policy disagreement as a legal conclusion.

59. J. W. Hirzy, "The Other Voice from EPA: The Role of the Headquarters Professionals' Union," *Environmental Law Reporter* 20 (1990): 10,057 (emphasis in original).

60. Ibid.

61. Thomas O. McGarity, "The Internal Structure of EPA Rulemaking," *Law and Contemporary Problems* 54 (1991): 78 (Table 1).

62. Ibid., p. 82.

63. James Q. Wilson, *Bureaucracy: What Government Agencies Do and Why They Do It* (New York: Basic Books, 1989), p. 284.

64. Bell, "The Attorney General," p. 1050.

65. *Congressional Globe*, 41st Cong., 2d sess. (1870), p. 3036. Similarly, a recent commission studying the role of the legal adviser to the Department of State noted "the perception—some would say widely shared—that legal advisers consider it their role to support and justify Administration policies, and that, in consequence, the legal opinions cannot be accepted as 'correct' statements of the law in at least some controversial cases." Joint Committee Established by the American Society of International Law and the American Branch of the International Law Association, "The Role of the Legal Adviser of the Department of State," *American Journal of International Law* 85 (1991): 358, 359.

One response to the complaint that agency lawyers lack sufficient independence is that the attorney general is no less prone to provide the sought-after answer—just for a different client. This, too, was offered in the 1870 debates:

> Does the gentleman think it peculiar to this country for a law officer to give an opinion to sustain the attitude of his superior? Has it not been done more than once in the office of the Attorney General of the United States?
>
> The gentleman will understand the idea I had in my mind, when I remind him of the anecdote of a former President who sent word to his Attorney General that if he could not find law for a particular policy he [the President] would find an Attorney General who could find a law for it.

Congressional Globe, 41st Cong., 2d sess. (1870), p. 3036 (remarks of Rep. Maynard). Maynard is referring to a famous (though likely apocryphal) story of political pressure on the attorney general. The president in question was Andrew Jackson, whose attorney general had expressed some doubt as to the president's authority to designate certain banks as repositories for United States funds. The usual version gives Jackson's statement as: "Sir, you must find a law authorizing the act or I will appoint an Attorney General who will." See, among many other sources, Luther A. Huston et al., *Roles of the Attorney General of the United States* (Washington, D.C.: American Enterprise Institute, 1968), p. 51.

66. 28 U.S.C. 512 (1988). This provision dates back to the Judiciary Act of 1789. Notice that only the head of the agency, not the general counsel, can ask the attorney general for an opinion.

67. Langeluttig, *The Department of Justice of the United States*, p. 147.

68. Nelson Lund, "Rational Choice in the Office of Legal Counsel," *Cardozo Law Review* 15 (1993): 489.

69. *House Oversight Hearings (Part 1)*, p. 254 (testimony of E. Donald Elliott, EPA general counsel).

70. In 1991, OLC gave 625 opinions to outside agencies, of which a quarter involved interagency disputes. McGinnis, "Models of the Opinion Function of the Attorney General," p. 423. That is a huge output for an office of two dozen lawyers, but it resolves only a tiny fraction of the legal issues confronting the federal government.

71. United States Office of Personnel Management, *The Complete General Counsel* (1981), p. 41.

72. See generally Michael Herz, "United States v. United States: When Can the Federal Government Sue Itself?" *William & Mary Law Review* 32 (1991): 893.

73. On the process of "negotiation" between the OLC and its client agencies, see Lund, "Rational Choice," pp. 494–95.

74. See supra, text accompanying note 38.

75. 467 U.S. 837 (1984).

76. Ibid., pp. 865–66.

77. Horowitz, *The Jurocracy*, p. 14; see also ibid., pp. 128–29.

78. Ronald M. Levin, "Identifying Questions of Law in Administrative Law," *Georgetown Law Review* 74 (1985): 43.

79. See *United States v. Stauffer Chemical Corp.,* 464 U.S. 165, 177 (1984) (Justice White, concurring).

80. 487 U.S. 654 (1988).

81. In her strikingly self-serving but probably not outright dishonest memoirs, Anne Burford describes how she and her chief of staff were willing to hand over whatever the committees sought. She displays deep bitterness that Robert Perry, then EPA's general counsel, was willing to withhold documents because the Department of Justice wanted him to, lamenting at one point that "it was becoming obvious that Perry, *my* General Counsel, was working more for the Justice Department than for me." Anne M. Burford and John Greenya, *Are You Tough Enough?: An Insider's View of Washington Politics* (New York: McGraw-Hill, 1986), p. 154. Nonetheless, even in Burford's account, Perry remained a reluctant participant in the Justice Department's strategy to pursue a test case. See, for example, ibid., p. 211.

For other accounts of this battle, also indicating the Justice Department's much greater determination to keep documents from Congress, see Clayton, *The Politics of Justice*, pp. 205–9; Peter M. Shane, "Legal Disagreement and Negotiation in a Government of Laws: The Case of Executive Privilege Claims Against Congress," *Minnesota Law Review* 71 (1987): 461.

82. *House Hearings (Part II)*, p. 474.

83. Ibid., pp. 482–83.

84. For the argument that the same dynamic underlies the failure to create a department of justice at all until 1870 and the highly decentralized legal arrangements in the early years of the Republic, see Lawrence Lessig, "Readings by Our Unitary Executive," *Cardozo Law Review* 15 (1993): 175, 192–99.

85. See Horowitz, *The Jurocracy*, pp. 114–16 (describing the Justice Depart-

ment's efforts to consolidate the counseling function with regard to Freedom of Information Act issues).

86. See generally *Opinions of the Office of Legal Counsel* 4a (1980): 69–114. This entire volume is devoted to OLC opinions arising out of the Iranian hostage crisis.

7

TOWARD AN UNDERSTANDING OF LEGAL POLICY-MAKING AT INDEPENDENT AGENCIES

NEAL DEVINS

Cases titled *Commodities Future Trading Commission v. Securities and Exchange Commission, U.S. Postal Service v. U.S. Postal Rate Commission,* or *U.S. v. Interstate Commerce Commission* make no sense to those who believe that the federal government should stake out unitary positions on issues of national concern. The design of the federal government, however, presupposes that different governmental interests will oppose each other in court. This state of affairs is a by-product of statutory grants of litigating authority to independent agencies—multimember governmental entities whose heads can only be dismissed "for cause" and not for failing to comply with presidential priorities. Unlike the federal legal policy-making of executive departments and agencies—where "the attorney's obligation is most reasonably seen as running to the executive branch as a whole and to the President as its head"[1]—independent agency attorneys are not bound to serve the White House. Instead, staff at independent agencies are obligated to advance whatever conception of the "public interest" garners majority support among the agency's heads.

Whether this disunity in federal legal policy-making is sensible is quite another matter. This chapter will explore that question by examining both the structure of legislative grants of litigation authority to independent agencies and the ways in which independent agencies use their litigation authority to fend off encroachments by other entities of the executive and legislative branches. This issue is critically important to the study of federal legal policy-making. One-third of all federal regulation emanates from independent agencies and commissions, including regulation of (among other areas) banking, securities, commodities, communications, antitrust, and labor.

POLITICS AND LEGAL POLICY-MAKING AT INDEPENDENT AGENCIES

The starting point of analysis is to sort out the structure and purposes of legal policy-making undertaken by independent agencies. This analysis, as will be shown, reveals little. Independent agency status seems to be established more as an accident of birth than as a purposeful decision by the Congress. Along the same lines, the scope (and indeed, the very existence) of independent litigation authority seems more haphazard than purposeful.

The circumstances surrounding the establishment of the Interstate Commerce Commission (ICC), the first independent agency, provides a useful point of departure. At first, the ICC—although governed by a board whose members served fixed terms—was to be housed within the Interior Department, under the supervision of the Secretary of the Interior. The precise relationship of the ICC to either the Congress or the president simply was not contemplated. "In fact," as the Senate Committee on Governmental Affairs recognized some years later, "there was an all but complete absence of discussion of the essential character of what was being created."[2] The ICC's 1887 design was dramatically altered in 1889. Without hearings or legislative debate, Congress dislodged the agency from the Interior Department and granted it independent authority over its own budget, personnel, and management. This dramatic transformation turned on political calculation, not some vision of the ideal structure of government. In 1888, Benjamin Harrison, a Republican railroad lawyer, was elected president. 'Democratic sponsors of the original legislation," again according to the Governmental Affairs Committee report, "feared Harrison's impact on the fledgling agency, subordinate as it would be to one of the new President's cabinet officers."[3]

Independence from presidential control thus appears to have been the original justification for creating independent agencies. The flip side of this coin is the immemorial desire of Congress to enhance its own influence by limiting presidential authority. The "arm of Congress" justification for independent agencies was stated succinctly by Senator Philip Hart (a Michigan Democrat) in 1973: "The commissions, if I may risk oversimplification, are ours. We have concluded that certain regulatory activities have gotten to a point where, on a day-to-day basis, Congress itself is inept and ill-equipped to make decisions. So we create a commission."[4] A third justification for the establishment of independent agencies is to transfer regulatory authority over complex and technical matters away from politicians and to "experts."

No coherent pattern explains Congress's decisions to locate some cessions of government authority within the executive and others with an independent agency, however.[5] Subject matter seems irrelevant, since independent agencies and executive agencies share responsibility over antitrust (Federal Trade Commission [FTC] and Justice Department), banking (Federal Reserve Board and Comptroller of the Currency), employment (Equal Employment Opportunity Commission [EEOC] and Justice Department), worker safety (Occupational Safety and Health Review Commission and Occupational Safety and Health Review Administration), and so on. The scope of operations, too, seems irrelevant. Independent agencies engage in the business of promulgating regulations, implementing those rules, and adjudicating enforcement actions; but executive agencies and departments—including the Environmental Protection Agency, the Food and Drug Administration, and the Department of Labor—perform similar functions. Congress's choice of making an agency independent or of locating it within the executive branch, finally, is rarely thought out. "Random selection" is the term Paul Verkuil uses[6]; Peter Strauss is more generous but no less critical, describing the diversity of agency forms as "characteristic of our pragmatic ways with government, reflecting the circumstances of the particular regulatory regime, the temper of presidential/congressional relations at the time, or the perceived success or failure of an existing agency performing like functions, more than any grand scheme of government."[7]

The absence of "any grand scheme of government" underlying Congress's choice to establish independent agencies is tellingly revealed in the roles and functions of the legal counsel's office in various independent agencies. Rather than following some discernable pattern, the general counsel's role varies tremendously from agency to agency. In some instances, the general counsel plays a pivotal role in defining agency policy-making; in others, the general counsel is more of a bit player. Needless to say, a broad range of political and structural factors explains this variation.

The most significant factor is the degree of importance that litigation has in agency policy-making. At the EEOC, for example, the principal forum for agency policy-making is the courts, and the general counsel's role is therefore pivotal. In contrast, the general counsel plays a key but less pronounced role at agencies such as the U.S. Postal Service, where litigation is a less central source of agency decision-making.

The relationship of the general counsel to the independent agency heads, especially the chair, also plays a prominent role in determining the general counsel's influence. The meshing or clashing of personalities is one factor here. The absence or presence of competing legal advisers is significant as well. At a small agency, such as the U.S. Civil Rights Commission, where the chair and the chief of staff have limited personal staffs, the general counsel and her cadre of attorneys may find themselves at the center of policy disputes. Where the personal staffs are larger, the need for general counsel advice is less acute and the impact of that advice is more diffuse. Another relevant factor is the process by which the general counsel is selected. When the general counsel is hand-picked by the agency head, as is the case at the FCC, the office typically plays a more direct role in shaping agency decision-making (especially where the chair is strong). In contrast, at agencies such as the EEOC, where the general counsel is appointed by the president to serve a set term, the general counsel's office may find itself isolated from the chair (although his or her relations with commissioners not allied with the chair may be somewhat stronger).

The most influential structural factor in defining legal policy-making at independent agencies does not hinge on the relationship between the general counsel and agency heads at all. Instead, the defining issue of legal policy-making is the relationship between independent agency counsel and Department of Justice officials. Where agency counsel are authorized to represent their own interests in court, independent agencies define both their substantive policy and their litigation strategy. When the attorney general controls independent agency representation, however, legal policy-making at the agency is defined by executive branch practices and preferences.

A Primer on Independent Litigating Authority

The absence of "any grand scheme of government" is also revealed in Congress's varied treatment of the litigation authority accorded to independent agencies. Government litigation, for the most part, is managed by the attorney general, not by the heads of agencies and departments. When Congress established the Department of Justice in 1870, it sought to secure "a unity of decision, a unity of jurisprudence . . . in the executive law of the United States."[8] The authorizing legislation establishing the Justice Department set the stage for massive centralization of government litigation, specifying that "[e]xcept as otherwise authorized by law, the conduct of [government] litigation . . . is reserved to officers of the Department of Justice, under the direction of the Attorney General."[9] Nevertheless, the initial caveat of the legislation ("[e]xcept as otherwise authorized by law") provided enough room for agencies to keep the debate over the appropriate level of Department of Justice control alive. Indeed, Congress's repeated exercise of its power to make exceptions to

Department of Justice control has substantially reduced the attorney general's role as chief litigator for the United States. That Congress would chose to make such exceptions should come as no surprise. When Department of Justice centralization frustrates legislative desires, Congress may protect its prerogatives by transferring litigation authority to an agency or department that is more likely to endorse congressional preferences.

Independent agencies would seem to be likely recipients of legislative grants of independent litigation authority. After all, the enhancement of legislative power and the diminution of presidential authority help explain the creation of independent agencies in the first place. Moreover, the "for cause" limitation on the president's removal authority presumably reflects Congress's intent that independent agency heads be able to reach policy decisions contrary to the White House's wishes without fear of dismissal. Since court action is a critical component of an agency's regulatory agenda, litigation authority would seem to constitute an essential attribute of agency independence. To put this point more bluntly: without independent litigation authority, the attorney general would be empowered to define legal policy-making for these entities and could thereby nullify much of their functional independence.

Congress is well aware of the importance of litigation authority to independent agencies and typically specifies some agency control over litigation. The reach and limits of this control, however, are extraordinarily varied. In some instances, there is no independent litigation authority.[10] This is the case with the National Transportation Safety Board, the Federal Reserve System, and others; it used to be the case with the FTC and the now-defunct Civil Aeronautics Board. In other instances, agency authority—sometimes depending on the solicitor general's refusal to participate, and other times irrespective of the solicitor general's action—extends up to and includes Supreme Court litigation. The Federal Election Commission, the FTC, the ICC, and (perhaps) the National Labor Relations Board, the Postal Service, and the Tennessee Valley Authority have such power. In most cases, there is some mixture of dependence and independence. Sometimes, as is the case with the Securities and Exchange Commission (SEC), the EEOC, and the Federal Energy Regulatory Commission, independent litigating authority extends to the federal courts of appeal. In other instances, as is the case (sort of) with the Consumer Product Safety Commission, independent litigating authority extends only to district court actions. In yet other instances, as is the case with the Nuclear Regulatory Commission and the Commodities Future Trading Commission (sort of), independent litigating authority is limited to appellate litigation. Finally, several agencies have arrangements that are so complex that they defy description. The Federal Communications

Commission (FCC) is one of these. In actions launched in district court (including suits to enforce commission orders), the Department of Justice has plenary responsibility over the matter. Appeals of radio and television licensing decisions are handled by the commission itself before courts of appeal, but by the solicitor general before the Supreme Court. Appeals of other FCC decisions are handled by the commission before the courts of appeal and—in some instances—before the Supreme Court up to the filing of a certiorari petition.

The fragmentary quality of independent agency litigating authority is typical, not exceptional. Independent agencies were formed at different times and by different groups of interests. Relatedly, the authorizing committees within Congress that helped create and currently oversee independent agencies are driven by substantive issues, not structural arrangements.

Take the case of the FTC. Prior to 1973, the Department of Justice represented the FTC on injunctive and mandamus proceedings, civil penalty suits, and—through the solicitor general—all Supreme Court litigation. Commission attorneys handled judicial review and enforcement proceedings. This division of responsibility proved problematic for the FTC, however. The antitrist division of the Department of Justice sometimes disagreed with FTC antitrust policy-making. Consequently, on matters referred by the FTC to the Department of Justice, significant delays in filing, unfavorable settlements, and refusals to file cases at all occurred with some regularity.[11]

The Department of Justice occasionally took issue with FTC positions in court, as well. In the 1968 *Federal Trade Commission v. Guigon* decision, for instance, the Justice Department argued that the FTC lacked statutory authority to enforce its own subpoenas and possibly lacked the power to appear in court at all.[12] The department's desire to protect its litigating authority at the expense of the FTC is certainly understandable. Eyebrows were raised, however, when—after the department's position prevailed before a federal appeals court—Solicitor General Erwin Griswold refused to file a certiorari petition for the FTC on the ground that "[w]hatever may be the merits of the Commission's position, I do not believe that the issue is of sufficient general importance to warrant requesting the Supreme Court to review it."[13] By not seeking certiorari, of course, the solicitor general shielded a Department of Justice victory from FTC attack. An earlier case that caused great distress at the FTC was *St. Regis Paper Co. v. United States,* a 1961 Supreme Court decision.[14] Here, the antitrust division agreed with the FTC's position that the FTC's interest in investigating possible antitrust violations outweighed confidentiality claims made by a company seeking to withhold reports filed with the Census Bureau. But the solicitor general sided with the Census

Bureau and the Bureau of the Budget, both of which opposed the FTC. In a remarkable and much criticized brief, rather than "burden the Court with briefs from different agencies," Solicitor General Archibald Cox, "attempt[ed]" . . . to set forth the competing arguments as effectively and objectively as possible."[15] Cox, however, disagreed with the FTC. Accordingly, the bulk of his brief, "while fully recognizing the delicate balance of opposing interests," explained why the FTC position was in error.

Conflicts between the FTC and the Department of Justice were finally settled by Congress, to the benefit of the FTC. In 1973 and again in 1975, Congress enacted legislation ensuring that the FTC could exercise independent litigating authority in enforcement actions, including the power to represent itself before the Supreme Court when the solicitor general would not represent the agency.[16] Tensions between the FTC and the Justice Department, exacerbated by the antitrust division's frontal (and apparently successful) attack on FTC litigating authority in *Guigon* and by the solicitor general's questionable advocacy in *Guigon, St. Regis,* and other cases, help explain this political response. That tension, however, is only a small part of the story. The House Committee on Interstate and Foreign Commerce concluded in 1974 that the Justice Department's concern that "the government maintains consistent positions on matters of common interest to all government agencies" outweighed the FTC's claim that "its litigation is conducted in the manner best calculated to achieve the agency's enforcement goals." The decision to transfer litigation authority to the FTC, therefore, cannot simply be tied to Congress's displeasure with the Justice Department's representation of FTC interests.

The ascendancy of independent FTC litigating authority, instead, is a by-product of political circumstances unique to a particular historical moment. First, White House opposition to FTC independent litigating authority was unusually restrained in both 1973 and 1975. In 1973, President Nixon was willing to concede litigating authority to the FTC in order to ensure congressional enactment of a bill establishing the Trans-Alaska Pipeline. In 1975, the specter of Watergate limited President Ford's ability to demand centralization of government litigation before the Supreme Court. Second (and relatedly), Congress's willingness to pursue decentralization of government litigating authority was part of a larger Watergate-era attempt to limit the "imperial presidency." At roughly the same time, Congress limited White House authority in fiscal policy through the 1974 Budget Act; considered making the Department of Justice an independent agency; and considered legislation to insulate independent agencies further from executive influence. Third, Congress was set to act on FTC-related litigation in both 1973 and 1975, regardless of the question of independent litigating authority. The costs to the FTC of raising the issue and to the Congress of adding it to much larger statutory reform efforts were therefore low. Fourth, after the Justice Department's successful attack on FTC litigating authority in *Guigon,* the FTC's independence was plainly at risk. These high stakes spurred legislative action in 1973. Fifth, public support for a powerful, independent FTC was strong during the mid-1970s' "age of consumerism."

This confluence of circumstances was clearly unique to the FTC. For instance, in 1973, Congress removed from proposed Security and Exchange Act amendments language that would have granted the SEC independent litigating authority before the Supreme Court. This refusal to grant the same type of litigating authority to the SEC that was extended to the FTC two years later is another by-product of political circumstance. Unlike the FTC, whose very independence was threatened by Department of Justice dominion over *all litigation,* the SEC already possessed independent litigating authority in all courts except the Supreme Court. With regard to its interests before the Supreme Court, moreover, the SEC was generally satisfied with the solicitor general's advocacy. In fact, when Congress held hearings on this question, former SEC Chair William Cary favored solicitor general control of the certiorari decision, and then-current SEC Commissioner Philip Loomis felt that the proposed amendment was of limited value because the solicitor general "has generally been sympathetic to the SEC" and has "been of value in obtaining consideration of our cases by the Supreme Court and in presenting cases to that Court."[17] The SEC presented a less convincing case to Congress for other reasons, too. Not only was the SEC's claim weak, but Solicitor General Erwin Griswold launched a strong counterclaim. Griswold, who served in both the Johnson and the Nixon administrations, invoked the prestige of both his office and himself in arguing that the proposed amendment challenged the integrity of the solicitor general's office. In contrast, in 1975, Solicitor General Robert Bork had to live down his role in the dismissal of special prosecutor (and one time solicitor general) Archibald Cox in the "Saturday Night Massacre" and so could not launch a comparable counterattack against FTC efforts.

Differences between the FTC and SEC experiences reveal the obvious. Specific political pressures and circumstances, not a unified vision of independent litigating authority, define the existence, scope, and sweep of legislative exceptions to Department of Justice control of government litigation. Before lower federal courts, these exceptions checker the landscape.

The seemingly random construction that typifies the present haphazard structure is likely to continue. Each agency serves a distinct set of constituencies, and these divergent interests are highly unlikely to agree to any joint effort to create uniform structural arrangements. Nonetheless the consequences of the existing patchwork structure of independent litigating authority are profound to federal legal policy-making. Congress's failure to subscribe to a "grand theory of government" places independent agency counsels in a no-man's land. While technically free to reach conclusions that reflect neither executive nor legislative branch preferences, the legal policy-making of independent agencies is subject to extraordinary political pressures from these two branches. Under the "arm of Congress" theory, congressional oversight committees may demand that independent agencies' legal policy-making match legislative preferences. Executive branch pressure is even more pervasive. When the Justice Department is authorized to represent the agency, executive branch interests—although sometimes held in check—may well overwhelm and replace independent agency interests, insofar as the two diverge. Nor do grants of litigating authority free independent agencies from executive branch attacks.

The uncertain status of independent agencies invites such challenges. Consequently, the process of federal legal policy-making at independent agencies is often a story of how independent agency concerns are balanced with competing legislative and executive branch preferences. These stories are idiosyncratic, hinging on the statutory specification of independent litigation authority and on other structural provisions, as well as on the expectations of independent agency counsel, Justice Department officials, and legislative overseers. A comparative analysis of the FCC and of the EEOC speaks to the ways in which structural provisions and political will separately contribute to legal policy-making by independent agencies.

CASE STUDIES

The experiences of the EEOC and of the FCC in wresting control over litigation from the Department of Justice represent two sides of the same coin. In both cases, the results turned as much on political will as on structural provisions. The EEOC undermined its own independence by giving in to White House pressures to cede complete control over state and local employment discrimination cases to the Department of Justice. In sharp contrast, the Department of Justice abandoned control over FCC litigation, to accommodate the president's recently named appointees and perhaps the president himself. In both instances, moreover, Congress played a critical role. With regard to the EEOC, Congress seemed indifferent to the White House's efforts. But in the case of the FCC, oversight committee pressures figured prominently in White House, Department of Justice, and agency calculations.

The EEOC

EEOC decision-making, like that of other independent agencies, is insulated from direct White House control. Each of its five commissioners serves a five-year term and presumably can only be removed for cause. Partisan controls are further limited by the requirement that no more than three commissioners may be of the same political party. This independence figures prominently in the agency's litigation authority: the EEOC has independent litigating authority before lower federal courts to initiate specified categories of employment discrimination lawsuits. EEOC litigation authority is further insulated from day-to-day executive control because the EEOC general counsel (a presidential appointee) serves a fixed four-year term.

The structural independence of the EEOC is far from complete. For one thing, the EEOC is technically located within the executive branch. More significantly, unlike independent regulatory agencies that possess quasi-adjudicatory and quasi-legislative authority, EEOC authority is exclusively executive. For the most part, the EEOC interprets various employment discrimination statutes and puts that interpretation into effect through litigation. The nexus between the EEOC and the executive branch is heightened further by an intermingling of functions both at the Department of Justice and at the commission.

Through a Carter administration reorganization, the EEOC took charge of several employment discrimination areas that had previously been the responsibility of executive departments and agencies. The EEOC was also dubbed the "lead agency" in employment discrimination matters and was authorized to coordinate the enforcement strategies of eighteen governmental agencies with Title VII enforcement power. Direct EEOC involvement with the executive is also a by-product of separate Department of Justice authority to enforce and interpret employment discrimination laws. Suits against state and local governments are the exclusive province of the department's civil rights division. The civil division—which represents the federal government when it is sued in employment discrimination matters—also has separate authority to interpret employment discrimination laws. Finally, at the Supreme Court level, all employment discrimination litigation is handled by the solicitor general. Since three separate offices within the Justice Department litigate in employment discrimination cases, the department has a very strong interest in controlling the government's voice with regard to this type of litigation. Needless to say, the likelihood of serious conflict between the Justice Department and the commission is also great. Clearly, this combination of concurrent authority was combustible; and the explosion occurred during the Reagan administration.

The triggering event was an amicus brief supporting a municipal policy of race-conscious affirmative action that the EEOC intended to file before a federal appeals court in *Williams v. City of New Orleans*.[18] The EEOC draft brief flatly contradicted an amicus brief that the Department of Justice's civil rights division had already filed in the case.[19] Indeed, the EEOC characterized as "deplorable" the failure of the Justice Department to have consulted the EEOC before filing its amicus brief. Rather than seeing the expression of conflicting views to be—as the EEOC put it—of "considerable public benefit," the Justice Department saw the EEOC brief as an outrageous challenge to the civil rights division's exclusive authority to manage employment discrimination lawsuits involving state and local government. In the civil rights division's view, the government must speak as one voice in cases involving state and local governments— and that voice belongs to the civil rights division. To prove its point, the civil rights division asserted that it would challenge in court the EEOC's right to file its amicus brief.

The civil rights division's claim contradicts the structural constraints that protect EEOC autonomy. Although the civil rights division has exclusive authority to initiate state and local cases, there are no statutory limits on the EEOC's independent authority to participate in lower court employment discrimination cases. And the structural limits on executive control encourage the EEOC to defend its interest in independently interpreting employment discrimination laws by participating in state and local cases. For the EEOC, *Williams* was not simply a state or local case. The Justice Department's position in *Williams,* if accepted, would have undermined the EEOC's private sector litigation strategy, including several EEOC-initiated private sector consent decrees. The EEOC understood the impact of *Williams* on its litigation strategy; the commission also recognized that the Justice Department's disregard of the EEOC's role "as the chief interpreter of Title VII" represented "a major . . . change in the government's civil rights policy."[20]

The EEOC's strong interest in *Williams,* buoyed by structural constraints on executive authority, suggested that the EEOC would stand firm in the face of the civil rights division's challenge and file its amicus brief. In the end, however, the EEOC capitulated to the Justice Department's power play. The pivotal event was a White House meeting between EEOC Chair Clarence Thomas and EEOC General Counsel David Slate with White House Counsel Ed Meese, Attorney General William French Smith, and civil rights division head William Bradford Reynolds. The factors that led to the EEOC's withdrawal in *Williams* are complex. The commission's stated reason was that the "public interest" was not served by the presentation of "conflicting [governmental] views on a legal issue involving a city government where the Justice Department has sole enforcement litigation responsibility."[21] This explanation, of course, flatly contradicts the EEOC's earlier assertion that the presentation of its conflicting views would be of "considerable public benefit." A more likely explanation is that the White House meeting convinced the EEOC that it would be politically unwise to do battle with the Justice Department. During the *Williams* controversy, the Justice Department's Office of Legal Counsel (OLC) issued an opinion in support of the civil rights division. This opinion went beyond the state and local authority issue to assert that, by transferring authority from the Department of Labor and the Civil Service Commission to the EEOC, the Carter administration's reorganization had de facto transformed the EEOC into an executive agency "subject to the supervision and control of the President." That the EEOC had earlier participated in public sector cases did not matter. The OLC viewed such appearances as having "been made with the approval of the attorney general whether implicit or explicit."[22]

The OLC opinion suggested that the Justice Department was prepared to use *Williams* as a vehicle to end EEOC independence in both public and private sector litigation. EEOC Chair Thomas accepted this line of argument, demurely commenting that "[t]his case has clarified our standing": "[i]t points out to Congress the chink in our armor . . . [that] we are in the executive branch which has its own opinions."[23] This concession is extraordinary. EEOC private sector litigation authority was not before the court in *Williams*. But rather than risk an adverse court ruling on its public sector authority, the EEOC effectively embraced defeat by failing to create the opportunity for a favorable court ruling. Ironically, the appellate court in *Williams* repeatedly referred to the EEOC's draft brief, a leaked copy of which had been submitted to the court through an amicus brief by the Center for National Policy Review.

The EEOC put up a remarkably feeble fight in *Williams*. It is difficult to know whether the Justice Department frightened the commission with its legal arguments or whether it convinced EEOC appointees that their political futures hinged on acquiescence to the Justice Department's position. In any event, the EEOC did not invoke on its behalf supposedly empowering structural constraints on executive authority. Instead, the interaction of various political players, their expectations, and their willingness to assert power provides insight into why the *Williams* scenario played out as it did.

The EEOC not only lost the battle over *Williams;* it lost a much larger battle with the Justice Department. In the wake of *Williams,* the department has subsumed the EEOC into the executive branch. Rather than serving as lead agency, the EEOC is now viewed by the department as its "whipping boy." For example, the solicitor general refuses to recognize the EEOC as an independent agency. While the EEOC may seek to persuade the solicitor general of the correctness of its position on a given issue (and indeed may influence the solicitor general's decision-making), the solicitor general today seems disinclined to allow the EEOC to advance competing arguments before the Supreme Court.

This behavior by the solicitor general can be linked to the *Williams* controversy. During the Carter years, the EEOC was allowed to file briefs that were at odds with the solicitor general's positions. During Reagan's first term, Solicitor General Rex Lee took note of disagreements between his office and the EEOC. Following the *Williams* dispute, however, the solicitor general has felt free to disregard competing EEOC perspectives—even in cases where the EEOC is a party to the litigation. This is precisely what occurred in the 1987 case of *Sheetmetal Workers v. EEOC.*

Sheetmetal Workers v. EEOC culminated the EEOC's assimilation into the executive branch (at least as far as the agency's litigating authority is concerned). Although the EEOC, a party in the case, had successfully defended the federal court's authority to order affirmative action hiring in an employment discrimination lawsuit, the solicitor general unilaterally reversed the EEOC's position in a brief it filed on behalf of the commission before the Supreme Court.[24] The fact that the EEOC was a party in the case mattered little to the solicitor general. Charles Fried, in his autobiography *Order and Law,* does not even mention the EEOC in his extensive account of the case. Moreover, when the EEOC explained its position to the solicitor general's office, it was flatly told that it was now part of the executive and would have to adapt itself to Department of Justice opposition to affirmative action. The only concession made to the EEOC was that the solicitor general opposed the granting of certiorari in the case, so that the Supreme Court could resolve the *Sheetmetal Workers* issue in an analogous case already before the Court. It is unclear whether this concession was rooted in a desire to accord some respect to EEOC positions or whether the solicitor general feared the repercussions of disregarding EEOC views. Once certiorari was granted, however, EEOC prerogatives played no apparent role in the solicitor general's handling of the case.

Sheetmetal Workers is an extreme example of the solicitor general's discounting of EEOC autonomy, but it is not altogether anomalous. In *Riverside v. Rivera*, the solicitor general rejected EEOC efforts to participate as an amicus in support of plaintiffs' claims in an attorney's fees case. Instead, the solicitor general filed an amicus brief in opposition to plaintiffs' claim, without mentioning the EEOC's conflicting position.[25]

Ironically, EEOC arguments were presented to the Court anyway: the NAACP Legal Defense and Education Fund reproduced as part of its amicus filing a leaked draft of the rejected EEOC brief. Another recent example of this solicitor general's unwillingness to note EEOC differences is *Price Waterhouse v. Hopkins*. In *Price Waterhouse*, the solicitor general did not note EEOC disagreement with its view that evidence of sexual stereotyping could be rebutted by a preponderance of the evidence, rather than by clear and convincing evidence.[26]

Solicitor General Fried's eagerness to accept the OLC opinion on the EEOC's executive branch status is hardly surprising. The solicitor general owes no deference to voices within the executive that contradict his own conception of executive branch desires; and the subordination of the EEOC to the executive branch appreciably enhanced the solicitor general's authority. On an issue as polarizing as affirmative action, where one would expect ideological consistency within the executive to be seen as especially important, the authority to advance a unitary governmental position is especially attractive. At the time of *Williams*, moreover, a campaign was launched within the Justice Department to challenge the constitutionality of independent agencies as being inconsistent with unitary White House control over the administration of government programs. That affirmative action was the agenda item for the civil rights division also lent support to intradepartmental solicitor general control. Indeed, at the time of *Williams*, the civil rights division was in the midst of challenging more than fifty affirmative action consent decrees between civil rights plaintiffs and state and local government. Finally, without any statutory claim to possess independent litigating authority before the Supreme Court, the EEOC had little leverage to use in combating the Justice Department's interpretation. In plain terms, the solicitor general had the power and was willing to use it. What is more, the EEOC's weak-kneed acceptance of Justice Department authority in *Williams* was the functional equivalent of wearing a "kick me" sign with regard to potentially conflicting Justice Department interests.

The battle between the Justice Department and the EEOC was, under the circumstances, inevitable. The Department of Justice perceived the EEOC as a threat to its own power, to the department's civil rights agenda, and to the ability of the administration to speak in a unified voice. With the Department of Justice ready and willing to rein in the EEOC and curtail its power, the EEOC was left wide open for attack. The control of government employment discrimination litigation is thus centrally a story about a Justice Department willing to launch a political broadside against the EEOC and about the commission's concomitant failure to fend off these political advances. Congress's acquiescence to this Justice Department power play also figures prominently in the saga.

Indeed, Congress's inability or unwillingness to create a truly executive or truly independent EEOC set the stage for the *Williams* controversy in the first place.

Congressional expectations regarding the EEOC's power were shaped by the tortuous evolution of the agency, from its creation in 1964 through its ultimate reorganization in 1978.[27] In 1964 and in 1972, Congress declined to grant the EEOC cease-and-desist authority in order to limit the scope of agency enforcement. In 1978, Congress remained silent when EEOC operations were integrated with those of executive departments and agencies. Congress apparently did not see any need to protect the EEOC's independent turf. By the time the big showdown between the Justice Department and the EEOC finally occurred, Congress understood the EEOC to be a relatively weak agency.

The *Williams* controversy occurred in the background of the Congress's inattentiveness to the EEOC's independent standing. The Justice Department's position hinged on Congress's acquiescence to the 1978 reorganization, claiming that only an executive EEOC could coordinate executive policy-making and receive Department of Labor and Civil Service Commission authority by way of an administrative transfer of power. *Williams* then presented Congress with an opportunity both to bolster EEOC policy-making authority and to clarify the commission's standing within the government.

But although Congress expressed dissatisfaction with the commission's withdrawal from *Williams,* it declined to do anything with this opportunity. Instead, Congress alternately cajoled and condemned the commission for its refusal to challenge the Justice Department. House Judiciary Committee chair Peter Rodino (a New Jersey Democrat) asked the commission to give Congress all relevant correspondence between itself and the Reagan administration. EEOC chair Clarence Thomas, moreover, was asked to testify about the *Williams* controversy before the House Judiciary and Labor Committees. Finally, the House Committee on Government Operations issued a report chastising the EEOC for failing to live up to its "obligation to participate in court cases, particularly controversial or precedent setting cases."[28] At the least, the report continues, the EEOC should "bring the issue of its independence before a court for resolution." Finally, in a remarkable bit of doublespeak, the report simultaneously speaks of the "EEOC['s] retain[ing] its independent authority to enforce Title VII" "[d]espite its status as an executive agency, subject to the authority of the President."

Instead of criticizing the EEOC, Congress should have done something about its own blemishes. Rather than protecting the EEOC through legislation that bolstered commission autonomy or limited Department of Justice authority to intervene, Congress did little more than urge the

EEOC to fend for itself. In short, Congress offered no genuine assistance. By asking the EEOC simultaneously to recognize presidential authority and to continue independently enforcing Title VII, Congress asked for the impossible. Clarence Thomas certainly recognized this dilemma, stating that "there is a contradiction [in having lead agency status without being in the executive branch] that has to be ironed out [by Congress]."[29] From its establishment of the EEOC in 1964 to its approval of the 1978 reorganization, however, Congress persistently left the EEOC in a never-never land with a part-executive, part-independent-agency status. That the EEOC landed in the executive branch should have come as no surprise to a Congress that never saw the EEOC as a strong independent voice.

The FCC

The FCC is a statutorily designated independent regulatory agency. Like the EEOC, it has five members who serve staggered five-year terms, thereby limiting the president's appointment power to one commissioner per year. Like the EEOC, the appointments power is further constrained by the requirement that no more than three commissioners may be members of the same political party. Finally, as with the EEOC, the president presumably (for the statute is silent) may only remove commissioners for cause. In contrast to the EEOC, however, the FCC possesses quasi-adjudicatory and quasi-legislative powers, including cease-and-desist authority. FCC functions, moreover, are not formally intermingled with executive branch operations.

    FCC relationships with the Department of Justice are difficult to characterize. This difficulty is a by-product of an extraordinarily confusing statutory scheme, which sometimes allows the FCC to appeal its cases directly to the Supreme Court, sometimes makes the FCC entirely dependent on Department of Justice attorneys throughout the course of litigation, and sometimes authorizes FCC representation before federal courts of appeals and solicitor general representation before the Supreme Court.[30] Department of Justice attorneys represent the FCC throughout the course of litigation in actions brought against the commission to enforce its orders, as well as in employment discrimination and Freedom of Information Act suits filed against the commission. In sharp contrast to these categories of cases stand cases where the FCC has a statutory right to seek certiorari before the Supreme Court in appeals of FCC declaratory orders. Finally, licensing decisions, handled by the FCC before federal appeals courts and by the solicitor general before the Supreme Court, involve a murkier division of responsibility between the commission and the Justice Department.

Policy disputes between the FCC and the Justice Department occur with some frequency. FCC licensing and regulations often conflict with the department's understanding of antitrust laws, as well as with its reading of the Constitution's free speech and equal protection guarantees. The prospects for such disputes being aired in court depend on the category of case and on the willingness of the Justice Department to shut the FCC out of cases within its control.

FCC views are accorded the least weight when Department of Justice attorneys represent the FCC throughout the course of litigation. These cases originate in federal district court and include actions brought against the commission to enforce its orders, as well as employment discrimination and Freedom of Information Act suits filed against the commission. Although FCC attorneys typically work with Department of Justice attorneys in preparing pleadings and other legal memoranda in these cases, policy-based disputes occasionally arise. One such dispute involved the League of Women Voters' challenge to a statutory prohibition of editorializing by public television and radio stations, culminating in the Supreme Court's 1982 *Federal Communications Commission v. League of Woman Voters* decision.[31] When the suit was first filed in 1979, the FCC and the Carter Justice Department concluded that the editorial ban was unconstitutional. Motions were filed in federal district court stating that the government would not defend the constitutionality of the ban. Before the case was dismissed, however, two critical events reinvigorated it. First, Congress amended the editorial ban rule so that it would apply only to public television and radio stations that received federally funded Corporation for Public Broadcasting grants. Second, the Reagan administration assumed office, and the Department of Justice at once softened its position on the constitutionality of editorial bans. That the FCC did not change its position did not matter. The Reagan Department of Justice unilaterally pursued this case from beginning to end. When the Supreme Court rejected the Department of Justice's defense and struck down the amended statute, the FCC rejoiced—calling the decision "a significant breakthrough."[32]

In sharp contrast to the Department of Justice's control of the *League of Women Voters* case stand cases where the FCC has a statutory right to seek certiorari before the Supreme Court in appeals of FCC declaratory orders. *Federal Communications Commission v. Pacifica Foundation* and *Federal Communications Commission v. MCI Telecommunications*—two Carter-era Supreme Court cases—typify such disputes. In both instances, the FCC and the solicitor general presented divergent views as statutory respondents before the Supreme Court. In the *Pacifica* case, the FCC successfully argued that certain words could be kept off the airwaves for most broadcasting hours and thereby withstood the solicitor general's challenge to the FCC order as being overboard because the commission did not consider "the context in which the offending words were used."[33] The *MCI* case involved an FCC order that MCI's corporate rival AT&T had no obligation to interconnect its facilities with those of MCI. The D.C. Circuit Court of Appeals invalidated this order. The FCC petitioned for certiorari, and the solicitor general filed a petition in opposition. The case, which was denied certiorari, is noteworthy because of a blistering footnote in the FCC brief "question[ing] exactly what interests of the United States the Solicitor legitimately represents in this case."[34] This statement of outrage exemplifies the power of independent litigating authority.

Licensing decisions, handled by the FCC before federal appeals courts and by the solicitor general before the Supreme Court, involve a murkier division of responsibility and are especially vulnerable to the specific circumstances surrounding them. This division of litigation responsibility enables the solicitor general to reverse FCC positions before the Supreme Court. In the EEOC context, where a similar division of responsibility exists, the solicitor general now views such conflicts as intraexecutive matters that are appropriately to be resolved by the Justice Department. This is precisely what occurred in the *Sheetmetal Workers* case. The FCC presents a more complicated scenario because the FCC is indisputably an independent agency. The FCC, moreover, is statutorily authorized to present its views before the Supreme Court in declaratory order cases.

Bureaucratic theory would resolve this conflict by having the solicitor general view the FCC as a client in need of representation.[35] This is precisely how the Carter administration resolved a dispute between the Justice Department and the FCC over commission rules governing the cross-ownership of television stations and newspapers in a single market. Specifically, the FCC was allowed to represent its own interests before the court, while the solicitor general filed a separate brief on behalf of the "United States." Proponents of the unitary executive, in contrast, would view the solicitor general's loyalties and obligations as running exclusively to the White House. According to this view, as the solicitor general did in *Sheetmetal Workers* and has done in several other cases involving independent agencies, the position adopted by the independent agency should be tossed aside in favor of executive branch interests.

The ability of the solicitor general to stare down the FCC and other independent agencies is a question of political will. *Metro Broadcasting v. FCC*, decided by the Supreme Court in 1990, exemplifies how political circumstances may limit Justice Department control. The *Metro Broadcasting* case called into question the constitutionality of FCC efforts to increase the number of minority broadcasters through preferences and set-asides. The case was a political battlefield because Congress had stat-utorily mandated the FCC to defend its preference policy in the wake of efforts by Reagan-appointed commissioners to reexamine these affirma-tive action programs. The FCC, therefore, could not argue in its own name that its preference scheme was constitutionally suspect. Further complicating this highly visible litigation was Bush administration Solici-tor General Kenneth Starr's commitment to Reagan administration chal-lenges to affirmative action. The initial resolution was for the FCC and the solicitor general jointly to oppose the granting of certiorari.[36] This ef-fort—as the certiorari petition stated—was designed to throw this politi-cally hot issue back to the Congress (where legislation repealing the pref-erence might be enacted) and to the D.C. Circuit Court of Appeals (where an apparent intracircuit conflict might resolve itself through new judicial appointees). This effort would also enable the solicitor general to duck the issue of whether he should allow the FCC to assert its position inde-pendently before the Supreme Court. Finally, for supporters of prefer-ences within the FCC and the solicitor general's office, this strategy would keep from the Court a case that most thought would drive an-other nail into the coffin of affirmative action.

Certiorari was granted, however. The solicitor general was set to file a brief challenging the constitutionality of FCC preferences. The question remained whether the FCC should be allowed to file separately. By this time, the commission—thanks to three pro-preference commissioners named by President Bush—strongly supported the preference program.

These commissioners, in fact, sought to strongarm the Justice Depart-ment in the *Metro Broadcasting* case, arguing that they would file their own brief before the Supreme Court with or without the solicitor's au-thorization. Bush's appointment of pro-preference commissioners while allowing his Justice Department to oppose racial preferences is certainly contradictory and definitely created a dilemma for a solicitor general dedicated to advancing presidential interests. The dilemma was resolved by allowing the FCC independently (and successfully) to defend its pref-erences before the Court, with the solicitor filing an amicus brief setting forth the executive's opposition to the FCC policy. The solicitor's interest in opposing preferences in *Metro Broadcasting* was as strong as it had been in *Sheetmetal Workers*. The FCC's threat to the solicitor general's statutory authority also raised the symbolic cost of acquiescence. In the end, however, ideological opposition to racial preferences gave way to political reality.

The question of why Bush would create this dilemma through his FCC appointments remains unanswered. Against the backdrop of ongo-ing battles between Reagan FCC appointees and the Congress, Bush's action appears politically expedient.[37] Reagan had appointed FCC commissioners who were committed to "unregulation," caricatured the commission as one of the "last of the New Deal dinosaurs," and viewed their jobs "as an important part of carrying out [the Reagan] mandate for a leaner, less intrusive federal presence throughout this country."[38] Congressional overseers, in contrast, admonished the commission to "follow our lead" and asserted that "[y]ou folks take an oath to regulate, not deregulate."[39] These competing philosophies resulted in an all-out war: FCC appointees perceived it "not possible to carry out the Reagan program and have amicable relations with Congress"[40]; oversight committee members thought that there was no way to "overly manage the commission," since the FCC was "a renegade agency" that needed Congress to step in as an "active participant" and "bring them back."[41] Congress's bite was as good as its bark this time. It enacted legislation at odds with commission policy, including funding bans freezing deregulatory initiatives; it blocked Reagan's appointments power by refusing to confirm FCC appointees for Reagan's last two years in office. For its part, the FCC antagonized Congress by, among other things, repealing the fairness doctrine and raising doubts about the propriety of several other congressionally supported regulatory programs.

The FCC's repeal initiatives, however, were sensitive to congressional preferences. Rather than directly overturn the fairness doctrine, the cross-ownership prohibition, and other regulatory programs, the commission sought to enlist the judiciary in helping to advance its deregulatory agenda. Specifically, the commission presented arguments in court that called into question the constitutionality of these programs. For example, in August 1985, the Commission issued a 111-page *Fairness Report* condemning the fairness doctrine as "unnecessary and detrimental."[42] Arguing that the fairness doctrine actually reduced discussion of controversial issues, the commission "questioned the permissibility of the doctrine as a matter of both policy and constitutional law." Despite these findings, the commission did not eliminate fairness standards. The FCC, however, did encourage the D.C. Circuit Court of Appeals to invalidate the fairness doctrine in litigation that grew directly out of its report. Congress vehemently disapproved of the efforts to have the courts do what the FCC refused to do on its own initiative. The FCC's indirect attack on fairness was labeled tricky "in the Nixonian Sense" and "a thinly veiled attempt to end-run Congress."[43]

The battle over race preferences exemplifies the bitterness of FCC-Congress relations. When the commission launched its reexamination of race preferences, it specifically requested comments on "whether [the FCC] is bound by, or may rely on, congressional findings of constitutionality."[44] Congress viewed this request as an attempt by the commission "to put itself above Congress."[45] Congress's outrage at the FCC was dramatically expressed at oversight hearings that occurred shortly after the announced reexamination. Congressman John Bryant (a Texas Democrat) characterized it as "almost pointless" to work with the commission; Congressman Mickey Leland (another Texas Democrat) referred to the need to draft "FCC proof" legislation as well as the need to "fight this Commission tooth and nail"; and Congressman Edward Markey (a Massachusetts Democrat) labeled the reexamination "a cloudburst in a storm of suspicion and distrust which seems to hover over this Commission."[46] To stop the FCC reexamination in its tracks, Congress prohibited the FCC from expending any funds on the reexamination.[47]

Comparing the FCC to the EEOC

Congress was a formidable opponent of the reexamination-minded FCC. Unlike with regard to the EEOC, where congressional threats could be dismissed, Congress took a proprietary interest in the FCC. The commission's independent status was not simply symbolic protection from an aggressive executive; it was a license for Congress to exert its will on FCC policy-making. For the Bush administration, telecommunications policy hinged on reestablishing dialogue between the FCC and Congress. Bush sought to achieve this objective in many ways, including sacrificing ideological consistency on affirmative action. The solicitor general could not ignore Bush administration efforts to normalize relations between Congress and the FCC. With the White House speaking out of both sides of its mouth on FCC preferences, it was appropriate that the solicitor general, too, sacrifice unitariness.

Department of Justice–FCC relations stand in dramatic contrast to Department of Justice–EEOC relations. The department, rather than endeavoring to persuade the FCC that the government should speak in the unitary voice of the Justice Department, empowered the FCC to speak in its own voice. Indeed, not only did the Justice Department make no effort to assume FCC authority, but the FCC sought to acquire additional power as a matter of right. Since both sets of conflicts involved race preferences, the Justice Department's assumption of power in one case and its ceding of power in the other are all the more staggering.

Structural differences are of limited use in explaining why the FCC fared so much better than the EEOC did. Although the FCC is more insulated from the executive than is the EEOC and although it possesses quasi-legislative and quasi-adjudicatory powers, statutory grants of independent litigation authority cut in favor of the EEOC in *Williams* and against the FCC in *Metro Broadcasting*. The principal difference between the EEOC and the FCC, instead, appears to be political will and the culture of political expectations. *Williams* was a severe threat to the

Justice Department's turf, in view of the civil rights division's exclusive authority to initiate state and local cases. *Metro Broadcasting* did not directly implicate the Justice Department's turf. At the time of *Metro Broadcasting,* moreover, the department had cooled its attack on affirmative action in the wake of its failed attempt to convince President Reagan to rescind affirmative action programs governing federal contractors. Congress's indifference to the EEOC's location in government and its unwillingness to protect the EEOC also contributed to the Justice Department's action in *Williams.* With respect to the FCC, Congress was an extraordinarily active and territorial player. Indeed, it effectively forced the FCC to defend racial preferences through appropriations legislation and through political pressures on the Bush White House. Bush's naming of pro-preference commissioners, moreover, signaled the Justice Department to leave the FCC alone in *Metro Broadcasting.* Unlike the Reagan administration, the Bush administration was less extreme in its policy agenda (especially its legal policy agenda) and less confrontational in its relations with the other branches.[48] In sharp contrast, the White House, in *Williams,* set up a meeting to pressure EEOC officials to comply with Department of Justice advances. That the EEOC did comply reveals another difference between *Williams* and *Metro Broadcasting.* The EEOC lacked a strong sense of its institutional identity. It bound itself to the executive in 1978 and could not easily toss aside those bonds in 1983. The FCC, in contrast, has always understood itself to be an independent agency. Supreme Court decisions upholding the constitutionality of the Commodities Future Trading Commission in 1986 and of independent prosecutors in 1988 further bolstered the FCC's sense of independence.[49]

Politics more than structure explains *Metro Broadcasting,* as well as the differences between the FCC and the EEOC. The failure of the government to speak a unitary voice in *Metro Broadcasting* also reveals that political compromise makes policy coordination especially difficult.

CONCLUSION

Congress, by creating independent agencies, seeks to insulate some regulatory decision-making from the control of elected government. The Senate Committee on Governmental Affairs, for example, commented that "[t]he multiple membership of these agencies, with terms expiring at staggering intervals, does tend to serve as a buffer against Presidential control and direction."[50] Limiting presidential control, however, does not mean—as some in Congress would like to believe—that independent agencies are mouthpieces for the Congress. The last word on independent agency decision-making, rather than lying with the Congress or the

White House, usually rests with the courts. A joint letter to President Carter, signed by the ranking majority and minority leadership of several Senate committees, expressed this sentiment, arguing that "in exercising the quasi-judicial and quasi-legislative authority which Congress has delegated to the agencies, agency actions shall not be subject to review or modification by either Congress or the Executive; only the courts may review final agency actions."[51]

Independent agencies, according to the Congress, are supposed to reach policy determinations according to their own dictates. While Congress recognizes that presidential power to submit budget requests, name the agency chair, and appoint at least some commissioners and key staffers ensures substantial White House influence, the final word on independent agency decision-making is typically spoken by Article III judges. Congress has not followed its own design, however. Rather than empowering independent agencies with independent litigating authority, Congress has crafted an extraordinarily incoherent system of varying, unpredictable degrees of litigating authority. Some agencies are virtually independent; others are entirely dependent; and most fall somewhere in the middle. Specific political circumstances, not cohesive thinking about the attributes of independent agency autonomy, explain this patchwork structure. In view of the supposed "last word" status of court edicts in defining independent agency decision-making, Congress's failure to sort out the litigation authority issue is extraordinarily troublesome.

No doubt, to expect Congress to have a coherent vision of the structure and purposes of independent agencies is to expect the impossible. The Senate Committee on Governmental Operations admitted as much, casually noting that "[a] decision on structure is after all a political issue, very much influenced by the prevailing political situation. And that situation can neither be quantified nor predicted."[52] The conclusion that "random selection" explains Congress's choice of an independent over an executive format is neither heartening nor surprising. The confluence of oversight committee preferences, interest group pressures, and legislative–executive relations inevitably yields different organizational structures. In the end, all one can say with certainty about independent agencies is that they are multimember bodies headed by individuals who cannot be appointed and removed "at will" by the sitting president.

The haphazard nature of independent litigating authority is certainly expected. Moreover, since the independent agency structure is far from preordained, Congress's decision to make some independent agencies more dependent on the executive than others seems to reflect an acceptable state of affairs. Nonetheless, there is something unsettling about the current arrangement. The case studies presented in this chapter reveal how the seeming haphazardness of structure and expectations that defines the creation and operation of independent agencies yields unpredictable legal policy-making by these agencies. This state of affairs will certainly continue. No interested parties—not Department of Justice officials, independent agency counsel, or Congressional overseers—have a fixed point of reference to use in sorting out appropriate from inappropriate legal policy-making by independent agencies.

NOTES

Portions of this chapter borrow from Neal Devins, "Unitariness and Independence: Solicitor General Control of Independent Agency Litigation," *California Law Review* 82 (April 1994): 255, and "Political Will and the Unitary Executive: What Makes an Independent Agency Independent," *Cardozo Law Review* 5 (1993): 273.

1. Geoffrey P. Miller, "Government Lawyers' Ethics in a System of Checks and Balances," *University of Chicago Law Review* 54 (1987): 1293, 1298.

2. Senate Committee on Governmental Affairs, "Study on Federal Regulation," 95th Cong., 1st sess., vol. 5, p. 27 (1977).

3. Ibid., p. 28.

4. *Congressional Record* (5/21/73; S16273).

5. See Geoffrey P. Miller, "Independent Agencies," *Supreme Court Review* (1986): 41.

6. Paul R. Verkuil, "The Purposes and Limits of Independent Agencies," *Duke Law Journal* (1988): 257, 259.

7. Peter L. Strauss, "The Place of Agencies in Government: Separation of Powers and the Fourth Branch," *Columbia Law Review* 84 (1984): 573, 584–85.

8. *Congressional Globe,* 41st Cong., 2d sess. 3036 (1870). See generally Olson, "Challenges to the Gatekeeper: The Debate over Federal Litigating Authority." *Judicature* 68 (1984): 71; "The Attorney General's Role as Chief Litigator for the United States," *Opinions of the Office of Legal Counsel* 6 (1982): 47.

9. 28 U.S.C. 516.

10. See generally Devins, "Unitariness and Independence"; Olson, "Challenges to the Gatekeeper."

11. See A. Everette MacIntyre, "The Status of Regulatory Independence," *Federal Bar Journal* 29 (1968): 1; U.S. Congress, House of Representatives, *Hearings Before the Subcommittee on Commerce and Finance of the Committee on Interstate and Foreign Commerce on H.R. 5050 and H.R. 340, Bills to Amend the Securities Exchange Act of 1934; to Provide Authorizations for Appropriations for the Securities and Exchange Commission for Fiscal Years 1974, 1975, and 1976; and for Other Purposes,* 93d Cong., 1st sess., 333, 343, 348–49, 352–52 (statement of FTC Commissioner A. Everette MacIntyre) [hereinafter 1973 House Hearings].

12. 390 F.2d 323 (8th Cir. 1968). For an FTC commissioner's view of this litigation, see MacIntyre, "The Status of Regulatory Independence," pp. 15–18.

13. Letter from Solicitor General Griswold to Chairman Dixon of the Federal Trade Commission (April 26, 1968).

14. 368 U.S. 208 (1961).

15. Brief for the United States, *St. Regis Paper Company v. United States,* 368 U.S. 208 (1968), p. 10.

16. Trans-Alaskan Pipeline Authorization Act of 1973, Pub. Law 93-153; 87 Stat. 591, 592; Federal Trade Commission Improvement Act of 1975, Pub. Law 93-637; 88 Stat. 2199.

17. See 1973 House Hearings, p. 232 (statement of former SEC chairman William Carey); ibid., pp. 299–300 (statement of SEC Commissioner Philip Loomis).

18. 729 F.2d 1554 (5th Cir. 1984).

19. The Justice Department brief argued that the affirmative action plan infringed on the rights of "innocent nonblack employees." "Justice Department Seeks to Overturn Promotion Plan for New Orleans Police," *BNA Daily Labor Report,* 10 January 1983, p. A-8. The EEOC brief castigated the Department of Justice for making this argument: "Contrary to this uniform body of case law approving the use of prospective employment goals, however, the Department of Justice asks this Court to hold that judicial relief under Title VII must be limited to [ ] actual victims of discrimination. . . ." Draft EEOC brief in *Williams v. The City of New Orleans* reprinted in *BNA Daily Labor Report,* 6 April 1983, p. E-1.

20. Quoted in "White House Pressure: Federal Agencies Differ Sharply over New Orleans Affirmative Action Plan," *BNA Government Employee Relations Report,* 14 March 1983.

21. Quoted in "White House Pressure."

22. Quoted in Ruth Simon, "Future Role of EEOC Questioned: A Shift of Authority," *National Law Journal,* 2 May 1983, p. 7.

23. Quoted in Fred Barbash and Juan Williams, "Administration Prods EEOC on Quotas Brief," *Washington Post,* April 7, 1983, p. A-1.

24. See Brief for the Equal Employment Opportunity Commission, *Local 28 of the Sheet Metal Workers' International Association and Local 28 Joint Apprenticeship Committee v. Equal Employment Opportunity Commission,* 106 S. Ct. 3019 (1986). Remarkably, then-acting EEOC general counsel Johnny Butler signed this brief. Butler, however, claimed in an interview that he and the EEOC vigorously opposed the solicitor general's position. Interview with Johnny Butler, 22 September 1992.

25. See "DOJ Rejects EEOC Advice and Tries to Limit Lawyers' Fees in Rights Cases," *BNA Daily Labor Report,* 9 January 1987, p. A-1; Brief for the United States as Amicus Curiae Supporting Petitioners, *City of Riverside v. Rivera,* 477 U.S. 561 (1986).

26. See Brief for the United States as Amicus Curiae, p. 23 n. 10, *Price Waterhouse v. Hopkins,* 490 U.S. 228 (1989). Respondent's attorneys noted this omission in their brief: "The Solicitor General's failure to comment on EEOC's position . . . is curious." Brief for Respondent, p. 42 n. 32, *Price Waterhouse v. Hopkins,* 490 U.S. 228 (1989).

27. See generally Hugh Davis Graham, *The Civil Rights Era* (New York: Ox-

ford University Press, 1990); Herman Belz, *Equality Transformed* (New Brunswick, N.J.: Transaction Press, 1991).

28. U.S. Congress, House of Representatives, Committee on Government Operations, Pay Equity, *EEOC's Handling of Sex-Based Wage Discrimination Complaints*, H.R. Rep. No. 796, 98th Cong., 2d sess., 5 (1984).

29. Quoted in Juan Williams, "Lawmakers Urge EEOC Not to Quit Rights Case," *Washington Post*, 10 April 1983, p. A-11.

30. See 47 U.S.C. 401, 504; 28 U.S.C. 516, 519; 47 U.S.C. 402(j); 28 U.S.C. 2350; 47 U.S.C. 402(b).

31. 468 U.S. 364 (1984).

32. Fred Barbush, "High Court Rules for Public TV; Right to Comment Upheld Despite Federal Funding," *Washington Post*, 3 July 1984, p. A-1 (quoting FCC general counsel Bruce Fein).

33. Brief for the United States, p. 14, *Federal Communications Commission v. Pacifica Foundation and United States*, 438 U.S. 726 (1978). Compare Petitioner's Reply Brief, p. 8, *Federal Communications Commission v. Pacifica Foundation and United States*, 438 U.S. 726 (1978) ("The [FCC] order seeks to protect parental and privacy interests . . . to the extent that this Court's constitutional options permit.").

34. See Brief for the United States in Opposition, *United States Independent Telephone Association v. United States of America and MCI Telecommunications Corp.*, 434 U.S. 1040 (1978); Petitioners Reply to "Brief for the United States in Opposition," p. 1 n. 1, *Federal Communications Commission v. MCI Telecommunications Corp.*, 439 U.S. 980 (1978).

35. See John O. McGinnis, "Principle Versus Politics: The Solicitor General's Office in Constitutional and Bureaucratic Theory," *Stanford Law Review* 44 (1992): 799.

36. See Brief for Federal Respondents in Opposition, *Metro Broadcasting, Inc. v. Federal Communications Commission*, 497 U.S. 547 (1990).

37. See generally Neal Devins, "Congress, the FCC, and the Search for the Public Trustee," *Law and Contemporary Problems* 56 (Autumn 1993): 145.

38. Mark S. Fowler, "The Federal Communications Commission 1981–1987: What the Chairman Said," *Comment Law Journal* 10 (1988): 409, 410–11, 414–15.

39. Quoted in "Congress Asserts its Dominion over FCC," *Broadcasting*, August 1989, p. 27.

40. "Micromanagement of FCC: Here to Stay," *Broadcasting*, 26 December 1988, p. 56.

41. Ibid.

42. *In re Inquiry into Section 73.1910 of the Commission's Rules and Regulations Concerning the General Fairness Obligations of Broadcast Licensees*, 102 F.C.C.2d 143 (1985).

43. Elanor Randolph, "FCC Scraps 'Fairness Doctrine,'" *Washington Post*, 5 August 1987, p. A-1; Bob Davis, "FCC Abolishes Fairness Doctrine, Arousing Debate," *Wall Street Journal*, 5 August 1987, p. 8 col. 3.

44. "In the Matter of Reexamination of the Commission's Comparative Li-

censing, Distress Sales and Tax Certificates Policies Premised on Racial, Ethnic or Gender Classifications," *F.C.C. Record* (30 December 1986), 1316, 1318.

45. *Congressional Record*, Senate, 133: 5494 (daily ed. 24 April 1987) (statement of Senator Lautenberg).

46. U.S. Congress, House of Representatives, *Hearings on H.R. 5373 Before the Subcommittee on Telecommunications, Consumer Protection, and Finance of the House Committee on Energy and Commerce,* 99th Cong., 2d Sess., 20, 22, 31 (1986).

47. 101 Stat. 1329–32 (1987).

48. See generally Cornell W. Clayton, *The Politics of Justice: The Attorney General and the Making of Legal Policy* (Armonk, N.Y.: M. E. Sharpe, 1992), pp. 172–220.

49. See *Commodities Future Trading Commission v. Schor*, 478 U.S. 833 (1986); *Morrison v. Olson*, 487 U.S. 654 (1988).

50. Senate Committee on Governmental Affairs, "Study on Federal Regulation," p. 75.

51. Letter from Bipartisan Senate Leadership to President Jimmy Carter, 16 December 1977, reprinted in U.S. Congress, House of Representatives, *Role of OMB in Regulation, Hearing before the Subcommittee on Oversight and Investigations, House Committee on Energy and Commerce,* 97th Cong., 1st sess., 170, 172 (1981).

52. Senate Committee on Governmental Affairs, "Study on Federal Regulations," p. 79.

8

GUARDIANS OF THE PRESIDENCY: THE OFFICE OF THE COUNSEL TO THE PRESIDENT AND THE OFFICE OF LEGAL COUNSEL

NELSON LUND

President Clinton's first White House counsel,[1] Bernard Nussbaum, was pressured into resigning his post after a special prosecutor began looking into meetings he had held with officials of an independent regulatory agency. These meetings, which related to the agency's investigations of financial dealings in which the president and his wife had been involved before they came to Washington, were immediately and almost universally denounced. Clearly bitter at having lost his job because of a standard of conduct having more to do with appearances of impropriety than with legal rules, Nussbaum claimed that he was the victim of people "who do not understand, nor wish to understand, the role and obligations of a lawyer, even one acting as White House Counsel."[2]

Nussbaum seems to have believed that the job of a lawyer—any lawyer—is to act as aggressively as possible to protect the interests of the individual who retains him, so long as his actions are "consistent with the rules of law, standards of ethics, and the highest traditions of the Bar."[3] Nussbaum's view was soon attacked by his predecessor (from the Bush administration), C. Boyden Gray, who said: "He confused his fiduciary role as a temporary occupant of that office with the no-holds-barred role a private litigant would have. He is not [the Clintons'] private lawyer. He is the lawyer for the Oval Office."[4]

Nussbaum's successor as White House counsel, Lloyd Cutler, also considered the private-lawyer model inapplicable. When the president announced his appointment, Cutler said: "The Counsel is supposed to be counsel for the President in office, and for the office of the presidency, as many people have said. Most of the time, those two standards coincide. Almost always the advice you would give the President is advice that is in the interest of the office of the Presidency. . . . When it comes to a President's private affairs, particularly private affairs that occurred before he took office, those should be handled by his own personal private counsel, and in my view not by the White House Counsel."[5]

As this is written (in October 1994), the Clintons and Nussbaum continue to insist that they have committed no illegal or unethical acts. Whatever may come to light in the continuing investigations of their conduct and the conduct of others with whom they have been associated, this will surely not be the last eruption of controversy about the ethics of the relationship between presidents and their legal advisers. Ever since Watergate made the distinctions among the president's various personal and official interests in his office a subject of close public scrutiny, the history of that office has looked as much like a battle among lawyers as it has like a contest between presidents and their political opponents.

One legacy of Watergate has been an intense interest (often politically motivated) in the ethics of those who serve in the upper reaches of government. And one consequence of that legacy has been a growth in the size of the office of the White House counsel, which plays a preeminent role in seeking to prevent ethical embarrassments from impeding the president's substantive agenda. Mr. Nussbaum wrecked his government career on the treacherous ethical rocks that have been thrown around the shores of the presidency—a fate that has become almost commonplace among senior officials during the last two decades.[6]

The preoccupation with ethics in government is the most obvious lingering effect of the Watergate affairs, but it may not be the most important. This chapter considers a less visible aftermath of Watergate: the increasing significance of politico-legal disputes that generally fall under the rubric of separation of powers. President Nixon, of course, tried unsuccessfully to invoke the constitutional separation of powers to prevent his own downfall. As emboldened congresses and a more belligerent press have sought to subject subsequent presidents to tighter and tighter controls, those presidents have also invoked the Constitution to protect themselves from encroachments on their freedom of action. Because these struggles between presidents and their adversaries have often been waged in legal and constitutional terms, lawyers who specialize in the separation of powers have become much more prominent than they once were. The function of articulating a principled defense of presidents and the presidency—mostly against congressional incursions—is carried out primarily by those who serve in the office of the counsel to the president at the White House and in the Justice Department's Office of Legal Counsel (OLC), to which the attorney general's legal advisory function has largely been delegated. The rise of this species of presidential lawyer is worthy of considerable attention both for its intrinsic intellectual interest and because it can be expected to have continuing effects on the political life of our nation.

FRAMEWORK FOR THE ANALYSIS

Legal Ethics and the Role of the President's Legal Advisers

Most commentaries on the advisory function of the presidential lawyer exaggerate the deep and inherent tensions that are supposed to exist between the political and professional obligations of those responsible for providing the president with legal advice. Real tensions between these obligations undoubtedly do exist, but in many cases the dilemmas are specious. Lawyers who work for the president without fully sharing his political goals have an obvious incentive to wrap their own political agenda in the guise of professional obligations. Similarly, those who wish to influence an administration's conduct have an obvious incentive to encourage the president's lawyers to resist his agenda in the name of supposedly objective professional criteria. Exaggeration of the tension in the role of presidential legal adviser has had real effects on the public discourse about the role of lawyers in government and on the academic literature about the functioning of legal bureaucracies.[7]

The principal alternative views about the professional obligations of the president's legal advisers are illustrated by the quotations provided in the previous section from the three lawyers who have most recently served as White House counsel. Gray and Cutler are clearly right in one respect: those who serve in this position are government employees who cannot properly act as personal counsel for their supervisors. In this respect, however, they are no different from lawyers retained or employed by institutional clients in the private sector. In some circumstances, the distinction between the interests of a corporation and the personal interests of its principal officers is genuinely difficult to draw. And counsel to a private corporation will sometimes be tempted to substitute loyalty to the officer who controls his remuneration for loyalty to the firm. Painful ethical dilemmas may arise and mistaken choices may be made by lawyers faced with them, just as they may in the government. Such problems are inherent in the business of representing institutional clients, however, and the underlying standard of conduct is the same in the public and private sectors: "A lawyer employed or retained by an organization represents the organization acting through its duly authorized constituents."[8] Thus, if Nussbaum undertook to represent the president or the president's wife (or both) in their personal capacities while he was on the public payroll, he acted improperly. This judgment does not depend on any peculiar ethical tensions created by government service in general or by the special demands of employment in the White House. The same impropriety would exist if Nussbaum, after returning to private practice, were to bill a corporate client for services performed in behalf of the personal interests of the client's chief executive officer.[9]

Although it is clear that government employees may not properly represent the personal interests of those who hire them, it is less clear exactly what interests they *are* supposed to represent. Gray and Cutler differ on this question, and their views represent the two alternatives most frequently presented. According to Cutler, the White House counsel must seek to balance the interests of the president as a politician against the interests of the office he holds. When these interests diverge, as they occasionally must, Cutler suggests that the lawyer must decide which interest is more important in the case at hand. Good judgment—a sensitivity to the competing demands of politics and principle, and an ability to resolve concrete dilemmas in a way that serves the interests of the nation as a whole—thus becomes the hallmark of excellence in a presidential legal adviser. Cutler's view is neither quirky nor indefensible. It is, for example, essentially the view taken by Nancy V. Baker in her extended study of the history of the attorney general's office.[10]

Gray articulates what seems at first to be a sharply different (and more glorious) view of the White House lawyer's job: that his client is the presidency itself, an entirely abstract entity whose needs and interests transcend the desires and concerns of any individual who happens to get elected to that post. When fully elaborated, this view provides a theoretical justification for the ascent—and ultimately, the ascendance—of government lawyers who specialize in the separation of powers. Tracing their intellectual roots to Alexander Hamilton, whose theory of energy in the executive gives intellectual respectability (and even a certain air of timelessness) to their endeavors, these lawyers present themselves as agents of the Constitution itself and as guardians of an office whose significance to our nation far outstrips the petty political disputes that consume the daily life of most of those around the president. Important elements of an academic theory supporting Gray's view are presented by Terry Eastland, who contends both that the Constitution itself largely dictates how presidents should conduct themselves in office and that these constitutional duties are largely bound up with defending the prerogatives of his office.[11]

What unites the views expressed by Cutler and Gray—and in my view unites them in error—is the assumption that mere lawyers should decide for the president how he should accommodate his political and policy agenda with the obligations he has to the office he occupies. Like the client of an attorney engaged in private practice, the president is responsible for his own decisions; and in fact he has the authority either to make his own legal determinations without consulting any of his lawyers or to proceed in the face of contrary advice from any lawyer he does consult.[12] It is true that the president has legal obligations that differ from those of any private citizen—or indeed from any other government official—but they are *his* obligations, not the obligations of his lawyers or subordinates.[13] If, for example, the president decides that furthering his political and policy agenda is more important to the future of the country than defending his office from constitutionally dubious legislative restrictions, no lawyer anywhere in the government has the authority to displace that determination. Like anyone else, his lawyers may argue that a particular judgment by the president is mistaken, and they may sometimes be right. But when lawyers presume to substitute their own judgment for the president's—as they must if "the Oval Office" (Gray) or the "office of the presidency" (Cutler) is their client—they are acting without legal warrant.

Although the president's lawyers have no legal right to substitute the presidency for the president as their client, they certainly do have the right to negotiate with the president for the privilege of making such a substitution. Lloyd Cutler may have done just that; it certainly appeared when he was appointed that President Clinton needed his services far more than Cutler wanted the job.[14] But even apart from such special circumstances, persistent forces encourage presidents to allow their closest legal advisers to view themselves as counsel for the presidency. If those forces were to produce a settled expectation that the president should be treated by his chief legal advisers merely as a kind of caretaker for the institution of the presidency, to which they owe their true allegiance, it might not matter much whether the president's lawyers could point to any legal basis for presuming to set themselves up as judges of his fidelity to his constitutional oath of office. Such an arrangement might even be thought to benefit presidents more than their lawyers, since the president would get to employ the authority that the lawyers were dedicated to defending and expanding.

The Bush administration provides a useful case study through which this possibility can be explored. When George Bush was elected president, various factors had established a pattern of conflicts in which unsettled constitutional issues involving the separation of powers provided the terms of debate for a struggle over control of the basic mechanisms of governance. In addition to the continuing repercussions of the Watergate scandals and the 1974 elections, these factors included the seemingly fixed disinclination of the voters to establish either political party in command of both the legislative and the executive departments of government and the fresh tensions generated by the Iran-Contra affair. Coming into office without a well-articulated substantive agenda, but with a strong sense of the disorder that can arise from congressional attempts to exercise naturally executive functions, President Bush took the unique (or at least very unusual) step of directing that a legal strategy be developed for enhancing the defense of his office. The record of this effort to close the gap between constitutional principle and administration policy can help illuminate the possibilities open to presidential legal advisers, as well as the limits on their role in government.

The Existing Literature and an Alternative Approach

A close study of the Bush administration's record on separation-of-powers issues also offers an opportunity to supplement a growing body of scholarship dealing with the behavior of legal bureaucracies. This scholarship, which has been produced mainly by political scientists, attempts to explain the behavior of lawyers in government in terms of various personal, institutional, and historical forces. Nancy V. Baker, for example, focuses on individual attorneys general and seeks to explain their performance in office according to whether they behaved more as a neutral law officer or as the president's advocate and supporter.[15] James Michael Strine's detailed study of the Justice Department's OLC concludes that both continuity and change within that office can be explained by its institutional structures, norms, roles, and rules.[16] Cornell W. Clayton emphasizes the impact on legal policy-making at the Justice Department of wider historical and political forces, such as the nationalization of governmental power, the judicialization of large areas of public policy, and the institutionalization of partisan conflict.[17]

The information included in these studies can explain a great deal, for government lawyers certainly do operate in environments that are severely constrained by factors ranging from the norms and expectations of the legal profession, to the balance of power that obtains among various political factions in and out of government at any given time, to the sheer growth in size and complexity of the federal administrative state. In my view, however, the existing literature does not adequately explain the operation of these factors, because it gives insufficient attention to the way in which incentive structures affect the choices made by individual lawyers and by those with whom they deal.

The absence of serious inquiry into the incentives that affect individual choice in legal bureaucracies appears to be the result primarily of constraints that the subject matter places on those who undertake such studies. First, the most accessible sources of information about the way legal bureaucracies operate are the memoirs of individuals who have served in high positions in the government. Such memoirs are obviously unreliable because their authors face an extremely strong temptation to understate the degree to which they engaged in self-serving or mistaken behavior while in office. When researchers try to supplement the accounts from such sources by means of interviews with more obscure officials, their research cannot escape the underlying problem. Many government lawyers take the confidentiality of their work seriously and are therefore reluctant to speak in useful detail about what they and others in the government do or have done. Those who do choose to speak with researchers, especially when they speak anonymously, cannot be assumed either to constitute a fair sample or to be unbiased reporters. On the contrary, it would be safer to suppose that a substantial number of those who are willing to provide information to outsiders do so because they have an ax to grind.[18]

Documentary evidence in the form of legal archives rarely provides much assistance in correcting the preceding problems. The documents that underlie the legal advice presidents receive are seldom available to researchers until after the decisions to which they relate are long past, and in many cases they never become available at all.[19] Much advice, moreover, is formulated in meetings and discussions that are never recorded, among people who will never have a reason to offer complete (or completely candid) accounts of what was said.

These difficulties can be especially serious when academic analysts are intent on formulating lessons that they wish to urge on policymakers, as most students of this subject have been. Clayton, for example, is extremely harsh in criticizing what he considers the "politicization" of the Justice Department under Presidents Reagan and Bush, and he concludes that serious consideration should be given to removing that department from the president's control.[20] Jeremy Rabkin, conversely, reviews most of what little is known about the history of the office of the counsel to the president and concludes by attacking the Clinton administration for relying insufficiently on the institutional wisdom of the Justice Department.[21] Such recommendations, however, can hardly be trusted beyond the limits of the explanatory models on which they are based; and scholarship in this area is very short on testable predictions. Indeed, one rarely sees any analysis that gets much beyond such completely obvious propositions as the following: when the executive and legislative departments are controlled by different political parties, conflicts over separation of powers increase; increasing conflicts between the executive and the legislature tend to increase the involvement of the judiciary in issues involving the control of governmental institutions; executive officials have less success in pursuing aggressive agendas if their private financial dealings create opportunities for their adversaries to attack their ethics; legal advisers who do not champion the president's agenda lose influence with the president, while those who do promote his designs invite attacks from the president's political adversaries.

I have tried to overcome some of the limitations in the existing literature. First, I employ a simple and fairly well-defined model of human behavior, drawn from the science of economics, that has proved to be extremely powerful in explaining a wide range of human conduct. I assume, as a hypothesis, that the president and his legal advisers, along with the other people with whom they deal in their professional lives, tend to behave as rational utility maximizers in an environment characterized by limited resources. This model implies, most importantly for present purposes, that people cannot have as much as they want of the most obvious things they desire—such as money, prestige, power, and leisure—and that they respond to changes in their environment by changing their own behavior in an effort to maximize their self-interest. One reason for regarding this model as especially useful in the present context is that it helps direct our attention to important causal influences that those who create the public record on which research must primarily rely have a motive to conceal, even from themselves. As everyone knows, people who serve in public office are inclined to explain their own behavior by reference to the "public interest" or "the law" or "the Constitution," rather than in terms of their self-interest. But there is no more reason to accept such protestations of disinterestedness from government lawyers—at least without critical examination—than from functionaries in the worlds of business or electoral politics.

One obvious danger involved in the use of a rational-choice model is that it tempts the analyst to discount any appeal to standards such as "the law" or "the Constitution" as self-serving camouflage, without giving sufficient attention to the fact that people may (at least in some circumstances) include fidelity to the law in their own utility functions. The law and legal principles, like the dictates of loyalty and justice, can and do operate as meaningful constraints on lawyers' behavior, even though this surely happens less often than lawyers say it does when they are explaining their own actions. To avoid the pitfall of unjustified cynicism, I have focused on the strengths and weaknesses of the legal arguments offered by the individuals whose conduct is being considered, and compared what they actually did with the explanations they offered for what they did.

The rational-choice model of human behavior generates a simple but somewhat counterintuitive prediction about the subject matter of this chapter: *a president should prove unsuccessful if he attempts to make the defense of the presidency an important element of his administration's agenda.* The rewards for a consistent and forceful defense of the legal interests of the office of the presidency would largely be abstract, since they would consist primarily of fidelity to a certain theory of the Constitution. To the extent that the rewards were manifested as actual increases in power to accomplish policy and political goals, the rewards would mostly be reaped at some remote period of time, after the defenders of the theory had left office. The costs of pursuing a serious defense of the presidency, on the other hand, would tend to be immediate and tangible. These costs would include the expenditure of political capital that might have been used for more important or more pressing purposes, the unpleasantness of increased friction with congressional barons and their representatives in the bureaucracy, and the sheer expenditure of time by extremely busy people on relatively dry legal issues.

Presidential lawyers who specialize in the separation of powers would tend to collect a relatively large share of the benefits, in the form of increased glory and increased job satisfaction, but the specialization of functions necessary to produce this result also means that the costs would largely be borne by others in the government—above all, the president. Accordingly, when the costs to the president (or to those of his advisers with a broader responsibility for governance than that allocated to separation-of-powers lawyers) become significant, we should expect that the lawyers' legal principles would be compromised or abandoned. Finally, because the costs of adhering to such principles will tend to be highest in the most important cases, we should expect to find a pattern in which the principles are adhered to most scrupulously in relatively trivial ways. The following sections of this chapter are devoted to testing these predictions.

The approach sketched here necessarily requires a more detailed level of analysis than one ordinarily finds in studies of the operation of legal bureaucracies. I have therefore limited the study in two dimensions. First, only issues involving the separation of powers are considered. Second, the analysis is confined almost exclusively to George Bush's four years in office. For the reasons offered earlier, I believe that this is a particularly illuminating example, but similarly detailed studies need to be made of other issue clusters and of other eras. In addition, this chapter presents a limited set of examples, and it describes them in a simplified form that is designed to render them accessible to a general audience.[22]

THE EFFORT TO IMPLEMENT CONSTITUTIONAL PRINCIPLE

In 1987, Vice-President Bush was introduced at a meeting of a group of conservative lawyers by C. Boyden Gray, who had served as his counselor throughout the Reagan administration. The vice-president then delivered a speech arguing that congressional "micromanagement" of foreign policy improperly substituted an unduly legalistic "regulatory" regime for the legislature's properly political oversight responsibilities. Bush believed both that this was a serious practical problem (because it threatened to "destroy our government's ability to function effectively") and that its amelioration required practical steps to establish relationships of trust between officials in the executive and legislative departments of government. Significantly, however, Bush contended that these practical steps should be taken in the context of a reexamination of the intent of the framers of the Constitution and of the "objective principles embodied in the law" they created.[23]

Soon after becoming president, Bush again addressed this same issue: "I am concerned about the erosion of presidential power, particularly in the fields of national defense and foreign policy, but I want to work with Congress," Bush said. "If they want in on the take-off, fine. I've got to make the decision. I have constitutional responsibilities and they have theirs, largely in the purse strings."[24] The president also moved quickly to establish a special working group of lawyers to devise legal strategies for carrying out his interests in these matters.[25] The ranking members of this group were C. Boyden Gray and William P. Barr, the assistant attorney general for the OLC, who was often described as Gray's protégé.[26] (The OLC is a relatively small office, usually staffed by twenty-odd lawyers, that carries out the attorney general's responsibility to provide legal advice to the president and to the heads of the executive departments.) Barr's reputation at the OLC came to rest largely on his aggressive defense of presidential authority,[27] and he enjoyed a meteoric rise from almost complete obscurity to the office of attorney general.

Defense of the constitutional authorities of the presidency continued to receive considerable attention throughout Bush's presidency. In a major address on the Constitution midway through his term, for example, the president talked mainly about relations between the president and Congress. In this address, he claimed that he had possessed the "inherent power" to use the armed forces during the Gulf War without congressional authorization; he said that, when Congress takes aggressive legislative action against specific presidential powers, "the President has a constitutional obligation to protect his Office and to veto the legislation"; and he boasted of having said on many occasions "that statutory provisions that violate the Constitution have no binding legal force."[28] At the very end of his term, moreover, President Bush engaged in an unusually direct and personal effort to assert authority over a federal agency (the U.S. Postal Service) that Congress had sought to insulate from the president's control.

This very high-level interest in shoring up the legal defense of the presidency distinguished the Bush administration from its predecessor. President Reagan's first attorney general, in a rare criticism of the president he served, wrote in his memoirs that the White House had not provided sufficient leadership in dealing with issues that could adversely affect the province of the executive.[29] This is not to say that the separation of powers had been given no thought during the Reagan administration or that there had been no willingness to act in defense of the presidency.[30] Indeed, that administration's constitutional lawyers—primarily those at the OLC—had worked out a detailed jurisprudence that was scarcely revised or supplemented during the Bush years.[31] At the beginning of his term, in fact, Bush may have seemed to be doing little more than elevating that preexisting jurisprudence to the status of administration policy. Alternatively one could say that Bush was endorsing the concerns and goals of the OLC in a way that would allow the body of legal principles developed in that office to be given a fair test outside the rarefied atmosphere of the OLC itself. If we want to obtain some idea of what can happen when the president allows (and even encourages) his leading lawyers to devote themselves to the interests of the presidency itself, the Bush administration offers an almost perfect case study.

I have argued elsewhere that the OLC faces certain constraints and incentives that prevent it from developing an institutional mission of the kind that is often observed in government bureaucracies, including such legal bureaucracies as the office of the solicitor general.[32] It is even more obvious that the White House counsel's office—which is completely reconstituted with each new administration, and which each president is free to shape in whatever way he sees fit—cannot be assumed to be driven by a stable institutional or bureaucratic culture. Even so, some "missions" may be so inherently appropriate or attractive to presidential legal advisers that they are adopted with a kind of inevitability that does not depend on the operation of bureaucratic imperatives of the usual kind. For the OLC, defense of the presidency constitutes an obvious candidate for such a mission, and separation of powers does seem to be regarded as the soul of that office's work.[33] For those who serve in the office of the White House counsel, moreover, adopting the mission of defending the presidency would offer a way of taking the edge off their slightly unsavory reputation for politically driven lawyering.[34] The Bush administration should therefore show us what can happen when lawyers with a commitment to the separation of powers are elevated, or get themselves elevated, to the role of serious policy players.

The record of the Bush administration also provides an opportunity to test an important hypothesis derived from game theory. As John O. McGinnis has pointed out, the actual practice of separation of powers can be described through "a model in which governmental powers are often distributed [not by the formal rules set out in the Constitution, but rather] by the branches themselves through bargains and accommodations that maximize their respective interests."[35] One corollary of this model seems to be that the president should be able to strengthen his bargaining position through a "precommitment strategy": by committing his prestige to the defense of a set of publicly articulated principles, the president can strengthen his own hand in future negotiations because everyone will know that departures from those principles are going to be more costly to the president than if his prestige were not already committed.[36] Under this view, President Bush's visible elevation of the roles of his constitutional lawyers can be seen as serving the president's interests at least as much as it served those lawyers' interests: "By articulating the principles that the executive will not concede, OLC generates commitments for the future that may strengthen the president's bargaining position vis-a-vis the other branches."[37] If this plausible suggestion about the usefulness of "precommitment strategies" actually helps explain the development of the separation of powers, we should expect to observe significantly more resolute and uncompromising behavior by the Bush administration than by the Reagan administration. For reasons indicated earlier, my own conclusion is that other incentives operating on the president and his advisers should be expected to render such a precommitment strategy untenable.

Implementation of the Legal Strategy: Veto Messages and Signing Statements

Without attempting to canvass every issue involving the separation of powers that emerged during the Bush administration or to compare systematically that administration's approach with others in the past, one can find a number of indications that the president's interest in promoting a coherent and forceful legal strategy did have observable effects. Perhaps the most visible results of President Bush's initiative emerged in his veto messages and in the signing statements he issued when approving new legislation.

President Bush vetoed forty-six bills, citing constitutional objections in at least eleven instances. In five of these eleven cases, the bills would certainly have been vetoed because of nonconstitutional policy issues anyway, and they might not have been vetoed on constitutional grounds alone.[38] In two of the eleven cases, however, the principal grounds for the president's objection to the bill were constitutional in nature[39]; and in four other cases, constitutional objections were the only apparent reason for his veto.[40] Remarkably, every veto that was based solely or primarily on constitutional grounds involved a claimed invasion of the constitutional authority of the president's office, while at least two other bills that the president deemed unconstitutional (although not a threat to his office) were allowed to become law.[41] President Reagan, in sharp contrast, seems never to have vetoed a bill because it infringed on the president's authority,[42] although he sometimes included objections to such infringements in messages dealing with vetoes that were based primarily on policy grounds.[43] Reagan, however, did veto at least two bills on constitutional grounds unrelated to presidential authority, including one that simply codified a regulation that the Supreme Court had previously upheld.[44] Reagan frequently approved bills containing constitutionally objectionable restrictions on his authority,[45] and he signed into law at least four bills that his administration later challenged in the courts as violating the president's constitutional powers.[46]

A pattern similar to that found in Bush's veto messages can be found in his signing statements. Unlike the president's veto messages, which are required by the Constitution, the statements that presidents sometimes issue when they approve new legislation are completely discretionary. Many presidents have issued such statements from time to time, but serious efforts to use them as a tool for advancing a coherent legal strategy began only in the Reagan administration.[47] Signing statements can serve as such a tool in three principal ways: by interpreting ambiguous statutory language in a manner that the president hopes will be treated by the courts as a legitimate form of legislative history[48]; by instructing the president's subordinates in the executive agencies to resolve statutory ambiguities in the way favored by the president[49]; and by creating a record that can later be used to refute claims that the president has approved of constitutionally dubious provisions of bills that the president has decided to sign because of his desire to see other provisions of the legislation become law.

During the Bush years, the constitutional issues addressed in signing statements dealt mostly with questions of presidential authority, and the statements seem to have been designed mostly to serve the third purpose mentioned above—namely, to avoid leaving the impression that the president approved of objectionable legislation. The Bush signing statements are pervaded by an amazing scrupulosity about the separation of powers. Even a cursory review of the record suggests that the administration tried to identify and deal with every such issue in every bill that was presented to the president. The lengths to which the Bush administration was prepared to go in applying legalistic analysis to enrolled bills, moreover, are suggested in the following droll passage from the signing statement for the 1991 defense authorization bill:

[S]ection 1409(a) refers to a classified annex that was prepared to accompany the conference report on this Act and states that the annex "shall have the force and effect of law as if enacted into law." The Congress has thus stated in the statute that the annex has not been enacted into law, but it nonetheless urges that the annex be treated as if it were law. I will certainly take into account the Congress' wishes in this regard, but will do so mindful of the fact that, according to the terms of the statute, the provisions of the annex are not law.[50]

This kind of hyperlegalistic interpretation was complemented by a grand attempt at comprehensive scrutiny. Each year, for example, the president issued a statement claiming that all of the numerous legislative veto provisions inserted in various bills would be treated as legal nullities.[51] Numerous signing statements challenged the legal validity of provisions that restricted the president's discretion, and the president sometimes seemed to threaten that he would act in defiance of the objectionable provisions. On at least four occasions, he went so far as to obtain a legal opinion from the OLC concluding that it would be lawful for him to defy a statutory provision,[52] and he seems actually to have done so in at least one case.[53] Although the president's constitutional objections to statutory provisions arose most often in the context of Bush's principal interest, foreign affairs,[54] many others dealt with matters, such as the arcana of the Appointments and Recommendation Clauses, that he could not possibly have taken a passionate interest in.[55]

It is impossible to assess with any confidence whether the Bush administration's veto and signing statement strategy will have any lasting effects. The strategy was defensive, consisting almost entirely in resisting new congressional encroachments into areas that the Bush administration thought were reserved by the Constitution to the executive's discretion. To measure the consequences of this resistance, one would have to determine what precedents would have been created if the resistance had not occurred, and one would have to determine what significance those precedents would have had in the future. Once the Clinton administration begins to establish its own approach to veto messages (if there prove to be any) and signing statements, some useful comparisons may begin to emerge. The evidence that now exists, however, leaves open the strong possibility that the Bush administration's strategy amounted to little more than a kind of gesturing by means of which it sought to signal its intention—or reserve its rights—to seize ground from Congress if the opportunity to do so ever arose. Absent evidence that such opportunities arose and were taken, Bush's veto messages and signing statements are not likely very important.[56]

Compromise of the Constitutional Vetoes

The four Bush vetoes that were apparently based solely on constitutional grounds reinforce this suspicion. They are therefore worth examining in some detail, for their contribution to legal and political developments can only be understood by examining the reasoning on which they were based and by seeing how the president subsequently dealt with what proved to be ongoing disputes.

The Appointments Clause. One minor piece of pork-barrel legislation sponsored by a Democratic senator was vetoed solely because it contained provisions that violated the Appointments Clause.[57] This bill, which was named in honor of former congressman Morris Udall, would have assigned authority to make determinations about eligibility for federal funds to a board dominated by members not appointed by the president. President Bush emphasized in his veto message that his refusal to approve the bill was based solely on constitutional grounds and that he had no substantive or policy objections to the legislation. But when the president was presented with a successor bill that he deemed constitutionally invalid because of a different type of Appointments Clause violation, he signed it anyway.[58] Fidelity to the constitutional analysis that had provoked the first veto thus proved to be less than thoroughgoing.[59]

President Bush's concession in this case can usefully be contrasted with another incident in which he was more successful in getting what he wanted. When he approved the National and Community Service Act of 1990,[60] Bush issued a signing statement discussing what he regarded as constitutional defects in the provisions establishing a commission created by the statute to administer the most important programs established by the act. Under the statute, various restrictions were placed on the president's freedom to choose nominees for this commission, and the president regarded these as violations of the Appointments Clause. In his signing statement, the president said that these restrictions were "without legal force or effect."[61]

As long as the president refused to nominate candidates for the commission, the congressionally mandated programs probably could not have been administered.[62] In the course of his signing statement, the president also indicated that he was not particularly enthusiastic about the programs that this commission was to implement, while he strongly favored a separate part of the act that authorized funding for one of his own favorite programs. Congress therefore had reason to believe that the president might refuse to make the nominations required by the statute. In a burst of speed that would otherwise have been mystifying, Congress passed remedial legislation to bring the statute into conformity with the president's view of the Appointments Clause, early in the next legislative session.[63] What distinguishes this case from the one involving the Udall bill is that here the president's political and policy interests were firmly aligned with his interest in the Appointments Clause, whereas his objections to the Udall bill seem to have been rooted solely in constitutional principle.

Presidential Control over Foreign Policy. In late 1990, President Bush vetoed a bill dealing with export controls on certain goods with military applications, because he objected to provisions requiring that sanctions be imposed on countries that use or distribute chemical and biological weapons. The president did not object to such sanctions as a matter of policy, and he made this clear by signing an executive order that directed the imposition of the same sanctions contained in the bill.[64] Rather, he objected to Congress's "rigid" and "mandatory" imposition on him (at a delicate diplomatic moment) of a legal obligation to impose the sanctions; this, he said, interfered with his "constitutional responsibilities" to conduct the nation's foreign policy.[65]

Although the president's objection to the export control bill was clearly rooted in his understanding of the constitutional separation of powers, he did not quite claim that such interference actually violated the Constitution. His constitutional concerns were also not clearly distinguishable from his concerns about immediate practical consequences that the bill might have during what proved to be the prologue to the Gulf War: "The mandatory imposition of unilateral sanctions as provided in this bill would harm U.S. economic interests and provoke friendly countries who are essential to our efforts to resist Iraqi aggression."[66] The relative importance of these practical concerns was confirmed, after the Gulf War had been successfully prosecuted, when the president signed a bill with mandatory sanctions provisions that differed only slightly from those to which he had objected earlier.[67] This outcome, together with the attenuated nature of the president's original constitutional objections, makes it impossible to regard his veto of the original version of the mandatory sanctions as an important sign of commitment to constitutional principles.

Congressional Responses to Iran-Contra. The two other vetoes that President Bush exercised on constitutional grounds were more significant, but they, too, were followed by compromises that undercut their importance substantially. The vetoed bills were part of a highly complex struggle between the Bush administration and Congress over legislative efforts to prevent a repetition of certain activities that had occurred in connection with the Iran-Contra affair. In simplified form, many individuals on the Hill were determined to make two requirements effective: that Congress be kept fully and contemporaneously informed about covert actions (like the arms sales to Iran); and that, when Congress placed limits on the president's ability to take certain foreign policy actions directly (like the limits placed at times on assisting the Contras), the president would not be able to take those same actions indirectly by imposing on other nations to carry them out.

In late 1989, President Bush was presented with a bill that made it a felony for any executive official to "assist" others (including foreign governments) in carrying out diplomatic initiatives that the executive itself was prohibited by statute from pursuing directly. The bill also required the president to notify Congress whenever an executive official "advocates, promotes, or encourages" the provision of material assistance by outside parties for activities that executive officials are forbidden by statute to undertake or assist in.[68] As President Bush noted when he vetoed this bill, its vague and sweeping provisions threatened to interfere with the conduct of foreign affairs by exposing diplomats and other officials to the threat of imprisonment for engaging in discussions that might later be found to constitute a prohibited form of "assistance." President Bush also observed that the threat to the president's constitutional role in conducting foreign relations was heightened by the fact that those who served in Congress would remain free to engage in the very diplomatic activities forbidden to the executive.[69] The resulting timidity and disarray in the conduct of foreign policy, said the president, would be "wholly contrary to the allocation of powers under the Constitution."[70]

The following year, President Bush vetoed another bill that would have had similar effects. This second bill contained a complicated set of provisions designed to force the president to notify Congress about covert actions more promptly than President Reagan had informed it about the secret arms sales to Iran during the 1980s.[71] As part of this effort to ensure greater congressional involvement in the conduct of covert actions, the bill defined such covert actions to include any "request" by the United States government to a foreign government or private citizen to conduct a covert action on behalf of the United States. This definition was sufficient to provoke the president's veto (although the provisions dealing with notifications to Congress about covert actions were no less important).[72] In language reminiscent of the wording he used the previous year, President Bush criticized the bill's vagueness about the meaning of reportable "requests," and complained that this vagueness "could have a chilling effect on the ability of our diplomats to conduct highly sensitive discussions concerning projects that are vital to our national security."[73] Because the contested provision of this bill did not actually forbid diplomatic discussions but only required that they be reported, and because it did not include provisions for criminal sanctions, it could not be easily characterized as unconstitutional (and the president's veto message did not use that term). President Bush's decision to veto the bill therefore could have been interpreted as signaling a serious determination to resist congressional meddling in the prerogatives of his office and to preserve the traditional separation of powers even beyond what he saw as the strict requirements of the Constitution.

President Bush was most aggressive in his defense of the authority of his office in the field of foreign relations, where his expertise and interest were greatest. The veto messages dealing with prohibited forms of "assistance" and with reportable "requests" reflect this emphasis, and they are also typical of the highly nuanced and sophisticated constitutional analysis that runs consistently through Bush's veto messages and signing statements. Viewed in isolation, however, these two veto messages could be quite misleading. First, the group of officials most directly threatened by these two bills consisted of career foreign service officers—a potent interest group within the government and one that counted among its own the man then serving as deputy secretary of state. Second, and more importantly, the Bush administration proved willing to compromise, in a very serious way, the principles that had seemed to be at the center of the president's decisions to veto these two bills.

This compromise occurred the same day the president vetoed the bill that would have prohibited U.S. officials from "assisting" others in certain foreign policy activities. That day, President Bush approved another bill containing a provision sponsored by Representative David Obey, under which U.S. officials were barred from providing appropriated funds to any foreign government or other person "in exchange for" that government's or person's undertaking an action that federal law expressly prohibited the U.S. officials themselves from engaging in.[74]

President Bush's signing statement recognized that the Obey Amendment, although somewhat less sweeping than the vetoed ban on "assisting" forbidden activities, also had the potential to chill the conduct of foreign affairs: "Many routine and unobjectionable diplomatic activities could be misconstrued as somehow involving a forbidden 'exchange.' "[75] Why then did the president sign the bill? Following a pattern characteristic of many Bush signing statements, in which he interpreted objectionable provisions so as to render them consistent with his view of the Constitution (though often completely inconsistent with the statutory language),[76] the president contended that the Obey Amendment covered only transactions "in which U.S. funds are provided to a foreign nation on the *express* condition that the foreign nation provide specific assistance to a third country."[77] The signing statement also maintained that, because the Obey Amendment was designed to apply only where U.S. law "expressly prohibits" American officials from taking an action, it would not apply where U.S. statutes "merely limit funding to undertake such an action."[78]

The president's interpretation was in some respects simply irreconcilable with the statutory language. The Obey Amendment, for example, unambiguously referred to exchanges with any "foreign person or United States person," not just to exchanges with "foreign nations." Similarly, the Obey Amendment prohibited U.S. officials from inducing others to undertake "any action" that the United States government is forbidden from taking, not just actions in which a foreign nation "provide[s] specific assistance to a third country." Where the president's interpretation of the Obey Amendment's text was not preposterous, it was far-fetched. The natural and obvious meaning of the phrase "in exchange for" clearly covers implicit agreements as well as transactions based on an express condition, especially when it occurs (as here) in a statutory provision that carefully distinguishes implicit from express prohibitions. And there is precious little room in the statute's language for the president's claim that laws that limit funding for certain activities do not expressly prohibit U.S. officials from providing funding in excess of those limits; on the contrary, it has long been a felony, pursuant to an express and general statutory prohibition, for government officials to make expenditures beyond the limits set in appropriations legislation.[79]

In a desperate attempt to shore up his utterly implausible interpretation of the Obey Amendment's language, President Bush sought to rely on the amendment's legislative history to show that his interpretation actually reflected congressional intent. But again he had little to rely on. Flouting standard canons of statutory construction, the Bush signing statement ignored the portions of the legislative history that courts consider the most reliable indicia of legislative intent, such as statements by the sponsor of the provision in question (which in this case was Representative Obey, who chaired the appropriations subcommittee with jurisdiction over the bill). Instead, President Bush referred vaguely to statements by Representative Mickey Edwards (the ranking *minority* member on the subcommittee), and to a colloquy between two *Republican* Senators (Kasten and Rudman).

When one actually examines the legislative history of the Obey Amendment, the flimsiness of the administration's legal argument becomes even more apparent. Representative Obey made it clear that his amendment was intended to prohibit appropriated funds from being "expended in any way to promote or entice other governments to support policies which would be illegal if followed by the United States."[80] Moreover, Representative Edwards, who helped negotiate the final version of the Obey Amendment and on whom the Bush signing statement purports to rely, never said that the amendment requires an express agreement. Rather, Edwards said that a violation of the provision would have to be based on a "quid pro quo," which is just another way of describing the provision of funds "in exchange for" some action.[81] The term "quid pro quo" no more excludes implicit agreements than the statutory "in exchange for" language does.[82]

The president's invocation of Representative Edwards's statements to support his narrow construction of the Obey Amendment was baseless, and his reliance on a colloquy between Senators Kasten and Rudman was not much better. Immediately after the House passed the bill containing the Obey Amendment, the Senate debate on the measure began. At the end of that debate, Senator Kasten offered a substitute amendment that would have replaced the Obey provision with language forbidding U.S. officials from providing appropriated funds pursuant to agreements under which, "as an express condition for receipt of such assistance," the recipients would undertake military or foreign policy activities that are illegal under American law.[83] Kasten, who was openly serving as the Bush administration's agent on this issue, withdrew this amendment after engaging Senator Rudman (who had generally opposed the administration's position on related issues) in a planned colloquy. Rudman asserted that violations of the Obey Amendment should not give rise to criminal penalties, and that the words "in exchange for" should be understood to refer to agreements under which U.S. aid is provided on the "express condition" that the recipient undertake an action that U.S. officials are legally forbidden to carry out.[84]

Because no objections were raised to Senator Rudman's interpretation, which the record indicates was offered on the floor immediately before the bill containing the Obey Amendment was passed by the Senate, the Kasten-Rudman colloquy is not completely worthless as an indicator of the Senate's intent.[85] But even if one assumes that the colloquy firmly establishes that the Senate's interpretation of the Obey Amendment was the same as the president's, the record in the House does not support that interpretation, at least with respect to whether a violation must be based on an express agreement. And since the meaning suggested by the debates in the originating chamber is more consistent with the language of the provision, a disinterested interpreter would almost certainly reject the construction of the statute offered in the Bush signing statement.

Even under a fair interpretation of its meaning, however, the Obey Amendment was less threatening to the president's conduct of foreign affairs than the provision against which President Bush used his veto the same day. The president's signing statement, moreover, may have helped prevent the new law from being used as a tool of partisan or ideological combat. But President Bush gave up a great deal when he signed the bill containing the second version of the Obey Amendment. To see how much he surrendered, one need only look at his signing statement's claim that the Senate record made it clear that "neither the criminal conspiracy statute, nor any other criminal penalty" would apply to violations of the Obey Amendment. Even if one assumes—somewhat heroically, perhaps—that the courts would apply the rule of lenity (which counsels that ambiguous statutes should be construed in favor of criminal defendants), such legislative history could not prevent an independent counsel from procuring indictments based on the general conspiracy statute.[86]

Lawrence Walsh had done this and more when he prosecuted Oliver North and others for conspiring to obstruct government functions by (among other things) evading two of the so-called Boland Amendments (which restricted federal aid to the Nicaraguan Contras),[87] and everyone concerned clearly understood that the Obey Amendment was an effort to make it easier (not more difficult) to discourage government officials from engaging in activities like those engaged in by the targets of Walsh's investigations. Nor could anyone who was involved in the conduct of foreign policy during this period have had less than an acute awareness of the costs that an independent counsel can impose on his targets even when he fails to make his criminal charges stick. Neither the president nor anyone else could assure U.S. diplomats that similar indictments for violating the Obey Amendment would not be brought or that the courts would rule against the validity of such prosecutions.[88] To the extent that U.S. diplomats chose to take their legal advice from the president's signing statement, or from the more elaborate but equally dubious legal opinion subsequently issued by the OLC,[89] the Obey Amendment could not have had much of a chilling effect. But when one considers how reckless or self-sacrificing a diplomat would have to be to take the president's statement as legal advice, any notion that the president's concession in signing the Obey Amendment into law was an unimportant surrender dissipates like the insubstantial haze of the legal analysis in the signing statement itself.[90]

President Bush's signing statements and veto messages displayed a consistent and relatively aggressive approach to the separation of powers issues that arose from congressional efforts to subject the administration to various statutory restrictions. In this sense, the Bush record represents a kind of triumph for the academically oriented lawyers responsible for crafting the president's statements.[91] Upon closer examination, however, this victory appears to have been more of form than of substance. The aggressive signing statements do not appear to have reflected much actual resistance to congressional control, and each of the vetoes based on constitutional objections was followed by substantial compromise of the principles on which those vetoes were based.

THREE RETREATS FROM THE ADMINISTRATION'S CONSTITUTIONAL PRINCIPLES

If the lawyers' "successes" do not suggest that their contribution to the development of separation-of-powers law was particularly important, the lawyers' "failures" provide even stronger evidence of their marginal influence. The Bush record shows that this administration was simply unwilling to defend its theories of the Constitution on several important occasions. A brief look at three departures from the principled jurisprudence articulated in the Bush signing statements and veto messages helps illuminate the forces that discourage the implementation of a thoroughgoing and principled jurisprudence of the separation of powers.

Legislative Vetoes

Early in its tenure, the Bush administration sought to dispose of the contentious matter of the Nicaraguan Contras, which it had inherited from President Reagan. After investing a significant amount of time in negotiations, the secretary of state reached an agreement with congressional leaders that provided temporary funding to support the Contras. Part of these so-called "Central American Accords" required the administration to promise in writing that no money would be used to support the Contras after a date certain unless the chairmen of four congressional committees approved the continued funding in writing.[92] Neither the OLC nor the counsel to the president (nor for that matter the State Department's own legal adviser) was consulted about this arrangement,[93] which incorporated a formal legislative veto device that would clearly have been unconstitutional under the Supreme Court's ruling in *INS v. Chadha,* had the device been adopted in legislation.[94] Press speculation intimated that personal factors may have contributed to the absence of advance consultations, and it can hardly be doubted that the secretary of state and the counsel to the president had an uneasy relationship.[95] But the agreement's adverse impact on the president's constitutional authority was evidently not overlooked. One State Department official who took part in the negotiations was quoted as saying that "the precedential aspects of this agreement were well and truly understood" by Secretary of State Baker and other negotiators.[96] Instead, the president seems to have decided that resolving the contentious issue of aid to the Contras was simply more important than maintaining a principled opposition to the use of legislative vetoes. The fact that the newly inaugurated president felt free to make this decision without consulting the OLC, the counsel to the president, or any other legal officer in the government strikingly illustrates how unlikely it is that a president would ever allow the concerns that lawyers have with the interests of his office to determine his conduct in that office.

The flap over the agreement to comply with a nonstatutory legislative veto attracted considerable attention because the counsel to the president mistakenly voiced his objections in the press.[97] During the ensuing years, however, no attention at all was paid to the fact that President Bush routinely signed bills containing legislative vetoes that unquestionably violated the *Chadha* rule, unlike the Contra funding agreement (which was not technically unconstitutional). Although the president also routinely issued statements denouncing the congressional practice of including such "legal nullities" in bills that were presented to him,[98] I have found no recorded instance of the Bush administration's refusing to comply with any of the innumerable legislative vetoes to which it was subjected. Nor, it appears, did the Bush administration take any other action that might have discouraged the Congress from flouting one of the few apparently significant post-Watergate Supreme Court victories for the office of the president.[99]

The Appointments Clause

It is easy to imagine why President Bush approved the trade-off between politics and principle involved in the Central American Accords, especially in view of the fact that the arrangement did not violate the Constitution. The same cannot be said, however, of another departure from well-settled principles of the separation of powers. On August 9, 1989, President Bush signed into law the Financial Institutions Reform, Recovery, and Enforcement Act of 1989 (FIRREA), which effected a massive restructuring of the regulatory regime governing the savings-and-loan industry. As part of that restructuring, an independent agency known as the Federal Home Loan Bank Board (FHLBB) had most of its functions transferred to a new entity, called the Office of Thrift Supervision (OTS), which was located within the Department of the Treasury. When he signed the bill, President Bush did not mention that the new statute contained a provision that purported to appoint as the first director of the OTS the individual who had been chairman of the FHLBB.[100]

Such a provision, under which an officer of the United States is appointed by statute, is as clear a violation of the Appointments Clause of the Constitution as one could hope to find. If one were familiar only with the fastidious attention to Appointments Clause issues that pervades the Bush administration's signing statements and with the president's decision to veto one bill solely because of a less clear-cut violation of the Appointment Clause,[101] the administration's acquiescence in the statutory appointment of a federal officer might be surprising or even shocking.

The president's failure to object to this element of the bill when he signed it, however, becomes easier to understand when one recognizes the still more extraordinary fact that the Bush administration had itself proposed the same kind of illegal statutory appointment in a savings-and-loan bill it had transmitted to the Congress a few months earlier.[102]

This blunder led directly to litigation brought by a thrift whose assets the OTS was threatening to seize.[103] In the course of the lawsuit, which challenged the OTS's authority to act, on the ground that its director had been unconstitutionally appointed,[104] the director resigned and was eventually replaced by an official appointed in the constitutionally prescribed manner. Before that happened, however, the Bush administration put forward the desperate argument that the statutory appointment was valid because the chairmanship of the FHLBB was the same office as the directorship of the OTS—a position emphatically rejected by the district court.[105] This litigation, which threatened serious disruption of the OTS's regulatory work, became moot when a new director was confirmed by the Senate and appointed by the president.[106]

Given the Bush administration's scrupulous attention to the Appointments Clause in other contexts, including one veto that was based solely on an Appointments Clause objection,[107] its flagrant disregard of constitutional forms in this case is striking. William P. Barr, who served at the head of the OLC when the president signed the bill enacting the violation into law, has publicly stated that the OLC "recognized an Appointments Clause problem" in the bill.[108] He also reports that many people in the Treasury Department and in Congress thought it was "absurd" to worry about such an issue, so that "the views of the Department of Justice were overridden. Political deals were made, and the bill passed."[109] Read carefully, Barr's account is highly revealing. First, it refers to the bill as one in which the OLC merely "recognized" a constitutional "problem." No mention is made of the fact that the Bush administration itself had formally proposed adopting the blatantly unconstitutional statutory appointment mechanism. Second, there is no indication that the OLC's constitutional objections were communicated to the president or to the White House counsel. And certainly there is no suggestion that the Department of Justice recommended that the president veto the bill, despite Barr's statement in the very same paragraph that "[w]hen a provision raises constitutional difficulties, in most cases the Attorney General should recommend veto."[110] It is hard not to infer that the Department of Justice was cutting its own "political deals" with officials at the Treasury Department and on the Hill who thought the OLC's concerns were "absurd."

What might the "political deals" involving the unconstitutional appointment provision have involved? Press speculation centered on the theory that the Bush administration—as the price for bringing the functions performed by the FHLBB under the control of the Treasury Department—acquiesced in a scheme to install the chairman of the FHLBB, who had close personal ties to a powerful Republican senator, as director of the OTS.[111] Thus the FIRREA episode suggests that, under certain circumstances, the president's constitutional lawyers themselves may bargain away the interests of his office for purposes of their own, even in an administration in which the president himself has made defense of that office an important goal. That this may have happened during the Bush administration illustrates that the president's lawyers have interests other than serving their client—even (or especially) if their client is assumed to be the presidency itself. The Justice Department's acquiescence in the unconstitutional statutory appointment therefore offers a useful counterpoint to the phenomenon illustrated by the Contra funding incident. Just as the president has interests of his own that he must weigh against the institutional interests of the office he holds, so his lawyers may be tempted to forgo the interests of his office to pursue an agenda of their own.

The Mask of "Complicated and Indirect Measures"

The Contra funding and FIRREA examples expose some important forces that necessarily limit any single-minded pursuit of the institutional interests of the presidency. Whatever intrinsic importance one may attach to the principles at stake in these incidents, however, neither departure from principle arose in circumstances that were likely to produce a large or enduring effect on the structure of government or on the law of the separation of powers. An illustration of the Bush administration's abandonment of constitutional principles when something very significant was at stake is provided by the history of the Supreme Court's decision in *Metropolitan Washington Airports Authority v. Citizens for the Abatement of Aircraft Noise, Inc.* (the *Airports* case).[112] This case proved to be an important victory for the interests of the president's office; in fact, it was probably the most important case involving those interests to be decided during the Bush administration. But the outcome was one that the president's lawyers opposed in the courts.

The *Airports* case arose from a congressional effort to create an ingenious substitute for the legislative veto device that the Supreme Court had declared unconstitutional in *Chadha*. To the extent relevant here, the story begins in 1984, when a consensus developed that capital improvements at Washington National and Dulles International airports could best be carried out if operating control and financial responsibility for the airports were transferred from the federal Department of Transportation to some sort of newly created state, local, or interstate entity.[113] In 1986, following consultations among executive agencies and interested congressional staffers over the best means of effecting such a transfer, the OLC reviewed three different proposals that would have given Congress substantial powers to supervise the new entity.[114] These powers were in the nature of legislative vetoes and were manifestly intended to substitute for the oversight powers that Congress and certain of its officers and committees had been exercising in the normal course of administration while control of the airports was vested in the Department of Transportation.

Under one proposal, state and local authorities would have been authorized to operate the airports, but Congress would have created a board of review comprising several members and officers of Congress; this board would have authority to veto the most important decisions of the new operating entity. The OLC emphatically rejected this proposal as creating a legislative veto in violation of *Chadha*. Under a second proposal, Congress would have required Virginia and the District of Columbia to establish the same kind of review board under state law, as a condition of their being allowed to gain joint control of the airports. Characterizing this proposal as one that presented "complex and novel questions involving the relationship between federal and state grants of authority," the OLC gave an elaborate legal analysis and concluded that, despite the office's "grave reservations" about the proposal's constitutionality, "a colorable argument" could be made in the proposal's defense.[115]

The third proposal was similar to the second proposal except in two particulars: the members of the review board would serve in their "personal capacities" as users of the airport, and not as representatives of Congress; and members of the review board would be members of Congress appointed by the new state operating authority from a list of names submitted by the congressional leadership. The OLC declared that this proposal would probably withstand constitutional scrutiny, and it declined to object to it on legal grounds.

The provision finally enacted in 1986 closely resembled the third proposal, which had been cleared by the OLC earlier that year. After Virginia and the District of Columbia enacted the required enabling legislation and the Secretary of Transportation entered into long-term leases with the new operating authority, the board of review was appointed from lists provided by the congressional leadership. In 1988, a citizens' suit was brought, challenging the new arrangement on the ground that the veto power granted to the board of review was unconstitutional.[116]

In 1989, after George Bush became president, the district court ruled that the legislative veto device created through the statute was constitutional. Appeal was taken, and the Department of Justice intervened in the court of appeals to defend the constitutionality of the statute.[117] The court of appeals, however, reversed the district court, holding that the device violated the separation of powers because the members of the board of review were in reality agents of the Congress.[118]

At this point, the Justice Department began behaving equivocally. Although it had intervened in the court of appeals to defend the constitutionality of the statute, it declined to join the airport authority's petition for certiorari.[119] When the Supreme Court granted this petition, the United States automatically became a respondent,[120] and it filed a brief on the merits that offered the Court little more than an expression of the government's ambivalence.

Indeed, the ambivalence might more accurately be described as incoherence. On the one hand, the Justice Department[121] argued that the fact that the board of review was created pursuant to state law did not preclude its being characterized as an agent of Congress and, therefore, unconstitutional under *Chadha* (which forbids legislative vetoes) or under *Bowsher v. Synar* (which forbids agents of Congress from exercising executive authority). The Justice Department's brief correctly observed that treating the board of review as a mere creature of state law would open "a massive loophole in the separation of powers." If such influence laundering were found to be constitutionally permissible, Congress could enact laws requiring the states, as a condition of receiving federal financial assistance, to appoint members of Congress to state offices controlling the administration of virtually all roads, schools, housing, and health care—thereby completely supplanting the federal agencies through which the president performs his central function of executing the federal laws. In a stunning effort to evade the compelling logic of this argument, however, the Justice Department then claimed that the statute at issue in the *Airports* case was constitutionally valid. Noting that members of Congress on the board of review were supposed to serve in their "personal capacities," the department contended that such individuals were especially well suited to represent the interests of all other users of the airports, since members of Congress must make frequent trips between Washington and their home districts. The Court was asked to suppose that members of Congress would somehow be appropriate representatives of airport users because they use the airports heavily, whereas they would not be appropriate representatives of constituencies that use roads, schools, and hospitals, because they merely partake in those programs to the same extent as other citizens.

The Supreme Court understandably dismissed this argument by observing that the facts of the case "belie the ipse dixit that the Board members will act 'in their individual capacities.'"[122] Rather than accept this "individual capacity" fiction, the Court affirmed the decision of the court of appeals, holding that the board-of-review device, although difficult to characterize, logically must either be an effort to exercise legislative power in violation of *Chadha* or be an attempt to exercise executive power in violation of *Bowsher*.[123] Repudiating the Justice Department's unprincipled suggestion that the Court uphold the statute while essentially confining the case to its facts, Justice Stevens forcefully explained that such ad hoc constitutional decision-making would invite abuses by the legislature, which "can with greater facility, mask under complicated and indirect measures, the encroachments which it makes on the co-ordinate departments."[124]

Perhaps the best that can be said about the Justice Department's brief is that it supplied the Supreme Court with the key argument needed for understanding the threat that the board-of-review device posed to the separation of powers. By contending that the argument did not apply in this case, however, the government's brief invited the Court to misapprehend how serious that threat was. The significance of the risk involved in the Justice Department's strategy is suggested by the fact that three dissenting justices emphasized how odd it was that the Court was reaching out to protect the president's authority from a threat that the president's own lawyers denied was real.[125]

How can the strange behavior of the Justice Department be explained? The first crucial step obviously came in 1986, when the OLC approved the scheme that was eventually invalidated by the Supreme Court. This approval seems manifestly inconsistent with the OLC's institutional propensity to resist congressional efforts to undermine the principles articulated in *Chadha* and *Bowsher*, and it is easy to imagine that the OLC's 1986 decision reflected policy pressures from the Department of Transportation and from the Office of Management and Budget. These agencies would undoubtedly have been more concerned about paying the price demanded by Congress for relieving the government of financial commitments and onerous operating responsibilities than about the niceties of constitutional law. Once the OLC's clearance was obtained and the statute was enacted, it is unremarkable that the Justice Department's litigating divisions defended the scheme when it was challenged in court. The department's litigation bureaucracies are strongly predisposed to defend the constitutionality of federal statutes, and they would have had little or no incentive to second-guess the OLC's earlier approval of this one.

It is somewhat surprising, however, that the Justice Department continued to take this approach even after President Bush came into office and began to give the defense of the presidency the kind of apparently serious backing that it had lacked during the Reagan administration. The

Bush administration could easily have abandoned its predecessor's position when the Justice Department first entered the case in 1989. Even if one assumes that the case did not at that time receive the kind of serious attention within the department that such a reversal of position would have required, the department could certainly have changed its position after the court of appeals bestowed on the president a significant and un-asked-for victory. Such "confessions of error" by the government are not common, but they are completely appropriate. Indeed, as long as they occur infrequently enough to avoid undermining the government's credibility in the courts, the only bad effect of these confessions of error is the embarrassment they cause to whichever individuals approved the position later abandoned by the government.[126] The fear of such embarrassment is the likeliest cause of the Justice Department's failure to change its position in the *Airports* case. Subsequent events, however, suggest that bureaucratic glitches and personal pride do not suffice to explain the way the *Airports* case was handled. A few months after the Supreme Court refused the Justice Department's invitation to create what the president's own lawyers called "a massive loophole in the separation of powers," Congress passed a pork-packed bill that included a provision amending the airport statute in response to the Court's decision. This bill included yet another desperate effort by Congress to retain its control over Dulles and Washington National airports by creating a new board of review that differed only superficially from the one that had been invalidated. Although membership on the new board was not expressly restricted to members of Congress, the board's members had to meet qualifications that few people outside Congress would possess, and the congressional leadership was given complete control over choosing candidates for the board. The new board also lacked an absolute veto over the operating authority's decisions, but it was given the power to delay (for up to six months) important actions with which it disagreed.

The persistence with which Congress pursued its unconstitutional goal in this situation can probably be explained by a strong, bipartisan fear that a state-controlled airports authority might inconvenience members of Congress by shifting some flights from the overburdened facilities at Washington National to Dulles (which is significantly farther from the Capitol). Members may also have been concerned that they might lose the reserved, free parking places that they now enjoy at both airports.[127] Although the president said that he considered this new legislative veto device unconstitutional, he signed the bill into law anyway, blandly commenting that the courts would have to deal with the constitutional problem.[128] At this writing, a federal district court has invoked the Supreme Court's decision in the *Airports* case to invalidate the new statute,[129] and the appellate courts are likely to reject the statutory refor-

mulation, as well. But if the courts again curb this congressional overreaching—an overreaching apparently motivated by the narrowest and
pettiest kind of self-interest—the Bush administration will certainly not
have been a significant contributor to that outcome.

The three examples discussed in this section show that the Bush administration was willing to tolerate and even advocate substantial losses
of presidential legal authority in response to perfectly ordinary—and in
some cases, remarkably trivial—political pressures. As the examples suggest, such pressures sometimes operated directly on the president and
sometimes seem to have had their effect at lower levels of the government. When one looks at these incidents together with the results of the
administration's strategy of using signing statements, veto messages, and
presidential addresses to articulate an ambitious agenda for defending the
presidency, there appears to be no evidence that this agenda was significantly furthered or even seriously pursued. Not only did the Bush administration fail to carry out a "precommitment strategy" of the kind described by John O. McGinnis, but it may actually have undermined its
credibility on the Hill by wrapping itself in high-flown rhetoric about
constitutional "principles" that, in the event, were abandoned as soon as
adhering to them became inconvenient.

DEBACLE IN THE COURTS

Perhaps the most remarkable example of the Bush administration's reluctance to act on its stated principles came to light after the president became a lame duck in the autumn of 1992. In a well-publicized series of
judicial decisions growing out of an arcane dispute over the litigating authority of the U.S. Postal Service, President Bush and his Justice Department suffered serious setbacks on several important issues involving
presidential legal authority.[130] What makes these losses especially significant for present purposes is that they could almost certainly have been
avoided if the administration had proceeded in a timely fashion according to the principles that it claimed to treasure.

On January 22, 1991, the U.S. Postal Service filed suit against the
Postal Rate Commission in the U.S. Court of Appeals for the District of
Columbia Circuit. Although suits by the Postal Service against the Postal
Rate Commission are specifically authorized by statute, they are constitutionally questionable because they assume that disputes within the executive establishment can legitimately be resolved by an entity outside the
president's control. The principle at stake—that the executive department of government is a unitary entity subject to the president's control
and supervision—implies that a suit brought by one executive agency

against another is a kind of absurdity, like a person bringing suit against himself. This principle is central to the constitutional vision to which President Bush committed himself at the beginning of his administration, and which he affirmed in numerous signing statements throughout his term.[131]

Despite the centrality of the unitary executive in the jurisprudence adopted by the Bush administration, the theory has met with a chilly reception in the courts, which have taken a relaxed attitude to the creation of independent agencies that are legally insulated from presidential control (at least when those agencies perform functions that do not seem to be at the core of the president's own constitutional responsibilities).[132] When confronted with the Postal Service lawsuit, the administration therefore had two obvious choices: it could let the suit go forward, hoping that nobody would notice the president's retreat from administration principles; or it could try to use the president's claimed authority over the two agencies to force them to resolve their dispute outside the courts. This should have been a relatively easy decision. The Postal Service is controlled by an eleven-member board of governors that comprises nine part-time governors together with the postmaster general and the deputy postmaster general (who are chosen by the governors). At the time of this dispute, all of the governors had been appointed by Presidents Reagan and Bush, and a majority were Republicans. Although the postmaster general and his deputy might well have resisted presidential control because they were full-time officials with a vested interest in their statutory independence, it should have been political child's play for a then-popular president to persuade a sufficient number of the part-time governors to defer to his wishes and thereby avoid a confrontation with him over an obscure legal issue that he considered important. Had this occurred, a useful administrative precedent would have been created, without any risk of adverse judicial decisions. And had the president failed to persuade the board of governors to go along with his wishes, the administration could have proceeded to make a considered decision about whether to risk litigation or to retreat to the passive role embodied in the first option.

The Bush administration took neither obvious path. Instead, it entered into a prolonged period of dithering, during which it relied on what one commentator has aptly called a strategy of "delay, threats, and prayers."[133] The public record does not indicate who was responsible for this policy, but there can be no doubt that it was indeed adopted. In any event, as the delay continued, the threats began to look empty, and the prayers went unanswered. Finally, some twenty months later, further stalling became impossible, and the Justice Department formally directed the Postal Service to withdraw its lawsuit. After this extremely tardy directive was (predictably) ignored, President Bush at last took action. On December 11, 1992, a president whose pre-election-day political re-sources had now evaporated took the extraordinary step of personally di-recting the board of governors to withdraw the lawsuit, on pain of dis-missal. The board voted six to five to defy the president, and the winning majority immediately went to court seeking an order to block their threatened removal. The president responded by attempting to use his recess appointment power to replace one of the governors, which might have led to a reversal of the board's narrow decision to refuse to carry out his directive.

The upshot of the litigation was a total victory for the Postal Service and a complete loss for the president. President Bush was subjected to an unprecedented court order forbidding him to discharge presidential ap-pointees,[134] and the court of appeals ruled that the Postal Service had the authority to bring suit against the Postal Rate Commission even in defi-ance of the president.[135] The court firmly rejected the Justice Depart-ment's theory of the unitary executive, concluding that the judiciary may indeed resolve disputes arising among executive agencies when autho-rized by statute to do so.[136] Furthermore, although the Clinton adminis-tration continued to defend Bush's recess appointment, that issue, too, was eventually resolved against the presidency.[137]

Thus ended George Bush's experiment with presidential commitment to the theories developed by constitutional lawyers who saw themselves as the guardians of the presidency. The Bush administration ended up es-sentially where the Reagan administration had so often found itself: beg-ging the courts for relief from impositions that it might have resisted through the exercise of political will. But whereas the Reagan administra-tion achieved some significant victories through litigation, as in *Chadha* and especially *Bowsher,* the Bush administration seems to have contrib-uted less than nothing to the few legal gains that the presidency made during Bush's four years in office.

CONCLUSION

Perhaps the most obvious question raised by the Bush record on separa-tion of powers is whether the absence of signal successes in enhancing or defending the office of the presidency resulted more from incompe-tence or from the operation of incentives that caused the administration to put greater value on achieving other goals. Examples such as the Postal Service case and the *Airports* litigation suggest that ineptitude played a significant role, for in neither case does any strong overriding political or policy goal seem to explain the administration's failure to defend the interests of the presidency. Incompetence, however, is probably not the sole or even the principal explanatory factor. In the *Airports* case, for example, the Justice Department became institutionally committed to defending the congressional board of review during the Reagan administration. One would therefore have expected this defense to continue during the Bush administration (as it did), unless the new president's special commitment to policing the separation of powers were being taken quite seriously. What this incident suggests more strongly than anything else is that the president's commitment was not (or was not perceived to be) strong enough to overcome ordinary forces of bureaucratic inertia and personal egotism at the Justice Department. Similarly, the Postal Service case is probably best explained in terms of an unwillingness by the Justice Department to request that the president take action in a matter that involved *only* separation-of-powers principles (with no prospect of collateral political or policy benefits), during a period when both the president and the department's senior officials had more politically promising and seemingly urgent items competing for their time and attention. Both cases might have seemed important to lawyers whose principal concern was constitutional law and the long-term effects of that law on the structure of government, but neither case promised the president or the attorney general any immediate political or policy payoff.

The same kind of explanation seems to fit the Bush record taken as a whole. Consider the compromises that followed the four vetoes that were based on the administration's objections to legislative encroachments on the president's authority; the administration's acceptance (and even defense) of an unconstitutional statutory appointment in the FIRREA legislation; and the virtually total unwillingness to violate—and thereby challenge—the many unconstitutional provisions (such as legislative vetoes) contained in legislation signed by the president. All of these suggest that the defense of the presidency never assumed real importance in the Bush administration. The president's public pronouncements, however, as well as the prominent role that he assigned in his administration to lawyers known especially for their interest in separation-of-powers issues[138] and the scrupulous attention that was given to these issues in his signing statements and veto messages, suggest that President Bush *deemed* these issues quite important. Since Bush had little or nothing to gain from feigning this interest in the defense of his office, there is no reason to suppose that his intellectual commitment to the issue was insincere. His administration's strong pattern of significant concessions, inaction at crucial moments, and downright self-destructiveness, therefore, almost certainly reflects the fact that a more resolute pattern of behavior would have imposed short-term costs that the president and others were simply unwilling to pay. One should expect other presidents and other administrations to be subject to the same incentives, and one should expect them to respond to those incentives in a similar manner. What makes the Bush administration unusual, I suspect, is only that the president (apparently) and some of his lawyers (almost certainly) seem to have thought at the outset that this time things could be different.

NOTES

1. Throughout this chapter, I will use the phrase "White House counsel" interchangeably with the more formal term "counsel to the president."

2. See Letter of Resignation from Bernard Nussbaum to President Clinton, reprinted in *New York Times,* 6 March 1994, section 1, p. 23.

3. Ibid.

4. Naftali Bendavid, "Whitewater Meets the Washington Legal Culture,"*Legal Times,* 14 March 1994, pp. 1, 14 (quoting C. Boyden Gray).

5. "Remarks Announcing the Appointment of Lloyd Cutler as Special Counsel to the President and an Exchange with Reporters," *Weekly Compilation of Presidential Documents* 30 (8 March 1994): 462.

6. The course that led Nussbaum to the White House counsel's office began when he worked for the House Judiciary Committee as it was considering the impeachment of President Nixon, where he supervised a young lawyer named Hillary Rodham. Stephen Labaton, "New Role for White House Counsel: De Facto Attorney General," *New York Times*, 9 March 1993, p. A14. Further research would be needed in order to determine whether the connection between Nussbaum's two ventures into national politics constitutes an odd coincidence or an example of poetic justice.

7. Perhaps the most spectacular recent example of the distortions that can result is Lincoln Caplan's *The Tenth Justice* (New York: Alfred A. Knopf, 1987). For discussions of the biases and conceptual mistakes in Caplan's book, see Roger Clegg, "The Thirty-fifth Law Clerk," *Duke Law Journal* (1987): 964; James Michael Strine, "The Office of Legal Counsel: Legal Professionals in a Political System," Ph.D. dissertation, Johns Hopkins University, 1992, pp. 8–14.

8. *Model Rules of Professional Conduct*, Rule 1.13(a) (1992). For a more detailed discussion, see Nelson Lund, "Rational Choice at the Office of Legal Counsel," *Cardozo Law Review* 15 (1993): 437, 450–51, and n. 25.

9. A separate set of questions, which I am not addressing here, might be raised about the propriety of White House involvement in specific cases that are being handled by independent regulatory agencies.

10. Nancy V. Baker, *Conflicting Loyalties: Law and Politics in the Attorney General's Office, 1789–1990.* (Lawrence, Kans.: University Press of Kansas, 1992).

11. Terry Eastland, *Energy in the Executive: The Case for the Strong Presidency* (New York: Free Press, 1992).

12. Presidents have been quite willing to exercise this right. See, for example, Robert H. Jackson, "A Presidential Legal Opinion," *Harvard Law Review* 66

(1953): 1353; Griffin B. Bell and Ronald J. Ostrow, *Taking Care of the Law* (New York: William Morrow, 1982), pp. 24–28.

13. Unlike other state and federal officers, who must avow that they will "support" the Constitution, the president is constitutionally required to take a unique oath through which he pledges that he will "to the best of [his] Ability, preserve, protect and defend" the Constitution. Compare U.S. Constitution Article VI with U.S. Constitution Article II. Although the president's oath implies that he has a special obligation to the Constitution that goes beyond the obligations of other government officials, it does not authorize any of these officials— be they lawyers, judges, or ethics specialists—to dictate how he should meet that obligation. The only legal method for enforcing the president's oath is through the impeachment process.

14. See, for example, "Remarks Announcing the Appointment of Lloyd Cutler."

15. Baker, *Conflicting Loyalties*.

16. Strine, "The Office of Legal Counsel," pp. 1, 318.

17. Cornell W. Clayton, *The Politics of Justice:The Attorney General and the Making of Legal Policy* (Armonk, N.Y.: M. E. Sharpe, 1992).

18. See, for example, Caplan, *The Tenth Justice*.

19. See, for example, John O. McGinnis, "Models of the Opinion Function of the Attorney General: A Normative, Descriptive, and Historical Prolegomenon," *Cardozo Law Review* 15 (1993): 376.

20. Clayton, *The Politics of Justice*, p. 236.

21. Jeremy Rabkin, "At the President's Side: The Role of the White House Counsel in Constitutional Policy," *Law and Contemporary Problems* 56 (1993): 95–97.

22. For a more detailed presentation of evidence supporting the thesis in this chapter, see Nelson Lund, *Lawyers and the Defense of the Presidency* (forthcoming, *Brigham Young University Law Review*).

23. George Bush, "The Interaction of the Legislative, Judicial, and Executive Branches in the Making of Foreign Policy," *Harvard Journal of Law and Public Policy* 11 (1988): 1.

24. "Bush Pledges to Work with Congress but Warns of Firm Hand," *UPI*, 21 January 1989. See also Robert Shogan, "Bush's Dilemma in Dealing with a Contrary Hill," *Los Angeles Times*, 16 April 1989, part 5, p. 3.

25. See R. W. Apple, "A Balance of Bush, the Congress and the Contras," *New York Times*, 2 April 1989, section 4, p. 1.

26. On Barr's relationship with Gray, see, for example, Phil McCombs, "Counsel's Last Hurrah: The Final Furious Days of C. Boyden Gray," *Washington Post*, 16 January 1993, p. G1; Sharon LaFraniere, "Barr Takes Center Stage at Justice Department with New Script," *Washington Post*, 5 March 1992, p. A19; Michael Wines, "A Counsel with Sway over Policy," *New York Times*, November 25, 1991, p. A16.

27. See, for example, David Johnston, "Washington at Work: Political Lifeguard at the Justice Dept.," *New York Times*, 30 August 1990, p. B8; col. 1;

Sharon LaFraniere, "For Nominee Barr, an Unusual path to Attorney General's Office," *Washington Post*, 12 November 1991, p. A6.

28. "Remarks at Dedication Ceremony of the Social Science Complex at Princeton University in Princeton, New Jersey," *Weekly Compilation of Presidential Documents* 27 (10 May 1991): 589.

29. William French Smith, *Law and Justice in the Reagan Administration* (Stanford: Hoover Institution Press, 1991), p. 222. The Meese Justice Department may have been more aggressive than its predecessor on separation-of-powers issues, and the pattern of White House behavior described by Smith may have changed somewhat as a result of the particularly close relationship between Reagan and Meese. What seems to set the Bush administration apart is the personal interest that the president himself took in the concerns that Smith identified.

30. Nor is this to say that the separation of powers and the defense of presidential prerogatives had been insignificant prior to the Reagan-Bush years. For example, Democratic and Republican administrations alike had consistently objected on constitutional grounds to legislative vetoes and to certain provisions of the War Powers Resolution. See *INS v. Chadha*, 462 U.S. 919 (1983); John W. Rolph, "The Decline and Fall of the War Powers Resolution," *Naval Law Review* 40 (1992): 85.

31. The OLC began contributing heavily to the legalization of separation-of-powers disputes at least as early as the Carter administration. Strine, "The Office of Legal Counsel." During the Reagan administration, however, the importance of the OLC's role seems to have increased. Geoffrey P. Miller, "From Compromise to Confrontation: Separation of Powers in the Reagan Era," *George Washington Law Review* 57 (1989): 410–12.

32. Lund, "Rational Choice at the Office of Legal Counsel."

33. This is illustrated in two recent articles written by OLC alumni: Douglas W. Kmiec, "OLC's Opinion Writing Function: The Legal Adhesive for a Unitary Executive," *Cardozo Law Review* 15 (1993): 337; and McGinnis, "Models of the Opinion Function of the Attorney General." Kmiec's article discusses seven major examples of the OLC's work, six of which are analyzed primarily as problems in defining the scope of the president's authority. Similarly, McGinnis's only extended discussion of the OLC's substantive legal analysis involves that office's effort to make a silk purse out of the earful that the Supreme Court gave the executive in *Morrison v. Olson*, 487 U.S. 654 (1988).

34. See, for example, Bradley H. Patterson, Jr., *The Ring of Power: The White House Staff and Its Expanding Role in Government* (New York: Basic Books, 1988), 141; Strine, "The Office of Legal Counsel," pp. 117–18 and n. 35.

35. John O. McGinnis, "Constitutional Review by the Executive in Foreign Affairs and War Powers: A Consequence of Rational Choice in the Separation of Powers," *Law and Contemporary Problems* 56 (1993): 294.

36. See ibid., pp. 312–14 and n. 106.

37. Ibid., p. 314.

38. See "Message to the Senate Returning Without Approval the Cable Television Consumer Protection and Competition Act of 1992," *Weekly Compilation*

of Presidential Documents 28 (3 October 1992): 1860; "Message to the Senate Returning Without Approval the National Voter Registration Act of 1992," *Weekly Compilation of Presidential Documents* 28 (2 July 1992): 1201, "Message to the House of Representatives Returning Without Approval the National Institute of Health Revitalization Amendments of 1992," *Weekly Compilation of Presidential Documents* 28 (23 June 1992): 1132; "Message to the Senate Returning Without Approval the Congressional Campaign Spending Limit and Election Reform Act of 1992," *Weekly Compilation of Presidential Documents* 28 (9 May 1992): 822; "Message to the House of Representatives Returning Without Approval the Textile, Apparel, and Footwear Trade Act of 1990," *Weekly Compilation of Presidential Documents* 26 (5 October 1990): 1531.

39. See "Message to the House of Representatives Returning Without Approval the Foreign Operations, Export Financing, and Related Programs Appropriations Act, 1990," *Weekly Compilation of Presidential Documents* 25 (19 November 1989): 1783; "Message to the Senate Returning Without Approval the Bill Prohibiting the Export of Technology, Defense Articles, and Defense Services to Codevelop or Produce FS-X Aircraft with Japan," *Weekly Compilation of Presidential Documents* 25 (31 July 1989): 1191.

40. See "Memorandum of Disapproval for the Morris K. Udall Scholarship and Excellence in National Environmental Policy Act," *Weekly Compilation of Presidential Documents* 27 (20 December 1991): 1877; "Memorandum of Disapproval for the Intelligence Authorization Act, Fiscal Year 1991," *Weekly Compilation of Presidential Documents* 26 (30 November 1990): 1958; "Memorandum of Disapproval for the Omnibus Export Amendments Act of 1990," *Weekly Compilation of Presidential Documents* 26 (16 November 1990): 1839; "Message to the House of Representatives Returning Without Approval the Foreign Relations Authorization Act, Fiscal Years 1990 and 1991," *Weekly Compilation of Presidential Documents* 25 (21 November 1989): 1806.

41. See "Statement on the Children's Television Act of 1990," *Weekly Compilation of Presidential Documents* 26 (17 October 1990): 1611; "Statement on the Flag Protection Act of 1989," *Weekly Compilation of Presidential Documents* 25 (26 October 1989): 1619. In both cases, Bush allowed the bills to become law, but withheld his approval. Despite Bush's refusal to approve the flag bill, however, his Department of Justice enforced it and defended its constitutionality in court. See Brief for the United States in *United States v. Eichman*, Nos. 89-1433, 89-1434 (U.S. Sup. Ct.).

42. On at least two occasions, President Reagan vetoed bills that contained provisions to which he objected because they improperly permitted entities other than the Congress to exercise legislative functions. See "Memorandum of Disapproval of S. 2166," *Weekly Compilation of Presidential Documents* 20 (19 October 1984): 1583; "Message to the House of Representatives Returning H.J. Res. 338 Without Approval," *Weekly Compilation of Presidential Documents* 19 (13 August 1983): 1133. This may or may not have reflected a principled concern with the separation of powers, but it does not imply a vigorous defense of the presidency.

43. See, for example, "Message to the House of Representatives Returning

H.R. 4868 Without Approval," *Weekly Compilation of Presidential Documents* 22 (26 September 1986): 1281; "Memorandum of Disapproval of H.R. 7336," *Weekly Compilation of Presidential Documents* 19 (12 January 1983): 38; "Memorandum of Disapproval of S. 2623," *Weekly Compilation of Presidential Documents* 19 (3 January 1983): 7.

44. See "Memorandum of Disapproval for the Children's Television Act of 1988," *Weekly Compilation of Presidential Documents* 24 (5 November 1988): 1456; "Message to the Senate Returning S. 742 Without Approval," *Weekly Compilation of Presidential Documents* 23 (19 June 1987): 715. S. 742 would have codified the so-called "fairness doctrine," which had been promulgated as a regulation by the FCC and then sustained against a constitutional challenge in *Red Lion Broadcasting Co. v. FCC*, 395 U.S. 367 (1969). President Reagan's veto message openly disputed the holding in *Red Lion*.

45. See, for example, "Statement on Signing a Bill on Veterans' Benefits," *Weekly Compilation of Presidential Documents* 24 (18 November 1988): 1548; "Statement on Signing S. 1874 into Law," *Weekly Compilation of Presidential Documents* 22 (4 August 1986): 1045; "Remarks on Signing S. 2603 into Law," *Weekly Compilation of Presidential Documents* 20 (9 October 1984): 1476; "Statement on Signing H.R. 5712 into Law," *Weekly Compilation of Presidential Documents* 20 (30 August 1984): 1201; "Statement on Signing H.R. 3222 into Law," *Weekly Compilation of Presidential Documents* 19 (28 November 1983): 1619.

46. See *Morrison v. Olson*, 487 U.S. 654 (1988) (independent counsel statute); *Bowsher v. Synar*, 478 U.S. 714 (1986) (statute that assigned an agent of Congress authority to determine cuts in the federal budget); *Ameron, Inc. v. U.S. Army Corps of Engineers*, 809 F.2d 979 (3rd Cir. 1986) (statute assigning a role in government procurement to an agent of Congress), *cert. dismissed*, 488 U.S. 918 (1988); Lear Siegler, Inc. v. Lehman, 842 F.2d 1102 (9th Cir. 1988) (same), *decision withdrawn in part*, 893 F.2d 205 (9th Cir. 1989); *National Federation of Federal Employees v. United States*, 688 F. Supp. 671 (D.D.C. 1988) (statute restricting president's authority to protect confidentiality of national security information), *vacated sub nom. American Foreign Service Ass'n v. Garfinkel*, 490 U.S. 153 (1989).

47. See, for example, Daniel B. Rodriguez, "Statutory Interpretation and Political Advantage," *International Review of Law and Economics* 12 (1992): 217; Frank B. Cross, "The Constitutional Legitimacy and Significance of Presidential Signing Statements," *Administrative Law Review* 40 (1988): 210–11.

48. Such hopes have rarely been realized. See, for example, Cross, "Constitutional Legitimacy," pp. 234–35; William D. Popkin, "Judicial Use of Presidential Legislative History: A Critique," *Indiana Law Journal* 66 (1991): 702–3 and nn. 14, 17.

49. See, for example, "Statement on Signing the Civil Rights Act of 1991," *Weekly Compilation of Presidential Documents* 27: 1701 (21 November 1991).

50. "President's Statement on Signing the National Defense Authorization Act for Fiscal Year 1991," *Weekly Compilation of Presidential Documents* 26 (5 November 1990): 1766. Similarly, the president claimed in another signing state-

ment that provisions in a bill that purported to give the force of law to language in a classified annex to the bill were legal nullities because the annex was not presented to the president along with the bill. "Statement on Signing the National Defense Authorization Act for Fiscal Years 1990 and 1991," *Weekly Compilation of Presidential Documents* 25 (29 November 1989): 1841.

51. See "Statement on Signing the Treasury, Postal Service, and General Government Appropriations Act, 1993," *Weekly Compilation of Presidential Documents* 28 (6 October 1992): 1873; "Statement on Signing the District of Columbia Mental Health Program Assistance Act of 1991," *Weekly Compilation of Presidential Documents* 27 (31 October 1991): 1575; "Statement on Signing the Department of the Interior and Related Agencies Appropriations Act, 1991," *Weekly Compilation of Presidential Documents* 26 (5 November 1990): 1768; "Statement on Signing the Treasury, Postal Service and General Government Appropriations Act, 1990," *Weekly Compilation of Presidential Documents* 25 (3 November 1989): 1669.

One student of the legislative veto counted more than 200 newly enacted legislative vetoes between the time of the Supreme Court's *Chadha* decision in 1983 and the end of the 102nd Congress in 1992. Louis Fisher, "The Legislative Veto: Invalidated, It Survives," *Law and Contemporary Problems* 56 (1993): 288.

52. Compare "Statement on Signing the Departments of Commerce, Justice, and State, the Judiciary, and Related Agencies Appropriations Act, 1992," *Weekly Compilation of Presidential Documents* 27 (28 October 1991): 1529, with "Issues Raised by sec. 129 of Pub. L. No. 102-138 and sec. 503 of Pub. L. No. 102-140," *Opinions of the Office of Legal Counsel* 16 (1993): 18 (preliminary print). Compare "Statement on Signing the National and Community Service Act of 1990," *Weekly Compilation of Presidential Documents* 26 (16 November 1990): 1833, with "Appointment of Members of the Board of Directors of the Commission on National and Community Service," *Opinions of the Office of Legal Counsel* 14 (1990): 173 (preliminary print). Compare "Statement on Signing the Omnibus Budget Reconciliation Act of 1990," *Weekly Compilation of Presidential Documents* 26 (5 November 1990): 1764, with "Constitutionality of subsection 4117(b) of Enrolled Bill H.R. 5835, the Omnibus Budget Reconciliation Act of 1990," *Opinions of the Office of Legal Counsel* 14 (1990): 170 (preliminary print). Compare "Statement on Signing the Foreign Relations Authorization Act, Fiscal Years 1990 and 1991," *Weekly Compilation of Presidential Documents* 26 (16 February 1990): 266, with "Issues Raised by Section 102(c)(2) of H.R. 3792," *Opinions of the Office of Legal Counsel* 14 (1990): 38 (preliminary print).

53. Despite a statutory requirement that representatives of a legislative body be included in the United States delegation to the Conference on Security and Cooperation in Europe, these negotiations appear to have proceeded without the inclusion of such legislative representatives. See McGinnis, "Constitutional Review by the Executive," p. 310 n. 81 (citing interview with former staff member of the National Security Council).

54. Among many examples, see "Statement on Signing the National Defense Authorization Act for Fiscal year 1993," *Weekly Compilation of Presidential Documents* 28 (23 October 1992): 2073; "Statement on Signing the Foreign

Relations Authorization Act, Fiscal Years 1992 and 1993," *Weekly Compilation of Presidential Documents* 27 (28 October 1991): 1526; "Statement on Signing the Foreign Operations, Export Financing, and Related Programs Appropriations Act, 1990," *Weekly Compilation of Presidential Documents* 25 (21 November 1989): 1810.

55. Among many examples, see "Statement on Signing the Reclamation States Emergency Drought Relief Act of 1991," *Weekly Compilation of Presidential Documents* 28 (5 March 1992): 413; "Statement on Signing the Bill Modifying the Boundaries of the Alaska Maritime National Wildlife Refuge," *Weekly Compilation of Presidential Documents* 26 (21 November 1990): 1897.

56. A pattern similar to the one that is manifest in the president's veto messages and signing statements can be found in his approach to the War Powers Resolution, which he said was unconstitutional but which he never directly challenged.

57. See "Memorandum of Disapproval for the Morris K. Udall Scholarship and Excellence in National Environmental Policy Act," *Weekly Compilation of Presidential Documents* 27 (20 December 1991): 1877.

58. See "Statement on Signing the Morris K. Udall Scholarship and Excellence in National Environmental and Native American Public Policy Act of 1992," *Weekly Compilation of Presidential Documents* 28 (19 March 1992): 507. Adding insult to injury, the second bill treated the president's pocket veto of the first bill as a nullity by purporting to repeal it.

59. The senator who sponsored the bill was chairman of the appropriations subcommittee with jurisdiction over the Office of Management and Budget, which may help explain the president's lack of policy objections to the bill as well as his compromise on the constitutional issues. For accounts of the influence of the director of the Office of Management and Budget during the Bush administration, see Charles Kolb, *White House Daze: The Unmaking of Domestic Policy in the Bush Years* (New York: Free Press, 1994); John Podhoretz, *Hell of a Ride: Backstage at the White House Follies 1989–1993* (New York: Simon & Schuster, 1993).

60. Pub. L. No. 101-610, 104 Stat. 3127 (1990).

61. "Statement on Signing the National and Community Service Act of 1990," *Weekly Compilation of Presidential Documents* 26 (16 November 1990): 1833.

62. See "Appointment of Members of the Board of Directors of the Commission on National and Community Service," *Opinions of the Office of Legal Counsel* 14 (1990): 173 (preliminary print).

63. See National and Community Service Technical Amendments Act of 1991, Pub. L. No. 102-10, 105 Stat. 29 (1991).

64. The executive order, which was signed before the bill was vetoed, was referred to in the president's veto message.

65. See "Memorandum of Disapproval for the Omnibus Export Amendments Act of 1990," *Weekly Compilation of Presidential Documents* 26 (16 November 1990): 1839.

66. "Memorandum of Disapproval for the Omnibus Export Amendments

Act of 1990," *Weekly Compilation of Presidential Documents* 26 (16 November 1990): 1839. The bill was presented to the president only a few weeks before American and allied troops invaded Iraq.

67. See Foreign Relations Authorization Act, Fiscal Years 1992 and 1993, Title V, Pub. L. No. 102-138 (1991); "Statement on Signing the Foreign Relations Authorization Act, Fiscal Years 1992 and 1993," *Weekly Compilation of Presidential Documents* 27 (28 October 1991): 1526.

68. The full text of the provision, which is summarized here, can be found in section 109 of H.R. 1487, which was vetoed on 21 November 1989. A complete legal analysis of this provision would require a more extended discussion of various terms and qualifications than is warranted here.

69. See "Message to the House of Representatives Returning Without Approval the Foreign Relations Authorization Act, Fiscal Years 1990 and 1991," *Weekly Compilation of Presidential Documents* 25 (21 November 1989): 1806.

70. Ibid.

71. The full text of the provisions can be found in Section 602 of S. 2834, which was vetoed on 30 November 1990.

72. The provisions of the bill dealing with the timing of the president's obligatory notification to Congress of covert actions were part of a separate constitutional and policy dispute between the Congress and the president. The story of that dispute's origins and development is quite complicated, and I will not address it here except to say that President Bush eventually made concessions on this issue, as he did on the others reviewed in this chapter.

73. See "Memorandum of Disapproval for the Intelligence Authorization Act, Fiscal Year 1991," *Weekly Compilation of Presidential Documents* 26 (30 November 1990): 1958.

74. The Obey Amendment included in this bill was a modified version of a provision contained in a bill that the president had vetoed two days earlier. That veto had been based partly on this earlier form of the provision and partly on a controversial abortion-funding provision. See "Message to the House of Representatives Returning Without Approval the Foreign Operations, Export Financing, and Related Programs Appropriations Act, 1990," *Weekly Compilation of Presidential Documents* 25 (19 November 1989): 1783.

75. "Statement on Signing the Foreign Operations, Export Financing, and Related Programs Appropriations Act, 1990," *Weekly Compilation of Presidential Documents* 25 (21 November 1989): 1810.

76. See, for example, "Statement on Signing the Reclamation Projects Authorization and Adjustment Act of 1992," *Weekly Compilation of Presidential Documents* 28 (30 October 1992): 2232; "Statement on Signing the Futures Trading Practices Act of 1992," *Weekly Compilation of Presidential Documents* 28 (28 October 1992): 2185; "Statement on Signing the National Defense Authorization Act for Fiscal Year 1993," *Weekly Compilation of Presidential Documents* 28 (23 October 1992): 2073; "Statement on Signing the Reclamation States Emergency Drought Relief Act of 1991," *Weekly Compilation of Presidential Documents* 28 (5 March 1992): 413; "Statement on Signing the Coast Guard Authorization Act of 1991," *Weekly Compilation of Presidential Documents* 27 (19

December 1991): 1873; "Statement on Signing the National Defense Authorization Act for Fiscal Years 1992 and 1993," *Weekly Compilation of Presidential Documents* 27 (5 December 1991): 1769; "Statement on Signing the National Earthquake Hazards Reduction Program Reauthorization Act," *Weekly Compilation of Presidential Documents* 26 (16 November 1990): 1843; "Statement on Signing the National Defense Authorization Act for Fiscal Year 1991," *Weekly Compilation of Presidential Documents* 26 (5 November 1990): 1766; "Statement on Signing the North American Wetlands Conservation Act," *Weekly Compilation of Presidential Documents* 25 (13 December 1989): 1949; "Statement on Signing the Department of Defense Appropriations Act, 1990," *Weekly Compilation of Presidential Documents* 25 (21 November 1989): 1809.

77. "Statement on Signing the Foreign Operations, Export Financing, and Related Programs Appropriations Act, 1990," *Weekly Compilation of Presidential Documents* 25 (21 November 1989): 1810 (emphasis added).

78. Ibid.

79. 31 U.S.C. 1341, 1350.

80. *Congressional Record* 135 (daily ed., 20 November 1989): H9088. See also ibid., H9089 (amendment says that "if this administration wants to try to accomplish a foreign policy purpose [that] is contrary to a specific prohibition in U.S. law, it cannot use money in this bill to do it") (statement of Mr. Obey).

81. See ibid. (statement of Mr. Edwards). One statement in the *Congressional Record* might seem to offer considerable support to the president's interpretation. The day after the bill containing the Obey Amendment was passed by the House of Representatives, Obey took the floor and declared (on behalf of himself and Rep. Edwards) that "the word 'exchange' should be understood to refer to a direct verbal or written agreement." *Congressional Record* 135 (daily ed. 21 Nov. 1989): H9231. This statement does not go as far as the Bush signing statement, for a "direct" agreement would not necessarily have to be an "express" agreement, but it does go further in the direction favored by the president than prior statements by Obey and Edwards had gone. Under standard canons of statutory construction, however, the statement of November 21 would be difficult to use as a meaningful indicator of congressional intent, because it was made *after* legislative action on the bill had been completed.

82. See, for example, *Evans v. United States,* 112 S. Ct. 1881, 1892 (1992) (Justice Kennedy, concurring in part and concurring in the judgment).

83. *Congressional Record* 135 (daily ed., 20 November 1989): S16361.

84. Ibid., S16362–63.

85. One commentator has attempted to make the Kasten-Rudman colloquy seem irrelevant by falsely asserting that "their colloquy concerned an amendment that Senator Kasten himself withdrew when it faced rejection by Congress." Charles Tiefer, *The Semi-Sovereign Presidency* (Boulder: Westview, 1994), p. 39. Although Kasten's amendment was before the Senate when the colloquy took place, the colloquy itself "concerned" the Obey Amendment. Kasten, moreover, withdrew his own amendment because he accepted the colloquy as an adequate substitute for his own amendment, and Tiefer does not demonstrate that "it faced rejection by Congress." Although it would be naive to think

that the Kasten-Rudman colloquy could be made to serve the administration's interests as well as the Kasten Amendment would have, it would equally be naive (or tendentious) to assume that the Obey Amendment would have been enacted without the concession to the president that was embodied in the Kasten-Rudman colloquy.

86. 18 U.S.C. 371. This statute authorizes prosecutions for conspiracies to commit offenses that are not themselves criminally punishable. See *United States v. Hutto*, 256 U.S. 524 (1921).

87. Walsh did not specifically charge North and the others with conspiracy to violate the Boland Amendments, but this seems only to have been a matter of trial tactics. In his final report, Walsh said: "Independent Counsel could as a matter of law have framed the conspiracy charge in that fashion, and its evidence at trial would have proved that the conspirators violated the Boland Amendment." Lawrence Walsh, *Final Report of the Independent Counsel for Iran/Contra Matters* (New York: Random House, 1994), p. 67.

88. The president's signing statement, together with a legal opinion based on it that was later issued by the Justice Department, might have been sufficient to justify the attorney general in refraining from seeking appointment of an independent counsel for alleged violations of the Obey Amendment. As the Iran-Contra prosecutions illustrated, however, an independent counsel appointed to investigate *other* alleged legal violations would be free to procure an indictment based on violations of the Obey Amendment.

89. "Criminal Penalties Under Pub. L. No. 101-167, Section 582," *Opinions of the Office of Legal Counsel* 14 (1990): 93 (preliminary print).

90. The Obey Amendment has been reenacted in subsequent appropriations bills. The current version can be found in Pub. L. No. 103-87, sec. 533, 107 Stat. 931 (1993). When he signed this legislation into law, President Clinton made no mention of the Obey Amendment. See "Statement on Signing the Foreign Operations Appropriations Legislation," *Weekly Compilation of Presidential Documents* 29 (30 September 1993): 1945.

91. For many years, the OLC has attracted lawyers with exceptional academic records, and many have gone on to academic careers. McGinnis, "Models of the Opinion Function," pp. 422, 424, and n. 185. During the Bush administration, C. Boyden Gray (himself a former Supreme Court clerk) broke with prior practice by hiring people with similar academic credentials to work in the White House counsel's office. See "Gray & Co.," *National Journal* 23 (17 August 1991): 2020.

92. See Robert Pear, "Unease Is Voiced on Contra Accord," *New York Times*, 26 March 1989, section 1, p. 1. Although the Central American Accords between the president and Congress were published by the executive, the part of the agreement discussed here was omitted from the published version. See "Bipartisan Accord on Central America," *Weekly Compilation of Presidential Documents* 25 (24 March 1989): 420.

93. See Pear, "Unease Is Voiced on Contra Accord."

94. See *INS v. Chadha*, 462 U.S. 919 (1983).

95. See, for example, Bernard Weinraub, "Gray-Baker Vendetta: A Long-Running Tale of Potomac Intrigue," *New York Times*, 29 March 1989, p. A16.

96. Pear, "Unease Is Voiced on Contra Accord." See also Helen Dewar and David Hoffman, "Baker Denies Contra-Aid Agreement Sets Precedent for Power-Sharing: Draft Letter on Assistance Plan Circulating Among Hill Leaders," *Washington Post*, 8 April 1989, p. A9; R. W. Apple, Jr., "A Balance of Bush, the Congress and the Contras," *New York Times*, 2 April 1989, section 4, p. 1.

97. See Pear, "Unease Is Voiced on Contra Accord"; Bendavid, "Whitewater Meets the Washington Legal Culture," p. 14 (" 'I was right to object,' Gray maintains. 'But Secretary Baker was mad, understandably so, because I had talked to the press before raising the matter in-house.' ")

98. See, for example, the sources cited in note 51.

99. The post-*Chadha* pattern, in which legislative vetoes are usually imposed in appropriations bills rather than in substantive legislation (probably because of the special powers of intimidation possessed by appropriators), suggests that the principal effect of *Chadha*—to the extent that it has had any effect at all—may have been to produce a slight shift in the relative power of congressional appropriations committees in comparison with authorizing committees. Legislative vetoes, especially committee vetoes, have continued to be exercised through extra-statutory mechanisms, as *Chadha* clearly permits. For examples of the use of extra-statutory mechanisms, see Fisher, "The Legislative Veto," p. 288.

100. Financial Institutions Reform, Recovery, and Enforcement Act of 1989, 301(c)(5), Pub. L. 101-73, 103 Stat. 183.

101. "Memorandum of Disapproval for the Morris K. Udall Scholarship and Excellence in National Environmental Policy Act," *Weekly Compilation of Presidential Documents* 27 (20 December 1991): 1877.

102. *Congressional Record* 135 (daily ed., 22 February 1989): S1513, S1535-36.

103. *Olympic Federal Savings and Loan Association v. Director, Office of Thrift Supervision*, 732 F. Supp. 1183, 1192–93 (D.D.C. 1990), *dismissed as moot*, 903 F.2d 837 (D.C. Cir. 1990).

104. The plaintiff that brought the constitutional challenge was represented by Charles J. Cooper, who had been assistant attorney general for the OLC during the Reagan administration.

105. *Olympic Federal Savings and Loan Association v. Director, Office of Thrift Supervision*, 732 F. Supp. 1183 (D.D.C. 1990). The court also rejected a number of efforts by the government to evade the Appointments Clause through bootstrapping arguments based on the Vacancies Act and on an alleged "inherent power" of the president to fill vacant offices without regard to the Appointments Clause. Ibid.

Ironically, one of the greatest differences between the OTS and the FHLBB is that the OTS falls clearly under the president's legal control, whereas the FHLBB did not. Still, the long-term benefits to the constitutional order that might result from the replacement of a single independent agency with an executive agency seem unlikely to outweigh the risks to that order posed by the Justice Department's defense of the unconstitutional statutory appointment.

106. *Olympic Federal Savings and Loan Association v. Director, Office of Thrift Supervision*, 903 F.2d 837 (D.C. Cir. 1990).

107. See "Memorandum of Disapproval for the Morris K. Udall Scholarship and Excellence in National Environmental Policy Act," *Weekly Compilation of Presidential Documents* 27 (20 December 1991): 1877. See also, for example, "Statement on Signing the Bill Modifying the Boundaries of the Alaska Maritime National Wildlife Refuge," *Weekly Compilation of Presidential Documents* 26 (21 November 1990): 1897; "Statement on Signing the National and Community Service Act of 1990," *Weekly Compilation of Presidential Documents* 26 (16 November 1990): 1833.

108. William P. Barr, "Attorney General's Remarks, Benjamin Cardozo School of Law, 15 November 1992," *Cardozo Law Review* 15 (1993): 38.

109. Ibid.

110. Ibid. Barr went on to say that an attorney general who believes that a bill is unconstitutional should recommend that it be vetoed even if he also believes that the courts would uphold it. He then cited an academic article (written by an OLC alumnus) contending that the President is *obliged by the Constitution* to veto such bills. Ibid., p. 38 n. 33. Absent from this passage is any discussion of whether the assistant attorney general for the OLC has an obligation to ensure that his view of the Constitution's requirements is conveyed to the president.

111. According to this theory, the unconstitutional appointment (which was strongly opposed in the House of Representatives) was essential to avoid the necessity of conducting confirmation hearings involving someone who had been intimately involved in the operation of the FHLBB. Senate support for this expedient, in turn, was motivated by concern that such hearings might embarrass other senators who were suspected of having improperly interfered with regulatory decisions of the FHLBB. See, for example, Robert A. Rosenblatt and Sara Fritz, "S&L Bailout Compromise Returns to Haunt Congress," *Los Angeles Times*, 6 April 1990, p. D1; editorial, "Trying Days for the Thrift Bailout," *Christian Science Monitor*, 27 March 1990, p. 20; editorial, "Another S&L Delay," *Washington Post*, 26 March 1990, p. A10; "Court Gives Thrift Agency a Reprieve," *Washington Post*, 24 March 1990, p. D12; Jerry Knight, "Court Ruling Disrupts Thrift Bailout: Judge Holds Top Regulators' Appointments Unconstitutional," *Washington Post*, 22 March 1990, p. A1.

None of this suggests what interests the Justice Department may have sought to serve by participating in any political deals, although various hypotheses might be formulated. For present purposes, however, the most important conclusion does not require a choice among such hypothesis.

112. 111 S. Ct. 2298 (1991).

113. See *Citizens for the Abatement of Aircraft Noise v. Metropolitan Washington Airports Authority*, 718 F. Supp. 974, 976 (D.D.C. 1989); Plaintiff's Exhibit 2 in the Joint Appendix filed with the Supreme Court in the *Airports* case. Dulles International and Washington National airports were the only two civilian airports operated by the federal government.

114. See Plaintiff's Exhibit 3 in the Joint Appendix filed with the Supreme Court in the *Airports* case. This document is a letter from the assistant attorney general for legislative affairs to the chairman of the House Subcommittee on Aviation Committee on Public Works and Transportation. The detailed constitutional argumentation in the letter, however, could hardly have been provided by any office other than the OLC, and the OLC does in fact routinely draft such letters. See Kmiec, "OLC's Opinion Writing Function," p. 338. Although the letter characterizes the three proposals reviewed in it as "alternatives proposed by your staff," there had apparently been some prior consultations, and it is not clear that all the ideas reflected in these alternatives originated with congressional staff. On the contrary, it is quite conceivable that the OLC itself devised one or more of the alternatives.

115. The OLC's reservations arose largely from *INS v. Chadha*, 462 U.S. 919 (1983), and *Bowsher v. Synar*, 478 U.S. 714 (1986).

116. See *Citizens for the Abatement of Aircraft Noise v. Metropolitan Washington Airports Authority*, 718 F. Supp. 974, 75 (D.C.C. 1989).

117. See the docket entries in the Joint Appendix filed with the Supreme Court in the *Airports* case.

118. *Citizens for the Abatement of Aircraft Noise, Inc. v. Metropolitan Washington Airports Authority*, 917 F.2d 48, 56–57 (D.C. Cir. 1990).

119. See 111 S. Ct., p. 2305.

120. Ibid., p. 2305 and n. 12.

121. Because the solicitor general himself was disqualified from this case, the brief was filed by one of his deputies.

122. 111 S. Ct., p. 2307.

123. 111 S. Ct., pp. 2311–12.

124. 111 S. Ct., p. 2312 (quoting *The Federalist* No. 48).

125. "Should Congress ever undertake such improbable projects as transferring national parklands to the States on the condition that its agents control their oversight, there is little doubt that the President would be equal to the task of safeguarding his or her interests." *Metropolitan Washington Airports Authority v. Citizens for the Abatement of Aircraft Noise, Inc.*, 111 S. Ct., 2298, 2321 (Justice White, dissenting) (citation omitted).

126. President Bush himself demonstrated no reluctance to order the Justice Department to change its position in the Supreme Court when something he cared about was at stake. Thus, after meeting with representatives of interests materially affected by a case that was before the Court, President Bush ordered his solicitor general to file a brief contradicting the position that the solicitor general had taken in an earlier brief to the Court in the very same case. See Reply Brief for the United States at *9–10 and n.*, *United States v. Mabus* (Nos. 90-1205, 90-6588). Linda Greenhouse, "Bush Reverses U.S. Stance Against Black College Aid," *New York Times*, 22 October 1991, p. B6; Ruth Marcus, "Bush Shifts Stand on Aid to Black Colleges: Administration Now Supports Increased State Funding in Mississippi Case," *Washington Post*, 23 October 1991, p. A6.

127. On April 20, 1994, the Senate rejected a proposal that would have invited the airport operating authority to stop providing free parking near the

Dulles and Washington National terminals to members of Congress. See *Congressional Record* 140 (daily ed., 20 April 1994): S4511–19, S4524. Five days later, the airport operating authority removed the signs at the reserved parking areas that read: "Reserved Parking/Supreme Court Justices/Members of Congress/Diplomatic Corps." The reserved parking areas were not altered, but new signs were installed that say: "Restricted Parking/Authorized Users Only." Karen Foerstel, *Signs Designating Members' Parking Are Removed from Both Airport Lots, Roll Call,* May 16, 1994.

128. See "Statement on Signing the Intermodal Surface Transportation Efficiency Act of 1991," *Weekly Compilation of Presidential Documents* 27 (18 December 1991): 1861. The Bush administration seems never to have cleared up its pathetic confusion about the *Airports* case. Shortly before leaving office, the president issued a signing statement evincing both an inability to articulate the principle of law for which the *Airports* case stands and an inability to distinguish between construing a statute to avoid constitutional issues and declaring a statute unconstitutional. See "Statement on Signing the Reclamation Projects Authorization and Adjustment Act of 1992," *Weekly Compilation of Presidential Documents* 28 (30 October 1992): 2232.

129. *Hechinger v. Metropolitan Washington Airports Authority,* 845 F. Supp. 902 (D.D.C. 1994).

130. The main-text discussion that follows presents a highly simplified account of an extraordinarily complex dispute. For a more complete presentation of the legal and factual details, and a thoughtful analysis of the issues, see Neal Devins, "Tempest in an Envelope: Reflections on the Bush White House's Failed Takeover of the U.S. Postal Service," *UCLA Law Review* 41 (1994): 1035.

131. See, for example, "Statement on Signing the Housing and Community Development Act of 1992," *Weekly Compilation of Presidential Documents* 28 (28 October 1992): 2186; "Statement on Signing the President John F. Kennedy Assassination Records Collection Act of 1992," *Weekly Compilation of Presidential Documents* 28 (26 October 1992): 2134; "Statement on Signing the Energy Policy Act of 1992," *Weekly Compilation of Presidential Documents* 28 (24 October 1992): 2094; "Statement on Signing the Treasury, Postal Service, and General Government Appropriations Act, 1993," *Weekly Compilation of Presidential Documents* 28 (6 October 1992): 1873; "Statement on Signing the Federal Deposit Insurance Corporation Improvement Act of 1991," *Weekly Compilation of Presidential Documents* 27 (19 December 1991): 1873; "Statement on Signing the Joint Resolution Settling the Railroad Strike," *Weekly Compilation of Presidential Documents* 27 (18 April 1991): 459; "Statement on Signing the Bill Modifying the Boundaries of the Alaska Maritime National Wildlife Refuge," *Weekly Compilation of Presidential Documents* 26 (21 November 1990): 1897; "Statement on Signing the Energy and Water Development Appropriations Act, 1991," *Weekly Compilation of Presidential Documents* 26 (5 November 1990): 1771; "Statement on Signing the Omnibus Budget Reconciliation Act of 1989," *Weekly Compilation of Presidential Documents* 25 (19 December 1989): 1970; "Statement on Signing the Treasury, Postal Service and General Government Appropri-

ations Act, 1990," *Weekly Compilation of Presidential Documents* 25 (3 November 1989): 1669.

132. See, for example, *Humphrey's Executor v. United States*, 295 U.S. 602 (1935); *Wiener v. United States*, 357 U.S. 349 (1958); *Morrison v. Olson*, 487 U.S. 654 (1988). There is a large academic literature dealing with various issues raised by the theory of the unitary executive. Good introductions to the underlying arguments on which the Bush administration's position ultimately rested can be found in Geoffrey P. Miller, "Independent Agencies," *Supreme Court Review* (1986): 41; and Steven G. Calabresi and Keven H. Rhodes, "The Structural Constitution: Unitary Executive, Plural Judiciary," *Harvard Law Review* 105 (1992): 1155.

133. Devins, "Tempest in an Envelope."

134. *Mackie v. Bush*, 809 F Supp. 144 (D.D.C. 1993), *dismissed as moot sub nom. Mackie v. Clinton*, 10 F.3d 13 (D.C. Cir. 1993).

135. *Mail Order Association of America v. U.S. Postal Service*, 986 F.2d 509 (D.C. Cir. 1993).

136. Ibid., p. 527 and n. 9. The Justice Department had also attempted to persuade the court that it had a statutory right to prevent the Postal Service from filing the lawsuit, but this argument was rejected.

137. *Mackie v. Clinton*, 827 F. Supp. 56, 58 (D.D.C. 1993).

138. The counsel to the president, C. Boyden Gray, was generally considered to be among the most influential members of the White House staff. See, for example, Anne Kornhauser, "Boyden Gray: Not Just George Bush's Lawyer," *Legal Times,* 12 November 1990, p. 1. Bush's first assistant attorney general for the OLC, William P. Barr, became known while in that office primarily for his defense of presidential authority; and Barr was eventually promoted to attorney general. Barr's successor at the OLC, J. Michael Luttig, was one of only three officials in the Bush Justice Department to receive a coveted appointment to a U.S. court of appeals.

9
COUNSELS TO THE PRESIDENT: THE RISE OF ORGANIZATIONAL COMPETITION

MICHAEL STRINE

From its origins in Franklin Roosevelt's administration to the present, the office of counsel to the president[1] has undergone a startling transition in terms of function and importance in White House policy-making. As late as 1980, one Justice Department official could say: "In general, the law-yering aspect of the job involve[s] internal White House questions which do not overlap with Justice Department business."[2] Yet the seeds of com-petition were sown in the pre-Watergate era. Since that time, with few ex-ceptions, counselors to the president have expanded the scope of the of-fice's powers and heightened tensions in working relationships with the Justice Department. This chapter traces the evolution of the role of the office of White House counsel—a role that has shifted from administra-tion to administration, but nonetheless has increasingly become institu-tionalized within the web of organizational and policy expectations of presidents, Congress, the Justice Department, and the public.[3]

Two forces have driven the evolution of White House counsel—one idiosyncratic, and the other reflective of a longer historical trend of presi-dents seeking to centralize control over legal policy. The role of White House counsel is idiosyncratic because it reflects the need Roosevelt and later presidents had to find a formal staff position for personal advisers and friends. Because these friendships often take different forms and serve different political or other functions, the role of the office has shifted over time. At the same time, the White House counsel has offered presidents a logical solution to the problem of how to assert central com-mand over sprawling federal legal administration and the increasingly im-portant area of legal policy.[4] Some observers attribute shifts in the role of White House counsel and in the role of its counterpart in the Justice Department, the Office of Legal Counsel (OLC), to their perception of how best to serve their client, the president. This client-centered approach, however, fails to account for long-term trends in government lawyers' roles.

This chapter places the idiosyncratic evolution of the White House counsel's office within the broader institutional context of the legal bureaucracy's development. By focusing primarily on lawyering functions—specifically, opinion writing—the chapter examines a function traditionally not subject to the direct intervention of White House officials. In addition, however, the chapter discusses expansion of counsel's power in three other areas: judicial and Justice Department appointments, legal policy-making, and litigation. In so doing, it moves beyond the presentism inherent in client-centered and rational choice models, and it argues that current practices within the office of White House counsel and the OLC do not reflect client-centered behavior, but rather a more long-standing dialogue among government lawyers seeking to define their roles in the context of competing demands and expectations. The evolution of the various roles played by presidential legal advisers is best seen as organizational differentiation in an embedded institutional context.

INSTITUTIONALISM AND THE EVOLUTION OF THE LEGAL ADMINISTRATIVE STATE

Competition between Congress and the presidency for control of the legal administrative state and of federal legal policy did not begin with the recent era of partisan and institutional conflict that peaked during the Nixon administration and again during the Reagan administration. Histories of the Department of Justice[5] illustrate the influence of early events on its subsequent growth. From the common origin of the attorney general's office in 1789, innumerable structures and offices within and outside the executive branch have emerged to carry out the government's legal business. At each stage of institutional development, the organization of legal administration has reflected an overtly political model of bureaucracy; that is, Congress and presidents have emphasized dual, but not competing, values in constructing the legal administrative state. Chief among these are political accountability and control, neutral competence, and professionalism.[6]

Recognizing the competition among the president, Congress, and the president's "own" Justice Department is also central to understanding the development of the White House counsel's role. Existing explanations of the evolution of the Justice Department perhaps overstate the impact of competition among particular elites within the executive branch.[7] Theories of elite behavior alone cannot explain the long-term evolution of the roles of and relations between White House and Justice Department lawyers. Instead, the general context of congressional–executive branch relations in the United States has been the most important force in shaping the organizational structures of government lawyers.

The attorney general and lawyers in the Justice Department historically have balanced competing political and professional values when administering federal law. Aware of the president's political agenda, they have tried to be sensitive to what they construe as the professional demands on them as lawyers. The emergence of the White House counsel's office as an institutional competitor to the Justice Department, however, fundamentally altered the roles of executive branch lawyers. Although that office was not originally created out of the demand for centralized control of executive branch legal policy, the growth and sprawl of the legal bureaucracy during the post–New Deal period has provided the context necessary for transforming the office from a generalist's position filled by personal advisers and friends to presidents to a specialist's position devoted to creating and effecting the administration's legal policy agenda.

World War I brought expansion of the administrative state. As part of this growth, Congress gave new agencies their own counsel and their own independent litigating authority. Concerned about disunity in the government's legal positions, President Wilson, invoking his wartime authority, gave the attorney general control over all agency litigation and made his legal opinions binding on the executive branch as a whole. Wilson's executive order centralizing government legal policy-making expired at the end of the war, however, allowing agency counsels to reassert their independence. By 1928, Attorney General John Sargent expressed his frustration at this outcome, noting that only 13 percent of agency counsels were under the statutory control of the attorney general.

During the 1930s, pressure to reassert centralized control over government lawyering reemerged. Administrative theories of the time emphasized the ideals of efficiency, neutral competence, and scientific administration that could only be accomplished through greater centralization. Indicative was the Brownlow Commission's report, which called for a general consolidation of administrative power in the presidency. At the same time, government lawyers increasingly became tied to the policies and ideology of the New Deal. Law professors loyal to Roosevelt's programs encouraged their students to go to Washington.[8] The professional community eagerly sought lawyers to help draft the regulatory statutes. Thus, political aspirations and professional idealism became mutually reinforcing.

In 1933, Roosevelt signed an executive order that, like Wilson's, attempted to consolidate the government's legal work and strengthen presidential control over it. Roosevelt's order required agency legal counsel to answer directly to the attorney general, and it also expanded the size of the Justice Department. Even with a generally supportive Congress of the same political party, however, Roosevelt's efforts to consolidate presidential authority over government legal work fell short. Congressional desire for political control and oversight of legal administration transcended party lines, and agency heads continued to resist the loss of their independent legal advisory and litigating authority. Congress continued the practice of creating independent counsel for different agencies. And in the wake of the New Deal, the number of agencies and independent regulatory commissions with separate counsel grew rapidly. At the same time, the Justice Department underwent a period of rapid expansion and reorganization.

Although not a direct response to increasing needs for control over the expanding legal bureaucracy, the emergence of the White House counsel's office during the Roosevelt administration marks a watershed in the administration of the government's legal business. Interestingly, Roosevelt, who created the forerunner to the Justice Department's OLC, to help the attorney general advise the president on legal matters, also created the White House counsel's office. A frequent visitor to Hyde Park and long-time family friend, Samuel Rosenman, served as Roosevelt's first counsel. Rosenman acted more as a general policy aide than as a legal adviser. Indeed, Roosevelt created the counsel's position so that Rosenman would have a formal title while continuing the advising and speech-writing functions he had first assumed while he was still a New York state supreme court judge.

During these early years, White House counsel handled the personal legal matters of presidents and served as an in-house link with Justice Department officials. Over time, however, presidents increasingly began to rely on the office for legal advice regarding the administration's programs and policies. A formal office for supplying legal advice became a permanent fixture in the White House during the Eisenhower administration.

THE PRESIDENT'S LAWYERS: THE RISE OF COMPETITION

Although both the Brownlow Commission and the first Hoover Commission were charged with finding ways to create an integrated, hierarchical bureaucracy, neither made recommendations for reforming the organization of legal services in the executive branch. Finally, the second Hoover Commission selected a panel of lawyers and jurists to examine the status of legal counsel and procedures for conducting administrative law hearings in the executive agencies. The Task Force on Legal Services and Procedures presented its report in March 1955. The report recommended strengthening Justice Department control over all executive branch attorneys, creating a centralized and separate civil service system for lawyers, and extending the Administrative Procedures Act to apply quasi-judicial procedures to more agencies.[9]

These recommendations reflected the prevailing view of the legal profession that law and politics could be neatly separated, as well as the belief that legal professionals should not be subject to control by politicians or career civil servants who were tied to agency policy goals. The commission also called for congressional review of the growing number of agency counsels who were hired without express statutory authority. The extension of quasi-judicial proceedings in the administrative process gave agencies increased independence from executive control. The reformers' goal of establishing a bureaucracy staffed by neutral, professional administrators, however, collided with the desires of both Congress and the president for greater political control and accountability. The result was rejection of the reform proposals in favor of the status quo. Competing between themselves for control over legal interpretation and procedure in the agencies, Congress and the president refused to accept increased autonomy of legal staffs in the executive branch.

The development of the White House counsel's office as a functional competitor to lawyers in the Justice Department was an outgrowth of presidential fears of a disloyal bureaucracy and the tensions that resulted when the professional values of department lawyers clashed with the political values of the White House. Presidential scholar Richard Neustadt noted this tendency in the relations among the Justice Department, the White House, and Charles S. Murphy, who serves as special counsel to President Truman:

> In the Truman administration, the Justice Department tended to be evasive, sometimes downright unresponsive in providing the Executive Office with forthright legal guidance on legislative or operational issues. This left a vacuum into which the Presidential Counsel was pressed to move, and on a number of occasions— particularly concerning controversial legislation and Executive Orders—Murphy's views were, in fact, decisive.[10]

Despite the president's need and desire for more direct control, the small size of the White House counsel's office and the office's lack of familiarity with the federal legal environment precluded it from assuming routine handling of government legal affairs. On the other hand, the lack of manpower and expertise was offset to some extent by the advantages of speed, proximity, and loyalty to the president. Increasingly, occupants of the White House counsel's office have acted as a filter between the Justice Department and the Oval Office.

Attorneys at the Justice Department, who resented what they perceived as an encroachment on their turf, fought to keep the OLC's advisory and opinion-writing functions from being usurped by the White House counsel's office. Still, the strategic value to the president of being able to obtain in-house legal advice has been extremely tempting; and as the advising function has shifted to the White House, the role boundaries of lawyers at the Justice Department have been disturbed. The OLC in particular was once accustomed to balancing professional obligations against the partisan advocacy inherent in advising the president on legal matters. But with the role of partisan advocate being transferred increasingly to the White House legal counsel, the OLC began to search for a way to readjust its role and retain an essential place in the system. The resulting competition heightened tension between the White House and the Justice Department. As one OLC member remarked:

> We certainly did not want some young, faceless twenty-five-year-old White House staffer taking issue with the attorney general of the United States, . . . and then taking the issue to the president in a memo which set forth two paragraphs and "Mr. President, check the box below."[11]

Bradley Patterson suggests that White House lawyers and the Department of Justice renegotiated a treaty at the outset of each new administration to establish functional boundaries.[12] In any case, however, the roles tend naturally to differentiate as a result of different institutional cultures and values—professional and political—within the two organizations.

Tensions Mount: The Battle over Legal Advice and Policy

The rise of competition between Justice Department and White House lawyers affects the quality and type of legal advice each gives the president. Expertise and research resources in the Justice Department give it an advantage over the White House counsel when authoring legal opinions. The OLC, for instance, maintains two deputy assistant attorney general posts: one for a holdover from the previous administration, and the other for an expert in a legal field relevant to the work of the office.[13] This practice provides continuity and encourages a high degree of professionalism. The career lawyers at the Justice Department also maintain an informal system of precedents regarding the implicit bargains and unwritten norms that structure presidential relations with Congress and bureaucratic agencies. Consequently, the department can provide essential information regarding the political topography and history of the federal legal environment that short-term officeholders in the White House counsel's office do not have.

By moving the legal advising function into the White House, presidents have freed themselves from the constraining influence of institutional memory and past presidential practice that informs the perspective and legal views of career lawyers at the Justice Department. But the lack of an adequate understanding of the structure of legal and administrative norms rendered presidents vulnerable to wrongly assessing the risks associated with action that violated long-standing agreements.[14]

The Watergate scandal accelerated the transfer of the legal advisory function to the White House and blurred whatever division of labor remained between the White House counsel and the Justice Department regarding who should provide legal advice to the president. President Nixon's personal legal troubles involved various issues of institutional power that the OLC had traditionally handled. The legacy of a contract-based attorney general left the line between professional and personal counsel extremely unclear.[15] Because the issues of executive privilege were intimately bound up with the executive branch's response to allegations against Nixon himself, however, responsibility for advising the president was assumed instead by White House counsel John Dean.[15]

The Justice Department's responsibility to investigate the Watergate charges also severely strained the channels of communication between the post-Mitchell Justice Department and the White House. As tensions grew worse over time, contacts between the department and the White House diminished. Blaming the souring relations on the Justice Department, White House policy adviser Geoff Shepard wrote:

Richardson's efforts to create an independent department have almost totally ended my contacts with Justice. I have yet to be invited to a single meeting; I know of no legislation or policy options currently under consideration within the Department (and, of course, none have been submitted to the President either); and I am led to believe that Richardson has strong reservations about legislation Justice already has pending on the Hill.[17]

Shepard felt that Richardson loyalists at the Department of Justice (including OLC chief Robert Dixon) were seeking to "reorient" the department away from Nixon's conservative policy agenda and could not be trusted as the sole source of legal advice for the administration. While Watergate effectively drove a wedge between the White House and the Department of Justice, Nixon's legal troubles were part of a larger evolution in the relationship between the two. The shift of advisory functions to the White House counsel's office reflected a deep and growing distrust by the president of career bureaucrats in general and ongoing presidential efforts to centralize administrative policy-making.

For its part, the Justice Department recognized that isolation from the White House would lead to diminished authority for itself and greater opportunity for presidents to avoid legitimate legal constraints on their actions. Antonin Scalia, then assistant attorney general for OLC, understood clearly the need to maintain status with the White House when he explained:

> The White House will accept distasteful advice from a lawyer who is unquestionably "on the team"; it will reject it, and indeed not even seek it, from an outsider—when more permissive and congenial advice can be obtained closer to home. And it almost always can be, if not from the White House Counsel then from one of the Cabinet members who is a lawyer, or from one of the Washington attorneys who soon become advisors of any administration.[18]

Nevertheless, following Watergate, pressures for reform and calls for an "independent" attorney general led President Ford to appoint Edward Levi as attorney general. Levi promised to restore the public's shaken confidence in the Justice Department and to buffer the department from improper White House influence. To observers, Levi and his Justice Department were not just independent, but entirely removed from the White House policy-making loop. Ford's long-standing and close personal relationship with White House counsel Philip Buchen also fed perceptions of a growing rift in Justice Department–White House relations.[19] Buchen's strong response to press inquiries only underscored his awareness of outside perceptions that White House–Justice Department relations had soured.

Ironically, the calls for an independent Justice Department in the wake of Watergate accelerated the transfer of legal advisory functions to the White House counsel's office and further removed presidential action from the constraints of legal professionalism in the Justice Department. By the end of the Ford administration, the norms that had governed the division of labor between the White House counsel and the Justice Department had all but evaporated. White House counsel handled all legal business submitted by members and offices within the executive office of the president. This included many functions traditionally reserved to the OLC: advising on legal problems with presidential action (including claims of executive privilege); appraising legislative programs; overseeing regulatory agencies; and examining the form and content of executive orders. In response to the perceived distance and disloyalty of the Justice Department, the White House counsel emerged as a functional competitor to the OLC and other units in the Justice Department.

Tension always had existed between presidents and attorneys general who were unwilling to justify presidential action. But the emergence of divided government and a fear of bureaucratic independence during the 1960s and 1970s, coupled with the growing desire for quick, partisan advocacy, drove the expansion of the White House counsel's role into areas once reserved to the attorney general. The emergence of that office as primary legal adviser to the president on matters of administration policy altered the balance of legal and political advice given to the president and disturbed the prescribed role of the Justice Department. No longer was Justice *the* president's lawyer. Lawyers in the OLC no longer balanced the constraints of legal professionalism against the need for partisan advocacy in providing legal advice to presidents.[20] The rise of the White House counsel balanced these competing values by redistributing the two roles between two separate organizational structures. The result was to institutionalize conflict and competition between the president's lawyers.

POST-WATERGATE REFORMS

The Democratic Congress of the post-Watergate period did not seek to achieve partisan gains by substantially altering the earlier patterns of legal administration. Rejecting proposals to statutorily reorganize the system, Congress instead reaffirmed the limited political checks on the president's power to administer the law. The major changes in the status of government lawyers resulted from internal reforms initiated within the White House or by the Justice Department. These internal reforms once again allowed Justice Department lawyers to differentiate their role from that of the White House counsel. The post-Watergate political environment reinforced the values of professionalism and independence at the department, especially within the OLC with regard to providing legal advice to the executive. Yet the reforms further exacerbated tensions among the White House, the Justice Department, and lawyers in various executive agencies.

Many observers point to Watergate and the demise of the Nixon administration as the turning point in relations between Congress and the executive. Post-Watergate reform measures, such as the War Powers Act and the Congressional Budget and Impoundment Control Act, attempted to restore checks and balances to the institutional system of separation of powers. Many opponents charged that these reforms ignored the president's constitutional authority and unduly constrained presidential power. Legal scholars have similarly suggested that the Nixon administration's abuse of the Justice Department led to fundamental changes in the organization and control of government lawyers. From this perspective, the era of conflict and reform immediately following the Nixon administration contributed to growing legal conflict between the president and Congress.

This interpretation of events in the 1970s, however, must be placed within the broader context of the evolution of the legal administrative state. Controversy surrounding government legal administration began well before the Nixon administration's abuses. President Kennedy's appointment of his brother Robert to the attorney generalship in 1960 and the participation of the Justice Department in the vanguard of civil rights movement heightened congressional interest in this area. By the end of the Johnson administration, members of Congress were closely scrutinizing the adequacy of the Justice Department's protection of congressional interests. The Nixon administration drew Congress's special attention to the Justice Department. The Watergate scandal, the criminal convictions of two attorneys general, and the widespread perception that Nixon to an unprecedented degree had politicized the Justice Department all spurred proposals to create an independent attorney general.

The outcome of the Watergate-era reforms did reshape the values of lawyers administering law in the executive branch. Calls for independent administration of law altered the normative climate in which government attorneys operated. Each congressional proposal, whether accepted or rejected, changed the environment and the perceptions of how government lawyers should function. By reemphasizing values of neutral competence in legal administration, the reforms ultimately exacerbated the emerging conflict between the Department of Justice and the White House counsel.

In the spring of 1974, Senator Sam Ervin offered S. 2803, a bill designed "to insure the separation of constitutional powers by establishing the Department of Justice as an independent establishment of the United States."[21] Although nothing in the Constitution compelled its rejection, the proposal met opposition from all sides. The bill called for appointing attorneys general, their deputies, and solicitors general to six-year terms. The power to appoint assistant attorneys general would rest with the attorney general, rather than with the president.

Former officials of the Justice Department, legal scholars, and members of Congress were unwilling to replace presidential control with an independent model of legal administration. The principal opponents of the proposals for an independent Justice Department and a permanent special prosecutor objected on normative grounds. While everyone agreed that the Nixon administration had abused the department for partisan political gain, few would endorse a Department of Justice answerable to no one. Democrats and Republicans alike—including Ted Sorensen, Kennedy's White House counsel, and Richard Kleindienst, an attorney general under Nixon—testified against the reforms.

This uniform opposition reflected a long-standing consensus regarding the desirability and practical need for maintaining political control over the administration of law. Archibald Cox, former solicitor general and Watergate special prosecutor, expressed this normative consensus in a statement to the Senate Subcommittee on Separation of Powers:

> It seems to me that the President should have the power and responsibility for making these decisions when they are important enough for him to make them, or at least should have someone who is attuned to his philosophy of government making them. The chief reason he should be involved in making such decisions is that there *should be* political responsibility for the decision, and it is through the President, in quadrennial elections and the impact of off-term elections, that political responsibility is made known.[22]

Cox also suggested that the independent department proposal would worsen the problem of excessive politicization, by detaching professional lawyers form the White House. "[S]uppose S. 2803 had been law," the Harvard law professor asked:

> The governmental philosophy of the Attorney General and the Assistant Attorneys General might have well been opposed to that of the President [Nixon]. Sometimes that might make no difference. Perhaps there would have been an effort at cooperation or at least consultation. . . . The inevitable consequence would be that Presidents would build up the White House staff or Executive Offices. . . . Such a trend would not merely result in expensive duplication, conflict, and confusion. It would also dangerously increase the size and isolation of the executive establishment.
>
> The same unfortunate consequences would follow in the area now occupied by the Office of Legal Counsel in the Department of Justice. Any President—every President—had need to consult with lawyers in whose wisdom and judgement he had absolute trust in securing legal advice about his powers and duties, with

whom he works emphatically in discussing the legal consequences of a course of action and in drafting executive orders.

If the Department of Justice were independent, this relationship might sometimes develop, but it seems unlikely to develop
often. A newly-elected President is unlikely to confide in an Attorney General or Assistant Attorney General chosen by the opposing party. Instead, he will provide himself with legal services by
building up his personal staff.[23]

In an era when presidential scholars expressed fear of an isolated president surrounding by sycophants, Cox's words rang true to many on the
Judiciary Committee.

Witnesses blamed the problems at the Justice Department on Nixon's
administrative style. For insiders, the politicization of the department
was an aberration that resulted from the appointment of campaign officials and other highly partisan individuals at its head. The blame thus lay
with people rather than with the system. The only statutory change that
resulted from the Senate hearings on an independent Justice Department
was the eventual establishment of a limited special prosecutor's office under the Ethics in Government Act of 1978. But despite the committee's
failure to produce major institutional reorganization, it and other post-
Watergate reform efforts significantly affected government legal administration.

REFORM FROM WITHIN

The atmosphere of reform following Watergate prompted voluntary
changes within the Justice Department during the Carter presidency.
President Carter and Attorney General Griffin Bell endorsed attempts to
depoliticize the Justice Department. Bell's theory of legal administration
emphasized multiple constituencies and professional norms. As Bell declared: "We're lawyers for the people of the United States, for the agency
heads and for the President—not just employees of the government. We
have to act professionally, give our best judgment and be ethical in what
we do."[24]

Bell established organizational barriers to White House influence over
Justice Department personnel. The attorney general's organizational directive prohibited White House staff members, cabinet members, and
members of Congress from having direct contact with Justice Department lawyers below the rank of deputy attorney general. Although it was
designed primarily to prevent intervention in criminal investigations,
Bell's order had widespread effects on relations between the White

House and all units in the Justice Department. Under the new arrangement, all White House staff contacts with lawyers at the department were filtered through the White House counsel's office. The directive also specifically barred direct contact between White House staff and OLC lawyers.

Bell's directive had some advantages for both the White House counsel and the Department of Justice. Lawyers at the OLC supported the proposal because it limited the number of contacts between the OLC and White House policy advisers and it gave the OLC greater freedom to make independent interpretations of the law.[25] The office's increased autonomy from White House policy directives encouraged OLC lawyers to develop a new role orientation. In contrast to attorneys in the White House counsel's office, lawyers in the OLC no longer saw themselves as functionally being the personal lawyers of the president. One attorney-adviser expressed sentiments common among OLC lawyers after the Carter administration: "I viewed our client as the Constitution, not the President."[26] In the OLC staff's eyes, White House lawyers were the president's hired guns.

White House counsel Robert Lipshutz and the staff counsel favored the proposal as well. By serving as the sole contact point between the White House and the Justice Department, the office of White House counsel could enhance and secure its role in coordinating all legal matters for the president. The White House lawyers jealously guarded this role. When Jody Powell contacted OLC lawyers directly to request a legal opinion on press passes for Soviet journalists, Lipshutz directed his anger at both Powell and the OLC for excluding his office from the decision.[27] The Justice Department and the OLC similarly guarded their turf. When White House lawyers requested that Markham Ball, general counsel to the Agency for International Development (AID), contact them before following the legal advice of the OLC, John Harmon, the assistant attorney general in charge of the OLC, informed Ball that AID was bound statutorily by the OLC's opinion.[28]

Griffin Bell's close relationship with Carter and Carter's commitment to reforming the Justice Department seemingly supported Bell's effort. If personalities and political loyalties were important ties, the problems that Richardson had with the Nixon White House should have been unlikely to occur under Bell. Nevertheless, tensions between the White House and the Department of Justice continued unabated. Organizational directives limited contact between White House staff and Justice Department units on policy and enforcement issues as well as in connection with legal advice. Members of the White House staff and the White House counsel objected to these new directives.[29] Continuing a policy developed in the Ford administration, Bell had the OLC serve as a filter for White House requests for updates on enforcement.

Bell's desire to modify relationships extended beyond the department's lawyering functions. In judicial selection, for example, Bell implemented a merit model, combined with an emphasis on racial and gender diversity, that altered existing norms dating to the 1950s. Prior to the Eisenhower administration, attorneys general and their subordinates handled judicial and Justice Department appointments in an ad hoc, informal manner. Herbert Brownell, Eisenhower's first attorney general, systematized the process to gain greater control over partisan screening of appointments to the bench. Presidents Kennedy, Johnson, and Nixon maintained these practices. President Carter supported Bell's reforms of the process, issuing two executive orders to create merit panels, located outside the Justice Department, to recommend nominations lists to the attorney general.

From Bell's perspective, the internal reforms fulfilled Carter's campaign promise to reestablish neutral administration of the law. "It is one campaign promise that has been absolutely carried out," he stated:

> The response we have had demonstrates that there ought to be a neutral, nonpartisan Justice Department, just as in the foreign intelligence area. And I'll say something else; it would be very difficult for anybody to change it back. The lawyers here would hardly stand for it. There might be an Attorney General with a political bent, but the people down the line would protest and so would the American people and members of Congress who want an independent Justice Department.[30]

Creating barriers between the Justice Department and White House staff was a shrewd political maneuver in the wake of Watergate. Bell thought that these reforms would increase the stature of the Justice Department by restoring congressional and public faith in the department. Bell attempted to use a favorable political environment to justify changes of degree, but the result of his efforts was to produce an unrealistic separation of politics and professionalism that further strained relations among lawyers throughout the executive branch.

Campaign promises often collide, as happened during litigation of the Tennessee Valley Authority/snail darter case. Faced with the prospect of breaking campaign promises to environmentalists, Carter attempted to reverse the solicitor general's position supporting the TVA's legal authority to build a dam despite its potentially adverse effect on an endangered species protected under federal law. Bell resisted White House intervention, but the rift between the Justice Department and the White House widened despite Bell's personal friendship with Carter. Similar conflicts occurred during litigation of affirmative action issues.[31] These tensions over White House intervention led Bell to issue a now-famous memorandum on the independence of the solicitor general.[32]

IMPACT: THE RISE OF TENSIONS

The rise of a more independent Justice Department during the Carter administration aggravated tensions with White House staff outside the counsel's office who believed that the neutrality and independence of the department often interfered with policy development. Members of Carter's Domestic Policy Council met to discuss the widespread dissatisfaction with the Justice Department among White House and executive agency personnel. Notes of this meeting written by a domestic policy staffer summarized the effects of the severed ties between the department and the president. Among general "perceptions about justice," she noted:

1. That concern about depoliticizing has affected relationships in program areas (Law Enforcement Assistance Administration, the Bureau of Prisons, Immigration and Naturalization Service)—interchange occurs only when we initiate.
2. That Justice has become its own client + often ignores view of the agencies it represents.
3. That Justice often resolves interagency matters in a manner contrary to views of all the agencies without White House involvement.[33]

For its part, the Justice Department continued to seek greater control over agency litigating authority and agency legal policy formulation. Two years into his term, Bell bluntly described the limits on his authority to coordinate federal legal policy: "Although I am the chief legal officer in the Executive Branch, I have virtually no control or direction over the lawyers outside the Department of Justice, except indirectly in connection with pending litigation." Bell felt that the Justice Department's independence uniquely qualified it to coordinate legal advice and litigation for the executive branch. Like the Hoover Commission's recommendations for consolidation, however, Bell's pleas for efficiency and coordination fell on deaf ears.

The growing distance between the Justice Department and the White House actually had the effect of diminishing the department's influence over administration policy-making by leaving room for the policy entrepreneurship of Lipshutz and his successor, Lloyd Cutler. Cutler was the consummate Washington insider. Relying in part on the connections he established while working as a lawyer in his firm, Wilmer, Cutler & Pickering, Cutler parlayed his experience and power into an expanded role in White House policy, both legal and otherwise. By defining problems as policy questions rather than as legal questions, Cutler successfully overcame Carter's commitment to an independent Justice Department.

During the first term of the Reagan administration, the White House counsel assumed a role that was more reminiscent of John Dean's than of Lloyd Cutler's or Samuel Rosenman's. Fred Fielding and Peter Wallison primarily focused on narrow legal matters, except in the area of judicial appointments. By chairing the President's Committee on Judicial Selection, Fielding exercised a final screen over nominations submitted to the president. This step would lay an important foundation for more permanently shifting the function into the White House. Presidents Bush and Clinton seem to have continued the practice of centralizing appointment screening inside the White House.

Defining a more limited role for White House counsel held promise for establishing goodwill with the Justice Department's lawyers. During this period, conflict over roles and policy came from another source: interbranch tensions. During the Reagan administration, such tensions exacerbated ill will between the White House and the Justice Department. After the Justice Department insisted on asserting executive privilege claims for Interior Secretary James Watt and for EPA administrator Anne Gorsuch,[34] attorneys in the White House counsel's office raised concerns about the political costs of continued confrontation with Congress. An earlier controversy involving James Watt had reinforced the office's feelings about direct confrontation over congressional demands for access. Intervention by the White House counsel followed an established pattern: counsel supported the executive's defense of constitutional prerogatives until the political costs became unbearable. Fried Fielding's negotiating led to a settlement with Congress, under the terms of which Congress received redacted versions of all withheld documents. As in past conflicts over executive privilege, Congress ultimately gained complete access to the executive papers at issue. By negotiating a settlement, Fielding saved some of the president's waning political capital with Congress but exacerbated tensions between the Justice Department and the White House over control of legal advising and policy-making.[35]

Resolving the Conflict? Appointing a Unified Team

Following the legal scandals surrounding Watergate, the roles performed by the White House counsel have greatly expanded. Because of its initial origins as either a personal legal adviser or political policy-maker, the office of White House counsel's power first expanded to compete with the Justice Department's opinion writing and policy-making roles. The blurred line between legal advice and legal policy later produced bitter inter- and intrabranch disputes over the legal advisory function. White House counsel staff compete with Justice Department lawyers for control of legal advice, judicial and Justice Department appointments, and legal policy-making. In the area of legal advice, the White House counsel's office serves as an alternate source of legitimation for presidential action. Traditionally, White House lawyers held legitimate and recognized (by Justice Department lawyers and Congress) claims to controlling legal policy. Attorneys general and presidents also recognized that, by statute, binding legal advice was solely the province of Justice Department lawyers. As the lines between policy and principle and between personal and professional legal advice grew indistinct, a battle raged between White House lawyers and Justice Department lawyers over the proper scope of their influence. In the role of legal policy-making and advising, White House counsel interacts with agency counsel and vies with the OLC for authority to dispense legal advice. In attempting to resolve these tensions, presidents sought to assemble a team of lawyers unified across the White House and the Department of Justice, through the appointment process.

Following Reagan's election to a second term, Edwin Meese shifted from working inside the White House to heading the Department of Justice, in an attempt to unify legal forces behind Reagan's agenda. During this period, Meese, like attorneys general before him, controlled appointments to the Justice Department and to the bench. Meese transformed an existing unit within the Justice Department into the Office of Legal Policy (OLP), which became responsible for pushing the administration's legal policy agenda. Although these moves gave conservatives greater influence over some units within the department, observers felt that Meese's influence on White House policy diminished after his move to the Department of Justice. Ironically, Meese constructed the model for White House–Justice Department relations for the Bush and Clinton administration. Gray and Nussbaum, however, managed to have a greater hand in Justice Department affairs while remaining inside the White House.

The pragmatic style of the Bush administration, particularly in domestic politics, was incongruent with the confrontational stance of the highly professionalized or politicized model of the Justice Department lawyers. As a result, appointing a unified team was essential to greater control over legal policy and advice. Unlike his predecessor, President Bush assembled a legal team that had established enduring friendships before coming to Pennsylvania Avenue. C. Boyden Gray joined Attorney

General Richard Thornburgh and OLC chief William Barr in renewing direct challenges to statutory limits on presidential power. The result was greater cooperation and a unified concept of the president's legal agenda. This development marked a significant departure from past practice. As Barr noted: "The Reagan administration never had this kind of cohesion."[36] Whereas preceding White House counsel had urged the president to avoid the political costs associated with frontal challenges, Gray openly criticized White House policy advisers for conceding a limited congressional veto in exchange for renewed funding of the Contras. The Justice Department continued to assert the president's authority not to execute unconstitutional legislation prior to judicial review.

White House political advisers, on the other hand, opposed direct confrontations over legal issues. Thus, John Sununu, Bush's chief of staff, and State Department officials ignored the pleadings of Gray and Thornburgh, and accepted the congressional veto in exchange for refunding of the Contras. By midway through the Bush administration, both the White House counsel and the OLC were backing away from direct confrontations with Congress. William Barr summarized the return to a balancing of political and professional norms when he declared in 1990: "The emphasis has not been on picking gratuitous fights, but to work out a standard approach. We try to accommodate as best we can. We look for compromise that will avoid violating our constitutional objectives."[37] On issues involving executive privilege and foreign policy, White House Counsel C. Boyden Gray and Justice Department officials began negotiating with Congress rather than seeking judicial review.[38] Conservatives derided the administration for bargaining away presidential authority. "My main criticism," said Bruce Fein, legal scholar at the Washington Legal Foundation and a former member of the Reagan Justice Department, "is that the President has refused to take a public stand on his prerogatives."[39]

In other areas, however, the White House counsel took positions mirroring those of the Reagan Justice Department. In 1991, for instance, Gray found himself at the center of a furor over civil rights policy. Gray had drafted a policy statement calling for an end to the use of racial preference in hiring federal government employees. Expressions of outrage by civil rights advocates and congressional leadership forced Bush to chastise Gray for his actions. The Justice Department was conspicuously absent from the controversy. As the White House counsel's office became increasingly ideological in the Bush administration, Gray became a conservative lightning rod, rerouting pressure and attention away from the OLC.[40] Gray's confrontational stance sharply contrasted with the actions of Lloyd Cutler and Fred Fielding (both of whom sought compromise with Congress), but also represented a reversal in the roles assigned to the White House counsel's office and to the Justice Department. More important, the criticism and the mobilization of opposition against positions taken on presidential power and on civil rights highlight the degree to which federal legal policies are institutionalized and the barriers that confront White House lawyers who seek dramatic changes.

The White House counsel also became the central player in the politics of judicial nominations and, as a result, the focus of criticism from the left and right. Democrats in Congress and liberal interest groups criticized Bush and Gray for extending the ideological screening process that had been revived during the Reagan administration. Conservatives criticized Bush for failing to screen candidates effectively and to fill vacancies on the bench quickly.[41] By the end of the Bush administration, over a hundred federal judgeships remained vacant.

By acting as a lightning rod for criticism of the president's legal agenda, Gray freed Justice Department lawyers from organizational competition, removed them from intrabranch and interbranch controversy, and allowed them to do a better job of balancing professional and political values. Gray's actions notwithstanding, the Bush administration's behavior in general reflects the more traditional practice of presidents, White House staffers, and Justice Department lawyers of the pre-Carter era, who attempted to avoid direct confrontations with Congress.

White House counsel Bernard Nussbaum's role in the Clinton administration appears to have paralleled Gray's in terms of power, if not in visibility. As Gray had, Nussbaum controlled many appointments within the Justice Department. In so doing, Nussbaum theoretically minimized conflict between the White House and the department. Zoe Baird, Kimba Wood, Philip Heymann, Lani Guinier, Webster Hubble, and Walter Dellinger are only the most prominent players placed in the Justice Department by Clinton and Nussbaum. The nominations of Hubble, Guinier, and Dellinger broke with the established practice of allowing attorneys general to pick their subordinates.

With the appointment of Janet Reno, who observers felt was more interested in the administrative and criminal justice divisions of the Justice Department, to the post of attorney general and the appointment of Walter Dellinger, a Duke University professor of constitutional law, to head the OLC, President Clinton entrusted Nussbaum with a central role in White House legal policy-making. Critical remarks on the Justice Department's tepid support for the administration's crime bill and on its position on child pornography, in addition to the resignation of Philip Heymann, illustrate that tensions over policy-making roles have not diminished. Still, it appears that the White House counsel's influence continues its rise. Despite her early success, Janet Reno now faces criticism of her management and policy-making skills, leaving the White

House counsel and Justice Department loyalists greater freedom to pursue the president's agenda. Nussbaum had cemented control of appointments in the White House, until Whitewater troubles forced him out. Staffers coordinated the selection process that resulted in the nominations of Ruth Bader Ginsburg and Stephen Breyer and are leading searches to fill numerous other vacancies on the federal bench. Still, the recent reluctance of the OLC to write a brief justifying presidential immunity illustrates the institutional roles of Justice Department and White House counsel lawyers. In the face of harsh criticisms of the appointment process and of policy-making roles, presidents seem quite willing to continue centralizing their administration's legal decision-making functions as a means to gain greater control over the legal agenda, leaving the Justice Department to search for an alternate role.

CONCLUSIONS

Since Franklin Roosevelt appointed Samuel Rosenman as counsel to the president, the role of the office has depended on the relationships among the president, the White House counsel, and the Justice Department. Despite these fluctuations, the duties and importance of the office of counsel to the president has consistently grown as presidents have sought to gain greater control over legal policy. As the office grows, however, it becomes increasingly embedded in the web of expectations, organizations, and interests that surround legal policy-making. Thus, rational choice and client-centered models overestimate the degree of freedom available to government lawyers in shaping their roles or legal interpretation.

In the presidency, a distinct set of limitations hinder efforts to change organizational arrangements of federal lawyering functions. The need for congressional approval of changes precludes presidents from constructing institutions to fit their needs. Presidents likely will continue to seek greater control over the legal policy created by various agencies and by Justice Department lawyers. Officeholders will determine the shifting bargains between the Department of Justice and the White House. The political and professional legal roles once performed by the Justice Department alone are now spread among the various government lawyers. The natural response of presidents seeking control over legal policy is to centralize these functions in the office of counsel to the president. The strengthening of the White House counsel illustrates the consistent desire of presidents to receive supportive (as distinct from independent) legal advice and to gain greater control over an increasingly decentralized legal bureaucracy. The response by the OLC reflects its need to define its organizational mission. The evolution of the roles of presidential legal advisers illustrates the embeddedness of government legal politics in a web of institutionalized expectations, both internal and external.

NOTES

1. The Office of Counsel to the President still is used as the formal title for the White House counsel's office. The term *White House counsel* is used more commonly to refer to the lawyers working in this office. In this chapter, *White House counsel* is used to refer to the lawyer who heads the Office of Counsel to the President.

2. Daniel Meador, *The President, The Attorney General, and the Department of Justice* (Charlottesville, Va.: White Burkett Miller Center of Public Affairs, University of Virginia 1980), p. 40.

3. On variations of institutionalist perspectives, see, for example, Walter W. Powell and Paul J. Dimaggio, *The New Institutionalism in Organizational Analysis* (Chicago: University of Chicago Press, 1991) (Organizational sociology); Stephen Skowronek, *Building a New American State* (New York: Cambridge University Press, 1981) (Historical/statist); Rogers Smith, "Political Jurisprudence, the 'New Institutionalism,' and the Future of Public Law," *American Political Science Review* 82 (1988): 90 (ideological/cultural).

4. Still, this chapter does not accept the rational choice models advanced by John McGinnis and Nelson Lund in separate articles at a recent symposium titled "Executive Branch Interpretation of the Law." John McGinnis, "Models of the Opinion Function of the Attorney General: A Normative Descriptive, and Historical Prolegomenon," *Cardozo Law Review* 15 (1993): 375; and Nelson Lund, "Rational Choice at the Office of Legal Counsel," *Cardozo Law Review* 15 (1993): 437. While each adds greatly to the knowledge about these offices, they overestimate the officeholder's ability to weigh alternatives in light of strategic incentives. Instead, this chapter argues that advances made by White House counsel evolve out of the expectations and institutions surrounding these functions and are less the product of individual or collective choice.

5. Nearly all who have written such histories did so after service in the Department of Justice. To some extent each presents an "official" history. See, for example, Arthur Dodge, *Origin and Development of the Office of Attorney General* (Washington, D.C.: U.S. Government Printing Office, 1929); Luther A. Huston, *The Department of Justice* (New York: Frederick Praeger, 1967); Griffin Bell, "The Attorney General: The Federal Government's Chief Lawyer or One Among Many?" The Sonnett Lecture, reprinted in Congress, Senate, Committee on the Judiciary, *Department of Justice Authorization,* 95th Cong., 2d sess., S. Doc. 95-911, 1978; and Meador, *The President, the Attorney General, and the Department of Justice.*

6. This view stands in contrast to existing theory on the growth of legal bureaucracy. The assumption of early studies of the Justice Department was that growing demands for government legal services led to the differentiation of

functions and growth of staff in the Justice Department. Dodge, *Origin and Development of the Office of Attorney General*; Albert G. Langeluttig, *The Department of Justice of the United States* (Baltimore: Johns Hopkins University Press, 1925), pp. 357–68. Later studies focused on the separation of powers as being central to the development of the structures of the department. Attorney General Griffin Bell provided the first sophisticated account of the political implications of the changing institutional arrangements. Bell, "The Attorney General." Drawing on Huston's emphasis on constraints created by Congress, the president, and the courts, Bell showed how these controls shaped the subsequent course of the Justice Department's development.

7. The rational competition model begins implicitly with Attorney General Griffin Bell's Sonnett Lecture. Today, John McGinnis and Nelson Lund extend the competitive model with explicit use of a rational choice model of organizational change and development. Their analysis extends Bell's focus on strategic action and reform downward to explain actions by lawyers within Justice.

8. Peter Irons, *The New Deal Lawyers* (Princeton, N.J.: Princeton University, 1982), pp. 6–9.

9. *Digest and Analysis of the Hoover Commission Report on Legal Services and Procedure* (Washington: Citizens Committee for the Hoover Report, 1955), pp. 72–76.

10. Unattributed quote, in Bradley H. Patterson, Jr., *The Ring of Power: The White House Staff and Its Expanding Role in Government* (New York: Basic Books, 1988), p. 141.

11. Ibid. (anonymous quote).

12. Ibid., p. 142.

13. Frank Wozencraft, "OLC: The Unfamiliar Acronym," *American Bar Association Journal* 57 (January 1971): 36–37.

14. This evidence suggests that the rational, economic calculations behind expanding the executive office of the president may be flawed. Terry Moe, "The Politicized Presidency," for example, suggests that presidents will create White House counterparts to counteract bureaucratic disloyalty and gain greater control over policy. Rational actor models do not include calculations of the professional and *political* expertise lost as a result of circumventing agencies.

15. Histories of the Justice Department show that early presidents hired attorney generals for particular assignments. Presidents often chose personal attorneys or others who could afford to accept sporadic work. Langeluttig, *The Department of Justice of the United States;* Homer Cummings and Carl McFarland, *Federal Justice: Chapters in the History of Justice and the Federal Executive* (New York: Macmillan, 1937).

16. Despite Lund's assertion that counsel ethically may not counsel the president on personal matters, this point has remained unsettled. In recent administrations, presidents have hired both a White House counsel *and* a personal attorney. This severed the White House counsel from one of its historical moorings. Yet the division between personal and political business remains unclear, and Clinton's personal attorney, David Kendall, drew press attention for his role in

managing the Whitewater legal issues. Naftali Bendavid, "Clinton's New Counsel: Quiet D.C. Superstar," *Texas Lawyer,* 17 January 1994, p. 10.

17. Memo, Shepard to Mel Laird, 3 October 1973, folder "Department of Justice [5 of 7 August–October 1973]"; memo, Shepard to Ken Cole, 8 November 1973, folder "Department of Justice [6 of 7 November–December 1973]" in Box 1, WHCF, Richard Nixon Presidential Materials Project.

18. Quoted in Meador, *The President, the Attorney General, and the Department of Justice,* p. 40.

19. Letter, Philip Buchen to Nina Totenberg, 31 March 1976, folder "FG 17 1 January–31 March 1976," Box 87, WHCF, Gerald R. Ford Library.

20. I suggest neither that this reorientation of OLC lawyers is normatively desirable nor that it is empirically grounded. Rather, OLC lawyers perceived and pursued this orientation as a means of delineating a distinctive role in legal politics inside the executive branch. Thus, this role is a social construct (as social role theory would suggest). To this extent, I agree with Nelson Lund. Where we disagree is with regard to Lund's interpretation that such behavior reflected strategic, self-interest pursuit. Indeed, OLC lawyers, including Assistant Attorneys General Harmon and Olson, paid the price for insisting on defending the prerogatives of the presidency against the interests of their president or his advisers.

21. Congress, Senate, Committee on the Judiciary, *Removing Politics from the Administration of Justice, Hearings Before the Subcommittee on Separation of Powers of the Committee on the Judiciary of the United States Senate,* 93d Cong., 2d sess. (1974), p. 3.

22. Ibid., p. 202 (emphasis added).

23. Ibid.

24. Dom Bonafede, " 'Judge' Bell Presides Over a Changed Justice Department," *National Journal,* February 10, 1979, p. 214.

25. Memo, Margaret McKenna to Robert Lipshutz, 10 February 1977, folder "JL 4-3 20 January 1977–20 January 1981," Box JL-13, WHCF, Jimmy Carter Library.

26. OLC attorney-adviser, interview with author, 30 January 1990. Other OLC members typically defined themselves by distinguishing their professional orientation as against the White House counsel's lawyers' political role or by reference to the quality of legal work done in the OLC compared to that done in the White House counsel's office or in executive agency counsel offices.

27. Memo, Margaret McKenna to Robert Lipshutz, 22 August 1978, folder "JL 4-1 20 January 1977–20 January 1981," Box JL-13, WHCF, Jimmy Carter Library.

28. Memo, Robert Lipshutz to Markham Ball, 27 May 1977; Memo, Robert Lipshutz to John Harmon, 27 October 1978; Memo, Ball to Lipshutz, 16 October 1978; Memo, Harmon to Lipshutz, 8 December 1978; and Letter, Ball to Harmon, 14 December 1978; all in folder "Veto, Congressional: February 1977–December 1978 Agency for International Development," Box 49, Staff Office-Counsel Lipshutz, Jimmy Carter Library.

29. Memo, Robert Lipshutz to the Attorney General, 12 September 1978, folder "Justice, Department of January 1977–September 1979," Box 30, Staff Office-Counsel Lipshutz, Jimmy Carter Library.

30. Quoted in Dom Bonafede, " 'Judge' Bell Presides over a Changed Justice Department," *National Journal,* 10 February 1979, p. 214.

31. For a first-hand account of these controversies, see Griffin Bell and Ronald Ostrow, *Taking Care of the Law* (New York: William Morrow, 1982).

32. United States Department of Justice, Office of Legal Counsel. "Memorandum Opinion for the Attorney General re: Role of the Solicitor General," *Opinions of the Office of Legal Counsel* 1977: 1 (Washington: Government Printing Office, 1977).

33. Notes, Domestic Policy Staffer, no date, folder "Justice Department-Relationship," Box 14, Domestic Policy Staff-Civil Rights & Justice-White, Jimmy Carter Library.

34. The Gorsuch document scandal eventually shook the foundation of Justice Department lawyers in the early years of the Reagan administration. Theodore Olson, OLC lawyer and advocate of the executive privilege claim, became the subject of an independent counsel investigation.

35. Elsewhere, I have documented the principle-oriented, test-case strategy of the OLC during the Carter and Reagan administrations. See James Michael Strine, "The Office of Legal Counsel: Legal Professionals in a Political System," Ph.D. dissertation, Johns Hopkins University, 1992. Some have taken this as an argument that the OLC endorses a professionalist, non-client-centered approach. Although (in the executive privilege cases and in others) the OLC took an approach contrary to the goals and interests of the president, they received explicit endorsement on the legislative veto case from President Carter. More consistent opposition to this strategy came from bureau chiefs reluctant to face congressional sanctions. Thus, the principled behavior does not represent a long-term orientation of the OLC, but rather an orientation driven by its organization context (namely, the post-Watergate environment at the macro level and the rising competition with and need for differentiation from White House counsel at the organizational level).

36. Quoted in Chuck Alston, "Bush Crusade on Many Fronts to Retake President's Turf," *Congressional Quarterly Weekly Report,* 3 February 1990, pp. 291, 292.

37. Ibid.

38. These incidents involved House member Jack Brooks seeking documents related to an investigation into allegations that Justice Department officials stole software from a private computer firm, involving access to documents in the Iran-Contra investigation, aid to the Contras, and limits on covert operations. W. John Moore, "The True Believers," *National Journal,* 17 August 1991, pp. 2018, 2021.

39. Ibid.

40. Ibid.; Andrew Rosenthal, "President Tries to Quell Furor on Interpreting Scope of New Law," *New York Times,* 22 November 1991, pp. A1, A20.

41. Bruce Fein, "The Flowering of David Souter," *Recorder,* 12 July 1993, p. 10; Stephen Trott, "This Reagan Judge Can't Be Pigeonholed," *Legal Times,* 8 November 1993, p. 2.

CONTRIBUTORS

CORNELL W. CLAYTON is an assistant professor in the Department of Political Science at Washington State University. He is author of *The Politics of Justice: The Attorney General and the Making of Legal Policy* (M. E. Sharpe, 1992) and *The United States Department of Justice and Federal Legal Administration* (Garland, forthcoming). He received his D. Phil. from Oxford University in 1990.

NANCY V. BAKER is an associate professor and chair of the Department of Government at New Mexico State University, where she teaches in the areas of public law and the presidency, specializing in the attorney general's office. She is author of *Conflicting Loyalties: Law and Politics in the Attorney General's Office, 1789–1990* (University Press of Kansas, 1992), as well as numerous book chapters and articles. She received a Ph.D. from Tulane University in 1989.

NEAL DEVINS is a professor of law and lecturer in government at the College of William and Mary, Williamsburg, Virginia. He is co-author (with Lou Fisher) of *The Political Dynamics of Constitutional Law* (West, 1992), editor of *Public Values, Private School* (Stanford Series on Education and Public Policy, 1989) and *Elected Branch Influence in Constitutional Decisionmaking* (Law and Contemporary Problems, 1993), and author of *Abortion Politics: The Role of Elected Government in Shaping Constitutional Values* (Johns Hopkins University Press, in progress). He has authored more than fifty articles on constitutional law, civil rights, and education topics.

KATY J. HARRIGER is an associate professor of politics and holds the Zachary T. Smith Professorship at Wake Forest University in Winston-Salem, North Carolina, where she teaches constitutional law and American politics. She is author of *Independent Justice: The Federal Special Prosecutor in American Politics* (University Press of Kansas, 1992), and she testified before a Senate subcommittee considering reauthorization of the independent and counsel statute in 1992. She received her Ph.D. from the University of Connecticut in 1986.

MICHAEL HERZ is a professor of law at the Benjamin N. Cardozo School of Law, Yeshiva University, where he teaches primarily in the areas of environmental and constitutional law. A graduate of Swarthmore College and the University of Chicago Law School, Professor Herz served as law clerk for Judge Levin Campbell of the U.S. Court of Appeals for the First Circuit and for Justice Byron R. White of the United States Supreme Court. He joined the Cardozo faculty after three years as an attorney with the Environmental Defense Fund. Professor Herz has written on a variety of public law topics.

NELSON LUND is an associate professor of law at George Mason University School of Law and executive editor of the *Supreme Court Economic Review*. Professor Lund received his Ph.D. in political science from Harvard University in 1981 and his J.D. from the University of Chicago in 1985. He served as law clerk for Judge Patrick E. Higgin Botham of the United States Court of Appeals for the Fifth Circuit (1985–1986) and for Justice Sandra Day O'Connor of the United States Supreme Court (O.T. 1987). In addition to having worked in the United States Department of Justice at the Office of the Solicitor General and at the Office of Legal Counsel, Professor Lund served in the White House as Associate Counsel to the President from 1989 to 1992.

JEREMY RABKIN is an associate professor in the Department of Government at Cornell University. He received his Ph.D. from Harvard University and is author of *Judicial Compulsions: How Public Law Distorts Public Policy* (Basic, 1989) and co-editor of *The Fettered Presidency: Legal Constraints on the Executive Branch* (American Enterprise Institute, 1989). His published articles have centered on public law and administrative politics.

REBECCA MAE SALOKAR is an associate professor in the Department of Political Science at Florida International University in Miami, Florida. She is author of *The Solicitor General: The Politics of Law* (Temple University, 1992). In addition to her work on the solicitor general, Salokar has published on the roles of the congressional legal counsels and the politics of abortion in the state of Florida.

MICHAEL STRINE received his Ph.D. from Johns Hopkins University and is an assistant professor in the Department of Political Science at the University of Colorado at Boulder. He currently is finishing a book on presidential counsel. His most recent research includes a study of presidential capacity to interpret the Constitution.

INDEX

Abortion, 14–15, 42, 51, 61, 75, 79, 120
Advocate-general (European Community), 60
Agency for International Development (AID), 269
Agency general counsel, 2, 8–10, 40, 67, 68, 72, 76–77, 117–18, 135, 143–70, 181–204
 relations with Justice Department, 8–11, 13–14, 40, 47, 62, 159–69, 184–204, 239–40, 258–77
 See also specific agencies and departments
Agriculture Department, 146, 147
Altman, Roger, 126–27
Antitrust law, 1, 19–21, 35, 183, 186, 197
Attorney general, office of, 2–4, 8, 17, 18, 31–49, 63, 65, 76, 86–87, 91–96, 99, 109–10, 118–22, 143–45, 150, 159–62, 168–69, 170, 192, 258–60, 262, 265–68, 275
 assistant attorneys general, 32
 associate attorney general, 32
 cabinet membership, 33, 39, 40, 168
 deputy attorney general, 32, 36, 63, 266, 268
 opinions of, 31–32, 130–31, 144, 147, 160–62, 178, 259–65, 273–76

relationship to independent counsel, 90–97
 relations with Congress, 13–16, 33, 35–36, 48, 109
 See also Justice Department
Ayer, Donald, 45

Baird, Zoe, 275
Baker, Howard, 112–13
Baker, James, 112, 130, 230
Baker, Nancy, 2–4, 22, 25, 212, 214
Baker v. Carr (1962), 66, 75
Ball, Markham, 269
Barr, William, 35, 57, 92, 119, 155–56, 218, 232, 253, 256, 274
Bean, Elise, 104
Bell, Griffin, 3–4, 19–20, 33, 34, 35, 36, 44, 46, 48, 107, 119, 120, 139, 159, 268–71, 278
Biddle, Francis, 34, 60, 63, 75–76
Blackmun, Harry, 15
Bob Jones University v. United States (1983), 47, 58, 63–64, 79, 121
Bork, Robert, 60, 63, 65, 73–74, 188
Bowsher v. Synar (1986), 78, 235, 240
Bristow, Benjamin, 63
Brock, William, 47–48
Brownell, Herbert, 42–43, 270
Browner, Carol, 172–73
Brownlow Commission, 259, 260
Brown v. Board of Education of Topeka (1954), 43, 75, 76, 138

285